Rebellious Passage

In late October 1841, the *Creole* left Richmond with 139 slaves bound for New Orleans. It arrived five weeks later minus the Captain, one passenger, and most of the captives. Nineteen rebels had seized the US slave ship en route and steered it to the British Bahamas where the slaves gained their liberty. Drawing upon a sweeping array of previously unexamined state, federal, and British colonial sources, *Rebellious Passage* examines the neglected maritime dimensions of the extensive US slave trade and slave revolt. The focus on south-to-south self-emancipators at sea differs from the familiar narrative of south-to-north fugitive slaves over land. Moreover, a broader hemispheric framework of clashing slavery and antislavery empires replaces an emphasis on US antebellum sectional rivalry. Written with verve and commitment, *Rebellious Passage* chronicles the first comprehensive history of the ship revolt, its consequences, and its relevance to global modern slavery.

Jeffrey R. Kerr-Ritchie is Professor of History at Howard University and author of *Freedpeople in the Tobacco South: Virginia, 1860-1900; Rites of August First: Emancipation Day in the Black Atlantic World*; and *Freedom's Seekers: Essays on Comparative Emancipation*.

Rebellious Passage

The Creole *Revolt and America's Coastal Slave Trade*

JEFFREY R. KERR-RITCHIE
Howard University, Washington DC

CAMBRIDGE
UNIVERSITY PRESS

CAMBRIDGE
UNIVERSITY PRESS

University Printing House, Cambridge CB2 8BS, United Kingdom

One Liberty Plaza, 20th Floor, New York, NY 10006, USA

477 Williamstown Road, Port Melbourne, VIC 3207, Australia

314–321, 3rd Floor, Plot 3, Splendor Forum, Jasola District Centre, New Delhi – 110025, India

79 Anson Road, #06–04/06, Singapore 079906

Cambridge University Press is part of the University of Cambridge.

It furthers the University's mission by disseminating knowledge in the pursuit of education, learning, and research at the highest international levels of excellence.

www.cambridge.org
Information on this title: www.cambridge.org/9781108476249
DOI: 10.1017/9781108616324

© Jeffrey R. Kerr-Ritchie 2019

First published 2019

Printed in the United Kingdom by TJ International Ltd, Padstow Cornwall

A catalogue record for this publication is available from the British Library.

Library of Congress Cataloging-in-Publication Data
NAMES: Kerr-Ritchie, Jeffrey R., author.
TITLE: Rebellious passage : the Creole revolt and America's coastal slave trade / Jeffrey R. Kerr-Ritchie.
DESCRIPTION: Cambridge, United Kingdom ; New York, NY : Cambridge University Press, 2019. | Includes bibliographical references.
IDENTIFIERS: LCCN 2018043005| ISBN 9781108476249 (hardback : alk. paper) | ISBN 9781108700009 (paperback : alk. paper)
SUBJECTS: LCSH: Creole (Brig) | Slave insurrections – United States – History – 19th century. | Mutiny – United States – History – 19th century. | Slaves – Emancipation – Bahamas – History – 19th century. | Slave trade – United States – History – 19th century. | Slave trade – Atlantic Coast (U.S.) – History – 19th century.
CLASSIFICATION: LCC E447 .K47 2019 | DDC 306.3/6209730904–dc23
LC record available at https://lccn.loc.gov/2018043005

ISBN 978-1-108-47624-9 Hardback
ISBN 978-1-108-70000-9 Paperback

To the Nineteen
Horace Beverley
Walter Brown
George Burton
Richard Butler
Adam Carney
Pompey Garrison
George Grandy
Williams Jenkins
Benjamin Johnson
Philip Jones
Robert Lumpkins
Elijah Morris
George Portlock
Doctor Ruffin
Peter Smallwood
Warner Smith
Addison Tyler
Madison Washington
America Woodis

Contents

Figures

Preface

One warm evening in late 1879, sexagenarian Elijah Morris sat on his porch in Gambier Village just outside the large town of Nassau in the Bahamas. Behind him stood a thatched roof cottage on ten acres of land for which he had recently purchased the deed. In front was West Bay Road hugging the northern end of New Providence. Ahead of him, Morris could see and hear the waves crashing from the northern Caribbean Sea. Far beyond the eye lay the shoreline of the southern United States where he had been born as somebody else's property.

As he gazed at the sunbeams of the setting sun playing in the waves, he reflected on his remarkable life's journey. He had been born enslaved in Virginia in 1818. In October 1841, he lay in a slave trader's pen in Richmond awaiting forced transportation to the Deep South through the bustling port of New Orleans. There he encountered other captives dissatisfied with their condition. With scores of other captives he was loaded onto a ship adorned with a figurehead in the shape of a lady. In early November, Morris along with eighteen other captives rose up, seized the slave ship, and directed it toward the Bahamas. Controlled by the British, this island had a reputation for liberating slaves. After several days of being kept aboard in Nassau harbor, the captives were allowed to go free. Morris recalled fondly that this liberation was undertaken by captives who walked to freedom assisted by hundreds of local Bahamians who had surrounded the slave ship and ferried its newly freed people to the mainland. This act of racial solidarity remained etched in his memory. He and his fellow conspirators had been lodged in the local jail because of the death of one of the white overseers and serious injuries to the ship's officers. Morris and his fellow rebels were eventually released after spending four months incarcerated in the Nassau jail. He stayed close to the city, raised a family, worked and saved, built a house, and eventually bought some land.

What was a former American slave doing in the Bahamas? Why was he where he was? What was the nature of the coastwise slave trade experienced by Morris and his fellow captives? Who were these enslaved people aboard the slave ship named the *Creole*? Who were the slave rebels and why did they rise? What were the reactions of a slaveholding nation deeply split over the issue of slavery? What were the reactions of a national abolitionist power that had recently terminated its slave trade and colonial slavery and was determined to pressure others to do the same? What were the consequences of the maritime revolt Morris helped to lead? What can this generation learn from a slave ship revolt in a faraway place in a faraway time? This book seeks to answer some of these engaging questions.

The *Creole* revolt generated a lot of attention among politicians, abolitionists, diplomats, newspaper editors, and others across the English-speaking Atlantic world throughout the early 1840s. This enthusiasm seems to have waned during the 1850s and after the legal abolition of American slavery in 1865. In contrast to commemorations of Lincoln's Emancipation Proclamation on January 1 and Juneteenth celebrations marking the termination of American slavery, the *Creole* revolt does not appear to have garnered much popular attention during the post-emancipation decades. The centennial of the *Creole* revolt in 1941 attracted little comment. This might have been because of the ongoing Second World War, and especially the fallout from Japan's surprise military attack on Pearl Harbor and America's subsequent entry into World War II in early December 1941. The exception was one journalist's suggestion that the *Creole* revolt would make a great movie. Unlike so many other movies that failed to cater to "colored people," this historical event would attract alternative patrons because it grew "out of their life in America."[1] The Black Freedom Struggle also does not appear to have generated much historical interest in the *Creole* revolt. This was in marked contrast to attention toward the *Amistad* rebellion with its emphasis on resistance and social history from below with ordinary men and women during the 1960s.[2]

[1] Louis Lautier, "$250,000 Movie Contest Shows Lack of Sepias," *Baltimore Afro-American*, Oct. 15, 1938.
[2] Marcus Rediker, *The Amistad Rebellion: An Atlantic Odyssey of Slavery and Freedom* (New York: Viking, 2012), 4.

Since the early 1970s, the *Creole* has been the subject of at least four journal articles, four book chapters, and two books.[3] This historical scholarship charts three major directions. The first concerns the *Creole* revolt's contribution to sectional division between proslavery southern states and antislavery northern states. In 1970, James Stewart's fine biography of Joshua Giddings highlighted the Ohio congressman's 1842 resolutions on the *Creole* rebels' natural rights of personal liberty.[4] Several years later, Howard Jones penned an important article on the *Creole* revolt as a "microcosm" of southern concerns over slavery and rebellion being encouraged by outside interference from northern states and foreign powers.[5] These works have proven influential in shaping subsequent writing on links between the slave ship revolt and antebellum sectionalism.[6]

---

[3] Clifton H. Johnson, "The Creole Affair," *The Crisis* vol. 78, no. 8 (Oct. 1971): 248–251; Howard Jones, "The Peculiar Institution and National Honor: The Case of the *Creole* Slave Revolt," *Civil War History* vol. 21, no. 1 (Mar. 1975): 28–50; Edward D. Jervey and C. Harold Huber. "The Creole Affair." *The Journal of Negro History* vol. 65, no. 3 (Summer 1980): 196–211; Anita Rupprecht, " 'All We Have Done, We Have Done for Freedom': The *Creole* Slave-Ship Revolt (1841) and the Revolutionary Atlantic," *Internationaal Instituut voor Sociale Geschiedenis* 58 (2013): 253–277; Philip Troutman, "Grapevine in the Slave Market: African American Geopolitical Literacy and the 1841 *Creole* Revolt," in Walter Johnson, ed., *The Chattel Principle: Internal Slave Trades in the Americas* (New Haven: Yale University Press, 2004); Maggie Montesinos Sale, "The Case of the *Creole* (1841)" in *The Slumbering Volcano: American Slave Ship Revolts and the Production of Rebellious Masculinity* (Durham: Duke University Press, 1997); Stanley Harrold, "Romanticizing Slave Revolt: Madison Washington, the *Creole* Mutiny, and Abolitionist Celebration of Violent Means," in *Antislavery Violence*, John R. McKivigan and Stanley Harrold, eds. (Knoxville: University of Tennessee Press, 1999); Roy Finkenbine, "The Symbolism of Black Mutiny: Black Abolitionist Reponses to the *Amistad* and *Creole* Incidents" in Jane Hathaway, ed., *Rebellion, Repressions, and Reinvention: Mutiny in Comparative Perspective*. (Westport, CT: Greenwood Press, 2001); George Hendrick and Willene Hendrick, *The Creole Mutiny: A Tale of Revolt aboard a Slave Ship* (Chicago: Ivan R. Dee, 2003); Arthur T. Downey, *The Creole Affair: The Slave Rebellion That Led the U.S. and Great Britain to the Brink of War* (Lanham: Rowman and Littlefield, 2014).

[4] James B. Stewart, *Joshua R. Giddings and the Tactics of Radical Politics* (Cleveland: Case-Western Reserve University Press, 1970), chap. 4.

[5] Jones, "Peculiar Institution."

[6] Sean Wilenz, *The Rise of American Democracy: Jefferson to Lincoln* (New York: W. W. Norton, 2005), 555–558, 909n25-9. Stanley Harrold argues that the cult of American romanticism encouraged non-violent abolitionists to embrace slave revolts like that of the *Creole* against southerners' defense of slavery. See Harrold, "Romanticizing Slave Revolt." The sixth and seventh editions of *From Slavery to Freedom*, the pioneering African-American history textbook by John Hope Franklin published in 1947 refer to US Congressman Giddings's political usage of the *Creole* revolt. For some reason, the textbook's ninth edition published in 2011 fails to mention the *Creole*.

The second route focuses on the diplomatic fallout between the United States and Great Britain over what is described as the *Creole* "affair." This approach has undergone a major shift from the slave ship revolt being a minor diplomatic irritant to its causing a full-blown crisis portending military conflict.[7] The most strident statement of the latter approach is Arthur Downey's 2014 book with the sensationalist subtitle, *The Slave Rebellion That Led the U.S. and Great Britain to the Brink of War*, proclaiming the author's thesis. The problem of fugitive slave flight during the American Revolution and War of 1812 – together with maritime disputes over impressment and right of search, and the release of slave cargoes from coastal slavers driven into British territorial waters that culminated in the *Creole* slaves' release – threatened a major military conflict between the two powers. Only deft American and British diplomacy resulting in the passage of the Webster-Ashburton Treaty in 1842 deflected "the potential for a third US–UK war."[8]

The historical literature's third pathway is that of heroic slaves engaged in a glorious liberation struggle. Social movement activists and rebels of the Black Sixties helped focus attention on the actions of their predecessors. Both Clifton Johnson, director of the newly formed Amistad Research Center in New Orleans during the early 1970s, and Vincent Harding's poetic *There Is a River* published at the end of the decade, depicted the *Creole* revolt as a rivulet in the long river of black resistance.[9] Edward Jervey and C. Harold Huber published a gripping narrative account of the *Creole* revolt based upon two key documentary sources that centered on slaves' actions.[10] Eugene Genovese's comparative examination of slave revolts in the western hemisphere did not mention the *Creole* but implied maritime

---

[7] E. D. Adams, "Lord Ashburton and the Treaty of Washington," *The American Historical Review* vol. 17, no. 4 (July 1912): 764–782; Thomas A. Bailey, *A Diplomatic History of the American People* (New York: Appleton-Century-Crofts, Inc., 1955), chap. 14; Wilbur D. Jones, "The Influence of Slavery on the Webster-Ashburton Negotiations," *Journal of Southern History* vol. 22, no. 1 (Feb. 1956): 48–58; Alexander Deconde, *A History of American Foreign Policy* (New York: Charles Scribner, 1963), 157–158; John O. Geiger, "A Scholar Meets John Bull: Edward Everett as United States Minister to England, 1841–1845," *The New England Quarterly*, vol. 49, no. 4 (Dec. 1976): 577–595.

[8] Downey, *Creole Affair*, vii.

[9] Johnson, "Creole Affair;" Vincent Harding, *There Is a River: The Black Struggle for Freedom in America* (New York: Vintage Books, 1983), 112–113.

[10] Jervey and Huber, "Creole Affair."

resistance.[11] Maggie Sale's discursive analysis of slave ship revolts pits masculine fighters depicted by antislavery politicians, activists, and press editors against the "implicit feminizing of the enslaved population," propagated by defenders of American slavery.[12] Walter Johnson's examination of the US domestic slave trade described the *Creole* rebellion as the consequence of "infrapolitics" in which a group of strangers formed themselves into a resistance collective.[13] Independent scholars George Hendrick and Willene Hendrick's *The Creole Mutiny* published in 2003 told the tale with a central focus on Madison Washington as the tragic hero who lost his wife but gained his personal liberty.[14] This book was clearly aimed at a popular audience. The desire to increase popular understanding of the *Creole* revolt has become even more evident with encyclopedia articles together with entries on Wikipedia.[15] Eric Taylor's *If We Must Die*, published in 2006, provides the first book-length survey of slave ship revolts. He situates the *Creole* revolt within a broader tradition of what he calls "second wave Atlantic shipboard slave resistance."[16] Marcus Rediker's *Amistad Rebellion* published in 2012 argues that the *Amistad* along with the *Creole*

[11] "And when, as in some noteworthy cases, slaves aboard ships in the domestic slave trade rebelled and steered for Haiti or for the protection of the British, they demonstrated that the appearance of favorable conditions and a genuine chance of success could trigger bold action," Eugene D. Genovese, *From Rebellion to Revolution: Afro-American Slave Revolts in the Making of the Modern World* (Baton Rouge: Louisiana State University Press, 1979), 6.

[12] Sale, "Case of the *Creole*," 134.

[13] Walter Johnson, *Soul By Soul: Life Inside the Antebellum Slave Market* (Cambridge, Mass.: Harvard University Press, 1999), 75–76. For influential studies of subaltern resistance through the notion of infrapolitics, see James C. Scott, *Domination and the Arts of Resistance: Hidden Transcripts* (New Haven: Yale University Press, 1990) and Robin D. G. Kelly, *Race Rebels: Culture, Politics, and the Black Working Class* (New York: Free Press, 1994).

[14] Hendrick and Hendrick, *Creole Mutiny*. Although well written and readable, the book lacks detailed archival research, employs guesswork, and narrates other revolts to fill in the gaps in the *Creole* story. One reviewer concluded, "the *Creole* story still stands as incomplete." "The Creole Mutiny: A Tale of Revolt aboard a Slave Ship by George Hendrick; Willene Hendrick," Review by Howard Jones, *The Journal of Southern History* vol. 70, no. 2 (May 2004), 427–428.

[15] Philine Georgette Vega, "Creole Case (1841)," in Junius Rodriguez, ed., *Encyclopedia of Emancipation and Abolition* vol. 1 (Armonk, NY: M.E. Sharpe, 2007), 148–149; "Creole Case," http://en.wikipedia.org/wiki/Creole_case.

[16] Eric Robert Taylor, *If We Must Die: Shipboard Insurrections in the Era of the Atlantic Slave Trade* (Baton Rouge: Louisiana State University Press, 2006), 156–159.

capped a "decade long wave of rebellion" in the "Atlantic geography of resistance."[17]

Rebellious Passage differs from previous scholarship in several distinct ways. First, it centers on slaves, rebels, and free blacks before, during, and after the shipboard revolt. It seeks to uncover the lives and experiences of captives in slavery, in confinement, aboard ship, and after emancipation. Most studies mention Elijah Morris but go no further. In contrast, we trace this important rebel leader through a documentary trail from Virginia to England to the Bahamas. The same is true for women and children captives whose personal stories help recast vital parts of a familiar narrative. We also bring to life those native Bahamians who engaged with the *Creole* in contrast to their usual depiction as blank ciphers. These central actors' voices, actions, and humanity are presented here as important parts of a historical drama that does not have to be fictionalized or occluded for more famous dramatis personae.

This study is also unique in its focus on the coastal trading career of the slaver *Creole* as a means to illuminate the maritime coastal business. Most studies start and finish with the 1841 voyage. Yet examination of ship manifests, together with enrollment and registration records, reveals that this coastal slaver had a lucrative career between its official registration in October 1840 and its spectacular demise in November 1842. Moreover, this ship was only one of many engaged in coastal slave trading. Between the illegalization of American participation in the Atlantic slave trade on January 1, 1808 through US congressional prohibition of the coastwise trade in July 1864, scores of thousands of captives were transported in thousands of sea journeys from ports in the Upper South down to ports along the Gulf coast. The maritime component of the domestic slave trade has been touched on by several scholars, but it demands much more thorough investigation. This book seeks to open up this important topic of the coastwise trade through the rise and fall of one particular coastal slaver and its remarkable odyssey.

The third way in which this book contrasts with previous scholarship is that it tells the Caribbean side of the story.[18] It seems rather strange that

---

[17] Rediker, *Amistad Rebellion*, 21.
[18] "...this book does not attempt to explore the impact of the *Creole* revolt on the slave and free black communities in the United States (or in the British Caribbean colonies)." Downey, *Creole Affair*, vii.

this aspect has been largely confined to the deck of the *Creole*. In other words, the sailing of the ship into Nassau, the boarding of the ship by British troops, the interrogations and confinement, and so forth represent the "Caribbean." Much less attention has been paid to the role of Bahamians in the liberation of the captives. Important relations between black Bahamians and former American slaves are rarely examined or commented upon.[19] The experiences of the newly liberated in the Bahamas and Jamaica have not been examined. The rebels go from being confined in the ship in early November to being released in mid-April without any comment on what happened to them in the Nassau jail and thereafter. These important parts of the story are rarely examined in detail and deserve much closer attention if we are to appreciate the broader spatial dimensions of the *Creole* revolt.

Finally, the book situates the *Creole* revolt within an international framework of clashing interests over slavery, slave trading, abolition, and empire building. In contrast to an older historical literature as well as some more recent works, it shows how slavery and slave trading permeated Anglo-American relations rather than being just peripheral or a minor irritant.[20]

But it goes beyond the familiar Washington–London axis by examining the broader world of clashing empires over slave trading, abolition, and post-emancipation. Events leading up to the *Creole* revolt, as well as the shipboard rebellion itself, cannot be explicated from a broader historical context in which Britain was seeking to expand its imperial power by using the Royal Navy to back its slave-trading treaties with other nations. This ran smack bang into Spain's expansion of colonial slavery in Cuba, Brazilian slaveholders' sustained efforts to circumvent the abolition of the Atlantic slave trade in 1830, and the emergence of Haiti as an antislavery state. In particular, this work draws attention to transcontinental clashes over slavery and abolition between British Canada, the United States, and Mexico especially during the decades of the 1820s and 1830s. This is a complicated history, but it must be broached if we are to appreciate the broader dimensions of the *Creole* rebellion.

---

[19] One exception is Rupprecht "All We Have Done."

[20] This is analogous to Matt Mason's salient point concerning slavery's sectional divide in American politics <u>prior</u> to political differences temporarily resolved by the 1820 Missouri Compromise. Mathew Mason, *Slavery and Politics in the Early American Republic* (Chapel Hill: University of North Carolina Press, 2006), 1–8.

The *Creole* revolt is a richly documented history. There are four important federal sources. The first emanated from the US Senate in 1842 and consists of forty-six pages of official correspondence, officer and crew depositions, and protests against mutiny, murder, and slave liberation collected at Nassau and New Orleans. It is a vital source for reconstructing the slave ship revolt as well as the process of slaves' self-liberation in Nassau, albeit from the perspective of those antagonistic toward the slaves' liberty. It is the source most used by scholars, but its bias against the captives and their actions requires careful exegesis.[21] The second was a US Senate report on the activities of the Anglo-American Commission (AAC) for the adjustment of outstanding civil claims and property disputes involving American and British citizens. Issued in 1856, its eighty pages detail the AAC's schedule, claims, and decisions. It is an excellent source for examining maritime disputes between the United States and Great Britain between 1812 and the early 1850s that has been overlooked by scholars.[22]

The third federal source consists of underutilized ship manifests. As a consequence of the outlawing of American citizens' participation in the Atlantic slave trade in 1808, Congress legislated that every ship involved in domestic transportation was required to sign manifests stipulating that no African slaves were being imported into the United States. *Rebellious Passage* draws on a small sample of thousands of these ship manifests stored in federal archives scattered in several northern, southern, and western states.[23] Finally, there are US consul dispatches from Nassau to Washington in 1841 and 1842 housed at the National Archives and Records Administration (NARA). The consul records are particularly revealing for the light they shed not only on the *Creole* revolt but also on America's political ambitions in the northern Caribbean.[24]

[21] US Congress, Senate, Executive Document 51, 27th Congress, 2nd Session, Message from the President of the United States, Communicating, in Compliance with a Resolution of the Senate Copies of Correspondence in Relation to the Mutiny on Board the Brig Creole, and the Liberation of the Slaves Who Were Passengers in the Said Vessel, January 1842, Washington DC, 1–46.

[22] US Congress, Senate, Executive Document 103, 34th Congress, 1st Session, Message of the President of the United States, Communicating the Proceedings of the Commissioners for the Adjustment of Claims under the Convention with Great Britain of February 8, 1853, Washington, 1856.

[23] Records of the US Customs Service, 1745–1997 Record Group 36
https://catalog.archives.gov/id/365

[24] Bureau of Marine and Navigation, Record Group 41; Dispatches from US Consul in Nassau, British West Indies, Record Group 59, National Archives and Records

There are also important documentary collections at the state level. The Virginia Library in Richmond is home to tax records that are useful for reconstructing the activities of local slave traders in the maritime business and to local newspaper reports of popular support for the extension of slave property rights beyond the municipality. New Orleans has several useful archives. The records of seven legal suits against insurance companies in the Commercial Court of Orleans Parish are available on microfilm at the City Archives in the New Orleans Public Library. They contain insurance contracts, slave lists, court documents, correspondence, and much more that tell us about the *Creole*'s slaves and slave-owners as well as the broader business of the US coastal slave trade.[25] The Amistad Research Center (ARC) at Tulane University holds photocopies of bills of lading, slave schedules, insurance contracts, court petitions, and memorials for compensation from the AAC that are essential for understanding the origins and consequences of the *Creole* revolt. The New Orleans Notarial Archives (NONA) is an important repository for reconstructing the selling histories of traders transporting captives aboard the *Creole* and other slave vessels. Certificates describing the age, sex, and origin of slaves that were attached to some of the bills of sale also shed some light on the humanity of those who were transported.[26] The Williams Center at Historic New Orleans holds the best collection of Louisiana newspapers on microfilm. Finally, there is a detailed report, published in 1845, of one of the major lawsuits together with its ruling and rulings on the *Creole* in the state Supreme Court. This source is indispensable for understanding the broader world of competing statute laws, property rights, financial obligations, and diplomatic differences in the eighteenth- and nineteenth-century Anglo-American world.[27]

Administration; US Customs Service, Record Group 36, National Archives and Records Administration (NARA).

[25] These seven lawsuits were: #4408 Thomas McCargo v. The Merchants Insurance Company of New Orleans; #4409 Thomas McCargo v. The New Orleans Insurance Company; #4410 Edward Lockett v. The Merchants Insurance Company of New Orleans; #4411 Edward Lockett v. The Fireman's Insurance Company of New Orleans; #4413 Andrews and Hatcher v. The Ocean Insurance Company; #4414 Sherman Johnson v. The Ocean Insurance Company; #4419 John Hagan v. The Ocean Insurance Company. The docket numbers are CCNO references. See http://nutrias.org/~nopl/inv/creole.htm.

[26] Ulrich B. Phillips, *Life and Labor in the Old South*, 1929, rpt., Little and Brown, 1963, 155–156.

[27] "*Thomas McCargo* v. *The New Orleans Insurance Company*," in Merritt M. Robinson, *Reports of Cases Argued and Determined in the Supreme Court of Louisiana*, vol. 10, (March 1 to June 20, 1845). Samuel M. Stewart, 1845, 202–354. These 152 pages report the lower court case, the appeal of insurance companies before the state Supreme Court,

There are two important archives in London for information pertaining to the *Creole* revolt and its broader political dimensions. The voluminous Aberdeen Papers at The British Library (BL) are indispensable for understanding Anglo-American difficulties and resolutions especially in the correspondence involving British special envoy Lord Ashburton, US Secretary of State Daniel Webster, and British Foreign Secretary Lord Aberdeen.[28] The National Archives at Kew is the other major repository. Its Colonial Office and Foreign Office records on relations between London and Nassau are essential for understanding imperial governance in general as well as the critical moment of transition from colonial slavery to abolition during the 1830s and its implications. There are also legal records from the Vice-Admiralty Court at Nassau, Bahamas, that enjoyed local jurisdiction over maritime affairs, as well as Bahamian Governor Sir Francis Cockburn's correspondence with the Foreign Office.[29] The focus of documentary research for *Rebellious Passage* has been on broader issues of maritime disputes over freedom on the high seas.

There are also useful records in the Caribbean. The Department of Archives at Nassau is indispensable for tracing the settlement patterns of a number of former captives from the *Creole*. Local histories, oral interviews, land grant records, village maps, and other records reveal not only where some of these people spent their lives but also interesting details on household and landholding patterns. This is particularly true of *Creole* rebel leader Elijah Morris who turned out to be one of the stimulating revelations from this local research. Indeed, Morris's archival footprint allowed me to move the narrative away from the heroic leadership model of Madison Washington toward a more meaningful engagement with real, existing freedoms of a former rebel who was at liberty, owned land, and raised a family independently.

These various archives scattered across the English-speaking Atlantic world pose challenges to the *Creole* scholar. The time, travel, and expense of international research, together with the need to work through several

---

the slave-owner's rebuttal before the state Supreme Court, and Judge Henry Adams Bullard's summation and rulings on the *Creole* and six other law suits. This 1845 report also reproduces documents and depositions contained in the 1842 US Senate document as well as materials from the Nassau investigation.

[28] Aberdeen Papers 85, Add MS 43123, British Library (BL), London, England. Enlarged photocopies of some of these papers, together with some additional papers, can be found in RP (Reserve Photocopy) 6981/13 also in the Aberdeen Papers. Wilbur Jones and Howard Jones appear to be the only *Creole* scholars who consulted this source.

[29] Bahamas National Archives, Nassau, Bahamas.

different historiographies on slave resistance, the antebellum United States, British colonial abolition, maritime business insurance, Atlantic empires, international diplomacy, and other details make for a demanding schedule. It might explain why scholars prefer to write up various aspects of the *Creole* rather than present a more complete historical analysis. This book seeks to provide the most thoroughly documented and comprehensive study in the hope of not only revealing more about the reasons, nature, and consequences of the shipboard revolt, but also addressing broader issues of empires clashing over slavery and liberty in the nineteenth-century Atlantic world. The bigger picture aligns with those recent works that trumpet transnational and comparative approaches toward unearthing the past as compelling correctives to historical studies characterized by an increasing academic over-specialization that is intellectually stifling and parochial.

Rebellious Passage is organized into eleven chapters and concludes with an epilogue. Each segment aims to tell a vital feature of this dramatic tale. The first one contours a series of clashes and tensions between the United States and the United Kingdom on land and sea between the 1770s through the 1830s. In particular, it seeks to contextualize the *Creole* revolt by focusing on maritime clashes between expanding British colonial abolition and American slavery. It insists that the British antislavery state pursued imperial interests by attacking slave trading and undermining slave societies. At the same time, the American slave state sought aggressive maritime expansion in the northern Caribbean and Gulf waters. Chapter 2 examines the maritime dimensions of the domestic slave trade. Apart from contributing to our knowledge about this understudied topic, it seeks to reveal the experiences of captives in the coastwise trade. What was a month aboard a coastwise slaver truly like? Moreover, it demonstrates how the roles in slave commerce of traders, captains, sailors, investors, and federal employees contributed to the expansion of the American Empire *along the coast*.

Chapter 3 narrates the stories of several US coastal slavers and the liberation of their captives in the British West Indies between 1830 and 1840, both contrasting and highlighting the clash between slavery and antislavery empires that were <u>both</u> expanding. Examination of the contest between American coastal slavery and British colonial abolition not only helps us better understand the *Creole* revolt and its consequences; it further illustrates how different national policies were of the same territorially expansive coinage.

Chapter 4 provides a detailed examination of the slaver *Creole* prior to the 1841 rebellion, one that is little known and often mistakenly presented. Based upon excellent federal shipping records, it also aims to narrate this history as exemplary of the Coastal Passage. The following chapter narrates the *Creole* revolt. My telling differs from several other narratives in its emphasis on oral communication and verbal exchanges to reproduce the voices of those captives who were historical actors but who did not testify or leave a written record. Moreover the focus on experiences of fighting, killing and maiming, hiding, fear, capture, release, and so forth aims to put a more human face on this dramatic shipboard revolt.

The next two chapters focus on events in the Caribbean. Chapter 6 examines the release of the captives from the American slaver in Nassau harbor. It argues that, contrary to the view depicted by biased contemporary accounts and repeated uncritically by most scholars, freedom was an opportunity that was acted upon rather than the gift of the British authorities. It further maintains that liberation emanated from the creation of a racial bond between former American slaves and black Bahamians recently emancipated by British colonial law. In other words, the act of liberation represented a diasporic connection in which freedom was a shared struggle. The next chapter examines the transition of former American slaves into new British subjects and the ways in which these new colonial subjects defined their freedom.

We then shift to the broader canvas of international and national politics. Chapter 8 demonstrates how local differences between expanding slavery and colonial abolition reverberated in the respective capital cities. These differences between Washington and London are pursued as imperial contestation rather than as a short spasm of fractured international relations. Scholars frequently focus on differences between London and Washington in the aftermath of the *Creole* revolt. But it is clear that there were far broader clashes over slavery and freedom involving the abolition of Atlantic slave trading, the future of slave societies in Cuba and Brazil, and so forth. The ninth chapter examines the ways in which newspapers and politicians used the *Creole* revolt to make alternative statements about the rights of property, sovereign domain, and human rights. Specifically, it illustrates how the maritime revolt revealed sectional differences – between northern antislavery proponents for whom slave laws were municipal versus southern slaveholders and their supporters for whom slave laws extended beyond states – were protected by the federal government, and subject to the law of nations. This chapter demonstrates how an international crisis seeped down to local levels through newspaper reports and politicians' actions, including several southern states protesting the *Creole* revolt, insisting on the sanctity of slave property, and rejecting British actions. It also offers brief analysis of British views on the ship revolt – especially concerning the rights of man discussed in local newspapers – for the first time. It further provides transatlantic dimensions to Mexican and Texan independence in contrast to conventional treatments of political struggles over annexation as sectional prelude to the Civil War.

Chapter 10 examines the protracted legal dispute that reached the Louisiana Supreme Court in 1845; this dispute was between slave merchants and owners versus insurance companies over culpability for the loss of the captives. Readers who desire the sexy stuff of ship revolt can skip this but they would miss some intriguing insights into the murky world of maritime insurance. Indeed, this aspect of the *Creole* story has drawn the least scholarly attention, yet it opens up a fascinating glimpse into the transatlantic world of slave trading, the insurance industry, legal traditions, and maritime property rights. Although it was the hardest chapter to research and write because of my lack of training as a legal historian, it proved to be the most edifying. Chapter 11 analyzes the origins, nature, and outcome of the 1853 Anglo-American Commission that decided the outcome of disputes over lost property claims by citizens of both nations, especially those concerned with coastal slavers. In the spirit of the expansive nature of the project, the epilogue shows some of the ways in which maritime issues that informed and emerged from the *Creole* revolt did not end but continued into subsequent decades. The nineteen figures have been whittled down from a larger collection and have been carefully selected for two main purposes: to illustrate a point or an event more graphically than the text does and to make obscure archival records accessible to the interested reader. The footnotes are not Edmund Wilson's "scholarly barbed wire," but identify sources, add comment on historians and debates, and occasionally try to amuse the reader.

The *Creole* revolt has attracted two previous book-length studies. Why bother with a third one? There are four major reasons. One key objective of *Rebellious Passage* is to use the *Creole* as a means to reveal the maritime dimensions of the domestic slave trade. The Coastal Passage was not simply incidental but central to the expansionist proclivities of the American slaveholding republic in the waning decades before the Civil War. My hope is that other scholars will be inspired to produce much more systematic analysis of the coastal dimensions of this massive and disturbing forced relocation of captive labor.

A further aim is to demonstrate past continuities. The traditional narrative of pre-1808 Atlantic slave trading followed by post-1808 US transcontinental slave trading must be replaced with a story of the continuous process of enslavement and resistance and its ramifications. The Coastal Passage was a continuation of the forced voyage of enslaved Africans along the southeastern US coast rather than a radical rupture as a consequence of the termination of the Atlantic slave trade. This is one reason why I prefer the nomenclature "US" slave trade to that of "domestic" or "internal" slave trade.

A third purpose is connecting histories. The American slaveholding republic and British colonial slavery are usually taught or researched as separate topics. The *Creole* revolt reveals how they clashed and why this was significant. Caribbean history is invariably presented in terms of national narratives from settlement to colonization to slavery to freedom to migration to independence – with the occasional bow to regional patterns – but this ship rebellion and its consequences link up the northern Caribbean with the British Empire and the antebellum United States. African-American history usually mirrors American history: revolution, war and emancipation, migration, civil rights, and so forth. The *Creole* revolt, however, reflects a very different scenario in which "outsiders" like colonial officials, Bahamian boatmen, and others, helped change the past. It is these connections between slavery and freedom across borders that are the most compelling part of the story.

Finally, this book seeks to make a contribution to historical methodology. Too many studies of the *Creole* revolt make the traders, diplomats, politicians, and lawyers the central actors of the drama. This might be due either to the nature of the evidence or to a preference for a particular historical approach. But surely this maritime rebellion by American captives in the northern Caribbean is a classic example of history from the bottom up. Slaves seized the slave vessel. Their action halted business as usual. Local authorities in Nassau responded. London and Washington responded to these local officials. Proslavery and antislavery adherents seized on the revolt for their own political and ideological purposes. Lawyers and jurists in New Orleans, and international commissioners in London, adjudicated the final settlement of the maritime upheaval. The point is that people in power were reacting to the actions of a rebellion aboard a coastal slave ship by ordinary people in extraordinary times.

Over the past decade, I have been researching and writing on the ways in which enslaved people took advantage of free soil by crossing either land or sea borders as part of the African Diaspora. Throughout the nineteenth century, colonies, nations, and empires either contained or juxtaposed un-free and free soil. Slaves who wanted liberty often gravitated from the former toward the latter with diplomatic fallout. This approach seeks to transcend ongoing debates in American historical studies about who freed the slaves, whether freedom made a difference, and so forth, by focusing on the dialectic between proximate borders of freedom and slaves' initiatives. It also tries to transcend conventional approaches in British abolition studies between London and the Caribbean by examining saltwater self-emancipators within the latter region. Slaves seized their freedom at the right time and in the right place with international ramifications. This is social and political history from the bottom upward. It drives my recent research and this project is the natural outgrowth.

Acknowledgments

It is with great pleasure that I express my heartfelt thanks to all of those who helped bring this book to fruition. Cheers to Dr. Kate McMahon, my former research assistant at Howard University from 2015 through 2017, who tirelessly tracked down important governmental and legal records at the Library of Congress, located and passed along valuable federal census records on Ancestry.com, and emailed me numerous unpublished documents and secondary source references online. Thanks to the staff at the British Library and the National Archives in London for their help, guidance, and professional assistance. In the Bahamas, I had the good fortune to meet Kathleen "Queenie" Barry who steered me through the materials of the Bahamas National Archives. We also had a memorable working lunch at the downtown Fish Fry in Nassau. Dr. Gail Saunders proved an invaluable guide to the Nassau archives. Dr. Rosanne Adderley provided pertinent information on the villages of liberated Africans in the Bahamas. Greg Osborn of the New Orleans Public Library brought me a vital microfilm on the *Creole* that contained a copy of the *Creole* manifest. It was located at the very end of the spool, and I stumbled across it one hour before the library closed. Another unforgettable archival memory was leafing through the *Creole* logbook to the sounds of the annual New Orleans music festival wafting gently into the reading room. Such are the joys of research! Sally Reeves at the New Orleans Notarial Archives is the expert on this collection and helped guide me through the arcane corridors of nineteenth-century legal records. Christopher Harter and Chianta Dorsey at the Amistad Research Center at Tulane University, New Orleans, brought me some important documents and microfilm records pertaining to the *Creole*.

The archivists at the Library of Virginia in Richmond – a model public research facility – provided assistance with newspapers and city tax records. Toward the end of the project, I received timely assistance from Mark Mollan at the National Archives and Records Administration in Washington, DC. I would also like to thank Troy Vallos, the Special Collections Librarian at Norfolk Public Library, for some last-minute information regarding the local slave trade in southeast Virginia.

The organizers of the British American Nineteenth Century Historians meeting at Rice University, Houston, Texas, in April 2014 allowed me to first present this project, for which I am grateful. Chapter 2 benefited from constructive comments from participants at the "Slavery, Memory, and the African Diaspora" seminar at Howard University as well as written comments from Joseph P. Reidy. Thomas Heinrich's invitation to present on the international dimensions of the *Creole* revolt to students and faculty at Baruch College brought great personal satisfaction. Thanks to the Amistad Lecture Committee at Central Connecticut State University – especially Dan Broyld, Gloria Emeagwali, and Olusegun Sogunro – for the opportunity to address a large audience on my research. Matt Mason provided some useful critical feedback on the domestic ramifications of the *Creole* revolt. He also offered some very constructive criticism of the entire manuscript on two occasions, for which I am most thankful. Thanks to several colleagues who supported, prodded, and pushed the project along the way: Richard Blackett, Edna Medford, Cassandra Newby-Alexander, Joe Reidy, and Ashraf Rushdy. Google Book Search, Hathi Trust Digital Library, and The Avalon Project are to be commended for digitizing older published materials as well as hard-to-find documents thus facilitating scholarly research from the comfort of one's home library. The same is true of Wikipedia: The Free Encyclopedia whose endnotes for topics often contain very useful primary source material and references. The Library of Congress continues to be one of the best research locations in the world in terms of research materials and a pleasant scholarly environment. My thanks to Howard University undergraduates who enrolled in my Black Diaspora lecture survey course and read Chapter 5 on the ship revolt. "Reads like a movie," quipped one! I would like to thank Cambridge University Press and its three reviewers for their constructive criticism. In particular, I would like to express my appreciation to senior editor Deborah Gershenowitz for her unflagging and unwavering support for this project from gestation through publication. *Kam ung* to Yen and Claudia Dai for putting up with me in Roehampton during several research trips to London. Cheers to Maggie and David Lindquist for helping out occasionally with their grandchildren so that I could write. Love to ERL for her total support, editorial assistance, and constant enthusiasm. Finally, to the boys NKR and AKR whose daily requests served as a pleasant reminder (mostly) of other important things in life.

JKR, Durham, NC

May 2018.

Abbreviations

AAC	Anglo-American Commission
ARC	Amistad Research Center
BL	British Library
BNA	Bahamas National Archives
CCNO	Commercial Court of New Orleans
CO	Colonial Office (UK)
FICNO	Fireman's Insurance Company of New Orleans
FO	Foreign Office (UK)
FWP	Federal Writers' Project
GBC	General Birch Certificate
HMG	Her/His Majesty's Government (UK)
HMS	Her/His Majesty's Ship (UK)
JP	Justice of the Peace
LSC	Louisiana Supreme Court
MICNO	Merchants Insurance Company of New Orleans
NOIC	New Orleans Insurance Company
NONA	New Orleans Notarial Archives
NOPL	New Orleans Public Library
OIC	Ocean Insurance Company
PM	Police Magistrate
RSPP	Race & Slavery Petitions Project
TNA	The National Archives (UK)
USS	United States Ship
VL	Library of Virginia
WIR	West India Regiment
WPA	Works Progress Administration

I

Eagle versus Lion

When people in the United States and the United Kingdom encounter the term "special relationship," several things often spring to mind: former colonial ties; English as a common language; cordial relations between presidents and prime ministers – Roosevelt and Churchill, Reagan and Thatcher, Clinton and Blair; and cultural exchange – Beatlemania and Motown to an older generation, and Michael Jordan, David Beckham, Beyoncé, and Adele to younger generations.

A more malevolent relationship is rarely evoked. The decades since the 1940s have seen the forging of an unprecedented level of military and intelligence cooperation between Washington and London. Between 1955 and 1975, the Vietnam War – the Vietnamese refer to it as the American War – claimed the lives of between 1.3 million and 3.1 million people, depending on which side you ask.[1] British Prime Minister Harold Wilson refrained from criticizing this bloodbath at the time by reportedly saying, "We can't kick our creditors in the balls." Since the 1990s, London has repeatedly supported American intervention in the Arab–Muslim world during wars on Iraq, Afghanistan, Libya, and now Syria that have claimed the lives of hundreds of thousands people.[2]

---

[1] "Vietnam War Casualties," Wikipedia, https://en.wikipedia.org/wiki/Vietnam_War_casualties

[2] Some of us disagree that the world is a better place as a consequence of US global power supported by its junior partner in London. A British diplomat visiting Howard University several years ago seemed a little taken aback by my disagreement. The chaos and bloodshed in the Arab-Islamic world, the blowback in European cities, and the extension of the security state into the lives of American and British citizens over the past two decades suggest that the axis of good could not have got it more spectacularly wrong.

On the other hand, 2016 produced some interesting political develop-
ments that might unsettle this relationship. On June 23, a majority of the
British electorate voted in a referendum to exit the European Union.
On November 8, Donald Trump won the American presidency. Both
results defied the bookies' odds spectacularly. It is too early to forecast
the implications for the special relationship. On the one hand, the military
alliance remains intact.[3] On the other hand, there are signs that
Washington will seek trade deals with the bigger market of Brussels before
it does business with London.[4]

This post–World War II cozy relationship is far removed from the
world of Anglo-American conflict some two centuries ago. Washington
and London fought each other on land and sea, repeatedly clashed over
maritime incidents, failed to mutually honor treaty terms, fumed when
their citizens were occasionally killed by the other, and could not resolve
outstanding claims over property disputes. These differences were shaped
partly by a new republic proud of its independence and an old empire
(Ireland, Caribbean, India) grappling with the massive loss of its mainland
colonies. The heart of this conflict, however, was slavery. From the 1770s
onward, Americans and Britons repeatedly clashed over the issue of
slavery on battlefields and merchant ship, as well as in convention hall,
courtroom, and consulate. The primary reason for this conflict, it is
argued here, was because of the emerging contestation between
a slaveholding republic and an antislavery state. Both were expanding.
Both were in propinquity. And both were affected by generational pro-
cesses. One cannot fully comprehend this Anglo-American clash without
analyzing competing differences regarding slavery over an extended period of time.

During the late 1830s, the British state finally terminated chattel slavery
after nearly two centuries of support for the lucrative colonial system.
Emancipation, however, was an evolutionary process rather than
a revolutionary transformation. Wartime measures designed to maintain
the British Empire by winning colonial wars in two Anglo-American

---

[3] "UK Government 'Fully Supports' US Air Strike in Syria," BBC News, April 7, 2017, www
.bbc.com/news/uk-39524685; "Syria Strikes: All the Latest Updates," Aljazeera, April 15,
2018, www.aljazeera.com/news/2018/04/syria-air-strikes-latest-updates-180414021423
479.html

[4] Sarah Ann Harris, "Donald Trump May Prioritize EU over UK for Trade Deal – And
Remainers Aren't Surprised at All," April 22, 2017, *The Huffington Post UK*, www
.huffingtonpost.co.uk/entry/donald-trump-may-prioritise-eu-over-uk-for-trade-deal-and-
remainers-are_uk_58fb345be4b018a9ce5bad1e.

conflagrations between 1776 and 1781 and also between 1812 and 1814 resulted in a small but not insignificant number of enslaved people seeking freedom within British territory. The outlawing of slave trading on British soil crept along beginning with England in 1772, Scotland in 1778 and Upper Canada (now Ontario) in 1793, culminating in parliamentary legislation against British participation in the Atlantic slave trade passed on March 25, 1807 and implemented on May 1, 1807. London's legislation was momentous less because it reflected self-proclaimed national values of liberty and its expansion, but more because it effectively terminated the prodigious activities of the busiest transatlantic slave-trading nation globally.[5]

The integrity of colonial plantation slavery in the West Indies was also increasingly undermined during the early decades of the nineteenth century through growing intervention by the British state. Actions included legislation for registering slaves, the passage of amelioration laws, and the combined might of military and naval power to defeat massive slave rebellions in 1816 Barbados, 1823 Demerara, and 1831–1832 Jamaica. An Act for the Abolition of Slavery, passed on August 28, 1833 and implemented a year later on August 1, 1834, was the logical consequence of this expansive state power. Its passage was made possible by compensating former slave-owners in the British West Indies with GBP 20 million largely drawn from an increase in foreign sugar duties. Special magistrates representing London's colonial office were responsible for overseeing the new labor system of apprenticeship. The system was terminated in 1838, two years prematurely, because planters and apprentices resisted the new "free labor" system. Planters thought the new system was too "free" and sought to control labor in old, coercive ways. Apprentices demanded access to land and compensation for their labor; they either used the state's representatives to make their claims or protested with their feet against a system they thought too closely resembled slavery. Consequently, an alternative labor system of recruiting and transporting indentured workers from British imperial India was organized and managed by the colonial authorities to provide replacement workers for sugar plantations in Trinidad, Guiana, Jamaica, and elsewhere in the Caribbean.[6]

---

[5] J. R. Kerr-Ritchie, *Rites of August First: Emancipation Day in the Black Atlantic World* (Baton Rouge: Louisiana State University Press, 2007), chap. 4; Richard Huzzey, *Freedom Burning: Anti-Slavery and Empire in Victorian Britain* (Ithaca: Cornell University Press, 2012), chap. 3.

[6] Kerr-Ritchie, *Rites of August First*, chap. 1, chap. 4; Michael Craton, *Testing the Chains: Resistance to Slavery in the British West Indies* (Ithaca, New York: Cornell University

Moreover, the British antislavery state expanded its international reach.[7] After clamping down on the nation's slave-trading activities, the British government robustly pursued a diplomatic front against the continuation of the Atlantic slave trade through a series of treaties with several major slave-trading countries. These anti-slave trade treaties took four major forms. The first concerned the mutual right of search over shipping. Where incriminating evidence was discovered, it would be directed to courts of mixed commission that ringed the Atlantic Ocean basin. Conventions with additional regulations were signed with Spain (1817, 1835), Portugal (1817, 1842), the Netherlands (1818, 1822), Sweden (1824), Norway (1835), Brazil (1826), and Argentina, Uruguay, Bolivia, Chile, and Ecuador between 1839 and 1841. The second type of treaty concerned the mutual right of search without the complementary superstructure of mixed commission courts. Navy cruisers were required to hand over suspected slave-trading ships to respective domestic tribunals of parties as agreed in 1831 and 1833 conventions between Britain and France. Numerous other states including Denmark, Haiti, and the European provinces joined these Anglo-French conventions. In exchange for ceding some sovereignty on the high seas, these nations gained financial aid, military support, and trading benefits. It is noteworthy that the United States refused to sign either of these two types of treaties. The third form consisted of a mutual obligation to strengthen coastal Africa squadrons. For example, the 1842 Webster-Ashburton Treaty (examined more fully in Chapter 8) committed the United States to an eighty-gun squadron off the West African coast. By the mid-1840s, the combined force of the anti-slave trade squadron reached nearly sixty British, French, and American cruisers while the Portuguese–Angolan squadron stationed four to five ships after 1843. The fourth type were anti-slave trade treaties between Britain and the African states of Madagascar, Zanzibar, and Muscat.[8]

Press, 1982), chapters 20–22; Madhavi Kale, *Fragments of Empire: Capital, Slavery, and Indian Indentured Labor in the British Caribbean* (Philadelphia: University of Pennsylvania Press, 1998); Richard S. Dunn, *A Tale of Two Plantations: Slave Life and Labor in Jamaica and Virginia* (Cambridge, MA: Harvard University Press, 2014), chap. 9; Legacies of British Slave-Ownership, University College London, www.ucl.ac.uk/lbs/.

[7] Chapter 3 of Huzzey's *Freedom Burning* outlines the global dimensions of the British antislavery state.

[8] David Eltis, *Economic Growth and the Ending of the Transatlantic Slave Trade* (New York: Oxford University Press, 1987), 85–89; Keith Hamilton and Patrick Salmon, eds., *Slavery, Diplomacy and Empire: Britain and the Suppression of the Slave Trade, 1807–1975* (Eastbourne: Sussex University Press, 2009), 1–10; Mathew

Eloquently presented as humanitarian philanthropy to meet its power-ful abolitionist lobby at home, London's key aims included restricting foreign competition with its own sugar-producing colonies as well as the expansion and consolidation of its global power through the gunships of the Royal Navy. By the late 1830s, most slave-trading nations, with the exception of the United States, had signed antislavery treaties with Great Britain. Washington's refusal was due partly to concerns about British interference with American commercial activity as well as fears of com-promising its own national sovereignty. Thus, numerous transatlantic slavers from Europe, Brazil, and elsewhere hoisted the American flag in the hope that this would protect them from interference from the Royal Navy.[9]

Sea power buttressed these numerous diplomatic protocols. By the mid-1840s, 15 percent of British warships and 10 percent of total naval power was allocated to anti-slave trade activities. By the 1850s, transat-lantic slavers were being pursued and intercepted by twenty-six ships and 2,000 personnel of the West African Squadron. Their impact on the Atlantic slave trade was substantial. Between 1807 (British slave trade abolition) and 1867 Spanish slave trade abolition), some 160,000 Africans were liberated from the holds of more than 600 slave vessels belonging to those who had broken treaties and agreements. Of this number, around 94,000 Africans were liberated from transatlantic slavers and settled in the new British colony of Sierra Leone between 1815 and 1835. Most were detained on British orders. Most were stopped outside British territorial waters suggesting the enthusiasm with which London's admiralty ignored comity.[10]

Mason, "Keeping Up Appearances: The International Politics of Slave Trade Abolition in the Nineteenth Century Atlantic World," *William and Mary Quarterly*, 66, no. 4 (Oct., 2009): 811–816; Jeremy Black, *Slavery: A New Global History* (Philadelphia, PA: Running Press, 2011), chap. 5.

[9] Foreign Office (FO), Oct. 2, 1855, *Slave Trade Ledger*, Jan.–Feb. 1855, vol. 16, FO 84/973, The National Archives (TNA), Kew, London; FO, Nov. 11, 1843, *Hayti Ledger*, FO 84/479, TNA; H. G. Soulsby, *The Right of Search and the Slave Trade in Anglo-American Relations, 1814–1862* (Baltimore: John Hopkins University Press, 1933); Mason, "Keeping Up Appearances," 820–822.

[10] Eltis, *Economic Growth*, 94–98; Huzzey, *Freedom Burning*, 42–51; Northrup, "Sierra Leone," 23; Andrew Lambert, "Slavery, Free Trade and Naval Strategy, 1840–1860," in Hamilton and Salmon, eds., *Slavery, Diplomacy, Empire*; Huw Lewis Jones, "The Royal Navy and the Battle to End Slavery," BBC, www.bbc.co.u k/history/british/abolition/royal_navy_article_01.shtml; Rosanne Marion Adderley, *"New Negroes from Africa": Slave Trade Abolition and Free African Settlement in the Nineteenth-Century Caribbean* (Bloomington: Indiana University Press, 2006), 2–3;

These antislavery actions were carried out by the world's mightiest maritime power. In October 1805, the Royal Navy defeated the French Navy at Trafalgar, thus ensuring domination of the seven seas that was to last for nearly a century until the rise of the Imperial German Navy in the last decades prior to the First World War. During the Napoleonic Wars, the Royal Navy boasted 500 ships and 100,000 seamen.[11] By the 1840s, New Orleans editor James D. B. De Bow estimated that the Royal Navy consisted of 636 vessels with 17,681 guns operated by 40,000 seamen with 141 war steamers. The magnitude of this maritime might is illustrated by comparison with the fifteen other naval powers with a combined total of 1,497 vessels bearing 28,802 guns with 122,098 men and 135 war steamers. In other words, De Bow's estimates suggest that London controlled 42 percent of the world's vessels and 62 percent of these ships' gun power, and employed 32 percent of all of the sailors. This is reflected in the words of James Thompson's popular nationalist song: *Rule Britannia, Britannia rule the waves.*[12]

While the British antislavery state was expanding, the American slaveholding republic was also on the march. The admission of Alabama, Missouri, and Arkansas to the Union in 1819, 1821, and 1836 respectively, together with the annexation of Florida and Texas and their joining the union in 1845, massively expanded the real estate of slaveholding states together with their political power in the US republic. Slaveholders dominated federal government posts. Between 1788 and 1850, they controlled the presidency for five decades, the House Speaker's chair for four decades, and chairmanship of the powerful House Ways and Means Committee for forty years. Eighteen of thirty-one Supreme Court justices owned slaves.[13] President John Tyler, the tenth president of the United

---

David Northrup, "Identity among Liberated Africans in Sierra Leone," in Jorge Cañizares-Esuerra, Matt D. Childs, and James Sidbury, eds., *The Black Urban Atlantic in the Age of the Slave Trade* (Philadelphia: University of Pennsylvania Press, 2013), 23.

[11] Alan Taylor, *The Internal Enemy: Slavery and War in Virginia, 1772–1832* (New York: W. W. Norton & Co., 2013), 122–124.

[12] James D. B. De Bow, "The Merchant Fleets and Navies of the World," *Debow's Review*, 6, no. 4 (Oct.-Nov. 1848): 331. Linda Colley reports that the Royal Navy employed more than 140,000 sailors in 1812 during the Napoleonic Wars. See her *Britons: Forging the Nation 1707–1837* (New Haven: Yale University Press, 1992), 287. Jeremy Black observes correctly: "Indeed, the navy became a global force for change, challenging not only slavers but also established maritime law" Black, *Slavery*, 184.

[13] Leonard L. Richards, *The Slave Power: The Free North and Southern Domination, 1780-1860* (Baton Rouge: Louisiana State University Press, 2000), 9, 23–25; Leonard L. Richards, *Who Freed the Slaves? The Fight over the Thirteenth Amendment*

States who served between 1841 and 1845, hailed from a traditional slaveholding Virginia family. Several electronic sources summarize succinctly his political career, although the reader has to look closely for references to his propertied inheritance and ownership of slaves.[14] There is little doubt that this slaveholding heritage helped shape President Tyler's enmity toward British actions in response to the *Creole* revolt. In late June 1842, British envoy Lord Ashburton informed British Secretary Lord Aberdeen that the "President, as a Virginian, has a strong opinion about *Creole* cases [*sic*], and is not a little disposed to be obstinate over the subject."[15] Virginia slaveholder Andrew Stevenson served as American minister to Britain between 1836 and 1841. He was serving in London when the United States sought compensation for the liberation of slaves from the slave ships *Encomium* and *Enterprise*.[16] He reported British opposition, no doubt because of the recent passage of colonial abolition.[17] John Forsythe hailed from Georgia where he owned slaves and supported American slavery. His reward for loyalty to President Andrew Jackson was the post of Secretary of State from 1834 to 1841 where he denied British claims to search American vessels for slaves.[18] Although his successor Daniel Webster hailed from New England's abolitionist heartland, the new Secretary of State repeatedly insisted on the maritime rights of US merchant ships, opposition toward

---

(Chicago: University of Chicago Press, 2015), 12; Sven Beckert, *Empire of Cotton: A Global History* (New York: Alfred A. Knopf, 2014), chap. 5, esp. 107–120; Edward E. Baptist, *The Half Has Never Been Told: Slavery and the Making of American Capitalism* (New York: Basic Books, 2014), 9.

[14] John Tyler, biography, www.biography.com/people/john-tyler-9512796, John Tyler, http://totallyhistory.com/john-tyler/, John Tyler, www.history.com/topics/us-presidents/john-tyler.

[15] Ashburton to Aberdeen, June 29, 1842, Folder 133–5, Add. MS 43123, Aberdeen Papers, British Library (BL).

[16] See Chapter 3.

[17] "*Thomas McCargo* v. *The New Orleans Insurance Company*," in Merritt M. Robinson, *Reports of Cases Argued and Determined in the Supreme Court of Louisiana*, vol. 10, (March 1 to June 20, 1845), Samuel M. Stewart, 1845: 281; Howard Jones, "The Peculiar Institution and National Honor: The Case of the *Creole* Slave Revolt," *Civil War History* 21, no. 1 (March 1975): 35; Howard Jones, *Mutiny on the Amistad: The Saga of a Slave Revolt and Its Impact on American Abolition, Law, and Diplomacy* (New York: Oxford University Press, 1987), 53.

[18] "Biographies of the Secretaries of State: John Forsyth (1780 – 1841)," Office of the Historian, US Department of State, http://history.state.gov/departmenthistory/people/forsythe-john; Robert E. Luckett, "John Forsythe (1780–1841)," *New Georgia Encyclopedia*, http://georgiaencyclopedia.org/articles/government-politics/john-forsythe-1780-1841; "John Forsythe (Georgia)," http://en.wikipedia.org/wiki/John_Forsythe_%28Georgia%29. Only the latter website refers to Forsythe as slaveholder.

interference with the coastwise slave trade, and the sanctity of property rights in slaves during his tenure in Washington.[19]

The political and judicial power of southern slaveholders was underpinned by enormous economic clout. By 1860, cotton exports were earning $192 million for the United States. Some 80 percent of all enslaved people worked in the fields, and nearly 75 percent worked on cotton-growing farms. Most important, nearly 60 percent of total exports from the United States consisted of slave-grown cotton.[20] When South Carolina senator and cotton planter James Henry Hammond proclaimed, "No power on earth dares to make war upon it. Cotton *is* king," he was not only stating the white stuff's global significance, but also the indispensability of southern slaveholder's political power in the American republic.[21]

Moreover, the slaveholding republic wielded substantial power beyond its national borders. In 1823, President James Monroe submitted his doctrine to Congress and the world. The Virginia slaveholder supported anticolonial movements in the hemisphere, pledged non-interference in European affairs in both old and new nations, and warned that European interference in the New World would be considered a threat to the national interests of the United States.[22] The rapid expansion of the national economy encouraged the establishment of a network of consular agents in seaports around the world. Their mission was to encourage trade opportunities for shippers as well as to deal with any problems that might emerge between merchants and the foreign nations in which they

---

[19] See Chapter 8.

[20] Jonathan Hughes and Louis P. Cain, *American Economic History*, 5th ed. (Reading, Mass.: Addison Wesley, 1998), 170; John Mack Faragher, Mari Jo Buhle, Daniel Czitrom, and Susan H. Armitage, *Out of Many: A History of the American People*, 4th ed. (Upper Saddle River, NJ.: Prentice Hall, 2005), vol. 1, 313; Peter Kolchin, *American Slavery, 1619–1877* (New York: Hill & Wang, 1993), 95; Gavin Wright, *Slavery and American Economic Development* (Baton Rouge: Louisiana State University Press, 2006), 84; Beckert, *Empire of Cotton*, 119, 140, 206.

[21] I explain to students that cotton expanded the antebellum US economy the same way automobiles drove the post–World War II US economy, and information technology has done since the 1990s. The key difference, of course, is that carmakers and IT firms are not officeholders the way cotton planters were.

[22] John Mack Faragher, Mari Jo Buhle, Daniel Czitrom, and Susan H. Armitage, *Out of Many: A History of the American People*, 4th ed., vol. 1. (Upper Saddle River, N.J.: Prentice Hall, 2005), 265. To be sure, this economic and military domination of the Western hemisphere was only realized from the early twentieth century onward. But we should not forget that successful secession by the Confederate States of America would have established the most powerful slaveholding nation in the modern world.

operated.[23] John Bacon in Nassau, Bahamas, was one such consul who had to deal with the fallout from the *Creole* revolt as we shall see in Chapter 6. The US Navy was much smaller than the Royal Navy with only seventy-seven vessels carrying 2,345 guns with 8,724 seamen and five war steamers by the late 1840s.[24] But canny southern editor De Bow already understood the key role maritime power played in empire building. The dress rehearsal would be the Union's successful naval blockade of the Confederate States of America during the early 1860s.[25] This understanding was fully implemented several decades later under the influence of naval strategist Alfred Thayer Mahan and the expansion of American naval power throughout the Caribbean and Pacific Oceans.[26]

Local officials occasionally declared their colonial convictions. Bahamas Governor Sir John Carmichael Smythe wrote to Lord Viscount Goderich, Secretary of State for War and the Colonies, informing him that, whatever decision was made about American captives whose slaver was grounded in the Bahamas as a consequence of foul weather, the governor would "not permit these eleven men to be taken away as slaves."[27] In 1840, Sir Edmund Lyons protested the practice of Greek vessels engaged in trading slaves on the Barbary Coast.[28] In his deposition to the Nassau commission in April 1842 concerning the *Creole* revolt, Attorney General George Campbell Anderson favored "general emancipation," even though he was a person of European, not African, descent. Moreover, he supported British colonial abolition unequivocally. As "slavery is abolished throughout the British dominions," the colonial jurist wrote, "the moment a vessel comes into a British port with slaves on board, to whatever nation such vessel may belong, and however imperious

---

[23] Charles Sellers, *The Market Revolution: Jacksonian America, 1815–1846* (New York: Oxford University Press, 1991), 81.

[24] De Bow, "Merchant Fleets," 331.

[25] According to a recent biography of Gideon Welles, secretary of the US Navy from 1861 to 1869, the federal fleet increased from ninety ships – with only forty-two in commission – in 1861 to 700 vessels in 1865, only second to Britain. See Spencer Tucker, review of *The Civil War Diary of Gideon Welles, Lincoln's Secretary of the Navy*, William E. Gienapp and Erica L. Gienapp, eds. (Urbana: University of Illinois Press, 2014), *Journal of American History* 102, no. 2 (Sept. 2015): 566.

[26] For classic and recent statements, see William Appleman Williams, *The Tragedy of American Diplomacy* (1959; New York: Delta, 1962); Gerald Horne, *Fighting in Paradise: Labor Unions, Racism, and Communists in the Making of Modern Hawai'i* (Hilo: University of Hawai'i Press, 2011).

[27] Smythe to Goderich, January 31, 1831, *Bahamas Ledger*, 1831, vol. 1, pp. 28–29, CO 23/84, TNA.

[28] Huzzey, *Freedom Burning*, 50.

the necessity may have been which drove her into such port, such slaves became immediately entitled to the protection of British laws, and that the right of their owners to treat and deal with them as slaves, ceases."[29]

Conversely, American officials defended slave interests beyond municipal boundaries. US Consul Bacon in Nassau went to great lengths to defend property rights in slaves as well as to secure the arrest, return, and trial of those responsible for mutiny and murder aboard the *Creole*. At the same time, however, it is fair to point out that not all officials toed the proslavery line in foreign relations. Henry A. Wise, US Minister to Brazil between 1844 and 1847, pursued a robust policy against illegal transatlantic slave trading under cover of the American flag during the 1840s.[30] George William Gordon – New England blue blood, failed merchant, and federal postmaster – served as US Consul to Rio de Janeiro beginning in 1844 and spent much of his time documenting, writing up, and protesting the barely legal as well as illegal activities of New England slavers in the South Atlantic slave trade between Central Africa and Northern Brazil.[31]

Although the state was a critical actor in the expansion of American slavery and British antislavery, it is important not to overlook the role of civil society – especially the actions of ordinary women and men – and how these differed from one another. Mass mobilization played a critical role in ending the British slave trade. It also contributed toward the abolition of colonial slavery as well as the early termination of the apprenticeship system that was condemned for its similarity to previous forms of forced labor. It was also mobilized to oppose Asian indenture – especially the slave-like shipping conditions with poor treatment and high mortality rates – although this particular unfree labor system survived until 1917.[32] During the 1830s through the 1850s, British men and women turned to mobilize against American slavery in multiple ways, including the organization of joint conventions, publishing and purchasing ex-slave

---

[29] *"Thomas McCargo v. The New Orleans Insurance Company,"* in Merritt M. Robinson, *Reports of Cases Argued and Determined in the Supreme Court of Louisiana,* vol. 10, March 1 to June 20, 1845 (New Orleans: Samuel M. Stewart, 1845), 250–251.

[30] Mason, "Keeping Up Appearances," 824. Wise went on to become the thirty-third governor of Virginia, and a brigadier general in the Confederate States of America.

[31] Kate McMahon, "The Transnational Dimensions of Africans and African Americans in Northern New England, 1776–1865," (PhD dissertation, Howard University, Wash. DC, 2017), chap. 3.

[32] Gelien Matthews, *Caribbean Slave Revolts and the British Abolitionist Movement* (Baton Rouge: Louisiana State University Press, 2006); Verene A. Shepherd, *Maharani's Misery: Narratives of a Passage from India to the Caribbean* (Kingston: University of West Indies Press, 2002).

narratives, hosting and supporting visiting former American slaves, as well as commemorating and organizing around slavery's abolition. They also supported slave revolt as the logical consequence of natural rights theory. In a memorial to Lord Aberdeen, the British Anti-Slavery Society stated that the *Creole* rebels rose up and "asserted their natural rights." Although murder was committed, they acknowledged "that homicide is to be traced to the resistance by those who endeavored by force of arms to retain them in slavery, not to a spirit of revenge on the part of the Negroes. They sought not life but liberty."[33]

In contrast to Great Britain, the abolitionist movement in the United States was small, regionally isolated, and usually on the defensive. Prominent abolitionists were often hunted, beaten, and sometimes murdered as was the case with newspaper editor Elijah Parish Lovejoy in Alton, Illinois, who was killed four years to the day before the *Creole* rebellion. There were many more adherents to the antislavery cause, but they were primarily opposed to the expansion of slave labor and its political representatives while not necessarily supporters of abolition. To coin the phrase: all abolitionists opposed slavery, but not all antislavery adherents supported abolition.[34] Far more ordinary Americans supported the institution of slavery. This was evident not only in popular opposition to abolition in its regional heartland, but also through the gradual expansion of slaveholding interests throughout the American South. Although the majority of white Southerners did not own slaves, there were about 385,000 slaveholders in 1860. Nearly two-thirds of them owned fewer than ten slaves. As Kenneth Stampp put it in the opening chapter of his classic study, the typical slave-owner worked a moderate-sized gang.[35] Moreover, it was thousands of small slaveholders who mostly transported captives in the Coastal Passage.

[33] Clifton H. Johnson, "The Creole Affair," *The Crisis* 78, no. 8 (Oct. 1971): 248–251; R. J. M. Blackett, *Building an Antislavery Wall: Black Americans in the Atlantic Abolitionist Movement 1830–1860* (Baton Rouge: Louisiana State University Press, 1983); Christopher Leslie Brown, *Moral Capital: Foundations of British Abolitionism* (Chapel Hill: University of North Carolina Press, 2006); Kerr-Ritchie, *Rites of August First*, chap. 2 and chap. 3; Jeffrey R. Kerr-Ritchie, "Black Abolitionists, Irish Supporters, and the Brotherhood of Man," *Slavery and Abolition* 37, no. 3 (Sept. 2016): 599–621; Huzzey, *Freedom Burning*, Chapter 1; Clifton H. Johnson, "The Creole Affair," *The Crisis* 78, no. 8 (Oct. 1971): 248–251 ("liberty").

[34] For this important distinction, see introduction to Robert F. Engs and Randall M. Miller, eds., *The Birth of the Grand Old Party: The Republicans' First Generation* (Philadelphia: University of Pennsylvania Press, 2002).

[35] Kenneth Stampp, *The Peculiar Institution: Slavery in the Ante-Bellum South* (New York: Vintage, 1956), 30.

In addition, non-slaveholders worked the slave system as overseers, skilled laborers (blacksmiths, carpenters), and shopkeepers, while seamen and officers manned slave ships in thousands of coastal passages over several antebellum decades.

Moreover, slavery played a vital role in wealth accumulation in the American South. Economic historian Gavin Wright persuasively argues that slavery created a profitable form of capital accumulation because human labor could be transported and could also provide the basis for extended credit markets. The physical wealth of the 1860 South amounted to $6,332 billion, of which human property constituted $3,059 billion or nearly half the total[36]. In addition, slavery consisted of an effective set of legally guaranteed and mobile property rights. Slave labor "could be purchased and carried to any location where slavery was legal; they could be assigned any task – male or female, young or old; they could be punished for disobedience, with no effective recourse to the law; they could be accumulated as a form of wealth; they could be sold or bequeathed."[37] Indeed, slavery "created a strong, regionally unified credit market within the South"[38] that was superior to that of family farm counterparts in the North.[39] The maritime transportation of these mobile property rights is under-appreciated in studies of antebellum economic expansion.

These contrasting empires also assumed ideological expression. The British abolition of the slave trade and of colonial slavery was immediately depicted as a royal gift from above. King George III received apotheosis after 1808, while youthful Queen Victoria radiated as Britannia after 1838. This was God's work in action.[40] By the mid-nineteenth century, the continental expansion of the United States had become divinely inspired – whether as Manifest Destiny believed in by many ordinary Americans or as the practice of slavery being a positive good as propagated by southern intellectuals

---

[36] Gavin Wright, *Slavery and American Economic Development* (Baton Rouge: Louisiana State University Press, 2006), 60.

[37] Ibid, 7. [38] Ibid, 70.

[39] Gavin Wright, *Slavery and American Economic Development* (Baton Rouge: Louisiana State University Press, 2006), 60, 70. For more on the complex links between credit and slavery, see the discussion on slavery and capitalism in Chapter 2.

[40] Jeffrey R. Kerr-Ritchie, "Slaves' Supplicant and Slaves' Triumphant: The Middle Passage of an Abolitionist Icon," in Ana Lucia Araujo, ed., *Paths of the Atlantic Slave Trade: Interactions, Identities, and Images* (New York: Cambria Press, 2011), 327–358; Linda Colley, *Britons: Forging the Nation, 1707–1837* (New Haven: Yale University, 1992), chap. 5.

like Thomas Roderick Dew, George Fitzhugh, and others. African slaves from pagan backgrounds benefited from their exposure to a superior, white Christian civilization; slothful, pagan, and savage Indians were best removed so that busy, productive, and inspired white immigrants could fructify the land. All this was done in the name of God. Of course, abolition and slavery could not both be divinely inspired, which only proves the Almighty's magnanimity in not discriminating between causes.

While it is evident that the British antislavery state was the most powerful adversary faced by the American slaveholding republic, it is important not to forget other antislavery states like Haiti that also clashed with Washington. Traditional interpretations of Haiti's pariah status, uniqueness, and insignificance have been recently challenged by new research that firmly anchors the former French slave colony within the currents and eddies of the Age of Atlantic revolutions.[41] The Haitian Revolution inspired slaves and disturbed slaveholders across the Americas.[42] The successful declaration of independence in 1804 and the writing and implementation of a new constitution in 1805 were followed by a bloody civil war that divided the new republic until 1820.[43] Civil conflagration, however, did not stop Haiti's new rulers from asserting their independence along with their antislavery credentials. Henry Christophe, who gained control over northern Haiti and crowned himself King Henry I in 1811, seized the property of several American merchants as reimbursement for the loss

---

[41] David Barry Gaspar and David P. Geggus, eds., *A Turbulent Time: The French Revolution and the Greater Caribbean* (Bloomington: Indiana University Press, 1997); Laurent Dubois and John D. Garrigus, *Slave Revolution in the Caribbean, 1789–1804* (Boston: Bedford, 2006); Maurice Jackson and Jacqueline Bacon, eds., *African Americans and the Haitian Revolution: Selected Essays and Historical Documents* (New York: Routledge, 2010); Ashli White, *Encountering Revolution: Haiti and the Making of the Early Republic* (Baltimore: John Hopkins University Press, 2010); Jeremy D. Popkin, *You Are All Free: The Haitian Revolution and the Abolition of Slavery* (New York: Cambridge University Press, 2010); Julia Gaffield, *The Haitian Declaration of Independence: Creation, Context, and Legacy* (Charlottesville: University of Virginia Press, 2016); Marcia Headley, "Imaging Haiti: Perceptions of Haiti in the Atlantic World, 1791–1875," PhD dissertation, Howard University, Wash. DC., 2012.

[42] Kerr-Ritchie, *Freedom's Seekers*, chapter 3.

[43] Alex Dupuy, *Haiti in the World Economy: Class, Race, and Underdevelopment Since 1700* (Boulder: Westview Press, 1979), chapter 4; David Nicholls, *From Dessalines to Duvalier: Race, Color and National Independence in Haiti* (New Brunswick: Rutgers University Press, 1979), chapter 2.

of a shipment of coffee detained in Baltimore.[44] Alexander Pétion, who assumed the presidency of the west and south departments called the Republic of Haiti, was particularly dedicated to challenging slavery in the Americas. In January 1816, President Pétion provided guns, munitions, supplies, ships, and money to the Spanish American liberator Simón Bolívar in exchange for a promise to abolish slavery in the new independent nations. In early 1817, slave pilots steered the schooner *Deep Nine* from Jamaica to Haiti. President Pétion refused all requests to return the former captives. The "moment they set foot in its territory," he explained, they were at liberty. Haiti's status as an antislavery state continued after the death of President Pétion and the termination of the Haitian Civil War. In February 1822, President Jean Pierre Boyer spearheaded an invasion of 12,000 troops into neighboring Santo-Domingo (now the Dominican Republic) leading to the liberation of 4,000 bondspeople and the promise of land redistribution. Some 6,000 African-Americans – mostly free but some self-emancipators among them – ended up in Haiti during the 1820s. The Haitian republic eventually joined the Anglo-French anti-slave trade conventions of the early 1830s.[45]

Indeed, one cannot overlook clashing empires between Washington and Le Cap. Commercial ties were stronger than is often recognized. In 1820–1821, commerce between the two republics amounted to $4 million, or 4 percent of all American trade. The American government sent agents to oversee commercial interests in Haiti. The first agent Septimus Tyler was transported on a warship to his new post in 1817. But there was never any realistic prospect that the new republic, born out of successful slave rebellion and subsequently engaged in antislavery actions, would gain official recognition by the slaveholding republic. Repeated requests by Haitian leaders for official recognition

---

[44] Dupuy, *Haiti in the World Economy*, 86; Don E. Fehrenbacher, *The Slaveholding Republic: An Account of the United States Government's Relations to Slavery* (New York: Oxford University Press, 2005), 114; Julia Gaffield, " 'Outrages on the Laws of Nations': American Merchants and Diplomacy after the Haitian Declaration of Independence," in Gaffield, *Haitian Declaration of Independence*, 171. Howard University PhD candidate Andrew Maginn kindly provided the Gaffield reference.

[45] Jeffrey R. Kerr-Ritchie, *Freedom's Seekers: Essays on Comparative Emancipation* (Baton Rouge: Louisiana State University Press, 2014), 62–71 "territory" (68) ; Gerald Horne, *Confronting Black Jacobins: The United States, the Haitian Revolution and the Origins of the Dominican Republic* (New York: Monthly Review Press, 2015), chaps. 4 & 5; Frank Moya Pons, *History of the Caribbean* (Princeton: Markus Wiener, 2007), chapter 12.

were either ignored or rejected. In response, Haitian leaders refused to acknowledge US commercial agents officially. Soon after the passage of the Monroe Doctrine the United States convened the Panama conference of American nations but failed to invite Haiti. South Carolina Congressman James Hamilton perhaps best summed up this opposition: "Haytien independence is not to be tolerated in any form . . . [such] recognition would be fatal to our repose . . . The municipal laws of many of the Southern States would conflict with the provisions of a treaty containing such a recognition, and produce a concussion which must end either in the annihilation of these States, or the destruction of the power of the General Government."[46] At the center of this opposition was the deleterious impact of antislavery actions pursued by an antagonistic state. Its roots lay two generations earlier during the American Revolutionary War.

The American Revolution represented an anticolonial struggle against a centralized monarchical power that taxed injudiciously and denied political liberties. One unintended consequence was a clash between the colonies and London over American slaves. During the war, British military commanders offered freedom to patriot-owned slaves who entered British lines and served in support or fighting units.[47] On November 7, 1775, the Royal Governor of Virginia John Murray, 4th Earl of Dunmore, issued a proclamation offering to make "all indentured Servants, Negroes, or others, (appertaining to Rebels,) free that are able and willing to bear Arms." Delivered from the Virginian brig *William* seized from local merchants, around eight hundred enslaved people responded to liberty's call. For this action,

---

[46] Rayford W. Logan, *The Diplomatic Relations of the United States with Haiti, 1776–1891* (Chapel Hill: University of North Carolina Press, 1941); Fehrenbacher, *Slaveholding Republic*, 111–116 (quote on 116); Nicholls, *Dessalines to Duvalier*, 6.

[47] There are some difficulties with the usage of the term "Negroes" during the Revolutionary era. Obviously, most scholars no longer use such negative terminology. The term "Black loyalist" assumes incorrectly that blacks were supporters of the British rather than primarily liberty-seekers. Benjamin Quarles made this important distinction back in 1961 although not always without acknowledgment by subsequent scholars. The terms "American fugitives," "Black fugitives," "fugitive slaves," are equally problematic because they either assume national and racial identities or accept uncritically the definition of slave runaways as criminals fleeing the law. In which case, why not view the patriots fleeing British colonial laws as "American fugitives" or "White fugitives?" My own preference for "self-emancipators" does not always work because it conflates those who ran away under their own steam with those who were either beckoned forth or transported by loyalist ships. Perhaps the best phrase is "former American slaves," used when applicable.

Dunmore subsequently earned the nickname the "Great Liberator."[48]
On June 30, 1779, British Commander in Chief Henry Clinton pub-
licly offered from Phillipsburg, New York, "to every Negro who shall
desert the Rebel standard . . . full security within these Lines [and] any
Occupation which [they] shall think proper."[49] This British policy of
offering liberation to rebel-owned slaves was motivated primarily by
the need to weaken the patriots economically as well as to strengthen
the loyalists militarily.[50] It had little to do with the recent legal ruling
by Lord Chief Justice William Murray, 1st Earl of Mansfield, in the
Somerset case of 1772 outlawing slaveholding in England.[51] People
being denied their natural liberty fled to the British lines en masse.
Between 80,000 and 100,000 former American slaves sought liberation within British lines during the Revolutionary War, while between
20,000 and 30,000 black males served the loyalist cause as laborers,
servants, soldiers, and sailors.[52] It is unlikely that Lord Mansfield's
1772 ruling in England trickled down in any great degree to those who

---

[48] Lord Dunmore's Proclamation, Encyclopedia Virginia, https://www.encyclopediavirginia
.org/Lord_Dunmore_s_Proclamation_1775; Benjamin Quarles, *The Negro in the Making
of America* (1964; New York, Collier, 1987), 53; Sylvia R. Frey, *Water from the Rock: Black
Resistance in a Revolutionary Age* (Princeton: Princeton University Press, 1991), 63, 114;
Simon Schama, *Rough Crossings: The Slaves, the British, and the American Revolution*
(New York: Harper Collins, 2006), 75–76; Philip D. Morgan and Andrew Jackson
O'Shaughnessy, "Arming Slaves in the American Revolution," in Christopher Leslie
Brown and Philip D. Morgan, eds., *Arming Slaves: From Classical Times to the Modern
Age* (New Haven: Yale University Press, 2006), 189; Douglas R. Egerton, *Death or Liberty:
African Americans and Revolutionary America* (New York: Oxford University Press, 2009),
6, 66, 70; Jennifer K. Snyder, "Revolutionary Refugees: Black Flight in the Age of
Revolution," in Brian Ward, Martyn Bone, William A. Link, eds., *The American South
and the Atlantic World* (Gainesville: University Press of Florida, 2013), 96. In a family visit to
Colonial Williamsburg in March 2015, the interpreter made no mention of this important
proclamation during the tour of the Governor's mansion until I broached the topic.

[49] Quarles, *Negro in the Making of America*, 53; Frey, *Water from the Rock*, 113–14;
Schama, *Rough Crossings*, 100; Morgan and O'Shaughnessy, "Arming Slaves," 190;
Egerton, *Death or Liberty*, 84.

[50] One historian's assessment that Dunmore's proclamation was "[p]ractical rather than
moral, it was rooted in expediency rather than humanitarian zeal" is essentially correct
(Frey, *Water from the Rock*, 63). The same was to be true of President Lincoln's
Emancipation Proclamation issued eighty-eight years later, although this important
document continues to be discussed in moral terms.

[51] James Walvin, *The Zong* (New Haven: Yale University Press, 2011), 130–136.

[52] Frey, *Water from the Rock*, 211; Schama, *Rough Crossings*, 6, 8; Morgan and
O'Shaughnessy, "Arming Slaves," 198; Egerton, *Death or Liberty*, 6, 64; Downey,
Creole Affair, 1. This compares to about 5,000 black men who served in the
Continental Army and about 1,000 blacks who served the patriots' cause at sea.

were enslaved in the American colonies thus motivating them to escape. Rather, many of these enslaved people saw liberation being offered by the enemy of their enemy and followed it with hopeful expectation. Some seventy years later, rebel slaves aboard the *Creole* likewise seized the initiative by striking out for potential British freedoms in the Bahamas over the reality of American slavery in New Orleans.

At the end of the Revolutionary War, and the success of the patriots' cause for independence, British ships began to transport former American slaves out of the mainland colonies. During the conflict, some had become the servants of military personnel, while many others had been promised liberty in exchange for services rendered. The British proceeded to evacuate former American slaves from coastal entrepôts under their stewardship. This massive evacuation began in July 1782 and was completed by August 1785. Contemporary American and British estimates differ as to the numbers of those who left, so we only have approximations. Between 3,500 and 6,000 former American slaves departed from Savannah, Georgia, in the summer of 1782. Between 5,000 and 10,000 were evacuated from Charleston, South Carolina, in December 1782. Some 3,000 to 4,000 sailed from New York City in April 1783. The last group of evacuees left St. Augustine in East Florida on the HMS *Cyrus,* which carried 3,398 white emigrants and 6,540 black emigrants on August 29, 1785.[53]

Many of these former American slaves carried the official stamp of British liberty. The General Birch Certificate (GBC) – named after the designing officer – provided the bearer with free passage as a consequence of promises contained in official proclamations made during the Revolutionary War. One blank GBC from New York City dated April 23, 1783 read as follows:

> This is to certify to whomsoever it may concern that the bearer hereof . . . [name filled in] a Negro restored to the British lines in consequence of the proclamation of Sir William Howe and Sir Henry Clinton, late Commanders-in-chief in America; and that the said Negro has hereby his excellency's [*sic*] Sir Guy Carleton's

---

[53] Frey, *Water from the Rock,* 172–82, 193; Egerton, *Death or Liberty,* 151–2, 200–1; Ira Berlin, *Many Thousands Gone: The First Two Centuries of Slavery in North America* (Cambridge, Mass.: Harvard University Press, 1998), 303; Quarles, *Negro in the Making of America,* 56; Schama, *Rough Crossings,* 133–5, 154–56; Downey, *Creole Affair,* 1.

permission to go to Nova Scotia or wherever else . . . [destination filled in] may think proper.[54]

These GBCs were printed en masse and subsequently filled in with the names and prospective destinations of former American slaves who wished to leave. Phillis Thomas, a free black woman from Charleston, was certified to "go to the island of Jamaica or elsewhere at her own option."[55] Cato Ramsey, a forty-five-year-old man formerly owned by Dr. James Ramsey of Norfolk, Virginia, had responded to Lord Dunmore's proclamation and eventually made his way north to New York. Cato's certificate, like many others, stated that having reached "British lines," the bearer "has hereby his Excellency Sir Guy Carleton's Permission to go to Nova Scotia, or wherever else He/She may think proper" signed by Brigadier General Samuel Birch.[56] These GBCs suggest that the colonial authorities were sincere in fulfilling their pledge to grant freedom to all those who had ended up in British lines during the war. Former American slaves obtained their liberty throughout various parts of the British Empire, the northeastern Canadian dominions, the Caribbean, and England. Others ended up in the new British territory of Sierra Leone in West Africa.[57] The forty-day journey from Nova Scotia to the West African coast in a free transport with the prospect of land ownership contrasted sharply with the dark terrors of transatlantic ship crossings in the opposite direction. The movement of former American slaves to other parts of the Atlantic world anticipated the relocation and encounters of those aboard the *Creole* several decades later.[58]

---

[54] Arnett G. Lindsay, "Diplomatic Relations Between the United States and Great Britain on the Return of Negro Slaves, 1783–1828," *The Journal of Negro History*, vol. 5, no. 4 (Oct. 1920), 399n30. Brigadier General Buck W. Williams signed the certificate. This 1920 scholarly article originated as the first master's thesis in the history department at Howard University and was supervised by Dr. Carter G. Woodson.

[55] Schama, *Rough Crossings*, 132.

[56] Ibid., 150. The inclusion of this gender distinction on an official form suggests extensive liberty-seeking by former American slave women and girls.

[57] Harvey Amani Whitfield, *Blacks on the Border: The Black Refugees in British North America, 1815–1860* (Burlington, Vt.: University of Vermont Press, 2006), chapters. 1 & 2; Jeffrey R. Kerr-Ritchie, *Rites of August First: Emancipation in the Black Atlantic World* (Baton Rouge: Louisiana State University Press, 2007), chapter 4; Frey, *Water from the Rock*, 172, 193–8; Egerton, *Death or Liberty*, 197; Berlin, *Many Thousands Gone*, 304. It is estimated that between 600 and 1,000 self-emancipators ended up in London. Egerton, *Death or Liberty*, 209.

[58] At the same time, we should not overlook the British government's interest in relocating former American slaves as potential laborers to expand its imperial reach.

The most striking expression of this official certification of freedom was the movement of black people from New York to Nova Scotia during 1783 under the direct auspices of the British authorities. Between April 23 and late July, more than eighty ships were assembled in the city's harbor. Officers conducted embarkation interviews with those who wished to leave. Many held GBCs. Some claimed to be freeborn. The result was the creation of the "Book of Negroes," a list of 3,000 black people by name, age, and description. Walley Waring, a "stout fellow" of twenty-three years, was formerly enslaved to Joseph Waring of Stono, South Carolina, and left him three years previously. He bore a GBC. Nancy Hill, described as a "likely girl" of twenty-seven years, claimed she was free and produced a GBC to prove it. Simon, a "fine boy" of twelve years, was formerly enslaved to Cyrus Griffin, Esq., Virginia, whom he had walked away from in 1780. All three embarked on different ships to different destinations at different times: Simon on the *Nancy* for Halifax, Nova Scotia, on July 29; Nancy on the *Blackett* bound for Quebec on July 10; and, Walley on the *Elizabeth* for St. Johns, Nova Scotia. Altogether, the "Book of Negroes" listed 1,336 men and 914 women with the rest being children. About 1,000 sailed as families. Sarah Willet of West Chester County owned twenty-three year-old Nancy and thirty-six year-old Pomp Willet. Sarah died in 1776 after which Nancy and Pomp entered British lines. Both carried GBCs. They embarked on the *Peggy* bound for St. John's on July 29, 1783. The last of these New York City ships departed for the east coast of British Canada four months later on November 30, 1783.[59]

Many former American slaves, however, ended up in new conditions of servitude in the British Caribbean as a consequence of this massive relocation.[60] An unrecorded number estimated to have reached several thousand were forced to relocate with their loyalist owners to Jamaica. Between 1775 and 1785, more than 65,000 new slaves entered Kingston

---

[59] "Book of Negroes, Black Loyalists: Our History, Our People" http://blackloyalist.com/cdc/documents/official/book_of_negroes.htm; Egerton, *Death or Liberty*, 203–204; Schama, *Rough Crossings*, 222–223. For a recent examination of the transatlantic dimensions of black loyalists, see Byron James Stewart, "Freedom's Orphans: A Discourse on the Fates of Black Loyalists from the Revolutionary Generation 1776–1836," PhD dissertation, Howard University, Wash. DC, 2016.

[60] As one recent scholar of black flight during the Revolutionary era put it: "The majority of southern Loyalist blacks remained enslaved and were shipped into the Caribbean." Snyder, "Revolutionary Refugees," 99n1. Another scholar estimates that of the 6,000 slaves who fled wartime Virginia, one-third died of disease, one-third returned to owners, and only one-third made it to freedom in Nova Scotia (Taylor, *Internal Enemy*, 28).

harbor. Many of them probably came from either the Atlantic or Caribbean trades, with some from the mainland.[61] Other loyalists brought their slaves to settle the Mosquito Coast in Central America, a small British outpost rather than an official colony. White settlers were encouraged to re-create a former slave society for the production of raw materials (indigo, cotton, rice, tobacco) for the greater benefit of the Empire. Loyalists Robert English, Samuel Harrison, James Yarborough, John Nicholson, and others relocated to the Mosquito Coast and Belize and brought along their human chattel. Lieutenant McCarras, on behalf of James Moncrief, moved hundreds of the latter's slaves to the Mosquito Coast. This was a troublesome time for the slave-owner. The frontier nature of the region encouraged the desertion of 350 enslaved men and women who either joined Spanish and native settlements or established independent communities.[62] Around 1,000 whites and 4,000 blacks left St. Augustine, Florida, for the Bahamas and settled primarily on the islands of New Providence, Abaco, and Great Exuma. Denys Rolle brought around 150 slaves from East Florida and settled them on two tracts at opposite ends of the island of Great Exuma.[63] These ship transports of former American slaves anticipated the activities of merchant slavers after the takeoff of the Coastal Passage during the early decades of the nineteenth century.

The movement of loyalists and their human chattel from the mainland to the Bahamas was facilitated by geographical proximity. The short distance also meant that American slaveholders protested the transportation of fugitive slaves. Governor John Maxwell of the Bahamas complained of "daily pestering" from loyalist slaveholders to reclaim their former slaves. The sudden death of Maxwell's successor brought the Revolutionary War's "Great Liberator" to the colonial governorship.[64] Lord Dunmore set up a special "Negro court" consisting of three persons charged with deciding "all questions of Negro

[61] Frey, *Water from the Rock*, 182–3. Frey claims this number came from the United States rather than the Atlantic slave trade because records indicate limited African imports. This overlooks possible imports from the intercolonial slave trade. See Gregory E. O'Malley, *Final Passages: The Intercolonial Slave Trade of British America, 1619–1807* (Chapel Hill: University of North Carolina Press, 2014).

[62] Snyder, "Revolutionary Refugees."

[63] Frey, *Water from the Rock*, 184–5; Michael Craton, "Hobbesian or Panglossian? The Two Extremes of Slave Conditions in the British West Indies, 1783–1834," in *Empire, Enslavement, and Freedom in the Caribbean* (Kingston: Ian Randle, 1997), 204–206; Morgan and O'Shaughnessy, "Arming Slaves," 200.

[64] Frey, *Water from the Rock*, 185–6.

property." Recent loyalist planters claimed they had been robbed of their property under recent laws and proclamations whereby "slaves have illegally and shamefully been inveigled, by persons in high office." Moreover, former American slaves in the Bahamas, allegedly with encouragement, "broke out into some Acts of open rebellion." Nassau was "overawed by a considerable body of runaway[s] and other Negroes," who remained close to Government House and Fort Charlotte. These colonial establishments offered former American slaves some sanctuary from the claims of loyalist slave-owners. Others took up arms in self-defense of their new freedoms in Nassau and Abaco Island.[65] Eventually, some thirty blacks showed up at the court, with only one documenting his freedom, and the rest being returned to servitude. The Tory planters expressed their "extreme gratitude" to his Excellency for "fair, candid, and impartial Trials."[66] Lord Dunmore was to vacate the governorship in 1796, and to enjoy a comfortable retirement in England from his extensive colonial duties.[67]

More generally, American slaveholders protested these fugitive relocations and demanded an immediate halt to the removal of their personal property. Virginia slaveholder and successful military commander General George Washington protested to the British senior commander Sir Guy Carleton that these fugitive slaves were the property of US citizens and should be returned immediately.[68] Sir Carleton responded that these fugitives had come under the flag of the British government and could not be returned to a system of slavery.[69] It was a pressing enough issue to be dealt with at the Treaty of Paris in 1783 that marked the official cessation of hostilities between the United States and Great Britain. The seventh article stipulated the mutual release of all prisoners "and his Brittanic [*sic*] Majesty shall with all convenient speed, and without causing any Destruction or *carrying away any Negroes or other property of the*

[65] William Wylly, *A Short Account of the Bahama Islands, Their Climate, Productions, &c* (London: n.p., 1789), 21–22; Frey, *Water from the Rock*, 186n72-3.

[66] Wylly, *Short Account*, 40–41.

[67] Snyder, "Revolutionary Refugees," 97–98; Egerton, *Death or Liberty*, 202; "John Murray: Fourth Earl of Dunmore, ca. 1730–1809," Encyclopedia Virginia, www.encyclopediavirginia.org/Dunmore_John_Murray_fourth_earl_of_c_1730-1809.

[68] General Washington owned more than 200. See Egerton, *Liberty or Death*, 5; Henry Wiencek, *An Imperfect God: George Washington, His Slaves, and the Creation of America* (New York: Farrar, Strauss, and Giroux, 2003), 46, 81.

[69] Quarles, *Negro in Making of America*, 56; Frey, *Water from the Rock*, 192–193; Lindsay, "Diplomatic Relations."

American inhabitants, withdraw all his armies, garrisons and fleets."[70]
Despite Sir Carleton's order to prevent further carrying away, together
with several meetings with General Washington over the issue, former
American slaves continued to disembark on British transports. This was
because the British stated their wish not to renege on prior agreements. Sir
Carleton explained that "delivering up the Negroes to their former masters would be delivering them up – some to execution and others to
punishments which would in his own opinion be a dishonorable violation
of the public faith."[71] Sir Carleton's position anticipated future Foreign
Secretary Lord Aberdeen's subsequent rationale for not returning the
rebel slaves and their fellows from the *Creole* to US jurisdiction, albeit
with the critical difference of a recently declared official policy of colonial
emancipation. Both nestled under the broad umbrella of the antislavery
state.

This dispute was compounded by further infractions of Article Seven
reported by US slaveholders. At the same time, Britain expressed concern
about American non-compliance with other articles of the treaty.
Consequently, General Washington appointed John Jay to settle these
disputes. The major bone of contention was over former American slaves
and their status as either British colonial subjects or US slaveholders'
property. There was a regional distinction between members of northern
states who were less pressing on the return of former American slaves
compared to those of southern states where owners insisted on retrieving
their human chattel.[72] Several other attempts to resolve this issue came to
nothing. In the end, US special envoy Jay's mission failed. Along with not
obtaining protection for America's neutral shipping rights or ending
impressments of US sailors into the Royal Navy, he did not secure compensation for slaveholders whose human chattel had deserted during the
Revolutionary War.[73]

[70] Italics added. "The Definitive Treaty of Peace 1783, Article 7" [Transcript], The Avalon
Project: Documents in Law, History and Diplomacy, http://avalon.law.yale.edu/18th_
century/paris.asp; Fehrenbacher, *Slaveholding Republic*, 91–92.
[71] Lindsay, "Diplomatic Relations," 396–397. British officialdom's hypocrisy is proverbial:
We will not return American slaves who entered our lines because we promised them
liberty; however, we will support the relocation of loyalists' slaves to the British
Caribbean in the name of property rights as well as the continued development of the
colonial plantation system.
[72] Lindsay, "Diplomatic Relations," 403–406.
[73] Sean Wilenz, *The Rise of American Democracy: Jefferson to Lincoln* (New York:
W. W. Norton, 2005), 66–67.

During the Second Anglo-American War of 1812–1814, self-emancipators once again thrust freedom on the agenda by voting with their feet on the institution of slavery.[74] British naval incursions along the coast as well as troop movements on terra firma encouraged slaves' flight up and down the southeastern Atlantic seaboard. Scholars remain divided on the exact number of enslaved people who gravitated toward British lines. Some estimate the flight of 3,000 to 5,000 from Virginia and Maryland.[75] A more recent calculation suggests around 5,000 escapees from the Chesapeake region.[76] This is clearly an undercount since it does not deal with other southern states' theaters of war in which slaves were involved, including the Georgia Sea Islands, the Mississippi delta, and elsewhere.[77] Many of these escapees served as sailors, spies, guides, messengers, laborers, cooks, laundresses, servants, and so forth for the British war effort.[78] Several hundred are estimated to have served in military combat against the Americans. These became a corps of Colonial Marines that were recruited and trained on Tangier Island near the mouth of the Potomac River. Tangier became a magnet for fugitive slaves as well as a jumping-off point for raids and incursions. These Marines were to see action in the Chesapeake and in Georgia. In one engagement in May 1814, Rear Admiral George Cockburn reported "the Colonial Marines, who were for the <u>first</u> time employed in Arms against their old Masters on this occasion . . . behaved to the admiration of every Body" (except, one assumes, white Southerners.) Elsewhere, Cockburn praised these "excellent men" who "make the best skirmishers possible for the thick woods of the Country."[79]

---

[74] This topic has attracted much scholarly attention over the last decade, no doubt due to the bicentennial of the War of 1812–1814, together with the emergence of a rich historical literature on wartime slave flight and its consequences during the Revolutionary War and the American Civil War.

[75] Frank A. Cassell, "Slaves of the Chesapeake Bay Area and the War of 1812," *The Journal of Negro History*, vol. 57, no. 2 (April 1972), 154; Downey, *Creole Affair*, 2; Whitfield, *Blacks on the Border*, 31–34.

[76] Taylor, *Internal Enemy*, 441–442.

[77] Mary R. Bullard, *Black Emancipation at Cumberland Island in 1815* (New Bedford: Alpha Graphics, 2008); Horne, *Negro Comrades of the Crown*, 46; Frank L. Owsley Jr., *Struggle for the Gulf Borderlands: The Creek War and the Battle of New Orleans, 1812–1815* (Tuscaloosa: University of Alabama Press, 2000), 103–135. It also ignores those who failed. For their gut-wrenching stories, see Taylor, *Internal Enemy*, 156–157.

[78] Cassell, "Slaves of the Chesapeake," 144; Horne, *Negro Comrades of the Crown* 39, 49; Taylor, *Internal Enemy*, 1–2; Downey, *Creole Affair*, 3.

[79] Whitfield, *Blacks on the Border*, 35; Cassell, "Slaves of the Chesapeake," 150–151. For British attempts to recruit black and Indian troops in the Gulf region for purposes of

Besides determining the precise number of escapees, the more intriguing task is tracing the dialectic between slaves calculating their chances of winning and maintaining their freedom against being recaptured and returned to American slavery and the transformation of British wartime strategy. At the onset of the conflict, the British used a few escaped slaves in various capacities as temporary expedients. British commanders in the Chesapeake, for example, were ordered not to incite servile rebellion. But as the war dragged on, and the British realized the enormous odds facing them, expediency was replaced by official policy of using American slaves as weapons of war.[80] This change was exemplified by the proclamation issued by Vice Admiral Sir Alexander Cochrane, Commander of the North American Station of the Royal Navy, on April 2, 1814:

> That all those who may be disposed to emigrate from the United States, will with their families, be received on board His Majesty's Ships or Vessels of War or at the Military Posts that may be established upon or near the Coast of the United States, where they will have their choice of either entering into His Majesty's Sea or Land forces, or of being sent as Free Settlers to the British possessions [sic] in North America or the West Indies, where they will meet with all due encouragement.

He sent 1,000 printed copies to his second in command, Rear Admiral George Cockburn, for distribution along the shores of the Chesapeake. Many American newspapers reprinted the proclamation thus expanding its reach. People of African descent were not referred to specifically – "those who may be disposed" – but the meaning of Sir Alexander Cochrane's proclamation was clear enough. Enslaved people were encouraged to seek British lines in order to weaken the American war effort, especially the economic support provided by slave labor in the southern states.[81] This was a similar "tactic" pursued during the First Anglo-American War: the refusal to return fugitive slaves was primarily

---

manpower and stoking fear, see Owsley, *Struggle for Gulf Borderlands*, 103–135. This work also describes the role of the First West India Regiment in the attack on New Orleans, most of whom were sick. Owsley, *Struggle for Gulf Borderlands*, 142–157.

[80] Cassell, "Slaves of the Chesapeake," 145, 150; Whitfield, *Blacks on the Border*, 33; Jeremy Black, *Slavery: A New Global History* (Philadelphia, PA: Running Press, 2011), 170; Taylor, *Internal Enemy*, 4.

[81] Whitfield, *Blacks on the Border*, 33–34; Horne, *Negro Comrades of the Crown*, 51; Taylor, *Internal Enemy*, 209; Lindsay, "Diplomatic Relations," 410n61; Matthew J. Clavin, *Aiming for Pensacola: Fugitive Slaves on the Atlantic and Southern Frontiers* (Cambridge, Ms.: Harvard University Press, 2015), 42–50. Alexander Cochrane's Proclamation of April 2, 1814, is reproduced in Smith, *Slaves' Gamble*, 100. George Cockburn was the older brother of Francis Cockburn who was Governor of the Bahamas when the *Creole* docked in 1841.

practical. The key difference, of course, was Great Britain's anti-slave trade practices after 1807.

What about the American response to slave flight and changing British tactics? This varied. Some state officials pressured the federal government for compensation for lost slaves. Some slaveholders approached British lines to seek the return of their lost property. This was often unsuccessful. American slave Charles S. Ball recalled going with some Maryland slaveholders to persuade some fugitives to return to their former servitude but noted "their heads were full of notions of liberty and happiness in some of the West India islands."[82] (Some *Creole* rebels' heads were likewise filled twenty-six years later.) Another response was the dissemination of armed patrols seeking to either return or shoot escaped slaves. In one such encounter, between twenty-five and thirty men, women, and children fled in several stolen canoes from nearby Hampton, southeast Virginia, before being spotted by a group of fishermen who opened fire, killing some and recapturing the rest and marching them back to captivity. In addition, harsher laws against free blacks were implemented, including the restriction of movements, abolishment of schools for people of color, and increasing state legislative appropriation for the execution and transportation of slaves.[83]

These policies helped reduce the number of slave escapees. The British strategy of fomenting slave revolt and sowing seeds of fear in the minds of slaveholders largely failed as the Americans successfully repelled Britain's second military invasion to retake their former mainland colonies. As a consequence, thousands of former American slaves evacuated seeking liberty in Britain's remaining empire in North America and the Caribbean. Again, the numbers are inexact. One scholar estimates that 892 men, 583 women, and 188 children – the majority of whom were from Westmoreland and Northumberland Counties in Virginia – were evacuated to Halifax, Nova Scotia, between April 1815 and October 1818.[84] Another scholar reports 3,800 former American slaves from at least seven states embarked with British forces and settled in Nova Scotia, New Brunswick, Trinidad and Tobago, and Britain.[85] Official British records estimate 4,192 slave runaways relocated to Nova Scotia,

---

[82] Taylor, *Internal Enemy*.
[83] Cassell, "Slaves of the Chesapeake," 146–149; Taylor, *Internal Enemy*.
[84] Whitfield, *Blacks on the Border*, 37.
[85] Horne, *Negro Comrades of the Crown*, 46, 48, 72. See useful map of evacuees from the US to British imperial outposts in Smith, *Slaves' Gamble*, 189.

Trinidad, and New Brunswick.[86] Whatever the precise figure, thousands of former American slaves gained new liberties as colonial subjects much to the chagrin of slaveholders who demanded the return of their human chattel from the former colonial power (as would US slaveholders after the *Creole* revolt).

The Treaty of Ghent, signed on December 24, 1814, officially recognized the end of hostilities in the Second Anglo-American War. The issue of fugitive slaves as expropriated property was deemed important enough to be included in the third sentence of the treaty's first article. "All territory, places, and possessions whatsoever taken by either party from the other during the war, or which may be taken after the signing of this Treaty," it stipulated, "shall be restored without delay and without causing any destruction or *carrying away . . . or any Slaves or other private property.*"[87] Despite the peace and this agreement to return former American slaves, more diplomatic wrangling over these people and their status as property ensued for the next several years.

Although the Treaty of Ghent settled the Second Anglo-American War, it failed to resolve the dispute over runaway slaves. According to British officialdom, the liberation, confiscation, and refusal to return fugitives did not violate the treaty. According to the Americans, the opposite was true and the British state was responsible for indemnifying US slave-owners. Both sides agreed to arbitration under Tsar Alexander I of Russia who decided that the United States was entitled to compensation for lost private property, especially slaves. In 1822, the Tsar declared: "That the United States . . . are entitled to a just indemnification from Great Britain for all private property carried away by the British forces; and as the question regards slaves more especially, for all such slaves as were carried away by the British from the places and territories of which the restitution was stipulated by the treaty."[88] Eventually, an Anglo-American Commission made up of South Carolinian Langdon Cheves, North Carolinian Henry Seawell, Virginian George Hay, and British representative George Jackson convened in Washington in August 1823. Its primary purpose was to determine the average value of former American slaves and to adjudicate the validity of individual claims. One year later, the

---

[86] Taylor, *Internal Enemy*, 441–442.

[87] Italics added. "Treaty of Ghent;1814" [Transcript], http://avalon.law.yale.edu/19th_century/ghent.asp

[88] Harold E. Berquist, "Henry Middleton and the Arbitrament of the Anglo-American Slave Controversy by Tsar Alexander I," *The South Carolina Historical Magazine*, 82, no. 1 (Jan. 1981), 30

Commission agreed on the following values: slaves in Louisiana were worth $580 each ($14,900 in 2016); slaves from Georgia, South Carolina, Alabama, were individually priced at $390 ($10,000); and, slaves from Maryland, Virginia, and other states, were reckoned at $280 ($7,190).[89]

This Anglo-American price chart for human beings is instructive in several ways. Both sides deemed slaves chattel and simply wanted to either maximize or minimize payments. It illustrates the limitations of Britain's anti-slave trade principles as well as the firm establishment of America's proslavery policy. Moreover, slave labor was determined to be more valuable in the sugar and cotton states of the Lower South than in the older tobacco and wheat-growing states of the Upper South. This portended the profitability of the westward expansion of the system of bonded labor that resulted in the slave trade and its maritime dimensions in subsequent decades. In addition, the leading advocate of compensation for fugitive slaves was not a southern slaveholder but John Quincy Adams. A non-slaveholder from Massachusetts arguing in support of the property rights of southern slaveholders illustrated the power of slaveholding in the US republic. It was on display two decades later through the staunch support of Massachusetts's son, Daniel Webster, for the slaveholding republic.[90] Finally, thousands of enslaved people had sought and gained their freedom outside of the United States as a consequence of wartime conflict. They were now at liberty from the chattel principle.

After further differences and negotiations, the British government agreed to compensate American slaveholders to the tune of $1,204,960. This equals around $30 million today. Many claims from Maryland and Virginia were denied because of poor records and scant information. Other claimants were more successful in gaining compensation, with about $600,000 (about $15 million) being distributed to approximately three-quarters of the claimants. The Commission met for the last time on August 31, 1828.[91] A diplomatic impasse from two wars over five

[89] Fehrenbacher, *Slaveholding Republic*, 94–96, Horne, *Negro Comrades of the Crown*, 77, Lindsay, "Diplomatic Relations," 415–416; Mathew Mason, *Slavery and Politics in the Early American Republic* (Chapel Hill: University of North Carolina Press, 2006), 92–93. All dollar conversions are for 2016 and are computed from http://www.measuringworth .com.

[90] Fehrenbacher, *Slaveholding Republic* 98, 133; Mason, *Slavery and Politics*, 93.

[91] Berquist, "Henry Middleton," 31; Fehrenbacher, *Slaveholding Republic,* 96–98; Downey, *Creole Affair*, 3; Lindsay, "Diplomatic Relations," 415–419.

decades between old and new empires had finally been resolved. But the
clash over American property rights in slaves and British colonial abolition was to re-emerge with new vigor over coastal slavers and free waters
during the 1830s.

These various military conflicts, and their fallout over compensation
for lost human property, illustrated clear differences over slavery in
Anglo-American relations. There were other differences that were smaller
but no less important: British maritime impressment and American objections; the Royal Navy's right of search of US merchant ships and
Americans' refusal to accept this breach of sovereignty; and southern
states' imprisonment laws against British seamen. All three topics are
complex and have been examined extensively by historians. Our primary
focus is on how they highlight friction at sea between these two powers as
a means for contextualizing the subsequent clash over the *Creole* revolt.

There was a long history of British impressment into the Royal Navy
due to manpower shortages. This was a maritime empire that required
seamen to man ships that crossed oceans, linked the capital city with the
colonies, and transported goods, merchants, clergymen, officials, and
troops to wherever they were required. As an older authority on the
subject once put it: "The power of pressing is founded upon immemorial
usage," but could not be "vindicated or justified by any reason but the
safety of the state."[92] By the mid-eighteenth century, the Royal Navy
required more than 40,000 seamen in time of war. These were raised
from the merchant marine, press gangs, and impressment.[93] Following
this older tradition, British impressment of American seamen soon began
after the Revolutionary War. In particular, impressment followed upon
desertion, which was motivated by a desire to escape the harsh service and
possible death in the Royal Navy as well as higher wages in the American
merchant marine. It should not be forgotten that although the two navies
were poles apart in terms of strength and numbers, the story was different
with regard to the merchant marine. During the mid-eighteenth century,
around 25,000 sailors worked the English deep-sea merchant marine.
By the early nineteenth century, 50,000 sailors manned the US merchant
marine, of which some two-fifths were British born.[94]

---

[92] James Fulton Zimmerman, *Impressment of American Seamen* (New York: Kennikat
     Press, 1925), 16.
[93] Colley, *Britons*, 65.
[94] Robin Blackburn, *The Making of New World Slavery: From the Baroque to the Modern,
     1492–1800* (London: Verso, 1997), 395; Taylor, *Internal Enemy*, 123.

The Royal Navy impressed men in mundane as well as more spectacular ways. William Lyman and R. G. Beasley served as American Agents for Seamen in Great Britain from 1805 to 1812. The former estimated that the Royal Navy held 15,000 American seamen in 1807 while the latter recorded 802 applications for release from impressment in 1811. In the spring of 1806, HMS *Leander* stationed off of New York City harbor, "halted as many as 20 merchantmen at a time, pending searches for deserters."[95]

More sensational was what became known as the *Chesapeake* affair. In early March 1807, four sailors left Royal Navy ships and enlisted on the USS *Chesapeake* in Norfolk harbor. Admiral Berkeley, British Naval Commander at Halifax, Nova Scotia, ordered all ships under his command to stop the USS *Chesapeake* and seize the deserters "without the limits of the United States." HMS *Leopard* under Captain Humphreys met the USS *Chesapeake* on June 22, 1807 off the coast of Cape Henry. In the ensuing engagement, three seamen were killed, eighteen were wounded, the American ship was boarded, and four men were seized including three Americans and one Briton. They were taken to Halifax, where the Briton was hanged and the Americans were jailed. To search an American warship for deserters during peacetime constituted an act of war. Popular discontent was aroused, fueled by fulminating newspaper editorials. On July 7, President Thomas Jefferson called for the removal of all British vessels from American waters. In December, Congress passed the Embargo Act in response to the attack. The American minister in London, Jefferson's fellow Virginia slaveholder James Monroe, called for reparations including restoration of the three seamen, punishment of the naval officer, the abandonment of impressment from merchant vessels, and a special mission in Washington to announce reparations. The issue remained unsettled primarily because of the failure to disconnect the *Chesapeake* affair from the broader issue of impressment.[96]

Differences over the right of search constituted a second maritime clash. As part of its crusade against Atlantic slave trading, the British anti-slave trade state passed a series of treaties with other nations in which

[95] Zimmerman, *Impressment*, 163–164. Wilentz, *Rise of American Democracy*, 66–7.

[96] Zimmerman, *Impressment*, 135–155; Paul A. Gilje, *Free Trade and Sailors' Rights in the War of 1812* (New York: Cambridge University Press, 2013), 156–159, 163, 180–181; Wilentz, *Rise of American Democracy*, 66–67. Matt Mason's *Slavery and Politics* usefully examines the popular rhetoric of slavery versus impressment, including ludicrous analogies in which those seized by Algerian corsairs were deemed "*far better than that of the Americans impressed by British cruisers,*" (88–92, italics in original).

mutual rights of search of each other's ships were agreed. This of course benefited the world's greatest maritime power. On the other hand, the United States refused to sign such treaties and consistently denied the British right of search of their merchant ships. When Stratford Canning, Envoy extraordinary and minister plenipotentiary to the United States, asked Secretary of State John Quincy Adams if he "could conceive of a greater and more atrocious evil than this slave-trade," Adams replied "Yes, admitting the right of search by foreign officers of our vessels upon the seas in time of peace; for that would be making slaves of ourselves." This was an interesting response on several levels. Most obviously, such actions were against the law of nations. Moreover, the right of search raised the issue of sovereignty over which the Americans had recently waged two successful armed struggles. Finally, the US official elided the real existing condition of enslavement with the rhetorical device of liberty from state tyranny. The issue continued to rankle Anglo-American relations, although it did not feature when British troops boarded the *Creole* in late 1841 because the local US consul had requested their presence.[97]

The third significant maritime clash was over the passage of southern laws against the liberties of British seamen. During the summer of 1822, free black carpenter and former seaman Denmark Vesey planned a slave revolt designed to seize Charleston, South Carolina, and to start a slave uprising. A betrayal foiled the plot and resulted in more than thirty rebels being executed. Due to the maritime dimensions of the plot, the South Carolina legislature quickly passed repressive new laws against the mobility and freedom of all incoming seamen. In December, an "Act for the Better Regulation and Government of Free Negroes and Persons of Color" stipulated "that if any vessel shall come into any port or harbor of this State" manned by "free negroes or persons of color as cooks, stewards, mariners, or in any other employment on board of said vessel," they "shall be confined in jail until said vessel shall clear out and depart from this State." If the Captain did not remove his sailors or refuse to pay for their detention, they would be "taken as absolute slaves, and sold."[98]

---

[97] Mason, "Keeping Up Appearances," 821–822; Downey, *Creole Affair*, 3; Zimmerman, *Impressment*, 19–20; Soulsby, *Right of Search*, 17–18. The Royal Navy also boarded US merchant ships along coastal southeast Africa during the 1830s, much to the chagrin of the Americans. For some recent research, see Jane Hooper, "American Yankees and Abolitionism in East Africa, 1840–1860," paper presented at African Diaspora Seminar, Howard University, Fall 2017.

[98] Jeffrey W. Bolster, *Black Jacks: African American Seamen in the Age of Sail* (Cambridge, Mass.: Harvard University Press, 1997), 191–195; Egerton, *He Shall Go Free*, 217–218;

Within a short period of time, all visiting free black seamen were incarcerated while their ships rode at anchor in Charleston harbor. A British ship from the Bahamas had its mate and four seamen taken to jail. They were released after some difficulty. Stratford Canning, British envoy in Washington, wrote to John Quincy Adams protesting this "most grievous and extraordinary" mistreatment of British subjects and requested that the American government act to "prevent the recurrence of any such outrage in the future." This proved hard. In August 1823, black Briton Henry Elkison was removed from his ship and jailed in Charleston. B. F. Hunt, a lawyer supporting the law, declared that South Carolina was entitled to act this way because it was a sovereign state. Judge Johnson, Circuit Judge of the United States for the Sixth Circuit, disagreed, declaring the state's violation of the United States to regulate commerce together with the "reciprocal liberty of commerce." The native-born judge was vilified, while Great Britain was condemned for sowing "tares of discontent in the South." Seaman Elkison was eventually freed along with several other jailed sailors.[99]

This maltreatment of British seamen in South Carolina was condemned in the homeland. One Peter Petrie of Liverpool expostulated: "No country shall ever be permitted to treat any of the subjects of Great Britain so hostilely."[100] After the incarceration of the crew from a British sloop from Nassau seeking rice, British Board of Trade member William Huskisson warned: "[T]hese Yankees may kidnap one another but they must not kidnap British subjects in violation of the law of nations."[101] These violations by southern states continued unabated, however, through the 1850s as thousands of black sailors were jailed upon entering southern ports. Most of these were from northern states, but others hailed from British shores. The London *Times* wrote scathingly of the Negro Seamen Laws as proof of "the utterly indefensible nature of those institutions which this particular law was directed to maintain."[102] Most importantly,

---

Manisha Sinha, *The Counter-Revolution of Slavery: Politics and Ideology in Antebellum South Carolina* (Chapel Hill: University of North Carolina Press, 2000), 15; Horne, *Negro Comrades of the Crown*, 97–98.

[99] Philip M. Hamer, "Great Britain, the United States, and the Negro Seamen Acts, 1822 to 1848," *Journal of Southern History* vol. 1, no. 1 (Feb. 1935), 3–9, ("most grievous" 4, "reciprocal liberty" 7); John Lofton, *Denmark Vesey's Revolt: The Slave Plot That Lit a Fuse to Fort Sumter* (Kent, OH: Kent State University Press, 1964), 198–199, 205.

[100] Horne, *Negro Comrades of the Crown*, 98   [101] Ibid.

[102] Huzzey, *Freedom Burning*, 33; Elizabeth Stordeur Pryor, *Colored Travelers: Mobility and the Fight for Citizenship before the Civil War* (Chapel Hill: University of North Carolina Press, 2016), 110–111.

these state laws demonstrated the power of slaveholding in the American republic and its potential for sowing conflict across borders. As an older authority succinctly stated the case: "To the federal authority the Constitution has given power and responsibility in the field of international affairs; yet a state, acting within its reserved sphere of power, may give offense to a foreign government and involve the United States in difficulties."[103]

The simultaneity of expanding American slavery and British antislavery raises the issue of the "second slavery" thesis. Its proponents argue for two main stages to New World slavery. The first was marked by slave workers' production of cash crop staples like sugar, tobacco, tea, coffee, and chocolate for western consumption that in turn sucked up more human and natural resources in the Atlantic world. Labor productivity was not advanced and credit markets were undeveloped; the most strident critics of this first slavery were Christian antislavery activists morally motivated against British participation in the Atlantic slave trade. The second stage represented a new form of bondage in the American South, Brazil, and Spanish Cuba during the nineteenth century. Its major commodities were cotton, coffee, and sugar for mass consumption in Europe and the Americas produced by enslaved Africans on large plantations. This second slavery was marked by improvements in labor productivity, technological improvements in production and transportation, and the search for innovative practices disseminated in new scientific agricultural journals. The system was largely based upon extended credit networks linking planters with traders and financial houses headquartered in New York City, London, and Paris. The key point of this second slavery thesis concerns linkages between slavery and capitalism, specifically the advance of industrial capitalism based upon the more violent appropriation and efficient mobilization of forms of slave labor. Moreover, this second stage of slavery co-existed with the emergence of antislavery initiatives in the Caribbean and in North America.[104]

---

[103] Hamer, "Great Britain," 3.

[104] Dale W. Tomich, "The 'Second Slavery': Bonded Labor and the Transformation of the Nineteenth-Century World Economy," in Francisco O. Ramirez, ed., *Rethinking the Nineteenth Century* (New York, 1988), 103–137; Dale W. Tomich, ed., *The Politics of the Second Slavery* (Binghamton: State University of New York, 2016); Anthony Kaye, "The Second Slavery: Modernity in the Nineteenth-Century South and the Atlantic World," *Journal of Southern History* 75:3 (August 2000), 627–50; Baptist, *Half Has*

This second slavery thesis provides a compelling challenge to several previous historical approaches toward New World slavery. First, linkages between nineteenth-century plantation slavery and industrial capitalism point to the limitations of older views of economic stages, or a clear break between the two social forms of production.[105] Second, the expansion of slavery in the Americas during the nineteenth century challenges teleological notions of emancipation starting with the Haitian Revolution during the 1790s and concluding with Brazilian abolition in 1888. Emancipation was clearly a more uneven, convoluted, and contingent historical process.[106] Third, linkages between New World slavery and transatlantic circuits of capital accumulation were important. For our purposes, of course, this concerns British cotton manufacturers' reliance on slave-grown cotton in the American South. In 1857, enslaved workers in the American South cultivated nearly two-thirds of the cotton entering British textile factories.[107] The key promise of the second slavery thesis is its links between the simultaneous expansion of slavery in the US South, Brazil, and Cuba, the emergence of abolition in the northern United States, and the French and British Caribbean, and the burst of industrial capitalism in northern Europe during the nineteenth century.

But the second slavery thesis raises two sets of problems. The first is on a more general level. It tends to flatten key distinctions between larger and smaller slaveries in New World slavery and their economic impacts. In 1860, there were around 6,000,000 enslaved people in the western hemisphere, of whom 3.9 million – about two-thirds – lived in fifteen slaveholding states in the United States, some 1.5 million in Brazil, and about 370,000 in Cuba.[108] In other words, US slavery was much more expansive than bonded labor elsewhere. More important, American slaves grew cotton that went to Britain, the most industrialized nation on earth. This linkage was considerably more consequential than slave-grown coffee in Brazil or slave-grown

---

Never Been Told, 49, 63, 73, 79, 112, 186. Recent works on slavery and capitalism in the United States are discussed in Chapter 2.

[105] The historical *oeuvre* of Eugene and Elizabeth Fox-Genovese during the 1970s and 1980s constituted the most influential expression of antebellum slavery being mercantile capitalism in the English-speaking literature.

[106] Kerr-Ritchie, *Freedom's Seekers*, 141–150. According to a colleague, my negative equation of slave systems falling sequentially with a popular pizza chain did not sit well with her undergraduates who adored the company's product.

[107] Beckert, *Empire of Cotton*, 84; and "All the way to the Civil War, cotton and slavery would expand in lockstep, as Great Britain and the United States had become twin hubs of the emerging empire of cotton" (103).

[108] Kerr-Ritchie, *Freedom's Seekers*, xii.

sugar in Spanish Cuba. As a leading scholar of these connections has recently reminded us: Commodity trades boomed during the nineteenth century, with coffee exports from Brazil increasing seven times between 1820 and 1860, but "the major economies of the world depended on the cotton trade."[109]

Moreover, this view of the era prior to the second slavery bypasses historical transformations of New World slavery established by several prominent scholars over the past few decades. One approach is the tripartite model of changing colonial slaveries. The first stage was the Baroque characterized by diverse forms of slavery implemented by Iberian conquest and colonization during the sixteenth and seventeenth centuries. The second was the colonial mercantilist stage identified with English and French plantation development from about 1650 to 1783. The third was the new American slavery in the US South, Spanish Cuba, and Brazil during the nineteenth century and linkages between slave labor and industrial capitalism.[110] Another careful historical approach is the model of changing generations. The history of slavery in mainland North America was an uneven, convoluted process that can best be encompassed in four distinctive experiences. First arrivals, their progeny, and grandchildren defined the *charter generations* during the seventeenth century. They were followed by the *plantation generations* who were forced to grow the great staples of tobacco, wheat, rice, and indigo during the eighteenth century. The *revolutionary generations* came next and grasped the promise of freedom while facing a resurgent slave regime during the age of revolutions. The final distinctive experience were *migration generations* that saw the forced relocation of slaves from the Upper to the Lower South, the making of an African-American people, and the expansion and consolidation of the most powerful slaveholding regime in the nineteenth century Americas.[111] These two models of the making of hemispheric and national slaveries offer far more sophisticated and nuanced approaches than the of overdetermined structuralism the second slavery thesis.

---

[109] Beckert, *Empire of Cotton*, 205; and, cotton had "two labor-intensive stages-one in the fields, the other in factories. Sugar and tobacco did not create large industrial proletariats in Europe. Cotton did" (xvii). It is striking that one prominent economic historian of New World slavery ignores the thesis altogether. See Bergad, *Comparative Histories*.

[110] Robin Blackburn, *Making of New World Slavery*, and its recent restatement in *The American Crucible: Slavery, Emancipation and Human Rights* (London: Verso, 2011), parts I, II, IV.

[111] Ira Berlin, *Many Thousands Gone: The First Two Centuries of Slavery in North America* (Cambridge, MA: Harvard University Press, 1998); Ira Berlin, *Generations of Captivity: A History of African-American Slaves* (Cambridge, MA: Harvard University Press, 2003).

In addition, the second slavery thesis represents an economic model of slave production and mass consumption that downplays the political dimensions of abolition and emancipation. The state, for example, seems a fairly passive player in New World slavery and emancipation. This economistic approach pays lip service to what one scholar succinctly describes as the "great political convulsions, class struggles, and acts of resistance" that ended up destroying New World slavery during the nineteenth century.[112]

Moving from the general to the specific, *Rebellious Passage* both supports and refutes the notion of a second slavery. The coastwise movement of captives clearly built up antebellum slavery. It might also be argued that the short duration, numerous investments, credit system, and insurance business reflected modern aspects of capitalism. But, the coastwise trade was less a break than a continuation of a traditional transportation method of slave trading at sea. Moreover, the rebellious passage was less new than a part of numerous unbroken attempts to gain liberty by enslaved people of African descent at sea. If the *Creole* was partly unique, this was because it succeeded. Finally, British factories that consumed US slave-grown cotton represented a clear linkage that challenges the stages theory of economic development between slavery and capitalism. But the British state mobilized its military forces to interrupt and stop the transatlantic trade. In the process, they both protected their own sugar colonies worked by cheap wage labor and expanded their imperial reach. Indeed, what is striking about this juxtaposition of new slavery and new abolition was the extent to which the British state policed the seas around Brazil, Cuba, and West Africa in order to prevent slave trading while, at the same time, not stopping fugitives and rebels from gaining their liberation on British free soil and accepting slave-grown cotton into its factories to manufacture the white gold. This was global imperialism.

Let us conclude this long chapter with its relevance for a subsequent slave ship revolt as well as engagement with other historical interpretations of slavery in Anglo-American relations during the first few decades of the nineteenth century. To begin with, the conflict over slavery was lodged firmly in Anglo-American relations from the Revolutionary era onward. This contestation certainly preceded the political crisis temporarily abated by the 1820 Missouri Compromise. Second, the American

---

[112] Blackburn, *American Crucible*, 25.

protest against British maritime interference, including the right of search and impressment of seamen, drew from a republican ideology honed during and after two Anglo-American wars. It clashed with an emerging anti-slave trade practice pursued by the British state for the purposes of extending and consolidating imperial power globally. This clash was to become especially prominent during the 1830s as American slavery and British abolition both expanded. Third, these expansions were not only spatial but also political. Neither Britain nor America spoke with one voice on slavery; but each nation-state became increasingly identified with particular interests. Indeed, it might be argued that as the power of British colonial slaveholders gradually diminished over the decades between slave trade abolition in 1807 and slave emancipation in 1833 as a consequence of the rising British antislavery state, the power of American slaveholders gradually increased in the executive, legislative, and judicial arms of the republican slavery state.

Fourth, the issue of compensation for escaped slaves remained unresolved throughout this era and both preceded as well as followed on from the *Creole* revolt. Indeed, the clash of property rights in man was to last from the early 1790s through the early 1850s – a remarkable two generations. Fifth, these escaped slaves were less comrades of the crown than new colonial subjects who were former chattel slaves. This transformation was gradual but important and wide-ranging across time and space. Sixth, many of the issues over fugitive slaves on ships, rights of search and seizure, federal control of commerce, laws of nations, and so forth, that erupted during the crisis over the *Creole* revolt, did not emerge sui generis so much as capped a long tradition of maritime conflict between the Eagle and Lion. Finally, this conflict over the decades must have been memorable. Both Virginian and British officials had been contesting the status and worth of fugitive slaves and the outcome of their flight over land and at sea from 1775 through to 1814 to 1822 to 1841 and beyond. Was there a theme here of Virginians' angst, even paranoia, over perceived British interference? Were the British boasts of liberty for fugitive slaves only an effort to continue fighting the lost cause of their mainland colonies?

2

The Coastal Passage

The opening decade of the twenty-first century marked the bicentennial of the abolition of the Atlantic slave trade in the United States and Great Britain. In 2007, to commemorate the termination of this nefarious practice in Britain's past, both the British government and civil society organized political events, public exhibitions, walking tours, academic lectures and talks, museum events, and media specials. These commemorations had multiple aims: acknowledging an important historical event; endorsing the multicultural nature of modern British society; and drawing attention to Britain's past international greatness.[1] The last objective was particularly pressing during an era of dwindling global influence. The 2007 bicentennial commemoration took place at the same time British Prime Minister Tony Blair was providing unflagging military and political support to American President George W. Bush in his unprovoked military assault on Saddam Hussein's Iraq and its people.

The following year marked the 200-year anniversary of the US termination of its active participation in the transatlantic slave trade. The contrast to Britain could not have been starker. National and state legislatures largely ignored the event. There were few conferences, public commemorations, and media events. This might have been because the transatlantic slave trade in the United States was considerably shorter and much smaller than that practiced by Great Britain. According to the *Voyages* database, 102,031 enslaved Africans arrived in North America

---

[1] Jeffrey R. Kerr-Ritchie, "Reflections on the Bicentennial of the Abolition of the British Slave Trade," *The Journal of African American History*, vol. 93, no. 4 (Fall 2008), 532–542.

of the 121,843 who embarked between 1776 and 1825. (Compare these figures with respective totals of 707,358 of 787,492 in the British Caribbean and 338,895 of 396,525 in the French Caribbean during the same period.)[2]

The fanfare might also have been less because anti-slave trade legislation prohibiting the American slave trade resulted from a closed-door political compromise agreed upon twenty years earlier, during the 1787 constitutional convention in Philadelphia; this was unlike the two decades of massive popular mobilization that preceded the British act. Article I, Section 9, of the Constitution of the United States stipulated that the "migration or importation of such persons [slaves] . . . shall not be prohibited by the Congress prior to the year one thousand eight hundred and eight." The prohibition itself came from legislation proposed by a Vermont Senator. Finally, it might have been a reflection of the fact that official remembrance of slavery has usually lagged behind other historical commemorations in the United States. The abolition of trading in people, after all, represents an uncomfortable truth that not all men were created equal during the nation's founding.

Despite these contrasting commemorations, however, both slave trade abolitions share a similar historical narrative. The ending of slave trading is seen as a major rupture. British citizens ceased slave trading. Enslaved Africans now moved from colony to colony within the Caribbean depending on labor supply and demand, the state of sugar market prices, and similar factors. Colonial slavery, however, continued until its legal termination in 1833.[3] Similarly, American citizens stopped seaborne slave trading. In its place arose the US slave trade that was to forcibly relocate between 800,000 and 1,000,000 people across the southern United States. This expansion was facilitated by the dispossession of native peoples from southern territories by aggressive Euro-American immigrants and led to the making of a new land-based empire.[4]

---

[2] Transatlantic Slave Trade Database (TASTD), Voyages, http://www.slavevoyages.org/assessment/estimates

[3] Hilary McD. Beckles, " 'An Unfeeling Traffick': The Intercolonial Movement of Slaves in the British Caribbean, 1807–1833," in Walter Johnson, ed., *The Chattel Principle: Internal Slave Trades in the Americas* (New Haven, Conn.: Yale University Press, 2004), 256–274; Eric Williams, "The British West Indian Slave Trade after Its Abolition in 1807," *The Journal of Negro History* vol. 27 (1942), 175–191.

[4] The scholarship is large. Peter Kolchin, *American Slavery, 1619–1877* (New York: Hill & Wang, 1993) and Ira Berlin, *Generations of Captivity: A History of African-American Slaves* (Cambridge, Mass.: Harvard University Press, 2003) offer useful surveys of the American South. Laird W. Bergad's *The Comparative Histories of Slavery in Brazil, Cuba,*

The American narrative, however, largely ignores the maritime dimensions of the US slave trade. Captives continued to be transported on US merchant ships in large numbers for decades after the abolition of the Atlantic slave trade. As we shall see later in this chapter, more than 50,000 captives were moved by ship to new destinations over several decades between the 1820s and 1850s. Hundreds of vessels transported men, women, and children in this lucrative coastal business. In the process, goods like tobacco and finished manufactured products from northern factories spread commerce and developed new markets. Especially significant was the role of slave commerce by owners, traders, insurers, captains, sailors, federal employees, and others in expanding the United States as a maritime empire. The rich historical scholarship on the US slave trade has either overlooked or downplayed its seaborne features.[5]

This chapter provides an alternative narrative of the US slave trade with a focus on the Coastal Passage. It is organized into oppositional categories of maritime traders and shipboard captives. The first part examines the mechanics of the Coastal Passage. What were its spatial dimensions? Who were the slave traders? How did they conduct the business of the coastwise trade? Where did they operate and why? What did a coastal slave ship look like? The second section turns to the captives themselves. Who were they? What were their experiences before boarding and especially during transit? How did the gender and age of these captives compare to those transported overland? It concludes with an evaluation of the extensiveness of the trade. The objectives are twofold: to reveal the hidden dimensions of this maritime business and to argue for the continued importance of American slave trading across the water *after* 1808 – in other words, to reimagine the existing spatial configurations of the internal slave trade as well as the temporal dimensions of maritime trading and its abolition.

The chapter title has been deliberately chosen to capture these maritime dimensions and their significance. It echoes the well-known title "Middle Passage," in particular the forced movement of enslaved people across the Atlantic from confinement in coastal West and Central Africa to chattel bondage in the Americas. This chapter seeks

---

and the United States (New York: Cambridge University Press, 2007) highlights some compelling similarities and differences across the nineteenth-century Americas.

[5] Recent studies of ship manifests in Calvin Schermerhorn's *The Business of Slavery and the Rise of American Capitalism, 1815–1860* (New Haven, Conn.: Yale University Press, 2015) and Hank Trent's *The Secret Life of Bacon Tait, a White Slave Trader Married to a Free Woman of Color* (Baton Rouge: Louisiana State University Press, 2017) suggest the tide is changing.

to understand what was similar and what was different about these two maritime passages in contrast to the conventional demarcation of pre- and post-1808 seaborne slave trading and its rupture in Anglo-American historiography. It also seeks to challenge the notion of the second and intercolonial movement of captives that constituted what has been referred to as the final passage between the Caribbean and the mainland colonies. If anything, the coastal movement of captives in the nineteenth century suggests many final passages.[6] Most importantly, it tries to evaluate the extent to which the Coastal Passage represented a form of slavery at sea that requires analysis in its own terms. In other words, it reveals the shipboard experiences of captives being transported southward across the water as part of being enslaved rather than focusing primarily on slaves' experiences before in the Upper South and afterward in the Deep South.[7]

Federal records provide the major database. In order to prevent the continuation of transatlantic slave trading, the federal legislature passed laws requiring that all coastal slave traders must be inspected at both ports of embarkation and disembarkation. On March 2, 1807, the US Congress passed An Act to Prohibit the Importation of Slaves into Any Port or Place within the Jurisdiction of the United States. Section Nine stipulated that the ship's captain "sailing coastwise," with "any negro, mulatto, or person of color, for the purpose of transporting them to be sold or disposed of as slaves," was required to provide "duplicate manifests" of the human cargo to be delivered to the collector of the port. He, along with the captain, must "severally swear or affirm" that the persons aboard "were not imported or brought into the United States" after January 1, 1808. The collector – a federal employee – was to certify the manifest, a copy of which was to be carried by the captain "authorizing him to proceed to the port of his destination." Failure to comply with this federal law would result in the ship's confiscation and the captain's "forfeit" of $1,000 per "negro, mulatto, or person of color." Section Ten required that the ship's captain "deliver to the collector" of the port of entry "the manifest certified by the collector" from the port of embarkation after which "a permit for unlading" the cargo would be granted. Failure to do

---

[6] Gregory E. O'Malley, *Final Passages: The Intercolonial Slave Trade of British America, 1619–1807* (Chapel Hill: University of North Carolina Press, 2014).

[7] Sowande' M. Mustakeem's *Slavery at Sea: Terror, Sex, and Sickness in the Middle Passage* (Urbana: University of Illinois Press, 2016), proposes the concept of "slavery at sea" to examine "the social space of ships and the ocean as epicenters in the making and unmaking of transported slaves" (4).

so would result in a $10,000 fine.[8] Thousands of these ship manifests currently lie dormant in National Archives and Record Administration (NARA) repositories in Georgia, Texas, Pennsylvania, and Washington waiting to disclose their secrets about America's Coastal Passage.[9] The ship manifests examined here reveal several of the hitherto barely acknowledged slave traders and their activities in the antebellum United States. They also cast light on the lives and experiences of hundreds of captive men, women, and children who would otherwise remain hidden in history's shadows.

Ports linked America's coastal slave trade. The key entrepôts in the Upper South from which captives embarked were: Baltimore, Maryland; Alexandria, DC (retroceded to Virginia in 1846); and Richmond, and Norfolk in Virginia. Further south, captives were transported from the ports of: Wilmington, North Carolina; Charleston, South Carolina; Savannah, Georgia; and St. Petersburg, Florida. The major embarkation ports lay on the Gulf and Mississippi, and included: Pensacola, Florida; Mobile, Alabama; and Galveston, Texas.[10] There was also a thriving Gulf Coastal Passage. Texas slaveholder Ashbel Smith purchased three slaves aged ten, twelve, and seventeen in New Orleans and shipped them westward along the Gulf coast to Galveston in 1838.[11] But most of the coastal trade began in ports in the Upper South, continued through southeastern Atlantic and northern Caribbean waters, and ended in New Orleans. The Coastal Passage essentially linked the ports and hinterlands of nineteenth-century United States. The critical point – and a central claim of

---

[8] "An Act to Prohibit the Importation of Slaves into Any Port or Place within the Jurisdiction of the United States," *The Avalon Project: Documents in Law, History and Diplomacy*, Yale Law School, http://avalon.law.yale.edu/19th_century/sl004.asp. See also Charles H. Wesley, "Manifests of Slave Shipments Along the Waterways, 1808–1864," *Journal of Negro History*, vol. 27, no. 2 (April 1942), 157–159; John R. Spears, *The American Slave Trade: An Account of its Origin, Growth, and Suppression* (New York: Charles Scribner, 1900), 173–174; Wendell H. Stephenson, *Isaac Franklin: Slave Trader and Planter from the Old South* (Baton Rouge: Louisiana State University Press, 1938), 39.

[9] Letters Received, National Archives Catalog, US Customs Service, Record Group (RG) 36 https://catalog.archives.gov/id/2790606

[10] Frederic Bancroft, *Slave Trading in the Old South* (Baltimore: J. H. Furst, 1931), 275; Ulrich B. Phillips, *American Negro Slavery: A Survey of the Supply, Employment and Control of Negro Labor As Determined by the Plantation Regime* (1918. Baton Rouge: Louisiana State University Press, 1966), 196; Walter Jonson, *Soul By Soul: Life Inside the Antebellum Slave Market* (Cambridge, Mass.: Harvard University Press, 1999).

[11] Randolph B. Campbell, *An Empire for Slavery: The Peculiar Institution in Texas* (Baton Rouge: Louisiana State University Press, 1989), 163.

Rebellious Passage – is that these ports served as sinews of American slavery's expanding empire. The transportation southward and westward of bonded people, together with commercial goods and expanding markets during the first half of the nineteenth century, was as much a maritime as a transcontinental enterprise.[12]

The Coastal Passage stretched thousands of miles from the Chesapeake Bay down around the Florida peninsula and up into the Gulf region of the southwest United States. It was a long and dangerous maritime journey. Slave ships had to avoid hazardous sand and rocks just below the waters off Capes Hatteras, Lookout, and Fear along the North Carolina coastline. Instead of hugging the coastline, slave ships would venture further out to sea, then head almost directly south for the Bahamas archipelago. Once there, these ships would skirt Grand Bahama Island and chart a line through the "Hole-in-the-Wall" passage. After proceeding south parallel to the southeastern coastline of Florida, they would turn southwest around the Florida peninsula. This sea lane could be treacherous: Its currents, winds, and reefs claimed numerous ships and lives. The greatest danger to US slave ships, however, was sailing close by Spanish and British colonies before disembarking captives in ports adjacent to the newly acquired southwest territory.[13]

The key operators of this coastwise trade were merchants who chose to transport their human cargo via sailing vessel rather than by riverine craft or overland coffle. The reasons for selecting ships to transport slaves varied. It was cheaper to move slaves by sea compared to over land. The human merchandise was thought to arrive in better condition due to the shorter and less demanding method of transit. Human capital could be relocated quicker

---

[12] For useful studies of transatlantic slave port linkages and their significance, see Jorge Canizares-Esguerra, Matt Childs, James Sidbury, eds., *The Black Urban Atlantic in the Age of the Slave Trade* (Philadelphia: University of Pennsylvania Press, 2013); Mariano P. Candido, *An African Slaving Port and the Atlantic World: Benguela and Its Hinterland* (New York: Cambridge University Press, 2013); David Richardson, Anthony Tibbles, Suzanne Schwartz, eds., *Liverpool and Transatlantic Slavery* (Liverpool: University of Liverpool, 2007); Robin Law, *Ouidah: The Social History of a West African Slaving 'Port' 1727–1892* (Athens: Ohio University Press, 2004).

[13] Schermerhorn, *Business of Slavery*; Phillips, *Life and Labor*, 158; and Damian Alan Pargas, *Slavery and Forced Migration in the Antebellum South* (New York: Cambridge University Press, 2015), 47. Compare this maritime route to the overland trail. During the 1830s, the Tayloe slaveholding family moved captives from southwest Virginia, across the Appalachian Mountains into Tennessee and down to Alabama. This particular trail of tears was estimated to have taken forty-five days. See Richard S. Dunn, *A Tale of Two Plantations: Slave Life and Labor in Jamaica and Virginia* (Cambridge, Mass.: Harvard University Press, 2014), 279.

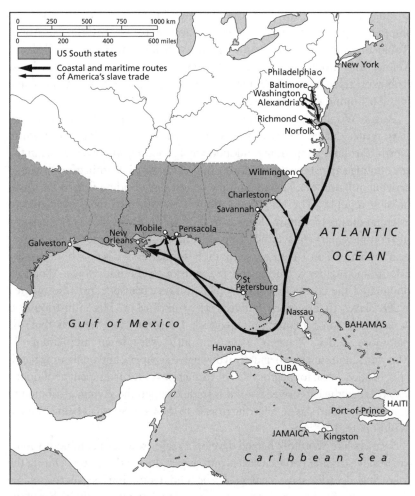

FIGURE 2.1 America's Coastal Passage, 1807–1864.
Cartographer: David Cox.

to a profitable marketplace. Besides, coastal slavers were available for hire while some large merchants had a fleet of ships ready for business.

This maritime trade displayed some recognizable decennial patterns. The decade immediately following the 1807 legislation did not see much coastal activity, probably due to the War of 1812 as well as to limited demand for enslaved labor on cotton and sugar plantations at this time.[14]

---

[14] Wesley, "Manifests of Slave Shipments," 160.

During the 1820s, however, the maritime business took off as traders shipped captives, especially from Baltimore to New Orleans. Abner Robinson shipped ninety-nine captives from Baltimore to William Kenner and Company in New Orleans in 1819. Thirteen years later, Robinson relocated to New Orleans in a migratory pattern than became familiar among slave traders.[15]

Austin Woolfolk, however, proved to be the most prolific and successful slave trader during the early stages of America's Coastal Passage. Born in North Carolina, he spent his childhood in Tennessee, where he served in the state militia against the British during the War of 1812. Within fifteen years of arriving in Baltimore, he had built the largest slave-trading firm in the slave-holding republic. The US slave trade was transformed from incidental to essential during his tenure. The key to the firm's rise was its owner's mastery of a complex marketplace and competitive advantage. Baltimore's Pratt Street near the Three Ton Tavern served as his headquarters – it is now buried under a four-lane highway. During the 1820s through the mid-1830s, Woolfolk dominated the coastwise trade from Baltimore, transporting an estimated 2,288 slaves to Louisiana between 1819 and 1832. His industriousness earned him some reputation. Frederick Douglass later recalled that the Baltimore trader's "agents were sent into every town and county in Maryland, announcing their arrival through the papers, and on flaming hand-bills, headed, 'cash for negroes'." The former slave and prominent abolitionist also recalled the extensiveness of this trade through the saying, attributed to eastern Maryland slaves, referring to sales to the Deep South as being "sold to Woldfolk [sic]."[16]

Traders like Woolfolk helped develop a major southern commodity market in slave trading between sellers and buyers during the 1820s. During the following decade, slave dealers in the Old Dominion began to assume domination of the Coastal Passage for reasons that are not altogether clear. George Washington Apperson, W. T. Foster, R. H. Banks, and R. L. Marsh were among the most prominent traders operating out of Norfolk. Both Banks and Marsh were masters of their own coastal slavers.[17] John and

---

[15] Phillips, *American Negro Slavery*, 196.

[16] Schermerhorn, *Business of Slavery*, chap. 2, " 'cash for negroes' " (39); Robert H. Gudmestad, *A Troublesome Commerce: The Transformation of the Interstate Slave Trade* (Baton Rouge: Louisiana State University Press, 2003), 26–27, "sold to Woldfolk" (26); Barbara Jeanne Fields, *Slavery and Freedom on the Middle Ground: Maryland during the Nineteenth Century* (New Haven, Conn.: Yale University Press, 1985), 17.

[17] Bancroft, *Slave-Trading*, 276n25; Troy Valos, Special Collections Librarian at Norfolk Public Library, email, July 19, 2017.

Sam Corby & Company as well as Lancaster, Denby & Company, and Thomas McCargo all operated out of Richmond – the latter two transporting captives on the *Creole*'s fateful voyage.[18]

One of Richmond's most prolific slave traders was Bacon Tait. Born in Lynchburg in 1796, Tait relocated to Richmond in 1828. His first recorded entry into the coastal slave trade occurred during the spring of 1828 when he transported twenty-nine men and eight women on the schooner *James Monroe* from Norfolk bound for New Orleans. The slaver carried 143 other captives and additional merchandise. In September 1835, Tait moved 144 captives aboard the brig *Adelaide* bound for New Orleans, where they were lodged and sold by his partner, Thomas Boudar. During the 1830s, Tait became "another dealer in human flesh and bones" in Richmond, building a new jail on the southeast corner of Cary and 15th Streets. In a notice advertising the new space, readers were assured "their NEGROES [would be] safely and comfortable taken care of." According to the 1840 federal census, Tait's household included a white man in his twenties, three enslaved adult women, one enslaved adult man, and three enslaved children. On September 19, 1841, about ten slaves escaped from his purportedly safe jail. Although he did not transport any captives on the *Creole* that departed a month later, Tait went on to become one of Richmond's wealthiest citizens and to lead an extraordinary personal life as we shall see in the epilogue.[19]

Along with Baltimore, Norfolk, and Richmond, Alexandria in the District of Columbia housed one of the most prolific slave-trading concerns. Franklin and Armfield was housed at a large three-story brick house on 1315 Duke Street in Alexandria, DC. Born in Tennessee the year of the French Revolution, Isaac Franklin served in the state's cavalry against the British during the War of 1812. Engaged in commerce on the Mississippi, Franklin turned to trading slaves. From 1828 onward, the firm used company ships to transport slaves from the Chesapeake to the lower Mississippi valley. Franklin was stationed in New Orleans and Natchez, where he received slaves. John Armfield, his brother-in-law, ran the shipping center and jail in Alexandria from whence slaves were transported.

[18] Bancroft, *Slave-Trading*, 276n25; Lancaster, Denby & Company, Richmond City Personal Property Book, 1836, 1837, 1838, 1839, Reel 365, Library of Virginia (VL).

[19] Trent, *Secret Life of Bacon Tait*, 2–3, 45–112, "flesh and bones" (61), "taken care of" (69); Elizabeth Kambourian, "Slave Traders in Richmond," *Richmond-Times Dispatch*, February. 24, 2014, http://www.richmond.com/slave-traders-in-richmond/table_52a32 a98-9d56-11e3-806a-0017a43b2370.html. This article lists the businesses and sites of fifty-five additional Richmond traders.

Rice C. Ballard ran the buying agency headquartered in Richmond and partnered with a trader in Fredericksburg. This was a massive and lucrative business. The jail at Natchez held between 600 and 800 slaves at any one time. They transported 1,000 slaves on the firm's ships in 1833, and expected a "much greater" number in 1834. According to one source, "they had agents in almost every large southern city, a fleet of ships, and earned more than $100,000 in profits annually through the sale of approximately 1,200 enslaved persons into the Southwest region." This business proved so lucrative that Franklin retired in 1836 owning several plantations comprising "8,500 acres and 550 slaves" in Tennessee and Louisiana worth nearly one million dollars.[20]

American slavery's merchants also worked the Coastal Passage from ports outside the Upper South. Hugh Macdonald traded from Charleston. He shipped 145 slaves to New Orleans between December 13, 1834, and March 19, 1835. Major shippers in New Orleans included Isaac Franklin (of Franklin and Armfield in Alexandria), Thomas Boudar, Edward Williams, Theophilus Freeman, R. W. Semington, Paul Pascal, Brander & McKenna, and Bullitt, Shipp, and Company. The year following the *Creole* revolt, Pitts & Clarke's Directory for 1842 listed forty-nine brokers, twenty-five auctioneers, and 185 slave traders in the Crescent City. One of these traders was prominent cotton factor and merchant trader John Hagan, whose five male and four female captives aboard the *Creole* were at liberty at the time the directory was published.[21]

The traders' initial task was to advertise their interest in buying "negroes" for the purpose of selling them into Lower South markets to meet the insatiable demand for plantation labor in the sugar and cotton fields. Newspaper readers would have encountered countless advertisements from Maryland, Virginia, and Washington, DC: "CASH FOR

---

[20] Schermerhorn, *Business of Slavery*, chap. 5, "550 slaves" (167); Gudmestad, *Troublesome Commerce*, 15–30; Bancroft, *Slave-Trading*, 276; Stephenson, *Isaac Franklin*, chap. 4; Pargas, *Slavery and Forced Migration*, 42–43; Donald Sweig, "Alexandria to New Orleans: The Human Tragedy of the Interstate Slave Trade," *Alexandria Gazette Packet*, October 2014, Parts I to IV; Franklin and Armfield, Virginia Foundation for the Humanities, http://www.aahistoricsitesva.org/items/show/1 57 . Earning state and national landmark status, the old merchant house now houses the Freedom House Museum.

[21] Bancroft, *Slave-Trading*, 276n25, 315; "Pitts & Clarke's Directory for 1842 New Orleans; and John Hagan, Bill of Lading, October 20, 1841, *in New Orleans Directory for 1842: Comprising the Names, Residences and Occupations of the Merchants, Business Men, Professional Gentlemen and Citizens of New Orleans, Lafayette, Algiers and Gretna*, New Orleans: Pitts & Clark, 1842).

NEGROES." "*Two Hundred* NEGROES WANTED." "CASH FOR 200 NEGROES, Including both sexes, from 12 to 25 years of age." "CASH FOR 400 NEGROES." A "liberal price in cash" for a "few Negroes." "CASH WILL BE GIVEN for a few likely NEGROES." "[C]ash for negroes." We "wish to purchase one hundred and fifty likely young negroes of both sexes between the ages of 8 and 25 years."[22]

These advertisements convey several important features about trading. The cash nexus pointed to the profitability of trading slaves. The demand was great as illustrated by the prolific number of these advertisements. Young men and women were preferred because they were in their prime working years. If shipped, these younger workers were likely to handle the sea voyage much better than older captives. Some readers would have noticed an advertisement placed by one Virginia trader in the final 1835 edition of the *Richmond Enquirer*:

CASH FOR 200 NEGROES. We will give the highest market price, in cash, for two hundred like-Negroes, from 12 to 25 years of age. Every person who intends to sell, will do well to give us a call, Seabrook Warehouse, where we are prepared to keep them safe and comfortable, whether for sale or otherwise. THOS. M'CARGO & CO.[23]

This notice highlights several key features of the trading business. Its profitability was indicated by the advertiser's readiness to pay cash. The traders sought young slave workers for the marketplace without regard to gender. Their security – that is to say inability to escape – was guaranteed. This particular dealer relocated to New Orleans and was to transport thirty-nine captives aboard the *Creole* six years later on its fateful voyage.

After successful transactions between sellers and traders, the recently purchased captives were moved to so-called holding pens. The most prominent of these were located in Baltimore, Alexandria, Richmond, and Norfolk – all of which provided easy access to the Coastal Passage. Both contemporaries and historians agree that these cells were invariably crowded, noxious, filthy, and disease-ridden.[24] Moreover, they were less

---

[22] These advertisements were taken from the following sources: Bancroft, *Slave-Trading*, 28; Wesley, "Manifests of Slave Shipments," 167–168; Schermerhorn, *Business of Slavery*, 36, 39, 165, 174–175; Winfield H. Collins, *The Domestic Slave Trade of the Southern States* (New York: Broadway Publishing, 1904), 51; Sweig, "Alexandria to New Orleans," Part I.

[23] *Richmond Enquirer*, December 31, 1835.

[24] Ethan Andrews, *Slavery and the Domestic Slave Trade in the United States* (Boston, Mass.: Light and Stearns, 1836), 80, 136–141, 164–165; Benjamin Drew, A *North-Side*

pens, cells, or "warehouses," than secure places of confinement or jails. Winfield Collins referred to the "slave prisons" of Alexandria, DC and Washington, DC.[25] Franklin and Armfield's establishment in Alexandria consisted of a solid phalanx of bolts, locks, doors, cells, and guards, illustrating the difficulty of breakouts. Ethan Andrews, professor and abolitionist based in Boston, described it as a "penitentiary."[26] Kidnapped New Yorker Solomon Northup recalled Williams's slave pen in Washington, DC as being twelve feet square with walls of solid masonry, a heavy plank floor, and "one small window, crossed with great iron bars, with an outside shutter, securely fastened."[27] Mr. Goodwin's "slave pen" in Richmond was similar.[28] These "comfortable" confinements awaited the newly purchased captives.

They were then transferred from stationary jails to floating prisons.[29] Franklin and Armfield operated a flotilla of ships from Alexandria through Richmond and Norfolk to New Orleans.

In 1828, the firm bought the *United States*, a brig with 158 tons burden and mastered by Captain Henry C. Bell for several subsequent years. Those wishing to transport slaves southward would have been interested in an advertisement placed in the *Phenix Alexandria Gazette* in 1829:

For New Orleans, To sail from this port, about the 15th of January the fast sailing packet brig UNITED STATES Henry C. Bell, Master Persons wishing to ship, will please make early application to Franklin & Armfield.

This brig made regular trips from Alexandria to New Orleans.[30] Another one of the firm's prominent ships was the *Isaac Franklin* – no doubt modestly named in recognition of the founder's commercial success.

View of Slavery. The Refugee or the Narratives of Fugitive Slaves in Canada. Related by Themselves, with an Account of the History and Condition of the Colored Population of Upper Canada (Boston: J.P. Jewett and Company, 1856), 82–84; Steven Deyle, *Carry Me Back: The Domestic Slave Trade in American Life* (New York: Oxford University Press, 2005), 115; Phillips, *American Negro Slavery*, 194; Schermerhorn, *Business of Slavery*, 127, 130, 136, 146.

[25] Collins, *Domestic Slave Trade*, 96–98.

[26] Andrews, *Slavery and Domestic Slave Trade*, 80. Civil War photographs of Franklin and Armfield's slave jail are reproduced in Sweig, "Alexandria to New Orleans," Parts II & III.

[27] Solomon Northup, *Twelve Years a Slave: Narrative of Solomon Northup, a Citizen of New York, Kidnapped in Washington City in 1841, and Rescued in 1853* (New York: Norton, 2017), 28–32.

[28] Ibid, 38.

[29] For transatlantic slave ships as floating prisons, see chapter 2 of Marcus Rediker's *The Slave Ship: A Human History* (New York: Viking, 2007).

[30] Stephenson, *Isaac Franklin*, 36.

Built in Baltimore shipyards in 1835, this 189-ton vessel measured eighty-nine feet and five inches in length, twenty-three feet in width, and ten feet and four inches in depth.[31] The ship had a square stern, one deck, and two masts. On April 22, 1836, Master William Smith of Alexandria signed a registry oath "that John Armfield of the town of Alexandria" was "the true and only owner of the Ship or Vessel called the Isaac Franklin."[32] Another member of the firm's flotilla was the *Tribune* – the Latin name drawing either from champion of the people or a Roman legionary officer. A visitor described the vessel in early 1834:

The hold is appropriated to the slaves, and is divided into two apartments. The after-hold will carry about eighty women, and the other about one hundred men. On either side were *two platforms* running the whole length; one raised a few inches, and the other half way up to the deck. They were about five or six feet deep. On these the slaves lie, as close as they can stow away.[33]

What's striking about this description is the organization of the space of this vessel designed to transport captives. The men were separated from the women. The platforms were designed to accommodate as many captives as possible within a relatively small ship. Later on that same year, this vessel and another were advertised as being ready for the season's business:

Brig TRIBUNE, Captain Smith, and Brig UNCAS, Captain Boush, will resume their regular trips on the 20th of October: one of which will leave this port every thirty days throughout the shipping season. They are vessels of the first class, commanded by experienced officers, and will at all times go up the Mississippi by steam, and every exertion [will be] used to promote the interests of shippers and comfort of passengers.[34]

A year later, the business of these ships was again advertised in greater detail:

Brig TRIBUNE, Samuel C. Boush, Master, will sail as above on the 15th inst., (Nov.); brig ISAAC FRANKLIN, William Smith Master, on the 1st December; brig UNCAS, Nathaniel Boush, master, on the 15th December.[35]

---

[31] The *Creole* was similarly proportioned.   [32] Stephenson, *Isaac Franklin*, 38.

[33] Stephenson, *Isaac Franklin*, 38, original italics; Bancroft, *Slave-Trading*, 275–276.

[34] Stephenson, *Isaac Franklin*, 37. This advertisement appears to distinguish between coastal vessels like the *Tribune* and "first class" vessels powered by steam that navigated internal waterways like the Mississippi River. See Bancroft, *Slave-Trading*, 280–283.

[35] Washington *Daily National Intelligencer*, November 6, 1835, quoted in Stephenson, *Isaac Franklin*, 37.

Readers would no doubt have been struck by the emphasis on the claims
for the interest of the traders as well as the comfort of the "passengers"
being forcibly transported. Ten weeks later, Captain Boush and Thomas
McCargo signed the *Tribune*'s manifest swearing that the sixty-five captives embarking from Alexandria and destined for New Orleans were
"held to serve or labor as Slaves" under the laws of Virginia and were
not imported in contravention of the 1807 legislation.[36]

A careful examination of several ship manifests provides a good sense
of the spatial, temporal, and human dimensions of the Coastal Passage.[37]
The brig *Ajax* – probably named after the legendary Greek fighter boastful
of his independence – had a "burthen" of 147 tons, and was mastered by
William Smith. On February 13, 1832, the ship's manifest was signed by
the captain, shipper Bacon Tait, and collector of the District and Port of
Norfolk and Portsmouth, with permission granted to proceed from
Norfolk to New Orleans. The brig arrived on February 29, 1832, having
been examined and found correct by the local inspector whose name is
unreadable on the manifest. There were a total of four different ship
manifests suggesting four sets of captives by different shippers and buyers.
Prominent Richmond trader Bacon Tait shipped twenty-year-old Adam,
nineteen-year-old Lightfoot, and sixteen-year-old Duke to Thomas Sloo,
Jr., of New Orleans. Moses Payne shipped seventeen-year-old Emanuel
and sixteen-year-old Caroline to W. B. Kenner and G. L. Duncan of New
Orleans. B. Ballard, who traveled with the ship to New Orleans, shipped
twenty-year-old Patsy, sixteen-year-old Louisa, nine-year-old Daniel, and
ten-year-old Betsy. Thomas McCargo shipped twenty-one-year-old
Maria, three-year-old Thomas, two-year-old Sam, twenty-one-year-old
Cecilia, three-year-old Emily, and two-year-old Catherine to A[bner?]
Robinson.[38]

On October 17, 1835, the schooner *Hunter* left Norfolk bound for
New Orleans with a human cargo of five captives. Richmond trader
Thomas McCargo shipped fifteen-year-old James Page, sixteen-year-old

---

[36] Manifest of Brig *Tribune*, January 18, 1836, *Slave Manifests of Coastwise Vessels Filed at New Orleans, Louisiana, 1807–1860*, Microfilm Serial *M1895*, Microfilm Roll 7, RG 36, NARA. The ship's manifest describes the captives as slaves under the laws of Virginia even though Alexandria was in the District of Columbia until its retrocession to Virginia in 1846.

[37] These manifests have been selected for their availability, readability, and representativeness.

[38] Manifest of the *Ajax*, February 13 and 29, 1832, *Slave Manifests of Coastwise Vessels Filed at New Orleans, Louisiana, 1807–1860*, Microfilm Serial *M1895*, Microfilm Roll 7, RG 36, NARA.

George Christian, fifteen-year-old Noah Nelson, fifteen-year-old Jerry Page, and sixteen-year-old Oliver Peyton to J & S Crosby of Richmond and E. Archinark of New Orleans. Captain Robert Benthall, shipper McCargo, and the port collector signed off on the manifest. The 119-ton vessel sailed three to four weeks before arriving at New Orleans on November 11, 1835, where it was examined, found in compliance, and signed over by the port collector.[39]

The *Caledonia* captained by D. W. [Slavey?] embarked from Petersburg, Virginia, on June 23, 1840, carrying thirty-five captives. They consisted of twenty-five males and ten females, most of whom were under thirty years of age. The shippers included Harrison Cook, Thomas B. Jackson, William H. Betts, George W. Brown, and Mr. Davies. The consignees were Thomas McCargo, Richard H. Beazley, Theo Apperson, and Mark Davies. The vessel arrived in New Orleans a month later on July 24 where it was examined and found correct by the port collector.[40]

Joseph Robinson skippered the schooner *Josephine* with a burden of 190 tons. On December 23, 1841, port collector Thomas Nelson along with the master signed the manifest for transporting seventy captives from Richmond to New Orleans. Forty-two were male and twenty-eight were female. It was a young group of captives with only eight being older than twenty-five years. The shippers were George Kephart, George Rust, James F. Purvis, George W. Barnes, Andrew Grimm – a suitable surname for such a sordid business – John W. Coleman, and Shields L. Somerville. The consignees were Thomas Boudar, Theophilus Freeman, and Robert A. Gramman – all of whom resided in New Orleans. John Coleman shipped twenty-one-year-old John Redman to Thomas McCargo of New Orleans. The vessel appears to have arrived on January 17, 1842, when the local inspector passed the vessel as being in compliance with the 1807 legislation.[41]

---

[39] Manifest of the *Hunter*, October 17 and November 9, 1835, *Slave Manifests of Coastwise Vessels Filed at New Orleans, Louisiana, 1807–1860*, Microfilm Serial M1895, Microfilm Roll 7, RG 36, NARA.

[40] Manifest of the *Caledonia*, June 23 and July 24, 1840, *Slave Manifests of Coastwise Vessels Filed at New Orleans, Louisiana, 1807–1860*, Microfilm Serial M1895, Microfilm Roll 7, RG 36, NARA.

[41] Manifest of the *Josephine*, December 23, 1841, and January 17, 1842, *Slave Manifests of Coastwise Vessels Filed at New Orleans, Louisiana, 1807–1860*, Microfilm Serial M1895, Microfilm Roll 7, RG 36, NARA. This manifest is divided into three pages. The third page notes that the port inspection occurred at "English town" which is an unclear reference. It is probably the correct page, though, because it also notes the same

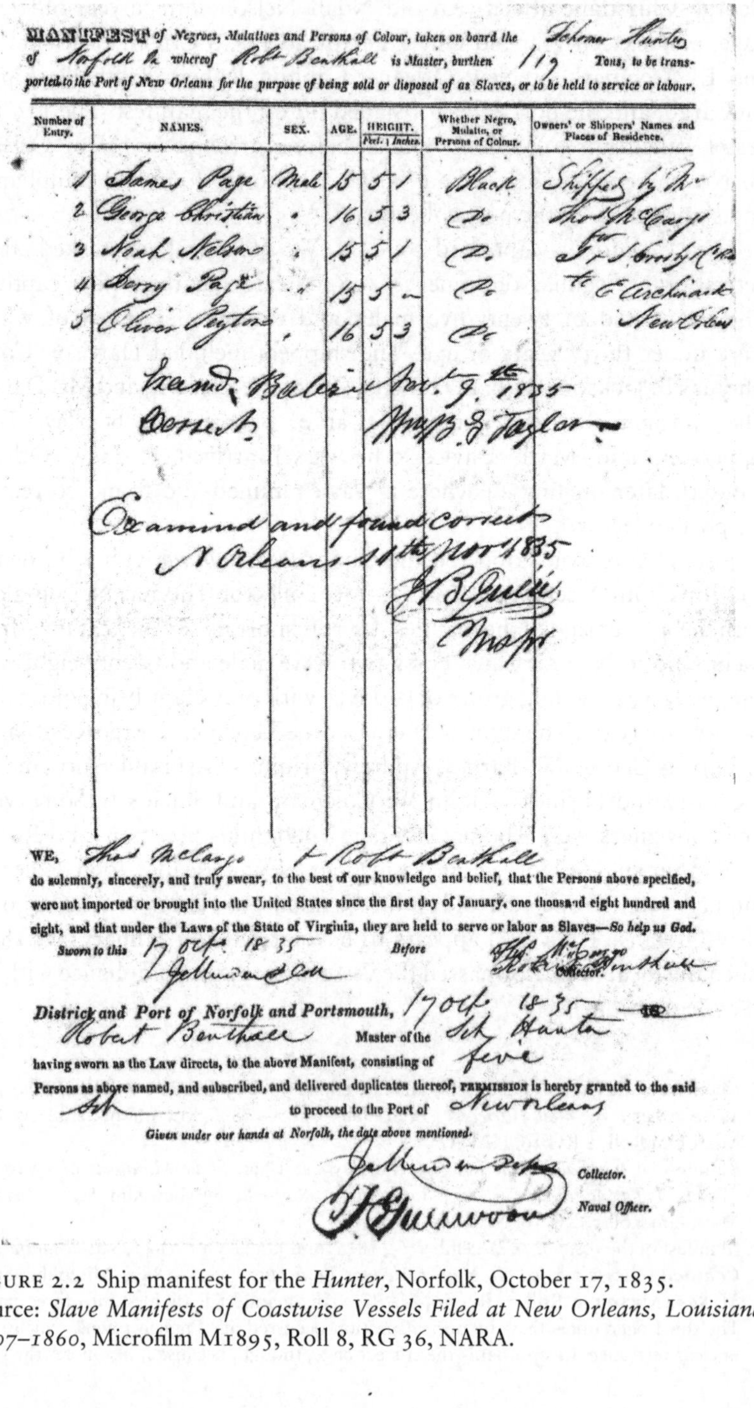

MANIFEST *of Negroes, Mulattoes and Persons of Colour, taken on board the* Schooner Hunter *of* Norfolk Va *whereof* Robt Benthall *is Master, burthen* 119 *Tons, to be transported to the Port of New Orleans for the purpose of being sold or disposed of as Slaves, or to be held to service or labour.*

Number of Entry.	NAMES.	SEX.	AGE.	HEIGHT. Feet.	Inches.	Whether Negro, Mulatto, or Persons of Colour.	Owners' or Shippers' Names and Places of Residence.
1	James Page	Male	15	5	1	Black	Shipped by Thos McCargo
2	George Christian	"	16	5	3	Do	for
3	Noah Nelson	"	15	5	1	Do	J. & S. Armfield & Co
4	Berry Page	"	15	5	–	Do	to E. Archinard
5	Oliver Peyton	"	16	5	3	Do	New Orleans

Examd, Balize Novr 9th 1835
Correct. Wm B. G. Taylor

Examined and found correct
N Orleans 11th Nov 1835
J. B. Quilie
Majr

WE, Thos McCargo & Robt Benthall do solemnly, sincerely, and truly swear, to the best of our knowledge and belief, that the Persons above specified, were not imported or brought into the United States since the first day of January, one thousand eight hundred and eight, and that under the Laws of the State of Virginia, they are held to serve or labor as Slaves—*So help us God.*

Sworn to this 17 Oct 1835 *Before* Thos McCargo
Jno Holloway Colr Robt Benthall
Collector.

District and Port of Norfolk and Portsmouth, 17 Oct 1835
Robert Benthall Master of the Sch Hunter having sworn as the Law directs, to the above Manifest, consisting of five Persons as above named, and subscribed, and delivered duplicates thereof, PERMISSION is hereby granted to the said Sch to proceed to the Port of New Orleans

Given under our hands at Norfolk, the date above mentioned.

Jno Holloway Colr *Collector.*
T. G. Broughton *Naval Officer.*

FIGURE 2.2 Ship manifest for the *Hunter*, Norfolk, October 17, 1835. Source: *Slave Manifests of Coastwise Vessels Filed at New Orleans, Louisiana, 1807–1860*, Microfilm M1895, Roll 8, RG 36, NARA.

These ship manifests reveal several striking features concerning the gender and age of the captives. A significant number were either women or children. They had been separated from families. They were considered to be important workers, probably destined for the cotton fields. Younger men were more likely to end up in the sugar cane fields. The younger workers were deemed future investments for buyers. The most striking characteristic was the balanced gender ratio. This confirms a recent survey of the listings of 3,500 captives listed on ship manifests for voyages organized by Franklin and Armfield between 1828 and 1836. Most of the captives were young men and women. Most of the women were without husbands or children and those with children were without husbands. Most were under twenty-five years old, and nearly half of the females were under sixteen years old.[42] The number of women and youngsters on these coastal slave ships challenges the familiar notion of males as "prime field hands" who constituted most of those transported during the US slave trade.[43] More generally, these shipping records suggest long-distance sales rather than the predominance of local transactions as argued by some scholars.[44]

These ship manifests outline the lives of captives, but they reveal little about the history of the shippers and consignees beyond names and residency. These federal sources are even quieter regarding sailors and officers. The dozen or so captains mentioned in these ship manifests were undoubtedly experienced in transporting slaves across the water. This was clear from trader advertisements of "experienced and accommodating officers" which were not necessarily inaccurate. They no doubt captained these ships for other traders and consignees. First officers were not named and did not sign the ship manifest, but were important because they were required to take over in an emergency – as proved to be the case after the severe wounding of the captain during the *Creole* rebellion. The sailors were employees of the ship's owners. They too were probably regulars with experience in the coastwise trade and its winds, currents, and treacherous conditions. Unlike their shipmates in the Atlantic slave trade,

date of December 23, 1841, which was when the *Josephine* departed. I examined numerous other ship manifests for this chapter including those of the *Architect, Mary, Cecelia, Zerviah, Ontario, Long Island*, and *Louisiana*. They followed the familiar routes during the winter seasons of the 1830s, but differed on vessel sizes and numbers of captives. See *Slave Manifests of Coastwise Vessels Filed at New Orleans, Louisiana, 1807–1860*, Microfilm Serial *M1895*, Microfilm Roll 7, RG 36, NARA.

[42] Sweig, "Alexandria to Virginia," Part II.
[43] Pargas, *Slavery and Forced Migration*, 43.   [44] Ibid, 32.

however, they experienced lower mortality rates from disease and unhealthy conditions because they were acclimated and unthreatened by pathogens from the African continent for which they lacked immunity.[45] But officers and crew still died during the Coastal Passage. Most importantly, these officers and sailors who manned coastal slavers functioned as conduits for the expansion of the American slaveholding republic.

Slave traders were key players in America's coastal business. Interpretations of their social position have shifted markedly over the decades. Both abolitionists as well as slaveholders frequently depicted them as ogres. Kidnapped New Yorker Solomon Northup believed his trader James H. Burch pursued the "disreputable calling" of "speculator in human flesh."[46] Visiting English novelist Charles Dickens wrote contemptuously of "buyers and sellers of slaves" who "own, breed, use, buy, and sell them at all hazards."[47] In contrast to these dealers, slaveholders claimed to exercise personal interest and professed paternalist care toward their servants. "As to willfully selling off a husband, or wife, or child," wrote prominent South Carolina cotton planter and politician James Henry Hammond, "I believe it is rarely, very rarely done, except when some offence has been committed demanding 'transportation.' "[48]

This disdain continued with the first professional historical scholarship on antebellum slavery. Ulrich B. Phillips clearly shared his contemporaries' contempt and "disesteem" for slave traders in his pioneering research.[49] But this moralistic view was most powerfully challenged during the 1970s by historical scholarship that focused on the ideological and economic imperatives of southern slaveholding society. Eugene Genovese was one of the most influential proponents of the argument for planter paternalism predicated on the view that slaveholders took care of their "servants" in an organic relationship defined primarily by the patriarchal household rather than the modern cash nexus exemplified by southern traders, northern factory owners, and industrial capitalists in Great

---

[45] Rediker, *Slave Ship*, chap. 8.   [46] Northup, *Twelve Years A Slave* (Norton ed.), 41.

[47] Charles Dickens, *American Notes* (1842, rpt., Heron Books: Centennial Edition, n.d.), 272.

[48] James Henry Hammond, *Letter to an English Abolitionist* (1845), in Drew Gilpin Faust, ed., *The Ideology of Slavery: Proslavery Thought in the Antebellum South, 1830–1860* (Baton Rouge: Louisiana State University Press, 1981).

[49] Phillips, *American Negro Slavery*, chap. 9, "disesteem" (200); Ulrich B. Phillips., *Life and Labor in the Old South* (1929. Boston: Little and Brown, 1963), chap. VIII. But Phillips also writes: "The dealers were not full of the milk of human kindness or they would not have entered upon their calling. On the other hand they cannot have been fiends in human form, for such would have gone speedily bankrupt" (*Life and Labor*, 158).

Britain. This was at the heart of his argument for a pre-capitalist mercantile antebellum American South.[50]

With the emergence of slavery and capitalism studies over the past two decades, slave traders have once again undergone a re-evaluation. In opposition to the view that the antebellum era was mercantilist, the new scholarship argues for a prewar slave society that was firmly ensconced within a modern capitalist market economy. In the words of one its leading proponents, it was "the expansion of slavery in both geography and intensity [which] made American capitalism."[51] Another adherent writes: "the transcontinental transfer of slaves in the antebellum period was a massive, rational, and lucrative capitalistic endeavor, its tentacles creeping into several sectors of America's market economy."[52] Slave traders operated within this world as capitalists who were "business insiders" rather than "social outcasts." These merchants, claims one enthusiast, "financed, traded, and transported enslaved people [and] chart the progress of nineteenth-century American capitalism more strikingly than any other enterprise." Capitalism is defined here as a "highly structured system of trade" with "debt obligations that bound borrowers' ambitions, expectations, and imaginations to future repayment."[53]

---

[50] Eugene D. Genovese, *Roll, Jordan, Roll The World the Slaves Made* (New York: Vintage, 1972); Eugene D. Genovese, *From Rebellion to Revolution: Afro-American Slave Revolts in the Making of the Modern World* (Baton Rouge: Louisiana State University Press, 1979); Eugene D. Genovese, *The Southern Front: History and Politics in the Cultural War* (Columbia: University of Missouri Press, 1995); Eugene D. Genovese, *The Slaveholders' Dilemma: Freedom and Progress in Southern Conservative Thought, 1820–1860* (Columbia: University of South Carolina Press, 1992). This pre-modern paternalist framework drew from the Marxian framework established in his first book *The Political Economy of Slavery: Studies in the Economy and Society of the Slave South.*

[51] Baptist, *Half Has Never Been Told*, 421. The half is the role of slavery in making modern American capitalism. Interestingly enough, the phrase itself was uttered by Wesley Burrell, a former slave in Washington County, Texas, interviewed by the WPA who recalled that a white lady rebuffed hearing about slavery time: "I told her the half hadn't been told if she didn't want to hear that, it wasn't nothing to tell." See Campbell, *Empire of Slavery*, 115. This is what critics of Baptist's book and its title mean when they say that the half has very much been told especially by generations of scholars.

[52] Pargas, *Slavery and Forced Migration*, 42.

[53] Schermerhorn, *Business of Slavery*, 124. James Oakes, Walter Johnson, Seth Rockman, Edward Baptist, and Sven Beckert, among others, have penned influential studies of slavery and capitalism. For slavery's subtle evocation as "simulation" of modernity on the global stage, see Blackburn's *Making of New World Slavery*, especially his opening epigraph from influential French sociologist Jean Baudrillard: "All of the above precedes the productive rationality of capital, but everything testifies already – not in production, but in counterfeit – to the same project of control and universal hegemony" (1). In other

This recent depiction of slave traders as capitalists is preferable to older moral and ideological viewpoints because of its insistence on the indispensability of slavery to the economic growth of the antebellum United States. It is evident that this economic expansion would not have occurred without the systemic exploitation of enslaved labor and land expropriation from American Indians facilitated by an expansionist state.[54] But the slavery and capitalism thesis is very debatable. Its emphasis on traders as wealth creators undermines an older essential viewpoint that it was the exploitation of slaves' labor that largely created the wealth that sustained slave societies. Moreover, traders – much like planters, factors, and farmers – were retainers of a financial system operated by masters located in financial centers in the northern United States as well as Europe. Economic historian Harold Woodman penned the classic statement on this financial dependency several decades ago and it remains compelling. The antebellum "South remained an agricultural section concentrating on land, slaves, and a few staple crops, and the North and Europe provided the manufactured goods, transportation, and many of the other commercial services necessary to market the crop."[55] Even "such wealthy factors as Maunsel White of New Orleans," he pointed out, "who was said to be worth a million dollars in 1850, could not support the credit needs of their customers from their personal assets and had to rely upon outside funds."[56] In addition, is slavery's role in capitalism to be equated with expanding free labor communities in northern and western states during the nineteenth century together with the expansion – not contraction – of the American economy after the abolition of slavery? Finally, the depiction of merchant traders as market-savvy makes the antebellum era suspiciously resemble our own era of financial speculation since the 1990s.

words, the seeds of earlier systems of New World slavery – first the Baroque, followed by mercantile colonialism – sprouted in the age of slavery and capitalism during the nineteenth century.

[54] Eric Williams' landmark *Capitalism and Slavery* first published in 1944 made a similar argument linking British economic development to New World sugar and slavery.

[55] Harold D. Woodman, *King Cotton and His Retainers: Financing and Marketing the Cotton Crop of the South, 1800–1925* (1968: Columbia: University of South Carolina Press, 1990), 152–153.

[56] Woodman, *King Cotton*, 154. Even Ed Baptist's *Half Has Never Been Told* does not ignore this external financial power: "Barings' money allowed [Vincent] Nolte to accumulate huge piles of cotton on the levee after 1815 . . ." (85); "Financial giants Baring Brothers, Hope and Company and other European cotton buyers injected millions of pounds of credit to pay Nolte and his peers" (92); "The factors themselves needed credit, and their financing came from New York banks, such as Brown Brothers" (353), and so forth.

It is no coincidence that this is precisely the era of the rise of studies of slavery and capitalism.[57]

The Coastal Passage also challenges the slavery and capitalism thesis in several ways. To begin with, coastal traders were as beholden to external power as everyone else in the antebellum southern economy. John Hagan, a factor to planter William S. Hamilton in Louisiana during the late 1820s, transported slaves aboard the *Creole* in late 1841 and was very much a retainer of King Cotton.[58] Furthermore, this external economic control was compounded by internal political weakness. Historian Joseph Reidy puts it succinctly: "Yet the profiteering slave traders' inability to keep the Union intact, thereby maintaining slavery's central role in the capitalist world economy, revealed their political marginalization."[59] The final issue concerns surplus extraction of some 50,000 or more maritime captives – many of whom were women and children – and represents a specific form of exploitation that gets lost in macro explanations for slavery's role in developing American capitalism.[60]

Much of the historical literature on the US slave trade examines its economic, political, and demographic dimensions. Scholars have only recently begun to focus to on the migratory experiences of slaves.[61] This second section turns from the mechanics of coastal slaving to the actual experience of captives in the Coastal Passage. It opens with confinement in urban jails and concludes with an assessment of the

---

[57] "The financial product that such banks as Baring Brothers were selling to investors in London, Hamburg, Amsterdam, Paris, Philadelphia, Boston, and New York was remarkably similar to the securitized bonds, backed by mortgages on US homes, that attracted investors from around the globe to US financial markets from the 1980s until the economic collapse of 2008." See Baptist, *Half Has Never Been Told*, 247–248. They were only similar if we assume parallel circuits of capital movement, banking strategies, technological resources, and transient national borders.

[58] Woodman, *King Cotton's Retainers*, 40, 45, 67, 114–115, 117.

[59] Joseph P. Reidy, Book Review, Calvin Schermerhorn, *Business of Slavery*, *Journal of American History* vol. 103, no. 2 (September 2016), 468.

[60] For useful conceptual explanations of this distinction, see Thomas Picketty, *Capital in the Twenty-First Century* (Cambridge, Mass.: Harvard University Press, 2014), 158–163; Gareth Steadman Jones, *Karl Marx: Greatness and Illusion* (Cambridge, Mass.: Harvard University Press, 2016), 194–199. For its conflation, see Baptist, *Half Has Never Been Told*, 175: ". . . we can see that in the 1820s enslavers had also come as close to fully monetizing human bodies and lives as any set of capitalists have ever done."

[61] Baptist's *Half Has Never Been Told* and Pargas's *Slavery and Forced Migration*. The latter draws on slave narratives, government interviews, and interviews with refugee slaves in the North and Canada to provide a compelling comparative analysis of the different experiences of slave migrants, the ways they rebuilt their lives after being transported, and dual identity formation.

extensiveness of maritime transportation in the US slave trade. Following historian Sowande' M. Mustakeem's fruitful study of the intimacies of the Atlantic slave trade, we examine captives' maritime transportation "as a tangible experience" zeroing in on "what really happened."[62] What follows is an attempt to reconstruct the coastal captives' experiences at sea and to evaluate its significance rather than simply treating the ship as just another form of transporting slaves in the US slave trade.

It is irrefutable that family separations caused pain and suffering whether the victims were marched overland or via coastal slaver. Newspaper advertisements that brought in captives for the coastwise trade clearly divided families and kin networks and removed people from their familiar surroundings and environment. One local scholar of the prominent trading firm of Franklin and Armfield argues that the latter regularly separated young women from their children and husbands so as to trade young, single individuals who would fetch the highest price in the New Orleans market. As historian Donald Sweig summarizes: "the sale and transportation of local Virginia and Maryland slaves resulted in many broken families and many separations from family and kin," especially because of "the high percentage of young, single, African-American slave men and women that Armfield shipped from Alexandria to New Orleans."[63]

It must have been a gut-wrenching experience for all those who were separated. It might have been even more traumatic for youngsters broken from their mothers at such a tender age.

Those slaves transported overland might have escaped the despair of prolonged confinement before beginning their long march southward. Life in jail for those about to be shipped was frequently disgusting and disheartening, marked as it was by disease, suffering, and occasionally death. This was also true for enslaved Africans in coastal barracoons awaiting transportation in the Atlantic slave trade. On the other hand, jails brought together captives. One unintended consequence was the bonding of slaves with the potential for plotting and participating in rebellion. Slave prisoners rose up against their English captors in 1667, their Danish captors in 1727, and other captors during the 1820s and 1830s in coastal West Africa.[64] Confinement before America's Coastal

[62] Mustakeem, *Slavery at Sea*, 5–6.
[63] Sweig, "Alexandria to New Orleans," Parts II & III.
[64] Eric Robert Taylor, *If We Must Die: A History of Shipboard Insurrections in the Era of the Atlantic Slave Trade* (Baton Rouge: Louisiana State University Press, 2006), 19–23.

Passage also resulted in plotting revolt. Seven captives – Madison Washington, Elijah Morris, George Portlock, Pompey Garrison, William Jenkins, Richard Butler, and Warner Smith – were among the nineteen rebels who seized the *Creole*. They were lodged together in trader Thomas McCargo's warehouse in Richmond.[65]

What about conditions on board these coastal slavers? Vessels engaged in the Atlantic slave trade were often "packed" with large numbers of enslaved Africans in quarters that were insufficiently spacious in order to maximize profits. One of the earliest victories of the burgeoning British anti-slave trade campaign was the passage of the Dolben Act, or Slave Carrying Bill, in July 1788. Pushed by Sir William Dolben, independent Member of Parliament for Oxford University who opposed the slave trade, its main provisions included compulsory attendance by surgeons on slave ships and three slaves per five tons for ships up to 200 tons and a one-to-one ratio thereafter.[66] In contrast to these regulations, the US Congress did not regulate the number of captives per tonnage as part of its legislation against the transatlantic slave trade or as part of its regulation of the Coastal Passage. The *Tribune*, one of Franklin and Armfield's slave ships, was built to carry 180 captives. It transported sixty-five captives on one of its voyages from Norfolk to New Orleans in 1836, suggesting the absence of the "packing."[67] On the other hand, coastal slavers could be packed like Atlantic ships. Captain Basil Hall compared a slaver with 200 slaves in New Orleans to an Atlantic slaver he had seen in Rio de Janeiro. Slave trade abolitionist, Joseph Holt Ingraham, quipped ironically that Virginia slaves were "shipped for New Orleans, with as comfortable accommodations as can be expected, where one or two hundred are congregated in a single merchant vessel."[68] The *Creole* weighed 187 tons and transported 139 captives during its fateful 1841 voyage. This slave-to-ton ratio was perfectly legal in the United States, although it would have failed the reformist measure prescribed by the Dolben Act.

Most accounts of captives' experiences are either by supporters of slavery or anti-slavery adherents and thus need to be used with caution. William H. Seward, New York abolitionist and future US Secretary of

[65] Manifest of the *Creole* 28 October 1841, Consolidated Cases, Docket Nos. 4413, 4414, 4419, NOPL; *Richmond Enquirer*, December 31, 1835.

[66] Rediker, *Slave Ship*, 59, 68, 291, 313, 317, 336, 337, 341; Walvin, *Zong*, 53; Brown, *Moral Capital*, 296; Huzzey, *Freedom Burning*, 40; Black, *Slavery*, 158–159.

[67] Stephenson, *Isaac Franklin*, 38. The *Tribune* manifest does not record the ship's burthen.

[68] Pargas, *Slavery and Forced Migration*, 116–117.

State under President Abraham Lincoln, observed human cargoes being prepared for transportation from Virginia to New Orleans in 1846. A white man led seventy-five young men, women, and children to the steerage cabin. The children bore nothing, but the adults carried bags, bundles, and chests containing their earthly possessions. They "huddled together on the lower deck, [and] looked with puerile [why must their look be childish, Mr. Seward?] curiosity and gratification at all that surrounded them." They joined 125 slaves already aboard ship. (A total of 200 captives was a large number for a US coastal slaver.) As the ship undocked, the captain turned to a clearly disturbed Seward, saying: "'Oh, sir, do not be concerned about them; they are the happiest people in the world!'" The future American Secretary of State expressed skepticism: "I looked, and there they were – slaves, ill protected from the cold, fed capriciously on the commonest food – going from all that was dear to all that was terrible, and still they wept not . . . And these were 'the happiest people in the world'!"[69] Their experiences of poor conditions, familial uprooting, and stoicism in the face of immiseration were no doubt shared by many thousands of coastwise captives between the 1820s and 1850s.

Recollections by survivors of the Coastal Passage do exist, although these also need to be treated guardedly. Interviewers controlled information through the questions they asked. Interviewees' memories were not infallible. Jim Crow and racial violence in the post-emancipation American South exerted powerful forms of control against freedom of expression. In 1902 and 1907, historian Frederic Bancroft interviewed fifteen "ex-slaves" near New Orleans, most of whom "had been brought down by traders." Nathan Ross of Donaldsonville, Louisiana, recollected being sold to a Richmond trader named Daniel B. Budder about 1846:

Budder brought 'bout 50 or 60 all de way by boat to New O'leens. We drifted down de Jeems [James] to Po'tsmouth an' den we was put on de New Orleens ship. Dere was 30 or 40 uthahs [others] owned by tradahs. On board de ship we was treated well; had plenty to eat. We was allowed to walk on deck. We was not in de hol' 'cep'n at night er when it sto'med. At New O'leens we was taken to a tradah's office. De yahd [yard] was walled up 13 er 14 feet high 'round to de front.

The original number of captives as well as those owned by traders is plausible. The route was a familiar one. The availability of food on this ship was not implausible. (Why would Ross embellish unless he was food-

---

[69] Bancroft, *Slave-Trading*, 278.

deprived when interviewed?) Daily walks on deck and nocturnal confinement confirms established practice. The formidable walls nearly three times the average height of captives were probably unforgettable to those who desired their liberty. Mr. Ross was confined for three months before being sold privately to a "Creole."[70]

Washington Taylor, another surviving witness interviewed by Bancroft when Taylor was seventy-two years old, had been born in Gloucester County, Virginia. In 1853, he was sold to a trader, handcuffed, and then sold to another trader in Richmond. Taylor, along with eighty other slaves, was shipped to New Orleans in a "sailing vessel." His interviewer reports they were treated well, except the food was not good. The interviewer thought this was "a doubtful criticism."[71] Food deprivation on Taylor's slaver, however, was as plausible as food aplenty on Ross's ship. William Seward noted the "commonest food" on the Richmond trader that he observed.[72] Fellow New Yorker Solomon Northup recalled being appointed steward of food and water aboard the *Orleans*. Jenny, one of his assistants, prepared "the coffee, which consisted of corn meal scorched in a kettle, boiled and sweetened with molasses." His other assistants, Jim and Cuffee, "baked the hoe-cake and boiled the bacon."[73]

What about shipboard conditions more generally? Most of the journeys occurred during the winter months. The captives on the *Ajax*, for instance, had to endure a three-week passage in February 1832.[74] Such voyages could not have been pleasant with cold, fierce winds, tempestuous waves, and rolling, pitching ships. Nathan Ross remembered being kept in the hold during storms. These harsh conditions brought on vomiting, diarrhea, and sickness, especially to those unacquainted with the harsh seas. One former slave recalled being on the ship "for weeks an' days. It were dark an' I were feared an' homesick an' seasick."[75] Solomon Northup reported that: "sea-sickness rendered the place of our confinement [aboard the

[70] Bancroft, *Slave-Trading*, 279n35.
[71] Ibid. Bancroft adds that Taylor and his fellow captives were put in a trader's pen on Esplanade Street. New Orleans trader John Hagan owned property on this street and it might have been his establishment.
[72] Ibid, 278.   [73] Northup, *Twelve Years A Slave* (Norton ed.), 42–43.
[74] Manifest of the *Ajax*, February 13 and 29, 1832, *Slave Manifests of Coastwise Vessels Filed at New Orleans, Louisiana, 1807–1860*, Microfilm Serial M1895, Microfilm Roll 7, RG 36, NARA.
[75] Schermerhorn, *Business of Slavery*, 46–47, 58–59, 130; Pargas, *Slavery and Forced Migration*, "an' seasick" (117).

Orleans] loathsome and disgusting."[76] Moreover, forced removal from families, homes, and communities must have made many feel sick at heart. And let us not forget that these awful journeys could last three to four weeks from Richmond and Norfolk to Mobile and New Orleans. The ships' manifests record numerous long voyages between port inspectors signing off at embarkation and port collectors' signatures at disembarkation.[77] The seasickness, separation, and poor conditions resembled the experiences of the Middle Passage. The captives' experiences in the Coastal Passage were different from those in the transatlantic crossing, however, because the journey was shorter, there was greater freedom on the ship's deck, and the slaves were American-born.[78]

Much like the Middle Passage, the Coastal Passage claimed lives. Twenty-five-year-old Jesse Botts died en route to New Orleans aboard the *Lafayette*. Twenty-two-year-old Rachel died on the *Tribune* voyaging from Alexandria to Natchez in January 1833. Youngsters Henry and Simon both perished while in transit.[79] Robert Jones died of smallpox aboard the *Orleans*. Tom died ten days into the journey onboard the *Clio*. Four of Baltimore trader Woolfolk's original thirty-two captives died aboard a merchant sloop in 1831.[80] The reasons for this shipboard mortality varied from drowning to cholera outbreaks to deaths resulting from shipboard revolts. Eric Taylor estimates an average number of slave deaths in 170 transatlantic uprisings to be around 32 per rebellion.[81] Numerous rebels lost their lives during ship revolts against the coastwise trade as we shall see in Chapter 5. It will be a while before we can generalize about death rates on the Coastal Passage with equal exactitude

---

[76] Northup, *Twelve Years as Slave* (Norton ed.), 43. I still recall my initiation into the green world of seasickness as a teen Sea Cadet in southwest coastal Britain.

[77] Philip Troutman, "Grapevine in the Slave Market: African American Geopolitical Literacy and the 1841 *Creole* Revolt," in Walter Johnson, ed., *The Chattel Principle: Internal Slave Trades in the Americas* (New Haven, Conn.: Yale University Press, 2004), 229n22; Johnson, *Soul by Soul*, 50.

[78] Muskakeem's *Slavery at Sea* describes transatlantic ship transports as leading to the "continued erosion" (15) of black bodies. This was less likely during the Coastal Passage. Maritime transportation spared captives' bodies compared to the overland coffle where people were forced to march on foot and in chains over several hundred miles for long periods.

[79] Stevenson, *Isaac Franklin*, 40; Pargas, *Slavery and Forced Migration*, 117.

[80] Schermerhorn, *Business of Slavery*, 187, 48, 66.   [81] Taylor, *If We Must Die*, 115.

as the Voyages Database does for the Atlantic slave trade. But at this stage, it is clear that claims for low mortality rates are inaccurate.[82]

These captives' experiences were extensive. Many thousands went through this American maritime trade over several decades with important consequences. Frederick Bancroft cites a newspaper report that at least 1,152 slaves were shipped from Baltimore to various southern ports between January 6, 1851 and November 6, 1852.[83] Donald Sweig estimates that John Armfield shipped "at least 5,000 Virginia and Maryland slaves" to his partner Isaac Franklin in New Orleans.[84] Drawing upon a detailed investigation of inward-bound slave manifests into New Orleans from Baltimore and other Maryland ports between 1818 and 1856, local historian Ralph Clayton counts 11,550 slaves shipped by water.[85] Ulrich Phillips estimates the scale of the coasting transit as ranging from 2,000 to 5,000 slaves per annum between 1815 and 1860.[86] This range seems ambitious. It would mean a minimum of 90,000 to a maximum of 225,000 captives over a forty-five-year period. In other words, the Coastal Passage would have accounted for anywhere between 9 percent and 25 percent of the entire US slave trade of 1,000,000 transported captives from the Upper South to the Lower South. Both the secondary literature on the US slave trade, as well as preliminary investigations of ship manifests, do not suggest in any way that around one in four slaves were transported by ship.

Historian Charles Wesley's pioneering examination of ship manifests provides a more modest total of 31,854 slaves transported in the coastwise trade between 1817 and 1852.[87] He also suggests persuasively that this was a minimum because of lost manifests and press reports of coastal trading during years with no extant manifests. Ancestry.com, the

---

[82] Bancroft notes "only one death" aboard the *Uncas* in 1835 and "lively" arrivals in New Orleans a few years earlier clearly implying low mortality rates. Bancroft, *Slave-Trading*, 279. Stephenson concludes that ship manifests "record very few deaths in transit," Stephenson, *Isaac Franklin*, 52,

[83] Bancroft, *Slave-Trading*, 276.

[84] Donald Sweig, "Alexandria to New Orleans: The Human Tragedy of the Interstate Slave Trade," *Alexandria Gazette Packet*, Parts I to IV, October 2014.

[85] Ralph Clayton, *Cash for Blood: The Baltimore to New Orleans Domestic Slave Trade* (Heritage Books, Inc.: Bowie, Maryland, 2002), 133–620. These 487 pages index all inward-bound ship manifests into New Orleans from Baltimore and other ports between 1818 and 1856, and are drawn from RG 36 in the US National Archives.

[86] Phillips, *American Negro Slavery*, 195.

[87] Wesley, "Manifests of Slave Shipments," 172–173. To be precise, he recorded the total number of slaves reported in the manifests as 38,847, of which 6,993 were from internal manifests. The latter recorded the riverine and not the coastwise trade.

genealogical website, has digitalized many of these ship manifests. It lists
50,638 slaves shipped between 1790 and 1860.[88] This represents about
5 percent of the total number of all forced migrants during the US slave
trade. Only detailed investigation of thousands of ship manifests online
and deposited at several NARA repositories will provide scholars with
a more accurate number of maritime captives together with their comparative significance. What is already clear, however, is that the existing
historical scholarship on the US slave trade has paid inadequate attention
to the magnitude of this maritime business and its significance in the lives
of captives.

But these statistics should not blow the historian away. It is impossible
to determine exactly how many captives were moved in the Coastal
Passage compared to riverine journeys or overland routes via coffle or
railroad. Moreover, numbers reveal little about the ebbs and flows of
maritime movements. Even if we estimate that around 1,000 persons
per year were moved in the Coastal Passage, this figure does not take
into account how that average varied annually or decennially.
The quantification of different methods of transportation is mute on the
lived struggle of enslaved human beings and the consequences. As one
trenchant critic of historians' preoccupation with counting once put it,
"the complexities of personal relationships are especially resistant to this
exercise," because quantification "press[es] the evidence into rude
classifications."[89] One can be forgiven for sometimes feeling that slave
trade enumerators are among the least polite of our colleagues! Indeed,
the numbers game in older studies of the Middle Passage, and its rejection
by more recent scholarship, should serve as a cautionary tale of trying to
reduce complex human experiences to sober statistical analysis.[90]

In sum, America's Coastal Passage represented the massive relocation
of captive people along the southeastern Atlantic seaboard and the Gulf
coast for nearly two generations. It wrought extensive profits for traders,
planters, and financiers, as well as the federal government. It linked ports

---

[88] *US Southeast Coastwise Inward and Outward Slave Manifests, 1790–1860*, Microfilm
Serial *M1895*, Microfilm Roll 7, RG 36, NARA.

[89] Edward P. Thompson, *Customs in Common: Studies in Traditional Popular Culture*
(New York: The New Press, 1993), 450.

[90] Philip Curtin, Joseph Inikori, Herbert Klein, David Eltis, et al. produced the classic
quantification studies in transatlantic trading. Recent works by Markus Rediker,
Stephanie Smallwood, Sylviane Douf, Sowande' Mustakeem, James Walvin, and Eric
Taylor provide an alternative focus on the brutality, horrors, and survivors of the
transatlantic slave experience with an ethical dimension missing in earlier historical
scholarship.

from the East coast to the South coast to the Gulf coast, expanding the American Empire along the way. It consumed hundreds of people's lives. It also generated resistance and historical agency – the topics of subsequent chapters. Most important, its extensive practice demonstrates that the maritime dimensions of American slavery continued rather than abated after the abolition of transatlantic trading.

3

"Several Cases"

On August 1, 1842, US Secretary of State Daniel Webster wrote to British special envoy Lord Ashburton requesting improved security of American merchant vessels sailing through the Bahamas Channel. He drew attention to "several cases" in previous years of US ships engaged in coastwise trading being forced off course and into British-controlled ports in the Caribbean due to bad weather. At issue was Americans' merchandise consisting of slaves being liberated by local colonial authorities. The British government, Secretary Webster noted, had provided compensation in some cases, "for interference of the local authorities with American vessels having slaves on board, by which interference these slaves were set free." In other cases, this compensation had been refused. Secretary Webster told Envoy Ashburton that US President John Tyler thought it in the best interest of the two nations that "recurrences" of such cases "should be prevented."[1] This important letter – examined in greater detail in Chapter 8 – focused on the *Creole* revolt. The momentous impact of this 1841 ship revolt on Anglo-American relations, however, can only be accurately understood within the broader context of these maritime disputes during the 1830s.

These cases are not unknown to scholars. This chapter also narrates the dramatic stories of these coastal slavers and captives' liberation in the British West Indies. But this chapter is distinctive in several ways. First, it provides new research on these ships, captives, traders, and consignees.[2]

---

[1] Daniel Webster to Lord Ashburton, August 1, 1842, Aberdeen Papers, BL.

[2] Special thanks to NARA archivist Mark Mollan for unearthing several original documents pertaining to the coastal slave ships as well as to Kate McMahon for locating ship manifests.

Second, it uses these cases to further highlight the mechanics of the Coastal Passage. Too often, the subject of maritime slave trading is pushed aside for discussion of Anglo-American rivalry.[3] Third, these several cases demonstrate the clash between an expanding slaveholding republic and British colonial abolition, especially over property rights and maritime slave trading. They are frequently narrated divorced from this critical broader context.[4] Fourth, it focuses on the advent of liberty as something in which captives played an active part rather than something that simply resulted from either stormy weather or benevolent British officialdom.

On January 26, 1829, the *Comet* with a burden of 138 and 76/95 tons, was cleared to sail from Alexandria to New Orleans. The Captain was Isaac Staples. John Armfield of the slave trade firm in Alexandria shipped fifty-seven captives to consignee partner Isaac Franklin in New Orleans. John W. Smith of Alexandria shipped thirty-six captives to J. B. Digg of New Orleans. John Meek of Georgetown shipped fifteen captives to someone (illegible name on the manifest) in New Orleans. The ship's total human cargo consisted of 110 captives, of which seventy-five were male and thirty-five were female. Only David Allen bore a surname; the rest were listed by first name only. Most were in their late teens and twenties. But there were a significant number of child captives – twenty-one in total – including the youngest, Kitty, at four years old. Twenty-four of the captives were described as "Brown," "Yellow," "Copper," or "Mulatto." Shippers provided these racial descriptions and, although in the eye of the beholder, they do imply American provenance. All of these captives were successfully transported into the long night of expanding American slavery.[5]

The ship's next voyage, however, was to have a very different outcome. In December 1830, the *Comet* embarked from Alexandria, Virginia, en route to New Orleans, Louisiana, carrying 165 captives bound for southern and western slave markets. Franklin and Armfield owned most of the captives. Mrs. Mudd and Colonel Tutt owned nine apiece. The ship's

---

[3] Don E. Fehrenbacher, *The Slaveholding Republic: An Account of the United States Government's Relations to Slavery* (New York: Oxford University Press, 2005), 104–111.

[4] Arthur T. Downey, *The Creole Affair: The Slave Rebellion that led the U.S. and Great Britain to the Brink of War* (Lanham: Rowman and Littlefield, 2014), 62–66; Gerald Horne, *Negro Comrades of the Crown: African Americans and the British Empire Fight the U.S. Before Emancipation* (New York: New York University Press, 2012), 99–101, 109–110, 133.

[5] Manifest of the *Comet*, Records of the US Customs Service, 1745–1997, RG 36, https://catalog.archives.gov/id/365.

maritime path took it through the Bahamas Channel. On January 2, 1831, poor weather conditions drove the brig onto a reef near Abaco Island in the Bahamas. Three small craft belonging to the colony rescued the captives and took them to Nassau. The Bahamas House of Assembly submitted an address to Governor Sir John Carmichael Smythe "requesting of me to direct the slaves in question to be forthwith restored to their American owners." The Governor contacted British Colonial Secretary Lord Viscount Goderich about these events and requested advice. On one point, however, Governor Smythe was adamant: "Eleven of the slaves from the American Brig made their escape on shore and came to the Government House to claim protection." Whatever Admiralty decided about the slaves in general, he would not "permit these eleven men to be taken away as slaves."[6]

The American vice-president, Martin Van Buren, vigorously protested these actions, "urging upon His Majesty's Government the alleged claims of certain Persons, Citizens of the United States for injuries which M. Van Buren states that they have sustained in consequence of proceedings of the British Colonial Authorities of the Bahamas." Since the local authorities had released the slaves and were not prepared to turn them over to "a Foreign Country for the purpose of being dealt with as Slaves," Vice President Van Buren "demands on the part of the United States Government that reparation be made to the Citizens of the United States, for the injury thus done to their Property, either by the restoration of the Slaves, or by compensation for their loss." British Foreign Secretary Lord Palmerston requested an opinion from the House of Lords on the actions of the local authorities and Vice President Van Buren's claim. The House of Lords – effectively the supreme court of the British Empire – informed Foreign Secretary Palmerston that Custom House Officers in the Bahamas had "seized these Slaves upon a charge that the [1807] British Statute for the abolition of the Slave Trade had been violated by their importation into New Providence." The esteemed jurists also considered the vice president's charge "well founded." They believed that the "entire loss of the Slaves to their Owners cannot be ascribed to any improper conduct on the part of the Americans, but was occasioned

---

[6] Governor Sir. John Carmichael Smythe to Lord Viscount Goderich, January 31, 1831, CO 23/84, TNA; Frederic Bancroft, *Slave-Trading in the Old South* (Baltimore: J. H. Furst, 1931), 277n29. The same Government House had been sought by self-emancipators during the mid-1790s. Bahamian political representatives adhered to the principle of property rights in man carried by the first generation of post-revolutionary loyalists.

by the Act of the English Custom House Officers, in seizing them." The "original illegal seizure," they concluded, was "sufficient ground for the demand of a compensation."[7] Meanwhile, former American slaves enjoyed liberty as new British subjects in the Bahamas. New Orleans insurance companies paid the traders for their losses.[8]

Nearly three years after eleven captives escaped the *Comet* to Government House in Nassau, local custom officials were judged to have illegally liberated the rest of the captives from the slaver, and the British high court deemed American slaveholders worthy of compensation, the *Encomium* embarked from Charleston, South Carolina, destined for New Orleans, Louisiana.[9] It grounded near Fish Key, Abaco Island, in the Bahamas due to poor weather conditions in early February 1834. Lieutenant Governor Balfour wrote London that "a party of 69 Americans landed here, having been taken from a Brig wrecked upon Abaco; among them were 45 slaves who were, by my desire, informed that they were free to stay here unmolested, or to depart at their pleasure – forty one or two have taken advantage of this and intend to remain."

This particular act of maritime emancipation resulted from wreckers assisting the captives from the grounded vessel together with a senior colonial official refusing to prevent their walking to liberty. Lieutenant Governor Balfour also provided rations to those rescued and housed them in the local barracks. This was done to prevent the possibility of the former captives "getting into any scrapes with the troops or others" – a reference that remains obscure. He further hoped that in a short while, "we shall be relieved from any trouble or expence [*sic*] by their finding

---

[7] Herbert Jenner, J. Campbell, C. C. Pepys to Viscount Palmerston, April 9, 1834, in Baron Arnold Duncan McNair, "Slavery and the Slave Trade," in *International Law Opinions* (London: Cambridge University Press, 1956), 80–81; W. E. B. Du Bois, *The Suppression of the African Slave-Trade to the United States of America, 1638–1870* (1896; New York, Library of America, 1986), 309; Howard Jones, *Mutiny on the Amistad: The Saga of a Slave Revolt and Its Impact on American Abolition, Law, and Diplomacy* (New York: Oxford University Press, 1987), 53; Arthur M. Schlesinger, ed., *The Almanac of American History* (New York: Barnes & Noble, 2004), 222; Horne, *Negro Comrades of the Crown*, 99–100;, Calvin Schermerhorn, *The Business of Slavery and the Rise of American Capitalism, 1815–1860* (New Haven: Yale University Press, 2015), 146–7. These sources are mute on the eleven captives' actions and Governor Smythe's resolve.

[8] According to federal records, the *Comet*'s last document was surrendered on February 24, 1831, and the "vessel lost." Documents Issued, Ship Registers and Enrollments of New Orleans, La, vol. II, NARA.

[9] NARA archivist Mark Mollan checked the Index to Enrolments for Richmond through Charleston in 1839 but could not locate the *Encomium*. Mollan, email, May 16, 2017.

means to provide themselves with a livelihood." In other words, state support was only temporary. These latest colonial subjects were expected to achieve economic self-sufficiency quickly and for the long term.[10]

Interestingly, three or four captives decided against walking to freedom in the Bahamas. We can only speculate as to why they chose to remain in captivity: Kin relations in New Orleans? Fear of retribution should the British return them to American slavery? The documentary record is mute on when and how these captives were moved from the Bahamas back to the United States since the *Encomium* was wrecked. The majority of captives, however, clearly took advantage of freedom's opportunity provided by the British colonial official and made that short walk to freedom.[11]

The name of the next coastal slaver will be immediately recognizable to Trekkies. The *Enterprise*'s early history, however, is unclear. A careful search of federal shipping records reveals several ships bearing the same name. One was built in 1805 at Hanover, Massachusetts, surrendered abroad in 1834, and the vessel lost. This was not the ship because our *Enterprise* sailed in 1835. A schooner, built in Berkeley, Massachusetts in 1825, operated between New Orleans and Pensacola throughout the 1830s. This may have been it, although it does not appear to have traveled the same route as our vessel. A third ship was a sloop with a burden of a 27 and 14/95 tons built in 1825 in Currituck County, North Carolina, captained by John O. Hoast, and enrolled in St. Petersburg on September 4, 1839. This vessel would have been too small for most coastal slave voyages.[12]

In early February 1835, the *Enterprise* left Alexandria, Virginia, for Charleston, South Carolina. This vessel bearing 127 tons transported seventy-eight captives under the captaincy of Elliot Smith. The gender ratio was fairly even with forty-one females and thirty-seven males. One

---

[10] Lt. Gvr. Balfour to Lord Stanley, February 18, 1834, CO 23/91/12, TNA.

[11] Du Bois, *Suppression of the Slave Trade*, 309; Fehrenbacher, *Slaveholding Republic*, 104; Downey, *Creole Affair*, 63. Downey's claim that local authorities "liberated the slaves" is inaccurate since the captives disembarked unimpeded. But this mistaken view was vital for contemporaries. American supporters of slavery protested what they saw as British interference. Captives on ships like the *Creole* were drawn to potentially liberating environments of free soil like British Caribbean colonies. Local authorities were serious about following colonial laws in their jurisdiction. Historian Gerald Horne reports that Bahamas' officials told the Americans on the *Comet* that the only thing against slave-owners seeking to remove their erstwhile property was they were "liable to be hanged." Horne, *Negro Comrades of the Crown*, 110.

[12] Documents Issued, Ship Registers and Enrollments of New Orleans, La, vol. 1, 1804–1820, vol. II, 1821–1830, vol. III, 1831–40. NARA; Mollan, email, May 16, 2017.

striking aspect of this batch of captives was their relative youth compared to those on many other slavers. Some forty-four of them – or more than half – were twelve years or younger. Of these, four were infants, including tiny three-week-old Richard Pinney. Furthermore, many of these captives were kin. Twenty-five-year-old Dinah Buckingham carried her infant. Twenty-year-old Eliza Butler travelled with her two-year-old, Harriet Ann Butler. Twenty-year-old Dafney Gray bore her six-month-old, Grace Gray. There were six captives with the last name of Pinney, headed by twenty-four-year-old Eliza and the rest between eight years old and three weeks, suggesting kinship. Twenty-five-year-old Matilda Ridgley traveled with her five children – ten-year-old Martha, seven-year-old Helen, five-year-old Mahaley, three-year-old Betsy, and five-month-old Ann.[13] Five children with the surname of Warfield were also on board. Bermudan historian Nellie Musson states these youngsters were kidnapped from the Warfield plantation in Maryland. Nine-year-old Mary Warfield on board the *Enterprise* recalled "her mother, an Indian squaw, wringing her hands and screaming for the children."[14] The owners of the ship's captives were John Strohecker and other South Carolina slave-owners, including unidentified "widows and orphans." They contracted with the Marine and Fire Insurance Company of Charleston to protect their investment against loss.[15] Rather than pioneer uncharted regions, the *Enterprise* pursued a common, popular, and lucrative business. Ordinary citizens invested in slave trading, protected their risk, and sought to expand American slavery (see **Appendix 1**).

On February 11, 1835, the vessel was knocked off course by a hurricane and forced to seek shelter in Hamilton, Bermuda. Now one of the smallest capital cities in the world, it was the scene of an important maritime liberation during early 1835. British customs officers who boarded the ship reported very poor conditions. The ship's manifest recorded tobacco, bricks, and food, but made no mention of the vessel's

[13] Nellie Eileen Musson, *Mind the Onion Seed: Black "Roots" Bermuda* (Hamilton, Bermuda: Musson's, 1979), 66–67; Du Bois, *Suppression of the Slave Trade*, 309; Horne, *Negro Comrades of the Crown*, 108. The Adjustment Claims Commission, Sen. Doc. No. 103, 1856, 187, mistakenly states there were seventy-three slaves onboard. Bancroft incorrectly reports seventy-five slaves. Bancroft, *Slave-Trading in the Old South*, 277.

[14] Musson, *Mind the Onion Seed*, 66.

[15] Petition by John Strohecker and others to South Carolina Senate, 1842, Petition 11384205, Race & Slavery Petitions Project (RSPP), http://library.uncg.edu/slavery/petitions/details.aspx?pid=1573. Bancroft lists Joseph W. Neal as one of the slave-owners, although his name is missing from the petition. Bancroft, *Slave-Trading*, 277.

seventy-eight captives. The colonial officials probably believed the *Enterprise* was an illegal transatlantic slaver like the *Comet* that had been knocked off course by poor weather conditions, although this belief is absent from the documentary record. They informed Captain Smith that slavery was now illegal in the British colony of Bermuda and the slaves were free to leave. He responded that the ship had been driven into Bermuda's waters, was en route between American ports, and that the British authorities had no right to interfere. The Royal Navy detained the vessel while West India Regiment (WIR) soldiers boarded the ship.[16]

All the while the *Enterprise* was in the harbor, a local benevolent organization called the Colored Friendly Society was taking an interest in these captives and their possible liberation. After the captives were brought ashore, the Society obtained a writ of habeas corpus from the chief justice of Bermuda to get the captives into court. The attorney general asked each captive individually if they wanted to continue on to Charleston, South Carolina, as a slave or obtain their freedom in Hamilton. Seventy-two of the original seventy-eight captives chose freedom in Bermuda over slavery in South Carolina. The exception was Matilda Ridgley, who opted to return with her five children to American bondage. In the absence of Matilda's own explanation, we can only speculate on her decision: Family at the plantation of destination? Kind owner? Retribution should the Bermudian authorities return the captives to the United States? The attorney general voiced the new imperative of the British anti-slavery state: "a slave was as much free when he arrived in the Bahamas or at Bermuda as if he had reached Portsmouth or Plymouth [England]." This was the culmination of the "several cases" in the context of imperial abolition during the 1830s. The city mayor found temporary accommodation in a storeroom, while Society members assisted with employment and took some of the youngsters into their homes.[17]

The American government protested British actions requesting either the return of the slaves or compensation to the slave-owners. The red-and-ermine-draped law lords ensconced in their exquisite aristocratic chamber

---

[16] Musson, *Onion Seed*, 65; Horne, *Negro Comrades of the Crown*, 107–8; Downey, *Creole Affair*, 63; Adjustment Claims Commission, Sen. Doc. No. 103, 1856, 187. For a fictional account of the British merchant ship *Son and Heir* bound for Barbados and broken up by a hurricane, see Dickens, *Dombey and Son*, 504. The maritime accident symbolizes beautifully the familial break-up at the heart of the novel.

[17] Musson, *Onion Seed*, 66; Horne, *Negro Comrades of the Crown*, 108; Downey, *Creole Affair*, 63–64; Richard Huzzey, *Freedom Burning: Anti-Slavery and Empire in Victorian Britain* (Ithaca, NY: Cornell University Press, 2012), 54.

in central London were once again consulted. They upheld US claims in the case of the *Encomium*, ruling: "the Slave Owner is entitled to Compensation when he has been lawfully in possession of the Slaves within the English territory, and he has been disturbed in his possession of them by a functionary of the English Government." In short, "the case of the *Encomium* does not substantially differ from that of the *Comet*." But, continued the law lords, American claims for compensation were "not well founded with respect to the *Enterprize* [*sic*]." The slave owner with property on this vessel "never was lawfully in possession of the slaves within the English territory." As soon as the ship "entered the port at Bermuda they were free, as slavery had been abolished throughout the British Empire." These slaves "had acquired rights which the Courts there were bound to recognize and protect." Indeed, the law lords informed the British Foreign Secretary of their "great satisfaction" that the cases of the *Comet* and the *Encomium* were the last of their sort since: "Slavery now being abolished throughout the British Empire there can be no well founded Claim for Compensation in respect of Slaves."[18] This alternative ruling, promoted by legal passage of British colonial emancipation with the continued passage of US coastal slavers into northern Caribbean waters, was to play a pivotal part in contrasting American and British responses to the *Creole* revolt.

Several years after the ship entered Bermuda waters and the captives gained their liberty, Strohecker and his fellow slaveholders petitioned the South Carolina Senate seeking compensation for "the loss of Seventy or Eighty negro slaves on Board the Schooner *Enterprize* [*sic*] "that had been 'forcibly seized, detained, or set at liberty'" in Bermuda by local authorities "in opposition to the determined efforts of the master and the crew of the vessel." The precise nature of the crew's determined efforts was unexplained and the result of their petition went unrecorded.[19]

---

[18] For the *Encomium* and *Enterprise*, see Keith Archibald Forbes, Bermuda Online, http://www.bermuda-online.org/history1800-1899.htm; Dodson, Campbell, R. M. Rolfe to Viscount Palmerston, Oct. 31, 1836, in Baron Arnold Duncan McNair, "Slavery and the Slave Trade," in *International Law Opinions* (London: Cambridge University Press, 1956), 81–5; Jones, *Mutiny on Amistad*, 53–4; Jonathan Levy, *Freaks of Fortune: The Emerging World of Capitalism and Risk in America* (Cambridge, Mass.: Harvard University Press, 2012), 26–7; Downey, *Creole Affair*, 64.

[19] Petition by John Strohecker and others to South Carolina Senate, 1842, Petition 11384205, Race & Slavery Petitions Project (RSPP), http://library.uncg.edu/slavery/petitions/details.aspx?pid=1573. One of the owners was asked why he did not go to Bermuda and claim his lost property. "Because," answered Neal, "*a nigger is just as free there and stands just as good a chance in their courts as a white man.*" Bancroft, *Slave-Trading,*

Five years later, the *Hermosa* experienced a similar interruption in its coastal slaving. This schooner had a burden of 133 and 66/95 tons and was captained by John L. Chattin.[20] On October 10, 1840, the master, port collector George Read, and several shippers signed the ship's manifest as required by the 1807 federal law. The vessel's business was to transport forty-seven captives from Richmond to New Orleans. L. C. Read of Richmond shipped forty-five-year-old Lewis Johnson to one J. H. Daly. As the eldest, he might have been marketed for work beyond the plantation. Prominent Richmond trader Lancaster, Denby, & Company shipped five boys and four girls aged between eleven and sixteen to consignee A. Ledoux. H. N. Templeman of Richmond transported the bulk of the captives. Twenty-one were males: the youngest – sixteen-year-old Reuben Francis – and the oldest – thirty-five year-old Edward Parker. Ten-year-olds Louisa Gibbs, Dicey Lumkin, France Toublin were the youngest of the sixteen females while thirty-year-old Betsy Green was the oldest. The age and gender of these captives suggest they were destined for plantation production. The list of names does not reveal much about possible familial relations. Some were listed by first name only. Others like Malinda and Louisa shared the same surname of Gibbs while William and another were both surnamed Smith. This similarity suggests either common ownership or kinship (see **Appendix 2**).[21]

Nine days later, the *Hermosa* wrecked off Abaco Island. Bahamas's Governor Cockburn reported that "every slave would have perished but for the gallant exertions of the Boatmen of that place [who] rescued [them] from a watery grave." After being towed to Nassau, Captain Chattin arranged with American Consul John Bacon to get another ship to take the captives to their destination in Louisiana. British magistrates, backed by armed troops from the Second West India Regiment, boarded the *Hermosa* and removed the captives. A local magistrate set them free – presumably arguing that the slaves were at liberty once they entered a British jurisdiction in compliance with the reasoning of Britain's highest courts in the previous case of the *Enterprise*. The Americans protested this decision,

---

277. For being "free there," and its continental consequences in nineteenth-century North America (United States, British Canada, Mexico), see Jeffrey R. Kerr-Ritchie, *Freedom's Seekers: Essays on Comparative Emancipation* (Baton Rouge: Louisiana State University Press, 2014), chap.1.

20 NARA archivist Mark Mollan checked the index to Enrolments for Richmond through Charleston in 1839, but could not locate the *Hermosa*. Mollan, email, May 16, 2017.

21 Manifest of the *Hermosa*, October 10, 1840, in Bahamas 1840 Vol. 1, January-December, Gvr. Cockburn, CO 23/107, TNA.

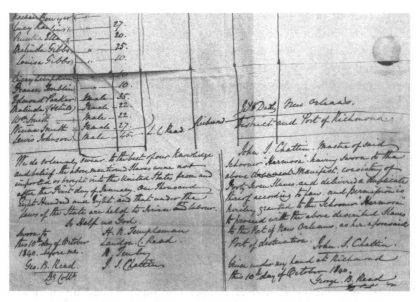

FIGURE 3.1 Detail of ship manifest for the *Hermosa*, Richmond, October 10, 1840.
Source: Bahamas, 1840, Vol. 1, Jan.-Dec., Governor Cockburn, CO 23/107, TNA.

arguing that they had broken no local laws and were just seeking aid for the protection of their private property. The Colonial Office regretfully informed Governor Cockburn that "no funds" were available from Her Majesty's Government for "remuneration" to the boatmen of Abaco "in saving the slaves."[22] Bahamian boatmen were also to play a decisive role in the liberation of captives from the *Creole* thirteen months later. Strangely enough, this objectionable act of slave liberation from the *Hermosa* led by British colonial authorities went unmentioned by US Consul Bacon in the aftermath of the *Creole* revolt a mere thirteen months later.

---

[22] Governor Sir Francis Cockburn to Lord ?, December 1, 1840, CO 23/107, TNA; Colonial Office to Cockburn, February ?, 1841, CO 23/107, TNA; Horne, *Negro Comrades of the Crown*, 133, 293. For incorrect reports of thirty-eight slaves aboard the *Hermosa*, see Downey, *Creole Affair*, 65, and Childress, "Hermosa Case (1840)" in the *Historical Encyclopedia of World Slavery*, ed. Junius P. Rodriguez. vol. 1 (Armonk, NY: M.E. Sharpe, 2007), 340. Howard Jones mistakenly refers to this vessel as the *Formosa*. Howard Jones, "The Peculiar Institution and National Honor: The Case of the *Creole* Slave Revolt." *Civil War History* vol. 21, no. 1 (Mar. 1975), 35.

All four of these incidents involving American coastal slavers bore striking similarities: poor weather conditions that drove the vessels off course into British waters and ports where captives' desires for liberation were facilitated by local authorities. In the first two cases, the British government subsequently compensated US slaveholders because colonial slavery still operated in its territories. In the latter two cases, US slaveholders failed to receive compensation because Great Britain had abolished colonial slavery. Any slave on either British soil or within British maritime borders was legally free due to the passage of colonial abolition in 1833. Although US slaveholders continued to press for compensation, these latter two cases remained unresolved until the final deliberations of the Anglo-American Commission during the early 1850s.

Before then, captives aboard the *Creole* had rebelled, commandeered the ship, killed a guard, severely wounded the captain and several crew, and steered for the Bahamas in the hopes of obtaining their freedom in free waters. This vessel's history was markedly unlike that of the *Comet, Encomium, Enterprise,* and *Hermosa.* The slaver ended up in British waters as a consequence of a successful slave insurrection whereas the previous slavers had been forced into British ports by poor weather after which their human cargo either walked or were transported to freedom. This latter action, it should be noted, resulted from similar expressions of racial solidarity between Caribbean boatmen and former American captives. Black consciousness across the water is rarely reported in the documents, but was instrumental to these several maritime acts of liberation.

4

"Engaged in the Business Ever Since She Was Constructed"

The *Creole* is the most immediately recognizable slaver involved in America's coastal slave trade, yet its life span at sea was remarkably short. It was constructed in the shipyards of Richmond in 1840. With a burden of 187 and 25/95 tons, the brig was ninety-five feet long, twenty-five feet and six inches wide, with a depth of eight feet and nine inches. The vessel had one deck and two masts. The stern was square. A lady's figure adorned the head of the ship. Hiram W. Taylor of Richmond, Virginia, and David Curry owned the vessel from November 14, 1840 to October 19, 1841. Captain Robert Ensor was the ship's master for most of its life at sea. The brig was officially enrolled and licensed for domestic trading at the Customs House in Richmond on November 14, 1840. On October 19, 1841, Isaac Davenport joined Curry in assuming joint ownership.[1]

---

[1] Enrollment No. 126, Brig Creole, November 14, 1840; Enrollment No. 137, Brig Creole, October 19, 1841; Finding Aid, Bureau of Marine and Navigation, RG 41, NARA. Several sources state inaccurately that Johnson & Eperson of Richmond owned the brig: Bacon to Webster, Nov. 30 1841, U.S. Sen. Doc. No. 51, 4; Edward D. Jervey and C. Harold Huber, "The Creole Affair," *The Journal of Negro History* vol. 65, No. 3 (Summer 1980), 196; Arthur T. Downey, *The Creole Affair: The Slave Rebellion That Led the U.S. and Great Britain to the Brink of War* (Lanham: Rowman and Littlefield, 2014), 10; George Hendrick and Willene Hendrick, *The Creole Mutiny: A Tale of Revolt aboard a Slave Ship* (Chicago: Ivan R. Dee, 2003), 77. The chapter title comes from lawyers Peyton and Smith in the 1845 Louisiana Supreme Court session, "*Thomas McCargo v. The New Orleans Insurance Company*" in Merritt M. Robinson, *Reports of Cases Argued and Determined in the Supreme Court of Louisiana*, Vol. 10, (March 1 to June 20, 1845) (Samuel M. Stewart), 1845, 287.

If the *Creole*'s beginnings were straightforward, its ending was rather enigmatic. According to the master abstract of ship registers, the ship's final document was surrendered on October 26, 1842, because the "Vessel [was] wrecked."[2] This is confirmed by a report in *The North American and Daily Advertiser* concerning a "late gale at Madeira" that "destroyed a great number of vessels" including the "brig Creole, of Richmond." Other newspapers also reported the ship's wreckage as a consequence of foul weather. But there were some oddities. The *Creole* was listed as hailing "from New York" in the *Cleveland Daily Herald*, and from New Orleans in the *Boston Courier*. It was the same ship because "Riddle" was named in the latter newspaper, and Alexander Riddle assumed mastership of the vessel after Captain Ensor's incapacitation.[3] Why was the *Creole* sailing from either New York or New Orleans? What was this US coastal slaver doing in a Portuguese-controlled archipelago of the northwest coast of Africa? Can it be that after a brief return to the coastal trade, the *Creole* switched to illegally engaging in the transatlantic slave trade?

Despite its short sea life, the *Creole* was very active. Between November 1840 and August 1841, surviving ship manifests suggest the brig voyaged between ports in Virginia and Louisiana at least five times. It usually transported large numbers of captives to the New Orleans marketplace. It returned to Richmond and Norfolk with smaller numbers of captives and owners traveling together.

On November 1, 1840, Captain Ensor signed the ship's manifest together with the port collector in Richmond for an outbound voyage to New Orleans. The manifest officially listed 152 slaves, but if we count the three infants traveling with their mothers then the total number of captives amounted to 155. There were more males than females – eighty-four to sixty-eight – or 55 percent and 45 percent respectively. Their ages ranged from infancy to forty years. But it was a young group with only fourteen captives being twenty-five years or older. We should exercise caution with these statistics because there is no documentary evidence to support the accuracy of these ages and this was a market that favored young captives. What we can say for certain is that these were mostly young workers who were traded for plantation production in the

---

[2] Finding Aid, Bureau of Marine and Navigation, RG 41, NARA.
[3] *The North American and Daily Advertiser*, January 3, 1843; *Cleveland Daily Herald*, December 16, 1842; *Boston Courier*, December 8, 1842. Thanks to Kate McMahon for these citations.

expanding slave economies of southwestern states and territories. The captives were divided into four racial categories of black, brown, yellow, and mulatto. There is no way to gauge the accuracy of these descriptions, although they were probably primarily based upon physical appearance. What seems clear is that the predominance of those not classified as black suggests that these captives were American-born. Moreover, their color either derived from the genetic pool or was biological evidence of coitus – coerced or otherwise – between enslaved women and white male owners, traders, or others.[4]

The shippers included George Bamb, An[n?e?] Notting, William N. Goodwin, Jason H. Birch, William Barret, Harris Edmundson, A. Mathews, Robert Lumpkin, T. B. Jackson, Abner Robinson, H. Davis, Richard R. Beasley, William Foster, William Harris, Hardy & Bros, William Francis, and E. Bannot. The consignees were Thomas McCargo, John Hagan, and Sherman Johnson, all resident in New Orleans. These traders included some well-known merchants as well as ordinary sellers. The range points to the normalcy of slave trading among numerous American southerners. It is also noteworthy that several of these traders were to subsequently invest in the coastal passage that failed. The *Creole* arrived safely in New Orleans on December 12, 1840, where it passed muster by the local port collector.[5]

Five weeks later, the *Creole* prepared to return to Virginia. On January 23, 1841, Captain Ensor co-signed the ship's manifest with owner Thomas Russell and the port collector of New Orleans. The manifest stated the ship was transporting four captives, although there were really five. Jesse was a twenty-eight-year-old male, five feet and eight inches tall, and described as "black." Ben was forty-eight, five feet and five inches, and "black." He was probably a domestic. George was either ten or sixteen (the writing is unclear), and described as "black." Anne was twenty-five and "black" and traveled with her eight-year-old. The shipper was slave-owner Thomas C. Russell who was traveling to the Chesapeake with his human chattel. It is not clear how much he paid for the transportation, although revenue from the return voyage presumably pleased the owners.[6]

---

[4] Manifest of the *Creole*, Nov. 1, 1840, *Slave Manifests of Coastwise Vessels Filed at New Orleans, Louisiana, 1807–1860*, Microfilm Serial M1895, Microfilm Roll 7, RG 36, NARA.

[5] Ibid. A comparison of the ship manifest and ship registration dates suggests the brig commenced its journey two weeks prior to its official enrollment.

[6] Manifest of the *Creole*, January 23, 1841, *Slave Manifests of Coastwise Vessels Filed at New Orleans, Louisiana, 1807–1860*, Microfilm Serial M1895, Microfilm Roll 7, RG 36, NARA.

On March 10, 1841, Captain Ensor and port collector Thomas Nelson signed the manifest for the slaver's next journey transporting fifteen captives from Richmond to New Orleans. Robert Lumpkin of Richmond was shipping fourteen captives to Thomas B. Small of New Orleans. Thomas B. Jackson was sending eighteen-year-old Jack to Thomas McCargo in New Orleans. Of the fifteen captives, thirteen had surnames different from those of the shippers suggesting that they were bought from planters and owners in the Upper South region. Fifteen-year-old Elvinia and sixteen-year-old Matilda shared the same surname of Bayly implying either former common ownership or kinship. Thirty-year-old Hannah and twenty-seven-year-old William also shared the same name of Robinson. The sex ratio was even with eight females and seven males. Their ages ranged between fifteen and thirty with the exception of Eliza who was eight years old. The height of the males was around the mid-five-feet range with the tallest being the five feet and nine inch Solomon Brown. The women were in the lower five feet range with the tallest being Elvinia at five feet and five inches. The slaver arrived at New Orleans port on April 9, 1841. The collector Bernard Hurt examined and found all correct. The captives were presumably sold into the long night of American slavery.[7]

The *Creole* returned at some point to Virginia, with or without human cargo. On July 1, 1841, it set out again for New Orleans. John Dickson transported three captives. Mary, aged twenty-six years, was five feet and two inches and described as "yellow." Ann was twelve years old, four feet and nine inches, and "brown." Sarah was nine years old, four feet and one and a half inches, and "yellow." None of the captives had surnames suggesting they were Dickson's property. Their complexions imply some form of miscegenation. Captain Ensor, owner Dickson, and port collector R. Walker of the District and Port of Norfolk and Portsmouth signed the ship's manifest, after which the vessel embarked for the Crescent City.[8]

On August 13, 1841, the *Creole* returned to Virginia. Captain Ensor shipped R. Freeman, aged twenty-eight years, five feet and ten inches, and described as "yellow" from New Orleans bound for Richmond. The master and shipper swore that the captive was not imported.

---

[7] Manifest of the *Creole*, March 10, 1841, *Slave Manifests of Coastwise Vessels Filed at New Orleans, Louisiana, 1807–1860*, Microfilm Serial *M1895*, Microfilm Roll 7, RG 36, NARA.

[8] Manifest of the *Creole*, July 1, 1841, *Slave Manifests of Coastwise Vessels Filed at New Orleans, Louisiana, 1807–1860*, Microfilm Serial *M1895*, Microfilm Roll 7, RG 36, NARA.

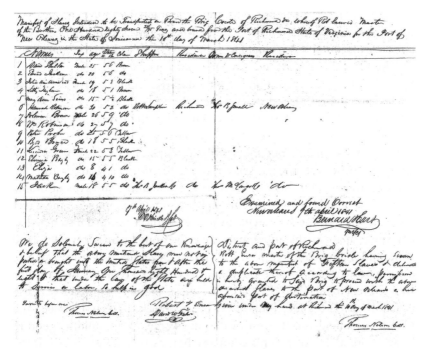

FIGURE 4.1 Ship manifest for the *Creole*, Richmond, March 10, 1841.
Source: *Slave Manifests of Coastwise Vessels Filed at New Orleans, Louisiana, 1807–1860*, Microfilm M1895, Roll 8, RG 36, NARA.

We can assume that they arrived without incident sometime in early September. This might well have been the *Creole*'s last successful passage before the rebellion.[9]

When the *Creole* sailed from Richmond in late October 1841, the ship's company consisted of three officers and six seamen. This was quite a reasonable compliment for a coastal slaver carrying that number of captives.[10] According to the 1840 US Census, Robert T. Ensor resided in

[9] Manifest of the *Creole*, August 13, 1841, *Slave Manifests of Coastwise Vessels Filed at New Orleans, Louisiana, 1807–1860*, Microfilm Serial *M1895*, Microfilm Roll 7, RG 36, NARA.

[10] Walter Johnson observes that coastal slavers such as the *Creole* carrying 135 slaves required thirteen sailors and three overseers. Johnson, *Soul By Soul: Life inside the Antebellum Slave Market* (Cambridge, Mass.: Harvard University Press, 1999), 61. Marcus Rediker notes the *Amistad* carried fifty-three slaves, five seamen, and two passengers. Rediker, *The Amistad Rebellion: An Atlantic Odyssey of Slavery and Freedom* (New York: Viking, 2012), 68.

Richmond, Henrico County, with two white females under five years of age – presumably his daughter and niece – and a white female aged twenty – presumably his wife. He does not appear to have been wealthy. The Richmond City Personal Property Book listed residents' tax returns for slaves, horses, mares, mules, colts, stallions, riding carriages, and so forth. Captain Ensor is unlisted for the years 1835 through 1840. The key point is that for two years, Captain Ensor led the *Creole* on numerous coastal voyages. This was to be his last journey.[11]

Below the captain came the first mate. Zephaniah C. Gifford was an experienced seaman having served at sea for thirteen years before the *Creole* voyage.[12] He was to play a central role in the subsequent drama of ship revolt and captives' liberation. He assumed command of the slaver in the absence of the incapacitated master. Officer Gifford also acted as key spokesman in the subsequent investigation. Lucius Stevens served as second mate behind Gifford.[13] William Deveraux was a free man of color who worked as cook and steward. Jacques Lecompts or Lacombe was a French member of the crew whose inability to speak English probably saved his life. John Silvy, Henry Speck, Francis Foxwell, and Blinn Curtis made up the rest of the ship's crew.[14] It would be good to know more about this ship's company but, as one lawyer noted at the 1845 Louisiana Supreme Court hearing, sailors wandered with the waves. What the record failed to show was that these seamen functioned as employees in the economy of slavery as well as maritime conduits of American empire building.[15]

Seven passengers boarded the *Creole* in Richmond for its October voyage to New Orleans. Captain Ensor brought along his wife, daughter

---

[11] 1840 US Census; Downey, *Creole Affair*, 208n14, Personal Property Tax Records for City of Richmond, Reel 365, 1835–1850, VL.

[12] Gifford's testimony, "*Thomas McCargo v. The New Orleans Insurance Company*," 206; Jervey & Huber, "Creole Affair," 196; Hendrick and Hendrick, *Creole Mutiny*, 7.

[13] Hendrick and Hendrick, *Creole Mutiny*, 7; Howard Jones, "The Peculiar Institution and National Honor: The Case of the *Creole* Slave Revolt," *Civil War History* vol. 21, no. 1 (March 1975), 30n6.

[14] Gifford's testimony," *Thomas McCargo v. The New Orleans Insurance Company*, 206; Hendrick and Hendrick, *Creole Mutiny*, 7.

[15] Despite useful studies by Markus Rediker, Jeffrey Bolster, and Emma Christopher, we still know little about these slave ship sailors. Sowande Mustakeem gives a good explanation for why this is so: "The inner lives of seafarers are most times inaccessible due to the predominance of illiteracy, but also due to the construction of narratives that silence the labor that seamen performed in the movement and brutal management of bondpeople." Sowande' M. Mustakeem, *Slavery at Sea: Terror, Sex, and Sickness in the Middle Passage* (Urbana: University of Illinois Press, 2016), 8.

and niece. This suggests he did not expect the captives to revolt or that the ship would flounder as a consequence of heavy weather. Theophilus J. D. McCargo was also aboard ship. He was the nephew of Richmond trader Thomas McCargo. He was too young to supervise the captives. John R. Hewell from Richmond was employed to guard those slaves traded by McCargo. Joseph or Jacob Lietener or Leidner – spelled variously in the documentation – was a Prussian who served as mate to the steward in exchange for free passage to New Orleans. Finally, William Henry Merritt acted as general guard for all of the slaves in exchange for free passage to the Crescent City. These three adult males contributed to the expansion of the slave economy through working the Coastal Passage.[16]

There is some disparity over how many shippers transported captives aboard the *Creole*. The ship's manifest signed by Captain Robert Ensor on October 28, 1841, lists four "owners or shippers" according to the certificate's rubric: George W. Apperson, John R. Hewell, Lancaster Denby & Company, and C. H. Shields & W. W. Hall.[17] The New Orleans Protest dated December 2, 1841, signed by the ship's officers and seamen, refers to nine shippers: Robert Lumpkin, John R. Hewell, Nathaniel Matthews, W. Robinson, Mr. Hatcher, Sherman Johnson, Edward Lockett, Thomas McCargo, and John Hagan.[18] At the Louisiana Supreme Court session in March 1845, Judge Henry Bullard identified six shippers: James Andrews and "another," Edward Lockett, John Hagan, Sherman Johnson, and Thomas McCargo.[19] The Anglo-American Commission (AAC) report from the early 1850s listed nine

---

[16] Hendrick and Hendrick, *Creole Mutiny*, 8, 77; Downey, *Creole Affair*, 9; Jones, "Case of Creole," 29; Conrad, Slidell, Benjamin, *"Thomas McCargo v. The New Orleans Insurance Company,"* 260; McCargo, deposition to Bacon, November 10, 1841, U.S. Sen. Doc. No. 51, 26; Lietener, deposition to Bacon, November 15, 1841, U.S. Sen. Doc. No. 51, 26; Merritt, deposition to Bacon, November 9, 1841, U.S. Sen. Doc. No. 51, 24.

[17] Robert Ensor, *Creole* manifest, October 28, 1841, Consolidated Cases: # 4413 *Andrews & Hatcher v. OIC*, # 4414 *Sherman Johnson v. OIC*, # 4419 *John Hagan v. OIC*, Microfilm, NOPL.

[18] New Orleans Protest, December 2, 1841, U.S. Sen. Doc. No. 51, 37, 40.

[19] *"Thomas McCargo v. The New Orleans Insurance Company,"* 332–335. But elsewhere in *"Thomas McCargo v. The New Orleans Insurance Company,"* 203, McCargo is credited with twenty-six slaves. Jervey and Huber rely on this source. Jervey and Huber, "Creole Affair," 196. For nineteen captives transported by McCargo listed by name, color, sex, and age, see Petition to Commercial Court of New Orleans, December 15, 1841, Petition 20884135, RSPP, http://library.uncg.edu/slavery/petitions/details.aspx?pid=16043. All of these people show up on Captain Ensor's manifest except for Milla Terretts.

shippers: Edward Lockett, John Hogun [Hogan], William H. Goodwin, Thomas McCargo, John Pemberton, G. H. Apperson and Sherman Johnson, P. Rotchford, and James Andrews.[20] The historians also do not agree. Some claim Johnson and Eperson owned the "majority" of the slaves.[21] Others identify Thomas McCargo as shipper of thirty-nine slaves, but are mute on the other transporters.[22]

Clarification concerning the exact number of shippers and who they were can be obtained from careful analysis of ship manifests, bills of lading, memoranda, slave schedules, and legal petitions located in the New Orleans Public Library (NOPL), Amistad Research Collection (ARC), and from the genealogical website Ancestry.com. This documentation consistently lists the same people: John R. Hewell, George W. Apperson, C. H. Shields & W. W. Hall, Robert Lumpkin, John Hagan, Nathaniel Mathews, Thomas McCargo, and Lancaster Denby & Company. This total of eight shippers is different from all the others and only adds further to the discrepancy over the number of shippers. But the failure to distinguish between traders, slaveholders, and overseers means that our understanding of those who moved captives aboard the *Creole* has been unclear until now.

Thomas McCargo was the most prolific shipper. In 1830, he was between twenty and thirty years in age and headed a household that included a forty- to fifty-year-old male (probably his father) and a thirty- to forty-year-old female (mother?) in Banister Township, Halifax County, in Virginia's Southside.[23] His business was marketing slaves. In 1831, McCargo sold twenty-three-year-old Julius, fifteen-year-old Harrison, and an unnamed thirteen-year-old for $500 each, together with other boys and girls worth between $275 and $550 to one Alfred I. Lowry of Concordia Parish, Louisiana.[24] That same year McCargo sold seventeen-year-old Usley to Agnes Tinsley, a free woman of color residing in New Orleans. According to the "certificate of good character" – a document required by Louisiana law adopted in 1829 to guard against the importation of rebellious slaves – Halifax County freeholders William Allen and Abraham Owen certified that Usley had been legitimately purchased from Jacob David, bore "no visible marks or scars," was of

---

[20] "Adjustment Claims," U.S. Sen. Doc. No. 103, 1856, 52.
[21] Jervey and Huber, "Creole Affair," 196.
[22] Hendrick and Hendrick, *Creole Mutiny*, 44; Downey, *Creole Affair*, 10.
[23] Halifax County, Virginia, US Census, 1830 returns.
[24] Phillips, *Land and Labor in the Old South*, 155–156.

"good moral character," and was not in the habit of running away. Around the same time, McCargo sold twenty-two-year-old Frank for $550 to Quentin Mauge of St. Mary, Louisiana. Halifax County freeholders John (Brown? Borden?) and Robert Tucker certified that Frank was not a criminal, was of good moral character, and not a runaway.[25]

Sometime during the 1830s, McCargo relocated to Richmond, where he became a prominent slave trader. In 1835, he was offering cash for slaves to be traded.[26] In 1836, he paid city tax of seventy-five cents on three slaves in Richmond.[27] Thereafter, he was no longer listed as a city taxpayer, and it was probably during this time that he relocated to the Crescent City.[28] It was from there that he directed the transportation of captives on two *Creole* voyages in November 1840 and March 1841.[29]

Thomas McCargo appears to have been a shrewd businessman who sought protection against risk. On November 15, 1841, he contracted with the New Orleans Insurance Company (NOIC) in the Crescent City for the insurance of "26 Negroes on the Brig Creole." The slaves were valued at $800 each for a combined value of $20,800. At 2 percent – $416 – and the policy at $2 – the total premium cost was $418. "THIS INSURANCE," read the contract, "is declared to be on Twenty-six negroes, at $800 each . . . This policy covers all risks & chiefly that of foreign interference. Warranted by the assured, free from elopement, insurrection & natural death."[30] The following day, McCargo took out a second insurance policy with the Norfolk branch of the Merchant's Insurance Company of New Orleans (MICNO) for the transportation of nineteen slaves valued at $15,200 from Norfolk to New Orleans aboard the *Creole.* This policy provided similar coverage of "perils, losses, and misfortunes" as McCargo's other policy with the NOIC, with the appended memorandum "that the Company are not liable for suicide, desertion, or natural death, but that it provides chiefly for the risk of

[25] William Boswell, Notary Acts No. 14, January 3 to March 25, 1831, page 76, page 79, NONA.

[26] *Richmond Enquirer*, December 31, 1835.

[27] Personal Property Tax Records for City of Richmond, Reel 365, 1835–1850, VL.

[28] Ibid.

[29] Manifest of the *Creole*, November 1, 1841, *Slave Manifests of Coastwise Vessels Filed at New Orleans, Louisiana, 1807–1860*, Microfilm Serial M1895, Microfilm Roll 7, RG 36, NARA; Manifest of the *Creole*, March 10, 1841, *Slave Manifests of Coastwise Vessels Filed at New Orleans, Louisiana, 1807–1860*, Microfilm Serial M1895, Microfilm Roll 7, RG 36, NARA.

[30] Marine Cargo No. 9430, NOIC & Thomas McCargo, November 15, 1841, Creole Affair Collection, ARC.

FIGURE 4.2 Thomas McCargo's insurance contract, New Orleans, November 15, 1841.
Source: Box 106, Creole Affair Collection, 1854–1941, ARC.

detention, capture, seizure of foreign powers."[31] Little did McCargo know that at precisely the same moment he was insuring his human cargoes, they were on the cusp of securing their liberty in the Bahamas.[32]

The other precaution taken by the New Orleans-based trader was to employ John Ragland Hewell to oversee the transportation of his captives from Virginia to New Orleans. The documentary record on this overseer is thin. On June 8, 1840, public notary Edward Barnet recorded that J. R. Hewell of Halifax County sold thirty-five-year-old George to Mistress Ann (Connarcher?) for $300. Attached to the notarized document was a form from the Recorder of Mortgages from New Orleans of the non-existence of a mortgage by Hewell against his slaves.[33]

---

[31] McCargo, Petition 20884135, RSPP, http://library.uncg.edu/slavery/petitions/details .aspx?pid=16043

[32] The combined number of slaves insured in these two contracts amounted to forty-five. According to the ship manifest, however, Thomas McCargo shipped forty-nine slaves. See Appendix 3.

[33] Edward Barnet, Notary Acts No. 12, May–July 1840, Act. No. 500, NONA. The law requiring certification of good character was ended in late 1831. Edward E. Baptist, *The Half Has Never Been Told: Slavery and the Making of American Capitalism* (New York: Basic Books, 2014), 175.

According to the ship manifest for the fall 1841 passage, Hewell shipped twenty-year-old William Carter, standing five feet and six inches and described as "black," and valued at $800. Hewell's most important task was to oversee Thomas McCargo's slaves aboard the *Creole*. He was probably paid well for his services, although it cost him his life.[34]

Robert Lumpkin was born around the same time as the prohibition of America's transatlantic slave trade and the regulation of the coastwise slave trade. During the 1830s, Lumpkin crossed the antebellum South trading in slaves.[35] By the late 1830s, Lumpkin was actively engaged in the Coastal Passage. He operated his business and private jail at the wall between Franklin and Broad Streets on Birch Alley.[36] In November 1840, he shipped captives aboard the *Creole*. In March 1841, he transported fourteen captives on the *Creole* to New Orleans.[37] Several months later, he shipped forty-three captives (31 percent of the total) aboard the *Creole* bound for New Orleans. This fateful November voyage included twenty-six males worth $20,800 and fifteen females worth $10,000 for a total of $30,800.[38] Unlike McCargo and other shippers, however, Lumpkin does not appear to have protected his large investment by contracting with insurance companies.[39]

When and where George Washington Apperson was born remains a mystery. He does show up in the federal census for 1830 as the head of a large household in Culpeper County, Virginia. The household comprised eleven free white males, eleven free white females, four free colored males, three free colored females, nine enslaved men, and nine enslaved women for a total of forty-seven people residing at that one address. It is not clear who all of the white residents were – family? lodgers? – but we may assume that those who were enslaved were associated with Lumpkin's' trading practices.[40] According to the Special Collections

---

[34] Several websites mistakenly report that Thomas McCargo moved only twenty-six slaves and that he also traveled aboard the *Creole*.

[35] Mathew R. Laird, "Lumpkin's Jail," Encyclopedia Virginia, https://www .encyclopediavirginia.org/Lumpkin_s_Jail#

[36] Elizabeth Kambourian, "Slave Traders in Richmond," *Richmond Times-Dispatch*, Feb.24, 2014, http://www.richmond.com/slave-traders-in-richmond/table_52a32a98-9 d56-11e3-806a-0017a43b2370.html

[37] Manifest of *Creole*, Nov. 20, 1840 and Manifest of *Creole*, Mar. 10, 1841, in *Slave Manifests of Coastwise Vessels Filed at New Orleans, Louisiana, 1807-1860*, Microfilm Serial M1895, Microfilm Roll 8, Record Group 36, NARA.

[38] Robert Ensor, Bill of Lading, October 20, 1841, Creole Affair Collection, ARC #16

[39] I found nothing in the ARC with the other insurance contracts. There is also no reference in the legal documentation.

[40] Culpeper County, Virginia, US Census, 1830 returns. Thanks to Kate McMahon for this citation.

Librarian at Norfolk Public Library, Apperson was to become "Norfolk's most prolific slave trader based upon the manifests and newspaper advertisements."[41] Sometime during the 1830s, he relocated to the Crescent City.

On March 3, 1838, Apperson sold twenty-year-old Rosetta to Eliza A. Gervais for $900. Both seller and buyer resided in New Orleans. There was no certificate for good character because the law had been terminated seven years earlier.[42] The former Virginia trader does not appear to have shipped captives on earlier *Creole* voyages. On October 28, 1841, Apperson "put on board" the *Creole* twenty-one slaves worth a combined total of $15,000. They were consigned to Sherman Johnson of New Orleans. Apperson took out an insurance policy with the Ocean Insurance Company at 2.5 percent rate "against all risks especially for interference warranted free from elopement, insurrection & natural causes."[43] He was to end up shipping forty-two captives in total – only second behind McCargo – aboard the *Creole*.

John A. Hagan was to become a very successful cotton factor and bank investor based in New Orleans. He was born in South Carolina in 1813.[44] By the late 1820s and early 1830s, the young businessman had provided Louisiana planter William S. Hamilton with information on the most profitable markets, transported three boxes of "Tomb Stones" from New York to Hamilton's plantation, and most importantly extended credit to the planter for his agricultural operations. In March 1828, for instance, Hagan informed Hamilton: "as we may not find it very convenient to lay out . . . this money during the summer months, we enclose a note for your signature for which if necessary we can obtain the funds through [the] Bank."[45]

[41] Troy Valos, email, July 13, 2017.

[42] William Boswell, Notary Acts No. 52, January–March 1838, Act. No. 206.

[43] Schedule of twenty-one slaves shipped in *Creole* by G. W. Apperson to Sherman Johnson of New Orleans put aboard at Norfolk October 28, 1841, Creole Affair Collection, ARC; Memorial of George Washington Apperson presented to Hon. Commissioners of AAC, March 14, 1854, ARC; Sherman Johnson contract with the OIC, November 23, 1841, ARC.

[44] Orleans Parish, Louisiana, US Census, 1850 returns.

[45] Harold D. Woodman, *King Cotton and His Retainers: Financing and Marketing the Cotton Crop of the South, 1800–1925* (1968: Columbia: University of South Carolina Press, 1990), 19, 39–40, 45 "Tomb Stones," 67, 114–115; "as we may" 117, 132. For Hagan's commercial and real estate dealing in New Orleans, see Friends of the Cabildo, *New Orleans Architecture,* vol. II *The American Sector (Faubourg St. Mary)* (Gretna: Pelican Publishing Company, 1972), 67, 69, 158, 161, 198.

Mr. Hagan also became a prolific "Negro Trader." On January 25, 1833, the slaver *Ariel* of Norfolk embarked with eighty-nine captives for New Orleans. Thirty-nine were consigned to Hagan.[46] On January 23, 1838, William Boswell notarized an act of sale in which Hagan sold twenty-five-year-old Lewis to Joseph Auguste Leveque of West Baton Rouge for $925.[47] Hagan was to ship nine captives worth $6,500 on the *Creole* on its fateful 1841 voyage.[48] On November 23, 1841, Hagan signed contract No. 3180 with the Ocean Insurance Company for slaves worth $6,500 at 2.5 percent for a $162.50 policy plus a fee of $1.50 for a total premium of $164. The contract was for risk against foreign interference and warranted free from elopement, insurrection, and natural death.[49] Little did the prominent slave trader know that at the same time he was signing this insurance contract, the *Creole* was four days out of Nassau harbor and on its way to New Orleans minus his personal property.[50]

We have limited information on the two other shippers. Lancaster, Denby & Company was a trading firm based in Richmond. According to the city property tax records, the business paid seventy-five cents in tax on three slaves in 1836 and 1837. In 1838, it paid sixty cents on two slaves. In 1839, it paid ninety cents on three slaves.[51] In October 1841, the company shipped twenty-eight-year-old Susan Shields described as five feet and one inch and "brown" aboard the *Creole*.[52] She might have been one of the taxable slaves the previous years. But her days of captivity were numbered, unbeknownst to her. All we seem to know about C. H. Shields and W. W. Hall is that they shipped eleven captives aboard the *Creole* in October 1841.[53] What's clear, however, is that the trading of slaves from

---

[46] Wendell H. Stephenson, *Isaac Franklin: Slave Trader and Planter from the Old South* (Baton Rouge: Louisiana State University Press, 1938), 36.

[47] William Boswell, Notary Acts No. 52, January to March 1838, Act No. 49, NONA. On this document, Hagan is listed as residing in Charleston, South Carolina.

[48] Certified Slave Schedule of 9 Negroes, John Hagan, Creole Affair Collection, ARC; appendix 3.

[49] Contract No. 3180, OIC and John Hagan, November 23, 1841, Creole Affair Collection, ARC.

[50] On the other hand, business continued. The day after the *Creole* limped into New Orleans harbor minus Hagan's nine captives, Hagan sold twenty-two-year-old Daniel and twenty-year-old Emanuel to James Anson Bradbury of Feneborne Parish, Louisiana for $850 each. Edward Barnet, Public Notary Acts No. 18, October to December 1841, Act. No. 860, NONA.

[51] Personal Property Tax Records for City of Richmond, Reel 365, 1835–1850, VL.

[52] Please see ship manifest entry in Appendix 3.

[53] Please see ship manifest entry in Appendix 3.

Virginia to New Orleans was profitable, and that the essence of this profitability had less to do with the wealth-creating abilities of slave traders and more with the existing and potential exploitability of the labor of the captives.

There is also some confusion in both the archive as well as the scholarship concerning the precise number of captives aboard the *Creole* on the October-to-November 1841 voyage. The New Orleans Protest listed "one hundred and thirty slaves."[54] Captain Ensor, Chief Mate Gifford, Seaman Stevens, passenger Merritt, US Consul Bacon, and Louisiana Chief Justice Bullard believed there were 135 slaves on board ship.[55] Most scholars accept this figure.[56] The ship's logbook reputedly recorded "150 slaves."[57] Appellant lawyers in the 1845 Supreme Court session argued that the logbook showed 186 slaves.[58] The Hendricks provide different figures: 129 "or more" on one page, and 135 "or more" on another page – the extra being made up of kidnapped free blacks and/or illegally trafficked slaves from Africa.[59] The larger figures are not documented and are exaggerations. For instance, the figure of 186 in the 1845 court session came from lawyers for the insurance company arguing that the ship was unseaworthy because it carried too many slaves.

[54] New Orleans Protest, December 2 1841, U.S. Sen. Doc. No. 51, 16.

[55] Ensor to British Magistrates Duncan and Burnside, deposition, November 18, 1841, in U.S. Sen. Doc. No. 51, 30, and Dispatches from US Consul in Nassau, Roll 5, RG 59, T475, NARA; Gifford to British Magistrates Duncan and Burnside, deposition, November 9, 1841, in U.S. Sen. Doc. No. 51, 30, and Dispatches from US Consul in Nassau, Roll 5, RG 59, T475, NARA; Stevens to British Magistrates Duncan and Burnside, deposition, November 10, 1841, in Dispatches from US Consul in Nassau, Roll 5, RG 59, T475, NARA; Gifford to Bacon, deposition, November 9, 1841, U.S. Sen. Doc. No. 51, 20; Gifford's testimony, *"Thomas McCargo v. The New Orleans Insurance Company,"* 218–219; Conrad, Slidell, Benjamin for the Defense, *"Thomas McCargo v. The New Orleans Insurance Company,"* 259–260; Merritt to British Magistrates Duncan and Burnside, November 9, 1841, U.S. Sen. Doc. No. 51, 28; Bacon to Webster, November 17 1841, in U.S. Sen. Doc. 51, 2; Judge Bullard's ruling, *"Thomas McCargo v. The New Orleans Insurance Company,"* 314.

[56] Eric Robert Taylor, *If We Must Die: Shipboard Insurrections in the Era of the Atlantic Slave Trade* (Baton Rouge: Louisiana State University Press, 2006), 156; Howard Jones, *Mutiny on the Amistad: The Saga of a Slave Revolt and Its Impact on American Abolition, Law, and Diplomacy* (New York: Oxford University Press, 1987), 29; Jervey and Huber, "Creole Affair," 196; Johnson, *Soul by Soul*, 61; Downey, *Creole Affair*, 10.

[57] *"Thomas McCargo v. The New Orleans Insurance Company,"* 339; Jervey and Huber, "Creole Affair," 196. Markus Rediker counts nineteen rebels and 130 fellow Africans and African-Americans (Rediker, *Amistad Rebellion*, 225).

[58] *Thomas McCargo v. The New Orleans Insurance Company*, 259.

[59] Hendrick and Hendrick, *Creole Mutiny*, 8, 77–78.

We can, however, be more precise. Several important documents archived at the ARC and the NOPL provide the best evidence for working out the exact number of captives aboard the *Creole* in late 1841. More importantly, beyond statistical counting these documents shed some light on the humanity of these human cargoes.

On October 20, 1841, Captain Ensor signed a bill of lading for nine slaves shipped by John Hagan from Richmond to New Orleans. This included four men, four women, and a nine-year-old boy with a combined market value totaling $6,500 ($182,000 in 2015).[60] That same day, Captain Ensor signed another bill of lading for forty-one slaves shipped by Richmond trader Robert Lumpkin to Edward Lockett on the same route.[61] Each cost $15 ($420) apiece to transport. There were sixteen females and twenty-five males. A supporting memo suggests the twenty-five male captives were worth $800 each for a total of $20,000. The female captives were valued at $666.33 each for a total of $10,661.28. The total value of the human cargo amounted to $30,661.28 – at least $731,000 in today's monetary.[62] On October 28, 1841, one week after signing these two bills of lading, Captain Ensor signed the *Creole* manifest as required by section nine of the 1807 law regulating coastal commerce. In total, eighty-six captives were transported.[63] There were forty-one females and forty-two males. The gender of one infant and two children is not recorded.[64] The number of captives from all three documents adds up to 135. If we add the two children belonging to Mary Anne Larson and Margaret Lattimore, together with the unlisted rebels, then the most accurate number of captives aboard the *Creole* on its fall 1841 passage was 139 (see **Appendix 3**).

---

[60] Copy of slave schedule by John Hagan, Box 106, Creole Affair Collection, 1854–1941, ARC. All dollar conversions are measured by the Consumer Price Index for 2015. See MeasuringWorth.com https://www.measuringworth.com/

[61] According to the documents in Appendix 3, Lumpkin shipped forty-two captives.

[62] Captain Robert Ensor, Bill of Lading, October 20, 1841; Memo of valuation of forty-one slaves shipped per the Creole, claim of Edward Lockett, n. d., Box 106, Creole Affair Collection, 1854–1941, ARC. The cost of one male captive aboard the *Creole* is equivalent to just less than one year's tuition and fees at Howard University for the 2017–2018 academic year.

[63] The manifest numbers eighty-four slaves. This includes one infant, but excludes two children who are grouped together with their mothers and not counted individually.

[64] Ensor, *Creole* Manifest; Thomas McCargo, Petition to Commercial Court of New Orleans, December 15, 1841, Petition 20884135, RSPP, http://library.uncg.edu/slavery/petitions/details.aspx?pid=16043. "Memo of Negroes Shipped on Board the Brig Creole by G. W. Apperson to Sherman Johnson of New Orleans, Put on Board at Norfolk on the 28 of Oct. 1841," ARC.

Let us get a little closer to these human beings. There were seventy-six males and sixty-one females on board (the two infants' gender was not given). This approximate gender ratio differed markedly from that of the Atlantic slave trade that usually figured two males for every one female.[65] But it approximated the gender ratio on other coastal slavers. The sex ratio is probably explained by the limited division of labor in cotton and sugar fields of the lower South as well as by the alternative trades in which some of these captives were put to work as domestics, skilled laborers, and so forth.

Most of the *Creole*'s captives were in their prime working years. Thirteen of the captives were twelve years old or younger (10 percent) including eight-year-old Adelaide Bell and nine-year-old Albert Hemming. (This excludes the infant and two children.)[66] Twelve of the captives were more than twenty-five years old (10 percent); these included thirty-seven-year-old Rachel Henley and forty-year-old Frankey Ferguson who were the eldest female and male captives. In other words, 80 percent of the vessel's captives were between the ages of thirteen (like Mary Collins) and twenty-five (like Hester Bell). These were the prime ages for agricultural workers. Together with the balanced gender ratio, this age range supports the argument of a limited sexual division of labor in US antebellum slavery unlike that in sugar-producing slave societies in the Americas.

According to demographic historian Richard Steckel's influential research on slaves' physical characteristics, most enslaved people in the American South grew four inches in height between the ages of ten and twenty-one years. This was largely due to their moving into the work force together with an improved dietary regimen including meat rations and calories from corn and vegetables.[67] Ship manifests and captains' bills of lading were static documents and obviously did not record changes in ages over time. Still, a comparison of the height ranges between these ages sheds some light on growth rates among captives. Ten-year-old female captives L. Clarke and Mary Loyde were four feet and six inches and four

---

[65] Gifford's testimony, "*Thomas McCargo v. The New Orleans Insurance Company*," 206, and Hendrick and Hendrick, *Creole Mutiny*, 8; both underestimate the number of female captives aboard the *Creole*.

[66] There were four youngsters aboard the *Amistad*. See Jones, *Mutiny on the Amistad*, 23, Rediker, *Amistad Rebellion*, 65.

[67] Richard H. Steckel, "Demography and Slavery," in *The Oxford Handbook of Slavery in the Americas*, eds., Robert L. Paquette and Mark M. Smith (New York: Oxford University Press, 2010), 654–656.

feet and seven inches respectively. Twenty-one-year-olds Lucy French and Melinda Joiner were five feet and five feet and three inches respectively. Ten-year-old male captives William Scott and Monroe White were four feet and seven inches and four feet and eight inches respectively. Twenty-one-year-old Harry Brown, Williams Jenkins, John Lindsay, Lewis Lonry, Jourdan Phillips, George Portlock, Lemis Sonry, and Edmond Tallafino all measured between five feet and six inches and five feet and eight inches. All of these examples point to growth rates exceeding four inches for these captives. They further confirm other scholarship that maintains enslaved people in the American South were taller than enslaved people in the Caribbean.[68]

Descriptions of the color of the captives ranged over several categories: black, dark, brown, yellow, and light black. Most of the captives were depicted as either black or brown. It has been stated that whites determined racial identity in several ways during this period: documented ancestry, collective identity, scientific definitions, slave status, and physical appearance.[69] Clearly, shippers decided what someone looked like based upon physical appearance. But it was also the case that racial description functioned as "proof" of American provenance on coastal slavers. The *raison d'etre* of the "color" category on the ship manifest was to determine that captives were <u>not</u> imported from Africa in accordance with the 1807 law. Thus we can say with some confidence that those described as brown, yellow, and so forth were born in the United States – although this still begs the question of the circumstances in which the birth took place. Was it sexual violence, rape, or enslaved women's resignation as a means of surviving the harshness of the slave system? It also does not explain why so many of the captives were described as black? Was this an accurate view? Was it careless ascription? Did it indicate that some captives were born in Africa? A. Bird, Frankey Ferguson, Rachel Henley, H. Overton – all described as being either black or dark – were more than thirty-three years old in 1841, meaning they could have been

---

[68] Ensor, Manifest of the *Creole*, October 28, 1841; Ensor, *Creole* Bills of Lading, October 20 (Richmond), October 28 (Norfolk), Creole Affair Collection, ARC; see sources in Appendix 3. Richard Dunn reports adult male and female slaves in the British Caribbean reached five feet and four inches and five feet and one inch respectively compared to a median height of five feet and seven inches and five feet and three inches respectively in the American South (Dunn, *Tale of Two Plantations*, 141).

[69] Nikki M. Taylor, *Driven Toward Madness: The Fugitive Slave Margaret Garner and Tragedy on the Ohio* (Athens: Ohio University Press, 2016), 101.

born outside the United States prior to the legal termination of the Atlantic slave trade.

What about the market value of captives being transported aboard the *Creole*? The evidence is incomplete but there are some insights regarding certain captives. The labor of captive male agricultural workers was valued at $800. That of prime female workers was worth between $666 and $700. These two categories were the majority of captives transported aboard the *Creole*. Those with particular skills were deemed more valuable. Blacksmith George Butt was valued at $900. Seamstress Melvina Wilson was also worth $900. The scholar who pores over these manifests and bills of lading, however, should never forget that these were market prices for slaves' labor power that had nothing to do with measuring the lives of liberty-less human beings.

Finally, what do the recorded names tell us about the identity of these captives? Most of them had surnames that were different from those of their shippers and owners, suggesting they had been sold from different places and had ended up being purchased by traders. The surnames were overwhelmingly British. Most were English (Brown, Clarke, Morris), with some Welsh (Evans, Jenkins, Jones, Williams), and some Scottish (Bruce, Ferguson, Gordon, Robinson). There were famous Virginia surnames – Carter, Tyler, and Washington – as well as American ones – Jackson, America, and so forth. Some were unusually named. Pompey Garrison mixed classical lore with modern antislavery. Many of the captives shared similar surnames: Bell, Brown, Butler, Carter, Clarke, Gaines, Glover, Grigsby, Jones, King, Moore, Robinson, Scott, Shields, Smith, Washington, White, and Wilson. This suggests common origins in plantations and owners. But some captives were clearly related by blood. Margaret Lattimore and Mary Ann Larson both traveled with their children. Twenty-four-year-old Rachel Glover was the partner of twenty-two-year-old Wiley, and they had nine-year-old Isah. Hester, Leonara, and Melvina all shared the same surname of Wilson and were shipped by George Apperson. Monroe and Pinkey were both surnamed Robinson and shipped by Thomas McCargo. Warner and Alley were Smiths and shipped by Apperson (see **Appendix 3**).

If accounts vary on the precise number of shippers, slaveholders, and captives aboard the *Creole*, there is much less discrepancy over the number and identities of rebel slaves who took over the vessel. The British troops who boarded the *Creole* moored in Nassau harbor on November 12, 1841, restrained nineteen suspects and subsequently incarcerated them in the local jail. C. A. Nesbitt, colonial secretary to

Governor Francis Cockburn, submitted a list of nineteen slave rebels to American consul Bacon two weeks later.[70] Bacon provided a list of "19" slaves "named and identified as leaders in the mutiny and murder on board the Brig Creole and imprisoned at Nassau Nov. 12 1841" in a November 30, 1841, letter to his superior in Washington.[71] The New Orleans Protest by the *Creole*'s crew and passengers in early December 1841 identified nineteen slaves who were incarcerated in Nassau.[72] At the April 1842 investigation in Nassau, the Attorney General for the Bahamas named nineteen persons accused of the revolt.[73]

We know little about these rebels beyond the information contained in the ship's manifest and the bills of lading.[74] All of them were young men between the ages of seventeen and twenty-six. This youthful age exemplifies protest movements from slave ship rebellions to Black Lives Matter. The height and color of these rebels does not reveal much about who they were and why they would revolt. Pompey Garrison – named after a famous Roman general as well as the fiery Massachusetts abolitionist – ended up taking his name seriously! Peter Smallwood towered over the rest at five foot and ten and one-half inches. One intriguing pattern, however, is that nearly all of the rebels were shipped by only three traders. Horace Beverley, Philip Jones, Dr. Ruffin, Peter Smallwood, and Addison Tyler were shipped by Robert Lumpkin. George Burton, Adam Carney, Benjamin Johnson, and America Woodis were transported by George W. Apperson. Richard Butler, Pompey Garrison, Williams Jenkins, Elijah Morris, George Portlock, Warner Smith, and Madison Washington were all moved by Thomas McCargo. What this pattern suggests is that many of the rebels were familiar enough to each other to think through and act out a shipboard revolt (see **Appendix 3**). More broadly, these nineteen compare to the twelve or thirteen slave

---

[70] Nesbitt to Bacon, November 26, 1841, U.S. Sen. Doc. No. 51, 28.
[71] Enclosure with Bacon's letter, 30 November 1841, Dispatches from US Consuls in Nassau, New Providence Island, 1821–1906, Roll 5, vol. 5, January 9, 1840 to December 28, 1841, ARC.
[72] New Orleans Protest, December 2, 1841, U.S. Sen. Doc. No. 51, 40.
[73] Anderson to Cockburn, November 13, 1841, U.S. Sen. Doc. No. 51, 9, *Thomas McCargo v. The New Orleans Insurance Company*, 250. The names of the rebels are spelled slightly differently in some of these documents. The names on the dedication page of this book are those most frequently used in the primary sources.
[74] A search through census records on Ancestry.com for rebel names unfortunately turned up nothing.

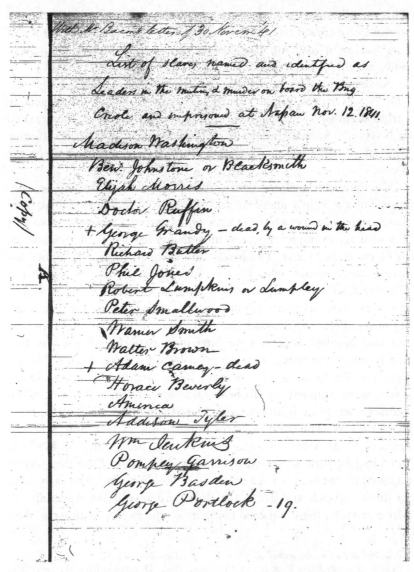

FIGURE 4.3 John Bacon's list of rebels, Nassau, Bahamas, November 30, 1841. Source: Enclosure with US Consul Bacon's Letter to Secretary Webster, November 30, 1841, Dispatches from US Consuls in Nassau, New Providence Island, 1821-1906, Roll 5, vol. 5, January 9, 1840-December 28, 1841, ARC.

rebels who seized the *Tryal*, to the group of at least thirty rebels who took over the *Decatur*, and to the hundred rebels who seized the *Lafayette*.[75]

What about rebel leadership? Nearly all of the documentation points to Benjamin Blacksmith (aka Johnson), Doctor Ruffin, Elijah Morris, and Madison Washington as the prime instigators. These four names cropped up repeatedly as leaders in depositions and protests by the *Creole* crew and passengers.[76] We know little about who they actually were or about their motivations for rebelling.[77] Johnson was twenty-three at the time of the rebellion, meaning that he must have been born around 1818. He appears to have been a skilled tradesman. Indeed, most of the testimony refers to him as Blacksmith rather than as Johnson, suggesting that this was his preferred name. It might also point to his trade and why he was able to access metal weapons.

Ruffin, who was the oldest of the rebels at twenty-five, must have been born around 1816. It is not clear why he earned his title of doctor. Was it medical know-how or knowledge in general? The documentary record does not tell us. Morris was also listed as twenty-three at the time of the rebellion and was born in 1818. We know little about him before the rebellion, but he seems to have played a vital role during the action. We also know much more about him afterward than about any of the other leaders.

Madison Washington, the fourth rebel leader, presents somewhat of a paradox. On the one hand, virtually every secondary account names him as being the prime instigator of the *Creole* revolt. On the other hand, there is very little verifiable information on him. Much of Washington's pre-revolt life – Virginia-born, escapee to Canada, return to free his wife, and recapture – draws from three sources published between 1842 and 1880.[78] Much of it is speculative. We know that Washington was lodged

---

[75] Taylor, *If We Must Die*, 141, 148, 150. These rebel numbers ignore the supportive roles other captives might have played in revolts. The ideological imperative of distinguishing between rebels and non-rebels by those hostile to the revolt is examined in Chapter 6.

[76] " . . . the four who took the most active part in the fight," New Orleans Protest, December 2, 1841, U.S. Sen. Doc. 51, 40.

[77] None of these four leaders show up on Ancestry.com. This is not surprising since only heads of household were listed in federal census records.

[78] "Madison Washington," *Liberator*, June 10, 1842; Frederick Douglass, *The Heroic Slave*, in *Autographs For Freedom* (Boston: John P. Jewett & Company, 1853); William Wells Brown, *The Negro in the American Rebellion: His Heroism and His Fidelity* (1880; Miami, Fl.: Mnemosyne, 1969), chap. 4. Much of this information is repeated uncritically in Hendrick and Hendrick, *Creole Mutiny*, chaps. 2 & 3, Downey, *Creole Affair*, 9–16, and "Madison Washington," Wikipedia, https://en.wikipedia.org/wiki/Madison_Washington#cite_note-williams-2

in the same jail as Morris. He was cook aboard the *Creole*. This post probably gave him ample opportunity to communicate with fellow captives while serving food as well as learning about the ship's routine and its crew. He was listed as twenty-two at the time of the revolt, meaning he must have been born sometime around 1819. It was probably in Virginia given his two names after prominent American presidents. Although we know little about him after the rebellion, he was to make a decisive contribution to its instigation and eventual success.[79]

Why some people rebel against oppressive conditions and others do not is a central question to all scholars interested in collective resistance. Clearly, decisions were shaped by backgrounds, personalities, risk assessment, and so forth. But it was the maritime rebellion that mattered, and it is to the burning decks on a sultry November night in the Bahamas Channel to which we now turn.

[79] Douglass's point about his fictional hero of a slave ship revolt is pertinent to Madison Washington: "Glimpses of this great character are all that can now be presented." Frederick Douglass, *The Heroic Slave*, in Ira Dworkin, ed., *Frederick Douglass: Narrative of the Life of Frederick Douglass, an American Slave* (New York: Penguin, 2014), 150.

5

"The Negroes Have Risen"

Historians agree that about one in ten slave ships experienced an attempted insurrection during the Atlantic slave trade.[1] This estimate corrects an older view that enslaved Africans rarely revolted at sea. It is undoubtedly an underestimate. Some ships that were illegally engaged in slave trading probably experienced attempted revolts that went unrecorded. Some captains could have failed to report an uprising that they successfully suppressed because such knowledge might compromise their chances of obtaining future commissions. Eric Taylor's important monograph – the first exclusively devoted to shipboard rebellions – estimates 493 cases of maritime revolts against the Atlantic slave trade between 1509 and 1865.[2] He goes on to argue that those that occurred in the nineteenth century constituted a "second" and "new" wave of shipboard rebellion.[3] This is a debatable proposition. Captives protested removal from families and homes, whether being transported from African or American shores. Both African-born and American-born captives were forced from their homes, families, kin, and communities resulting in the need to establish new relations and networks. Most important, captives

---

[1] Emory University, The Voyages Database, http://www.slavevoyages.org/voyage/; David Richardson, "Shipboard Revolts, African Authority, and the Transatlantic Slave Trade," in Sylviane A. Diouf, ed., *Fighting the Slave Trade: West African Strategies* (Athens: Ohio University Press, 2003), 201; Hugh Thomas, *The Slave Trade: The Story of the Atlantic Slave Trade* (New York; Simon and Schuster, 1997), 424; Sowande' M. Mustakeem, *Slavery at Sea: Terror, Sex, and Sickness in the Middle Passage* (Urbana: University of Illinois Press, 2016), 4.

[2] Eric Robert Taylor, *If We Must Die: Shipboard Insurrections in the Era of the Atlantic Slave Trade* (Baton Rouge: Louisiana State University Press, 2006), 3, 9, 139, 179–213.

[3] Ibid, 139–163.

transported in the Coastal Passage during the nineteenth century rose against their captors in ways similar to their cousins during the previous three centuries of the Middle Passage. This was less a division of chronologically and spatially discrete actions than a long rebellious tradition against the unnatural state of slavery.

That being said, the Coastal Passage was not exactly awash with slave ship revolts. Insurrections aboard the *Amistad* in 1839 and the *Creole* in 1841 were unusual, successful, and consequently significant. But they were by no means isolated. We would do well to recall historian Frederick Bancroft's earlier point that "actual or attempted slave mutinies by sea or land" were "frequent."[4] His aim was to draw attention to the dangers posed to slave traders using ships to transport their human cargoes. Our concerns are a little different: How did captives use the sea to effect their escape, did they succeed, and what was the significance of maritime spaces of freedom?

In April 1826, Maryland trader Austin Woolfolk led thirty-one captives from their Baltimore prison and boarded them on the *Decatur* bound for New Orleans. Among them was twenty-four-year-old William Bowser, alias William Hill, born at West River, who had already attempted to escape from the Harrison plantation before he was caught and sold to Woolfolk. On the morning of April 25 off the Georgia coast, Bowser led other captives in an attempt to seize the ship. The rebels grabbed Captain Walter R. Galloway and Chief Mate William Porter and tossed them overboard where they apparently drowned. Having seized control of the vessel, the rebels ordered one sailor to take them to Haiti where they expected freedom and protection. The rebels tried to avoid all other vessels but were unsuccessful. (They had unfortunately thrown overboard the two best navigators.) They encountered the US whaler *Constitution* that removed one sailor and about half of the captives before sailing away. On May 5, the *Rookes* commanded by Captain Atwood seized fourteen of them and placed an officer on deck to take the ship into port. Once the ship moored, the fourteen captives escaped with the exception of rebel leader Bowser who was taken to New York City to face trial. After seven months of incarceration, Bowser was convicted for the murder of the drowned captain and first mate of the *Decatur* and sentenced to hang. At his execution, Bowser reportedly forgave the slave trader who was present. Woolfolk, however, was unrelenting, telling the rebel leader that he was going to get what he

---

[4] Frederick Bancroft, *Slave-Trading in the Old South* (Baltimore: J. H. Furst, 1931), 277.

deserved "and he was glad of it." This hatred for the liberty seeker encouraged Benjamin Lundy – the abolitionist editor of the *Genius of Universal Emancipation* – to condemn the Baltimore slave trade and the trader's iniquitous business. Some months later, Lundy was accosted by Woolfolk in the streets and beaten violently to the point of incapacitation. Charged with assault, the slave trader got off with a one-dollar fine and court costs largely as a consequence of a sympathetic judge.[5]

The *Lafayette* was a regular transporter of captives. On October 4, 1828 the schooner left Norfolk with 161 captives bound for New Orleans.[6] After depositing its human cargoes, the ship returned to Virginia. On December 26, the *Lafayette* transported sixty-seven captives from Norfolk arriving eleven weeks later in the Crescent City.[7] A much bloodlier journey ensued twelve months later. On November 14, 1829, the *Lafayette* left Norfolk with 197 slaves bound for the New Orleans market. The major shippers were C. W. Diggs & James B. Diggs, and John B. Prentis & William Priddy. The ship also carried 150 kegs of pickled oysters for the market in the Crescent City. The male captives were separated from the female captives by an overturned boat close to a cask of water for them to drink. Three days into the passage, three of the male

[5] Robert H. Gudmestad, *A Troublesome Commerce: The Transformation of the Interstate Slave Trade* (Baton Rouge: Louisiana State University Press, 2003), 46; Ralph Clayton, *Cash for Blood: The Baltimore to New Orleans Domestic Slave Trade* (Bowie, MD: Heritage Books, Inc., 2002), 71–73; Taylor, *If We Must Die*, 147–149, 211; Steven Deyle, *Carry Me Back: The Domestic Slave Trade in American Life* (New York: Oxford University Press, 2005), 255; Calvin Schermerhorn, *The Business of Slavery and the Rise of American Capitalism, 1815–1860* (New Haven: Yale University Press, 2015), 60–62; Anita Rupprecht, " 'All We Have Done, We Have Done for Freedom': The *Creole* Slave-Ship Revolt (1841) and the Revolutionary Atlantic," *Internationaal Instituut voor Sociale Geschiedenis.* vol. 58 (2013), 263; Philip Troutman, "Grapevine in the Slave Market: African American Geopolitical Literacy and the 1841 *Creole* Revolt," in Walter Johnson, ed., *The Chattel Principle: Internal Slave Trades in the Americas.* (New Haven: Yale University Press, 2004), 209; William Calderhead, "The Role of the Professional Slave Trader in a Slave Economy: Austin Woolfolk, A Case Study," *Civil War History* vol. 23, No. 3 (September 1977), 205.

The same year as the *Decatur* revolt, captives aboard a flatboat on the Ohio River ninety miles west of Louisville, Kentucky, rebelled, killed the crew, sank the boat, and headed north for Indiana. Five were killed, more than fifty were captured, but twenty-one eluded captivity. See Johannes Postma, *Slave Revolts* (Westport, CT: Greenwood Press, 2008), 83; Taylor, *If We Must Die*, 211. In other words, self-emancipators also used rivers, streams, and internal waterways to escape American slavery.

[6] Charles H. Wesley, "Manifests of Slave Shipments along the Waterways, 1808–1864," *The Journal of Negro History*, 27, no. 2 (April 1942), 164.

[7] Wendell H. Stephenson, *Isaac Franklin: Slave Trader and Planter from the Old South* (Baton Rouge: Louisiana State University Press, 1938), 35.

captives jumped over the boat to get some water. Upon investigation by Captain Benjamin Bissell, the captives "seized him, threw him down and commenced fight, with handspikes, knives, billets of wood, etc." Mr. Thomas Balls, a traveling grocer, "jumped below and awoke the mate, armed himself with a cutlass, and soon as possible rushed to the assistance of the captain." The crew managed to suppress the revolt and trap the rebels in the hold. Upon being questioned, the rebels revealed their plan to seize the ship and "force the crew to take them to St. Domingo [Haiti] or New York." Twenty-five of the rebels were ring-bolted to the deck and the rest were incarcerated in the ships' hold. The rebels were arrested once the ship arrived in New Orleans, with four sentenced to ten years hard labor and three rebels to five years.[8]

The schooner *Orleans* was built in Baltimore, Maryland, and launched in 1838. The following year, the vessel jointly owned by Richard Haskins and Luther Libby transported 135 captives bound for the Crescent City. In the spring of 1841, recently kidnapped Solomon Northup was put aboard the *Orleans* under Master William Wickham. The ship's manifest listed its slave cargo under false names. Solomon Northup was registered as Plat Hamilton. They sailed down the James River and anchored outside of Hampton Roads where they picked up several more captives. One was Arthur Curtis. He stood five feet and ten inches tall, was dark-skinned, and bore a swollen face. This local resident had been beaten up while resisting capture by several men on a Norfolk street. After being subdued, Curtis was forcibly delivered to the ship and transported by renowned

---

[8] This narrative of the *Lafayette* revolt draws from Hank Trent, *The Secret Life of Bacon Tait, a White Slave Trader Married to a Free Woman of Color* (Baton Rouge: Louisiana State University Press, 2017), 63–64. All of the quotes come from this source. The major sources for the revolt were newspapers in which the actions of the captain, grocer, and crew are heralded. There is little comment on what the rebels thought, how they planned their attack, what their tactics were, and how they felt after being defeated. For additional comments, see *Niles Register*, January 9, 1830; Taylor, *If We Must Die*, 150–151, 212; Stephenson, *Isaac Franklin*, 52n40; Michael Tadman, *Speculators and Slaves: Masters, Traders, and Slaves in the Old South* (Madison: University of Wisconsin Press, 1996), 81. The *Lafayette* continued its coastal trading. On March 31, 1831, John Armfield consigned eighty-nine captives to the vessel to be sent to New Orleans. Seventy captives ended up with Franklin, thirteen to Woolfolk, three to Abner Robinson, and three to one C. Castangent. On January 16, 1833 Armfield shipped eighty-three captives aboard the *Lafayette*, with forty going to Franklin, twenty-four to John Hagan, eighteen to an unknown person, and one to William Thompson. See Stephenson, *Isaac Franklin*, 35. The transportation wing of the National Museum of American History in Washington, DC has a reproduction of a ship manifest for the *Lafayette* listing eighty-seven captives being transported from Alexandria to New Orleans in 1833.

Norfolk trader George Apperson. The *Orleans* was steered by a master, mate, and six seamen. It carried fifty captives who were unchained during the day, and locked in the hold at night. When the schooner stalled in the Bahamas Channel, Curtis and Northup plotted to seize the ship and take it to New York City. This might seem like an odd decision given the proximity of free soil under British control over the last several years. Why not just steer for Nassau port? Northup was probably determined to head northward to his home and family in upstate New York.[9] The plot evaporated through an outbreak of smallpox that ended the life of one of the conspirators, Robert Jones, and blew the wind out of the sails of the plotters. In May 1841, the *Orleans* successfully unloaded its human cargo where most of its people ended up in the long night of American slavery. Northup was eventually to gain his liberty after serving twelve years in bondage.[10]

On Monday, October 25, 1841, the *Creole* left Richmond at midnight towed by the steamer *Ben Sheppard*. Madison Washington, Elijah Morris, Pompey Garrison, and Andrew Jackson were part of the original group of slaves who had boarded at Richmond.[11] The next morning, the vessel cast off from the steamer and set sail at 10:00 a.m. Under fresh winds from the southwest, the *Creole* worked its way down the James River, anchoring off of Hog's Island around 9:00 p.m. At 6:00 the following morning, the vessel got underway, wending downriver under light breezes from the southeast amid clear skies. At 6:00 p.m. "three negroes" were boarded, and Captain Ensor took the steamboat for Norfolk. On Thursday, October 28, the ship got underway under the same weather conditions as the day before. At 5:00 p.m. the *Creole* anchored at Newport News, where Captain Ensor returned with "thirty three negroes."[12]

---

[9] Solomon Northup, *Twelve Years a Slave: Narrative of Solomon Northup, a Citizen of New York, Kidnapped in Washington City in 1841, and Rescued in 1853* (New York: Norton, 2017), chap. 1.

[10] Northup, *Twelve Years a Slave,* 67–76; Schermerhorn, *Business of Slavery,* 182–188.

[11] "Marine Journal," *Richmond Whig,* October 26, 1841; Gifford's testimony, *"Thomas McCargo v. The New Orleans Insurance Company,"* in Merritt M. Robinson, *Reports of Cases Argued and Determined in the Supreme Court of Louisiana,* vol. X, March 1 to Jun. 20, 1845 (New Orleans: Samuel M. Stewart, 1845), 206, 219.

[12] Armaci Adams, a former slave interviewed by the Federal Writers Project (FWP), later recalled being taken to Norfolk to be sold. She "saw a man up on a block an' a lot o' people was jes a-hollerin' 'roun' him, biddin' on 'im, I guess." Mrs. Adams did not end up being sold because of "burn scars' from her dress catching fire from a stove. Adams to Frances Greene and Claude W. Anderson, June 25, 1937, in Charles L. Purdue Jr., Thomas E. Barden, Robert K. Phillips, ed., *Weevils in the Wheat: Interviews with Virginia Ex-Slaves* (Charlottesville: University of Virginia Press, 1976), 3.

The following day, the ship sailed for three hours, from 1:00 p.m. to 4:00 p.m., anchoring at Sewell's Point. On Saturday, the ship worked down the bay from 11:00 a.m. to 8:00 p.m., halting at Linhaven Bay alongside the American brigs *Orleans, Long Island*, and several other "sail." The next day, the *Creole* proceeded to sea with the logbook recording "nothing of importance."[13]

This otherwise mundane account of the *Creole*'s daily itinerary glosses over two notable points. The shoreline pick-up of slaves along the James River resembled pick-ups along the West African and Central African coasts. Atlantic slavers rarely sailed into one port, loaded up with human cargoes, and then embarked for slavery's markets in the Americas. Rather, they would wait, search, and buy enslaved Africans here and there until the ship's captain determined they had either reached their full complement of slaves or that it was better to get under way for the purposes of time, weather, and other conditions.[14] Moreover, Captain Ensor's time in the Hampton region suggests he obtained slaves from southeast Virginia. This bordered the area of Nat Turner's bloody slave revolt in Southampton County a decade earlier. It is not inconceivable that some captives who boarded the *Creole* from this region were aware of the previous uprising and that it motivated them to act.[15]

---

[13] Gifford's testimony, "*Thomas McCargo v. The New Orleans Insurance Company*," 206, 339–340; Edward D. Jervey and C. Harold Huber, "The Creole Affair," *The Journal of Negro History* vol. 65, no. 3 (Summer 1980), 196; George Hendrick and Willene Hendrick, *The Creole Mutiny: A Tale of Revolt Aboard a Slave Ship* (Chicago: Ivan R. Dee, 2003, 77, 78; *Creole* Logbook, LSM.

[14] See the works of Elizabeth Donnan, Markus Rediker, David Eltis, and David Richardson for details of these pick-ups along the West African coast. For a vivid fictional account, see Barry Unsworth, *Sacred Hunger* (New York: Norton, 1993). These pick-ups were also risky because they could incubate maritime rebellions. Indeed, most of the ship revolts against the Atlantic slave trade occurred within eyesight of the coastline. See Taylor, *If We Must Die*; Diouf, ed., *Fighting the Slave Trade*.

[15] According to former soldier and newspaper editor John Hampden Pleasants, Turner's revolt was confined to Southampton County and not the broader region of Southeast Virginia. His castigation of those newspaper editors, however, who "seem to have applied themselves to the task of alarming the public mind as much as possible by persuading the slaves to entertain a high opinion of their strength and consequences," suggests broader ripples. See *The Constitutional Whig*, September 3, 1831, in Kenneth S. Greenberg, ed., *The Confessions of Nat Turner and Related Documents* (New York: Bedford St. Martins, 1996), 72. Vincent Harding, in *There Is a River: The Black Struggle for Freedom in America* (New York: Vintage Books, 1983), 112–113, writes of the *Creole*'s pick-up of slaves at Hampton Roads "(with all its memories of Gabriel [Prosser], Turner, Ferebee, and more)."

After putting out to sea, the captives were separated by sex. Women were put in the aft (back) hold of the vessel, while men were placed in the fore (front) hold. This gender division resembled the practices of Franklin & Armfield's *Tribune* as well as that of other coastal slavers. It has been suggested that the reason for this separation was to prevent slaves from diminishing the value of other slaves through passing venereal disease or impregnating women.[16] It seems more likely that male captives were placed in the forehold close to the cabin and crew where they remained under constant supervision. Security concerns trumped sexual behavior on coastal slavers. John R. Hewell – McCargo's enforcer – and William Merritt guarded the slaves, or, in the words of the first mate, "together attended the negroes."[17]

The captives aboard the *Creole* do not appear to have been chained. According to First Officer Gifford, the "men were allowed to come on deck night and day if they wished."[18] Presumably this was also true for the female captives. But this does raise the question of why these captives were not in irons. The absence of such an important precautionary measure suggests that the captain, officers, and crew did not believe that rebellion was imminent. The short voyage, together with sufficient food and water, made revolt seem less probable. On the other hand, there had been slave ship revolts on the *Decatur*, the *Lafayette*, and the *Amistad* off coastal North America and Cuba during the previous fifteen years. This was slightly longer than Chief Mate Gifford's thirteen years of experience at sea. Could the *Creole* revolt have been nipped in the bud if the captives had been forced to waste valuable time removing their chains?[19]

Boxes of manufactured tobacco separated the male and female slaves.[20] Tobacco leaf produced by slave labor on plantations and farms in piedmont and southside Virginia was transformed in factories in

---

[16] Walter Johnson, *Soul By Soul: Life inside the Antebellum Slave Market* (Cambridge, Mass.: Harvard University Press, 1999), 62.

[17] Gifford's testimony, "*Thomas McCargo v. The New Orleans Insurance Company*," 206.

[18] Gifford's testimony, "*Thomas McCargo v. The New Orleans Insurance Company*," 206; Jervey and Huber, "Creole Affair," 197; Hendrick and Hendrick, *Creole Mutiny*, 79.

[19] That "[t]hirteen men & four boys Slaves should attempt to rise upon Seven White Men" in a revolt aboard the *Cape Coast* in September 1721 was "unaccountable history" according to one eyewitness, "was it not that it seems they were all out of Irons by ye Master's orders." Stephanie E. Smallwood, *Saltwater Slavery: A Middle Passage from Africa to American Diaspora* (Cambridge, MA: Harvard University Press, 2007), 33. Compare this to the *Amistad* rebels who had to free themselves from "irons" (Jones, *Mutiny on Amistad*, 24) and faced an "iron dilemma" Rediker, *Amistad Rebellion*, 75.

[20] Gifford's testimony, "*Thomas McCargo v. The New Orleans Insurance Company*," 206, 260, 314; Jervey and Huber, "Creole Affair," 197.

Richmond, Petersburg, and Lynchburg. This was one of the largest manufactured products in antebellum Virginia. Nearly 13,000 men, mostly
enslaved, worked these tobacco factories by the 1850s. Many of the men
were hired out to firms by owners seeking greater profits from renting out
enslaved labor rather than employing that labor in agricultural production in the tidewater region. It should not be forgotten that these hired
slaves acted as "cultural and economic go-betweens and interpreters"
linking urban areas with rural plantations.[21] The manufactured article
consisted of snuff, chew, and pipe tobacco; it was in great demand in the
burgeoning new regions in the Gulf region of the southwest United States.
Recent immigrants were also mass consumers whose tastes helped to
reproduce the fruits of slavery and empire. The movement of tobacco
goods aboard the *Creole* – much like that of oysters on the *Lafayette* and
similar shipments – indicates the extent to which slavers played a critical
role in the expansion of markets and commerce in empire building.[22]

The *Creole* spent the next week sailing through the Bahamas Channel.
About 9:00 p.m. on the evening of November 7, 1841, the *Creole* "laid
to" off Abaco Island in the Bahamas at latitude 27 degrees 46 minutes
north and 75 degrees 20 minutes west. There was a fresh breeze and hazy
sky with no trade clouds.[23] Chief Mate Gifford was on watch and must
have been enjoying the balmy evening. Captive Elijah Morris informed the

---

[21] Lynda J. Morgan, *Emancipation in Virginia's Tobacco Belt, 1850–1870* (Athens:
University of Georgia Press, 1992), 57–76; Jeffrey R. Kerr-Ritchie, *Freedpeople in the
Tobacco South, Virginia, 1860–1900* (Chapel Hill: University of North Carolina Press,
1999), 19, 260n16.

[22] James Walvin, *Fruits of Empire: Exotic Produce and British Taste, 1660–1800*
(Basingstoke, Hants.: MacMillan, 1997); Jordan Goodman, *Tobacco in History:
The Cultures of Dependence* (London: Routledge, 1993), chap. 4; Robin Blackburn,
The Making of New World Slavery: From the Baroque to the Modern, 1492–1800
(London: Verso, 1997), 558–561.

[23] The narrative of the *Creole* revolt is fairly well established in the historical literature with
minor alterations and differences. See Jervey & Huber, "Creole Affair," 197–201;
Hendrick and Hendrick, *Creole Mutiny*, 11–12, 77–96; Downey, *Creole Revolt*, 12–14;
Rupprecht, "All We Have Done," 257–261. My account differs in three ways. It focuses
on oral communication and verbal exchanges to reproduce the voices of those captives
who were historical agents but did not testify or leave a written record, and were
invariably described in hostile terms. For instance, the chapter title comes from the
alarmist account of First Officer Gifford. Second, contemporary accounts and written
evidence are critiqued for contradictions, inconsistencies, and problems. It is one thing to
draw upon the evidence to narrate the *Creole* revolt. It is quite another to break down
some of the problems presented by this evidence. Third, and most important, it seeks to
put a more human face on the nature of this shipboard battle. It transcends existing
accounts that range from pedestrian descriptions of quite a dramatic event to ideologi-
cally inspired narratives of heroic slave resistance. Simply put, what was it like to be

ship's watch that a male slave had entered the aft hold where the women were being held. Since Morris was subsequently revealed to be one of the rebel leaders, it is not implausible that this was part of the initial plan to weaken the crew by separating them. Gifford awakened guard William Merritt who brought a lamp and a match. While Merritt went into the hold with the lamp, Gifford stayed by the hatch. The lamp illuminated "a very large and strong slave," Madison Washington, who was discovered to be among the women captives. Merritt asked: "Madison, is it possible that you are down here! You are the last man on board of the brig I expected to find here." It is not clear why Merritt thought this way. Washington replied: "Yes, sir, it is me." He quickly jumped out and on to the deck exclaiming: "I am going up, I cannot stay here." Gifford and Merritt tried to restrain him but without success. As soon as Washington was free, Morris fired a pistol, "the ball of which grazed the back part of Mr. Gifford's head." The fact that a captive had a gun suggests preparation. First Mate Gifford awoke Hewell saying: "John, I am shot, and the negroes have risen." Washington shouted: "We have commenced, and must go through; rush, boys, rush aft; we have got them now." He was also reported to have called to the slaves below: "Come up, every damned one of you; if you don't, and lend a hand, I will kill you all and throw you overboard." We shall return to this distinction between rebels and the other captives in the evidence and its implications below. The rebel leader was urging his fellow rebels to *carpe diem* without delay because speed was vital to any successful maritime revolt.[24]

The chief mate ran to the cabin and awoke the captain, seamen, and passengers. The rebels rushed aft and surrounded the cabin reportedly yelling out: "Kill them when they come up; kill the damn captain, kill the damn sons-of-bitches." The guard Merritt emerged from the hold and was

involved in a slave ship revolt with its attendant hopes, fears, mishaps, dangers, and unknowns?

[24] New Orleans Protest, December 2, 1841, Sen. Doc. No. 51, 37–38; McCargo to Bacon, deposition, November 10, 1841, Sen. Doc. No. 51, 26; Gifford to British Magistrates, deposition, November 9, 1841, Sen. Doc. No. 51, 30; Gifford testimony, *"Thomas McCargo v. The New Orleans Insurance Company,"* 206–207. It is striking that the captive Washington invariably appears as "large and strong" in both contemporary and historical accounts. Fredrick Douglass's fictional Madison Washington had "the strength of the lion." See Frederick Douglass, *The Heroic Slave*, in Ira Dworkin, ed., *Frederick Douglass: Narrative of the Life of Frederick Douglass, an American Slave* (New York: Penguin, 2014), 152. Why this was so? Racial stereotype? Physical manhood? Rebellious imperative? It is hard to fathom. The twenty-two-year-old rebel leader stood five feet and nine inches, about one inch shorter than former heavyweight boxing champion Mike Tyson.

seized by one of the rebels who exclaimed: "Kill him, God damn him, he is one of them." One rebel tried to strike Merritt with a handspike but missed and hit one of his fellow rebels. Merritt managed to escape. Howell emerged firing a musket that the rebels seized. He then wielded a handspike – a heavy wooden bar used as a lever but an effective club in a fight – and fought for a minute before it too was taken from him. The rebels fell on him with clubs, handspikes, and knives. He was knocked down and stabbed in twenty places by Johnson, Washington, and Morris. The guard staggered back to the cabin exclaiming either: "I am dead – the negroes have killed me," or "The d—d negroes have killed me at last." Trader Thomas McCargo's guard perished within the hour.[25]

The tenacity of the rebels encouraged some of the crew and passengers to hide. Passenger Merritt explained that because of the "noise on deck, and the number of slaves there," he tried to conceal himself with some bedclothes with "two colored females sitting on him." Some of the rebels entered the cabin calling: "Come out here, damn you." The women scarpered and Merritt bolted under a mattress where he was discovered. His life was saved for his navigational skills.[26] The ship's crew later recalled a slightly less courageous Merritt. He hid himself in one of the berths "crying and praying," while three female domestic slaves covered him with blankets.[27] Both accounts leave it unclear whether these women were hiding the man or restraining him.[28]

Second Mate Stevens ran on deck only to be struck with a flagstaff and stabbed at with a knife. He quickly retreated to the fore-royal yard. He was discovered at 4:30 a.m. Rebel leader Morris shouted to him: "Come down, you damned son-of-bitch, and receive your message." Stevens descended and asked why they wanted to kill him. (Was this legitimate or naive?) After carrying on with his regular duties, he was ordered below

---

[25] New Orleans Protest, December 2 1841, Sen. Doc. No. 51, 38; Stevens to British Magistrates, deposition, November 10, 1841, Sen. Doc. No. 51, 32; McCargo to Bacon, deposition, November 10, 1841, Sen. Doc. No. 51, 26; Gifford's testimony, "*Thomas McCargo v. The New Orleans Insurance Company*," 206–207.

[26] Merritt to Bacon, deposition, November 9, 1841, Sen. Doc. No. 51, 25; Merritt to British Magistrates, deposition, November 9, 1841, Sen. Doc. No. 51, 29.

[27] New Orleans Protest, December 2 1841, Sen. Doc. No. 51, 39.

[28] Hendrick and Hendrick speculate that these female slaves protected Merritt because they were expected to grant sexual favors and he may have treated them humanely and given them gifts and privileges. See Hendrick and Hendrick, *Creole Mutiny*, 88. During the *Amistad* revolt, wounded slave trader Pedro Montes hid behind a food barrel and covered himself with an old sail. See Jones, *Mutiny on Amistad*, 25; Rediker, *Amistad Rebellion*, 77–78.

decks at the point of a musket by Johnson who exclaimed: "You had better go below and stay there, or you will be thrown overboard, as there are a number of bad negroes on board." A little later, Morris came to the fore-hatch and said: "Stevens, I do not want to see you hurt, but they talk strong of heaving you overboard tonight." Later, one of the rebels fired in Stevens's direction. On being instructed to climb the rigging to look for the Abaco Island lighthouse, one rebel loaded a gun while another said: "Make haste, be quick," after which they did not fire but "only laughed." Clearly, the second mate was not popular with some of the rebels. This was probably due to a disinclination to distinguish between owners, traders, guards, and seamen – all of whom derived a living from American slavery in general and the Coastal Passage in particular.[29]

After hiding in one of the staterooms with Stevens, Seaman Curtis also made a beeline for the rigging. One of the rebels asked: "Who is that going up?" Curtis replied: "It is Jim." Rebel voice: "Come down, you shall not be hurt." It is not entirely clear why this ordinary seaman should have earned a more familiar name or have faced less physical danger from the rebels than did other crewmen. Maybe these were small acts of kindness in the heat of battle that will always remain unfathomable.[30]

Along with the cabin, the ship's rigging appears to have been quite a popular place during the *Creole* rebellion.[31] A few minutes after the initial alarm was raised, several rebels attacked Captain Ensor. Rebel leader "Blacksmith" stabbed him in two places. The ship's master also witnessed "Blacksmith," Garrison, Burden, and Portlock "murder" Hewell. Captain Ensor climbed to the maintop with difficulty. He told the first mate who joined him ten minutes thereafter: "Mr. Gifford, I am stabbed, and believe I am dying." The skipper remained there for eight hours, in his own words "bleeding and entirely helpless."[32] This must

[29] Stevens to Bacon, deposition, November 10, 1841, Sen. Doc. No. 51, 23; Stevens to British Magistrates, deposition, November 10, 1841, Sen. Doc. No 51, 32–33. This reference to "bad negroes" suggests determined, deliberate, and motivated rebels.

[30] Curtis to Bacon, deposition, November 10, 1841, Sen. Doc. No. 51, 24; Curtis to British magistrates, deposition, November 10, 1841, Sen. Doc. No. 51, 34. The rebels did not pursue these sailors into the vessel's rigging because they would have been hard to dislodge and would have to descend eventually.

[31] One Captain Codd found sanctuary in the ship's foretop during rebellion aboard the English slaver *Marlborough* in 1752. Some seamen "run up the Tops, where they were infamous Spectators of the whole Transaction" during another revolt aboard the *Black Prince* in 1757. See Taylor, *If We Must Die*, 119–120, 123.

[32] Ensor to Bacon, deposition, November 18, 1841, Sen. Doc. No. 51, 20; Ensor to British Magistrates, deposition, November 18, 1841, Sen. Doc. No. 51, 30; Nassau Protest, November 17, 1841, Sen. Doc. No. 51, 17; Gifford to Bacon, deposition, November 9,

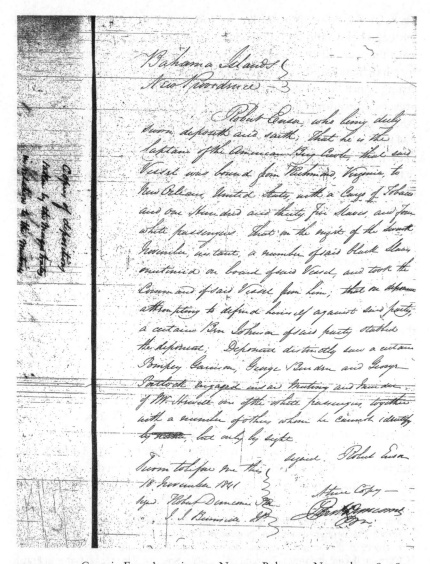

FIGURE 5.1 Captain Ensor's testimony, Nassau, Bahamas, November 18, 1841. Source: Dispatches from the US Consul in Nassau, British West Indies, RG 59, NARA.

have been quite an ordeal for the ship's two leading officers. They were

1841, in Sen. Doc. No. 51, 20–21; Gifford's testimony, *Thomas McCargo v. The New Orleans Insurance Company*, 207–208.

both injured – one severely – and witnessed a slave revolt unfolding sixty-plus feet below about which they could do nothing. The ordeal must have been quite terrifying, although their subsequent testimony suggests otherwise.

From their perch, the captain and first officer would have witnessed three or four of the rebels go aft to kill the French seaman Lecompts who was at the steering wheel. They overheard Washington tell his men not to hurt him because "he was a Frenchman and could not speak a word of English." This was an interesting personal amnesty. After supposedly telling the rebels to kill all the white men, Washington then made an exception for one of the crew. Was it because he was French and thus not an American citizen complicit in slave trading? Or did his knowledge as helmsman make him too valuable to be sacrificed on the altar of revenge? The rebels were reported to have searched the rest of the ship for "white people," threw water down the skylight, and doused the cabin lights. They then stationed men in different parts of the vessel to look out for Gifford and Ensor with instructions to kill them on sight.[33]

The rebels made one of the seamen bring the lantern from the bowsprit (front of the ship) that served to prevent other vessels from hitting the vessel. They took it down into the cabin where they came across the mortally wounded Howell. After bringing him up on deck, Gifford reported that one of the rebels "cut his head off as near as they could with a knife." It is not clear if the man was already dead or if the decapitation finished him off. The first mate overheard the rebel say: "We will separate the old son of a bitch somehow." They then ditched Howell's body overboard.[34]

It is not clear who was responsible for this act. In subsequent testimony, Captain Ensor identified Garrison, Burton, and Portlock. Seaman Lucius believed that Morris, Ruffin, Washington, Leatherwood, and Lyle were all accessories to the death. Leatherwood is probably Smallwood since the only other name close to this in the

---

[33] New Orleans Protest, December 2, 1841, Sen. Doc. No. 51, 39; Gifford to British Magistrates, deposition, November 9, 1841, Sen. Doc. No. 51, 30; Gifford's testimony, "*Thomas McCargo* v. *The New Orleans Insurance Company*," 207–208. Spanish slave trader Montes' life was spared only so that he might sail the *Amistad* back to West Africa. See Jones, *Mutiny on Amistad*, 26.

[34] Gifford's testimony, *Thomas McCargo* v. *The New Orleans Insurance Company*, 208; Jervey and Huber, "Creole Affair," 199; Hendrick and Hendrick, *Creole Mutiny*, 87–88. This act of decapitation is not mentioned in any of the depositions or the Nassau Protest and the New Orleans Protest in Sen. Doc. No. 51.

ship's documents was Martha Leatherbury whose youthful thirteen years made her an improbable participant. Seaman Carter thought "Grundy" (George Grandy) stabbed Hewell.[35] The most accurate assessment is that several of the rebels played a part in stabbing and knifing the Virginian overseer to death.

Recent videos by the self-proclaimed Islamic State of Iraq and the Levant showing their fighters decapitating western journalists, aid workers, and captured soldiers depict gruesome scenes. This is the theater of horror designed to appall and provoke Western/Christian nations' retaliation for the purpose of galvanizing *jihad*. John Howell's beheading was quite different of course. It probably represented an act of revenge. He was hired to police the transported slaves, a job that must have constantly provoked those he was guarding. According to passenger Leitner's subsequent testimony to British magistrates, Hewell had committed "various other acts of violence" toward the slaves on board the *Creole*.[36] Did this include sexual violence toward female captives? His killing was certainly different from the Mende ritual of *kootoo* performed after the death of Captain Ferrer aboard the *Amistad*.[37] Still, it must have struck fear into the hearts of Ensor and Gifford watching from the sails above. It should be noted, furthermore, that the decapitation of the overseer is ignored in some secondary accounts of the *Creole* revolt.[38] Is this because the unsavory act of decapitation fits awkwardly with a narrative of heroic slaves fighting for their freedom? It should be added that media coverage of decapitations today is also selective. Recent brutal beheadings by ISIS get western corporate media saturation, yet the decapitation of more people

---

[35] Ensor to British Magistrates Duncan and Burnside, November 18, 1841, Dispatches from US Consul in Nassau, Roll 5, RG 59, T475, NARA; Steven to Duncan and Burnside, November 10, 1841, Dispatches from US Consul in Nassau, Roll 5, RG 59, T475, NARA; Carter to . . . November 10, 1841, Dispatches from US Consul in Nassau, Roll 5, RG 59, T475, NARA.

[36] Lightener to British Magistrate Duncan & Burnside, November 12, 1841, Dispatches from US Consul in Nassau, Roll 5, RG 59, T475, NARA.

[37] Rediker, *Amistad Rebellion*, 78. In 1727, William Smith ordered a captured slave rebel aboard the *Elizabeth* to be hoisted on the foreyard arm, shot by firing squad, cut down, "the head cut off," and the body thrown overboard. In 1709, the ringleader of a failed revolt aboard the Dutch slaver *Fredericus Quartus* had his right hand cut off, followed by his left hand, and then his head. Hugh Thomas, *The Slave Trade: The Story of the Atlantic Slave Trade* (New York: Simon & Schuster, 1997), 426, 427. Were these demonstrations of power, savage acts against Africans who were deemed less than human, or both?

[38] Jones, *Mutiny on the Amistad*, 30; Taylor, *If We Must Die*, 157. Downey, *Creole Affair*, 13, refers to the "nearly decapitated" Hewell.

in Saudi Arabia has received far less comment and, by extension, less suitable condemnation.[39]

By 1:00 a. m. on Monday, November 8, 1841, the rebels had effectively taken control of the *Creole*.[40] For the next three hours, Chief Mate Gifford subsequently testified, the rebels talked in the cabin, although he could not hear what they were saying from his perch aloft. At around 5:00 a.m. the rebels spotted Gifford in the mast, presumably because of the sun breaking from the early dawn sky. They ordered him to descend, otherwise he would be shot by musket. Gifford descended and reportedly said: "I am here now, you can do with me what you please." This seems a pretty cool response after the night he had gone through and what he had witnessed. The rebels asked for the location of the captain. He was bleeding in the main top and strapped to the mast to prevent him from falling into the heavy sea swell that night. Gifford's request to retrieve the wounded man was met by one rebel's response: "Damn him, let him stay there till day-light, and we will then finish him." After a brief discussion, Gifford was told to bring the captain down; then the wounded man was laid on a mattress on the quarterdeck. The rebels then proceeded to take Gifford, along with Ensor, his wife, and Second Mate Lucius Stevens to the forehold. The entrance to the hold was covered with a grate, locked, and guarded by two rebels, one of whom was Williams Jenkins.[41] The hold was originally designed for male captives but now served as a floating prison for the ship's officer, crew, and passengers.

Scholars have passed lightly over several important questions concerning the *Creole* rebellion that demand our attention. First, *why* exactly did the captives revolt? The brutal hardware of bondage, the long duration of

[39] As of October 2014 the Saudi state had decapitated fifty-nine people in that year alone (Angus McDowall, "Saudi Arabia Steps Up Beheadings; Some See Political Message," October 2014, http://www.reuters.com/article/2014/10/20/us-saudi-execution-idUSKCN0I91G220141020).

[40] Compare the four hours of revolt aboard the *Creole* with the eight hours of rebellion on *L'Annibal* in 1729 in Gwendolyn Midlo Hall, *Africans in Colonial Louisiana: The Development of Afro-Creole Culture in the Eighteenth Century* (Baton Rouge: Louisiana State University Press, 1992), 90. Howard Jones states the *Amistad* revolt was successfully accomplished within "minutes." See Jones, *Amistad*, 25.

[41] Gifford to Bacon, deposition, November 9, 1841, Sen. Doc. No. 51, 21; Gifford to British Magistrates, deposition, November 9, 1841, Sen. Doc. No. 51, 31; Gifford's testimony, "*Thomas McCargo* v. *The New Orleans Insurance Company*," 208–209; Leidner to British Magistrates, November 12, 1841, Sen. Doc. No. 51, 36; McCargo to Bacon, deposition, November 10, 1841, Sen. Doc. No. 51, 26.

the voyage, and the scarcity of provisions drove slaves to revolt aboard the *Amistad*.[42] But conditions were quite different on the *Creole* because the captives were unchained, their voyage was short, and provisions were not lacking. The vessel was well stocked with barrels of beef, pork, and navy bread, and plenty of additional provisions for its crew, passengers, and captives.[43] Indeed, while it is hardly surprising that the crew failed to report harsh conditions aboard the *Creole* in their subsequent testimony, it is noteworthy that the British authorities did not report encountering emaciated and brutalized slaves upon boarding the ship in Nassau harbor.[44] Thus, we can rule out the severity of material conditions or deprivation as a causal factor in the uprising.

Another possibility was the fear of forced relocation from the relatively benign conditions of servitude in the Upper South to the reputed horrors of plantation slavery in the Deep South or even in Spanish Cuba. Samuel Walter Chilton, who was interviewed by the Federal Writers' Project (FWP) in 1937, recalled the days of slavery: "When you was sol' hit was de end of you. Dey carry you down south." Cornelius Garner remembered: "Boys git to cuttin' up on Sundays an' 'sturbin' Marsa and Missus an' dey comp'ny" after which the slave-owner descended on the quarters and threatened to "sell all dem chillun." "Dat threat was worsen prospects of a lickin'. Ev'ybody sho keep quiet arter dat." Virginia Hayes Shepherd of Norfolk never forgot a slave auction in Norfolk in which a woman was taken to Richmond "and sold down South . . . Now wasn' that cruel. Nothing worse could have happened to her."[45] Jacob Stroyer, formerly enslaved in South Carolina, believed that Louisiana was "considered by the slaves as a place of slaughter."[46] But there is no evidence from the *Creole's* officers and crew, the US consul in Nassau, or the Bahaman authorities suggesting that the transported slaves' fears of being sold "south" motivated their revolt.

---

[42] Rediker, *Amistad Rebellion*, 69–70; Taylor, *If We Must Die*, 152, 154. According to Jones, *Mutiny on the Amistad*, 15, 23–24, more than a third died from sickness and disease due to poor provisions and unhealthy conditions.

[43] Gifford's testimony, *"Thomas McCargo v. The New Orleans Insurance Company,"* 215–216, 231, 245.

[44] Officials had reported poor conditions upon boarding the *Enterprise* in 1835.

[45] Chilton to Susie R. C. Byrd, May 21, 1937, in Purdue, ed., *Weevils in the Wheat*, 71; Garner to Emmy Watson and Claude W. Anderson, n.d., in Purdue, ed., *Weevils in the Wheat*, 99; Shepherd to Watson and Anderson, May 18, 1937, in Purdue, ed., *Weevils in the Wheat*, 258.

[46] Damian Alan Pargas, *Slavery and Forced Migration in the Antebellum South* (New York: Cambridge University Press, 2015), 60.

Another explanation that has been put forward for why the slaves rebelled was Madison Washington's desire to reunite with his wife who was below decks; she was the one he was looking for when the revolt broke out. This romantic explanation has its appeal and can be traced back to the sensibilities of the nineteenth-century abolitionists' imagination.[47] Except the documentary record suggests otherwise. His wife's name has been given as Susan, but the *Creole*'s manifest and bills of lading only list fifteen-year-old Sarah Washington. Furthermore, although Sarah and Madison shared the same surname, it was obviously a popular one in Virginia, and might have been a coincidence. Finally, Robert Lumpkin traded Sarah while Thomas McCargo shipped Madison, suggesting the two captives were from different locales.

Another explanation is the successful example of the *Amistad*. According to one scholar, Madison Washington saw Nathaniel Jocelyn's portrait of rebel leader Cinque hanging in the home of Philadelphia abolitionist Robert Purvis. Washington questioned the Philadelphia abolitionist about Cinque and the slave ship revolt. He never forgot the story and it inspired him to act.[48] The *Amistad* revolt as inspiration for the *Creole* revolt continues to resonate.[49] But the evidence is debatable. It is not at all clear that Washington visited with Purvis. Moreover, the copious documents on the *Creole* revolt lack any acknowledgment of the role of the *Amistad* in inspiring the rebels to act. More inspirational was captives' knowledge of US coastal slavers being knocked off course onto British colonies and captives gaining their freedom from the British. The proximity of the *Creole* in the free waters of the Bahamas, I would argue, was more powerful incentive to rebel than following the *Amistad* rebels.

Judah Philip Benjamin – whom we shall later encounter as the stalwart legal defense counsel for the insurance companies sued for the loss of the *Creole* slaves – provided the most plausible explanation for the maritime revolt. At the Louisiana Supreme Court session in 1845, he stated rhetorically:

---

[47] William Wells Brown, *The Negro in the American Rebellion: His Heroism and His Fidelity* (1880; Miami, FL: Mnemosyne, 1969), chap. 4; Hendrick and Hendrick, *Creole Mutiny*, chaps. 2 and 3.

[48] Rediker, *Amistad Rebellion*, 224–225.

[49] This issue came up during the Q and A session after my talk on the *Creole* revolt at Central Connecticut State University, New Britain, in February 2018.

Will any one deny that the bloody and disastrous insurrection of the *Creole* was the result of the inherent qualities of the slaves themselves, roused not only by their condition of servitude, but stimulated by the removal from their friends and their homes, for the purpose of sale by their owners in an unknown land, and encouraged by the lax discipline of the vessel, the numerical weakness of the whites, and the proximity of a British province?[50]

Although the rebels and the other captives on board would have undoubtedly challenged the lawyer's description of the revolt as being "disastrous" since it led to their liberation from American slavery, the advocate's focus on the slaves' natural rights, self-determination, forced relocation, lax supervision, and proximity to free soil is sound.[51]

Second, why did this maritime revolt occur *when* it did? All accounts agree that the catalyst for the revolt was the discovery of Washington in the aft hold with the women.[52] This was followed by a call to arms by Washington. First Officer Gifford – and many scholars who rely on his account – implied that this was a spontaneous outbreak; but it is more plausible that there was a plot in the making, either set off prematurely by the discovery of one of the rebel leaders or planned deliberately.[53] A number of the captives were familiar with each other because they either shared the same owner or boarded together in the same trader's jail. Prisons can incubate solidarity. Rebels Morris and Johnson obtained arms very quickly. They were well led (more on this later). And their bolt for freedom in the Bahamas Channel was not accidental. Louisiana's Chief Justice during the case of the *Creole* in 1845 was not far off the mark when he explained:

the contest, which took place in the darkness of the night, but was brought about so suddenly, and yet with such evident readiness of preparation at the first signal [Washington's call], as to leave no doubt that the arms used were already loaded, and the plot formed so as to explode on reaching the vicinity of the Bahama Islan.[54]

[50] Conrad, Slidell, Benjamin, defense, *Thomas McCargo v. The New Orleans Insurance Company*, 266.

[51] In Frederick Douglass's fictional account of the *Creole* revolt, Madison Washington explains: "We have struck for our freedom." See Douglass, *Heroic Slave*, 188.

[52] The catalyst for the *Amistad* revolt was Celestino's threat that the slaves were to be cannibalized. Rediker, *Amistad Rebellion*, 71–72.

[53] Hendrick and Hendrick also think the rebellion was "likely planned." Hendrick and Hendrick, *Creole Mutiny*, 83.

[54] Judge Henry Adams Bullard's summation, "*Thomas McCargo v. The New Orleans Insurance Company*," 315. The implication of a leading jurist of a southern slave state legitimizing slave revolt is discussed in Chapter 10.

Many slave ship rebellions took place at night when the crew and guards were asleep. Careful preparation was vital for maritime revolts if they were to be successful. The rebellion on the *Amistad* was preceded by a Mende palaver.[55] The revolt on the *Decatur* took four days of planning.[56] The rebellion on the *Lafayette* was originally planned on the adjacent *Ajax* in Norfolk harbor.[57]

Third, what role did *leadership* play in this maritime revolt? How to motivate captives to rebel? How to deter people who suffered from enslavement from exacting bloody revenge? How to deal with oppressors, especially the possibility that they might rally a counter-offensive? It is not improbable that Washington used his position as ship's cook as a means to communicate openly and secretly on a regular basis with fellow captives both in and out of the galley. In other words, Washington did not simply languish in a warehouse in Richmond, or act impulsively one warm night, but used his position effectively to help rally captives to possible liberation.[58] As we have seen, some rebels did take their revenge, but many were prevented from doing so by resolute leadership.[59] Washington and his lieutenants stopped the killing of the French sailor as well as that of Gifford, Stevens, and Ensor. Mrs. Ensor, the captain's wife, begged for her life to which Morris replied: "We will not hurt you, but the damned captain and mate we will have, by God."[60] The crew and passengers were not killed but incarcerated. The rebels began the revolt after Washington's signal. The rebels were led into revolt and then directed to particular actions and stations in order to secure the vessel. The newly captured ship was now steered toward a destination that offered a good chance of realizing and confirming liberation for all former

---

[55] Rediker, *Amistad Rebellion*, 73; Jones, *Mutiny on the Amistad*, 24.

[56] Taylor, *If We Must Die*, 148.

[57] Taylor, *If We Must Die*, 150–151. Rebellions on transatlantic slave ships were often planned. Revolts aboard the *Robert* in 1721 and the *Ferrers* in 1727 were both plotted. Harding, *There is a River*, 12, 20; Taylor, *If We Must Die*, 90; Douglas Grant, *The Fortunate Slave: An Illustration of African Slavery in the Early Nineteenth Century* (London: Oxford University Press, 1968), 57; Trent, *Secret Life of Bacon Tait*, 64.

[58] Compare to the isolation of Joseph and the caboose experience of black cooks in the American merchant marine. Jeffrey W. Bolster, *Black Jacks: African American Seamen in the Age of Sail* (Cambridge, MA: Harvard University Press, 1997), 30, 33, 81–82. Charles Dickens provides a fictional comparison: "a black cook in a black caboose up to his eyes in vegetables and blinded with smoke," aboard the poorly prepared *Son and Heir* bound for Barbados from London. Dickens, *Dombey and Son*, 299.

[59] McCargo to Bacon, deposition, November 10, 1841, Sen. Doc. No. 51, 26.

[60] McCargo to Bacon, deposition, November 10, 1841, Sen. Doc. No. 51, 26.

captives. Indeed, it is not unlikely that many maritime revolts failed because of the absence of such resolute leadership.

What about the interaction with those who did not rebel? In the subsequent testimony to the American consul in Nassau as well as to the authorities in New Orleans, some seamen claimed that the captives were "afraid" of the rebels and appeared to stay away from them as much as possible during the voyage to Nassau.[61] But this testimony should be treated with caution. It was uncorroborated. There is no evidence of rebels abusing captives. And such a claim substantiated the view that the revolt was neither legitimate nor popular because it was restricted to a few "bad Negroes."

Fourth, what were *relations* between rebels and crew and passengers and were some non-confrontational? Two or three women might have hidden Merritt. Mary, an enslaved women traded by Thomas McCargo, asked Washington to stop other rebels from killing Merritt.[62] The youngster McCargo, nephew to the New Orleans trader, was protected by a rebel named "Jim" or "Jem" and escorted to the hold by his uncle's slave steward Lewis.[63] As we have seen, Seaman Curtis went unharmed. Passenger Lietener asked Morris, with whom he was familiar, "Will you kill me, Morris?" He replied, "No, he should not be hurt, but to go down into the after-hatch."[64] Andrew Jackson, traded by McCargo, wanted nothing to do with the revolt. He jumped into the rigging asking Seaman Foxwell where to go to save his life "saying that he was fearful they [rebels] would kill him."[65] The popular narrative of slave revolt understandably pits freedom's seekers against oppressors. But human relations during chaotic moments can be a little less predictable.

Fifth, what role did *female* captives play in the rebellion? No women were listed among the nineteen rebels. The documentary record is virtually silent on the activities of the sixty-one women captives. It is not entirely clear whether some women protected or restricted some seamen. What is evident is that there is no supporting evidence that female captives actively

---

[61] William Joseph Poole, Jr., "The Creole Case," M.A. thesis, Louisiana State University, Baton Rouge, 1970, 18.

[62] New Orleans Protest, December 2, 1841, Sen. Doc. 51, 39–40.

[63] McCargo to Bacon, deposition, November 10, 1841, Sen. Doc. No. 51, 26; McCargo to British Magistrates Duncan and Burnside, deposition, November 10, 1841, Sen. Doc. No. 51, 35.

[64] Lietener to Bacon, deposition, November 15, 1841, Sen. Doc. No. 51, 27.

[65] New Orleans Protest, December 2, 1841, Sen. Doc. No. 51, 40. It is not clear why Jackson feared for his life. Maybe he refused to go along with the rebels.

participated in the *Creole* revolt. On the other hand, there is also no evidence supporting the view that these women captives "dodged" the rebels as well as the crew as a "survival strategy."[66] Nor is there any evidence to suggest that those captives who did not join the revolt were simply "free riders" who stayed put in the hold.[67] We have no documentary evidence on what most female captives did during and after the revolt. It is most probable that they bided their time carefully the way many people do during struggles against oppressive systems. This changed once the brig reached Nassau harbor as these women became much more visible through decisions concerning movement, freedom, and the future destiny of families.[68]

Sixth, what was the nature of the *body wounds* and their treatment in this ship fight? The rebel's weaponry was not the hardware of bondage (manacles, shackles, neck-rings, chains, padlocks),[69] but rather muskets, pistols, knives, sticks, clubs, belaying pins, and handspikes. In his report on the revolt to American Secretary of State Webster, Consul Bacon wrote that the rebels were "prepared with pistols, bowie knives and clubs made of handspikes."[70] The latter were heavy wooden bars used to turn the windlass.[71] These could easily smash a human skull if wielded with enough force. Two of the rebels were "severely wounded by handspikes."[72] It was handspikes, along with bricks and fists by four white apprentices that had burst Frederick Douglass' eyeball and bloodied his face in an unprovoked attack in a Baltimore shipyard a few years earlier.[73] It was also a handspike that finished off Celestino during the *Amistad* rebellion.[74] Muskets were fired during the *Creole* revolt but

---

[66] Marjoleine Kars, "Dodging Rebellion: Politics and Gender in the Berbice Slave Uprising of 1763," *American Historical Review*, 121, no. 9 (February 2016), 39–69.

[67] Jonathan Levy thinks that the slaves who stayed in the *Creole's* hold were free riders. See Levy, *Freaks of Fortune: The Emerging World of Capitalism and Risk in America* (Cambridge, MA: Harvard University Press, 2012), 42.

[68] For some useful comments on women rebels against the transatlantic trade and the bloody price they paid, see Taylor, *If We Must Die*, and Mustakeem, *Slavery at Sea*, chap. 4.

[69] Rediker, *Amistad Rebellion*, 75.

[70] Bacon to Webster, November 30, 1841, US Consul Dispatches, Roll 5, RG 59, T475, NARA.

[71] Dean King, *A Sea of Words. A Lexicon and Companion for Patrick O'Brien's Seafaring Tales* (New York: Henry Holt, 1997), 224.

[72] New Orleans Protest, December 2, 1841, Sen. Doc. No. 51, 40.

[73] Laurence Fenton, *Frederick Douglass in Ireland: The Black O'Connell* (Cork: Collins Press, 2014), 24.

[74] Rediker, *Amistad Rebellion*, 75–76.

seemingly without much success. It seems that knives were the most effective weapons used in the revolt. These were either taken from the crew or came from the ship's galley that had served as Washington's workplace. After the revolt had succeeded, Jacob Leitener recalled: "Ben Blacksmith [Johnson] sat in the cabin with a large bowie-knife covered with blood, and said he had sent some of them to hell this night with this knife."[75] Overseer John Howell had his head sawed off with a knife. The rebel George Grundy was mortally wounded – by either a knife or handspike – in the fight.[76] Zephaniah Gifford, Henry Speck, and Binn Curtis were knifed. Captain Ensor was stabbed multiple times to the point of severe injury. This was no doubt due to where the knives struck the body and the resulting loss of blood. Being atop for several hours in a swell must have exacerbated the captain's wounds. Interestingly, the crew stated that the "wounds of the sailors were dressed by the negroes."[77] The best treatment for such wounds would have been a tourniquet to stanch the flow of blood, saltwater dousing to keep the wound from becoming infected, and the drinking of alcohol – if available – to help alleviate the physical pain.[78]

Finally, why was this slave ship revolt a *success*? At the 1845 legal session in New Orleans, defense lawyers argued it was because the ship was poorly manned and ill prepared.[79] This explanation seems unpersuasive. The *Creole* was a seasoned slaver that had made several previous trips to New Orleans and was as well prepared as any other slave ship. There is no reason to doubt the crew's subsequent claim that the ship was

---

[75] Leitener to Bacon, deposition, November 15, 1841, Sen. Doc. No. 51, 27.

[76] Nesbitt to Bacon, November 26, 1841, in Sen. Doc. No. 51, 28; New Orleans Protest, December 2, 1841, Sen. Doc. No. 51, 40; Gifford's testimony, *"Thomas McCargo v. The New Orleans Insurance Company,"* 207–209.

[77] New Orleans Protest, December 2, 1841, Sen. Doc. 51, 40. Captain Ferrer of the *Amistad* was less fortunate: he was repeatedly stabbed with a cane knife after which he was decapitated. Rediker, *Amistad Rebellion*, 78.

[78] Compare to the violence inflicted by the mutinous crew against officers aboard HMS *Hermione* on September 21, 1797. Captain Pigot was stabbed, cut, knocked in the head, and bayoneted before being pushed out of a cabin window. Third Lieutenant Henry Foreshaw was beaten on the head "with streams of blood running down his face," before being dumped overboard. Second Lieutenant Douglass had about "twenty Tomahawks, Axes and boarding pikes jagged into him," before being thrown overboard through a porthole." Niklas Frykman, "The Mutiny on the *Hermione*: Warfare, Revolution, and Treason in the Royal Navy," *Journal of Social History* 44, no. 1 (Fall 2010), 165–166.

[79] Conrad, Slidell, Benjamin, defense, *Thomas McCargo v. The New Orleans Insurance Company*, 266.

"tight and strong, well manned and provided, in every respect, and equipped for carrying slaves."[80] Rather, the rebels succeeded due to several factors: careful preparation; a plan that was not revealed, discovered, or betrayed; the element of nocturnal surprise; the absence of the hardware of bondage; quick access to weapons; the rapid overpowering of the enemy; speedy implementation of revolt; and resolute leadership.[81]

The most important demonstration of this success was the rebel's capture of the *Creole*. On Monday, November 8, 1841, the sun's rays dawned upon a very different ship. The former coastwise slaver was now under the command of some of its former captives. According to First Mate Gifford's testimony, nineteen rebels "kept strict orders over the rest of the negroes, exercising the same sway over the rest of the negroes that they did over the whites, threatening to whip them if they disobeyed their orders."[82] We should be skeptical of this claim for indiscriminate tyrannical rule for several reasons. It is a singular and uncorroborated view. Those who were enslaved often built solidarity from common oppression in slave ship revolts. And it is unlikely that the rebels would have failed to distinguish between the white crew and their recently enslaved black brethren. What characterized most maritime revolts was the construction of fictive kinship based upon common enslavement and the desire for liberty.[83] Moreover, it seems hardly surprising that slavery's defenders should distinguish between a passive mass and a small group of illegitimate criminals since such division vindicated the US slave trade as legitimate commerce and slavery as a *bona fide* institution.[84]

The rebels appointed a new cook for the ship's company. They also stationed men at different parts of the vessel, no doubt to ensure complete control of the *Creole*. Four of the nineteen rebels remained on the

---

[80] New Orleans Protest, December 2, 1841, Sen. Doc. No. 51, 37.

[81] According to Eric Taylor's analysis, 120 out of 493 cases of shipboard revolts led to the liberation of all or some of the slaves. For further comment, as well as some interpretive problems with these insurrections, see Taylor, *If We Must Die*, chap. 6.

[82] Gifford's testimony, *"Thomas McCargo v. The New Orleans Insurance Company,"* 209, 219.

[83] Rediker, *Amistad Rebellion*, 74, Harding, *There is a River*, 113; Rupprecht, "All We Have Done," 256.

[84] This "invidious distinction" (Vincent Harding's phrase) often failed. Captain Hopkins commanding a ship belonging to the Brown brothers of Newport, Rhode Island, sailed from Africa to Antigua in 1765: "On the way, sickness so depleted the crew that the captain impressed some of the slaves to help man the ship. But the Negroes, seizing the opportunity to gain their freedom, released some of their fellows and fell upon the crew." Lorenzo J. Greene, "Mutiny on the Slave Ships," *Phylon*, 5, no. 4 (1944), 352; Harding, *There is a River*, 21.

quarterdeck at all times armed with knives and a pistol. One rebel remained forward in the gangway (a narrow platform from quarterdeck to forecastle) with a musket and bayonet. These armed rebels prevented communication among the former crew. All of the rebels remained on guard, "relieving each other" in turn.[85] This former slaver was run in an organized and disciplined fashion. The rebels made sure that the ship's former crew and passengers were precluded from retaking the *Creole*. Theirs was no idle precaution. In 1829, the crew had regained control of the *Lafayette*. A century earlier in 1729, recently enslaved Africans rebelled aboard *L'Annibal* in the mouth of the Gambia River. After their leader was killed and the rebels forced to retreat, the French crew retook the ship, after which they shackled the slaves, and hung the leaders from the masthead.[86] The *Creole* rebels did not have to be told that the price of freedom was eternal vigilance.

There was much talk of "killing whites" according to Gifford's testimony. He had overheard Washington and other rebels talk of indiscriminate killing. He also claimed to have heard Ben Johnson threaten to throw the crew overboard.[87] What is striking is that these threats failed to materialize. Rebel leader Morris warned Lucius Stevens: "They talk strong of heaving you overboard tonight." The second officer was spared, although one of the rebels fired a pistol at him while he walked on the quarterdeck.[88] Both Merritt and Gifford were not killed, probably because they were deemed useful to sailing the ship. This reflects sensible leadership and strict discipline. During the slave revolt aboard the *Decatur* in 1826, the slave rebels killed two seamen who might have steered them toward their desired destination of Haiti.[89]

---

[85] Gifford's testimony, *Thomas McCargo v. The New Orleans Insurance Company*, 219, 315; Jervey and Huber, "Creole Affair," 200–201.

[86] Hall, *Africans in Colonial Louisiana*, 91.

[87] Gifford's testimony, "*Thomas McCargo v. The New Orleans Insurance Company*," 207–209.

[88] Stevens to Bacon, deposition, November 10, 1841, Sen. Doc. No. 51, 23.

[89] Taylor, *If We Must Die*, 148. Slaves revolted aboard the Portuguese slaver *Misericordia* in 1532 killing all the crew except the pilot and two seamen who escaped in the longboat. The ship was never heard from again, possibly because the slaves did not know how to sail her. Thomas, *Slave Trade*, 424. We should be careful, however, to always assume the indispensability of the crew. Slave rebels who seized the *Little George* in June 1730 steered the ship back to the West African coast after being at sea for six days. Darold D. Wax, "Negro Resistance to the Early American Slave Trade," *The Journal of Negro History*, 51, no. 1 (January 1966), 9.

Moreover, the *Creole* crew's mortality rate was small compared to other slave ship revolts. Twenty-five members of the crew of the *Tryal* lost their lives during and after a maritime rebellion.[90] Captain Peter McQuay and many of the crew aboard the Liverpool slaver *Thomas* were killed, butchered, or driven overboard as a consequence of slave revolt in the late summer of 1797.[91] Four members of the crew were killed in the rebellion aboard the *Annibal* in 1729.[92] Two of the crew died during the *Amistad*'s rebellion in 1839.[93] A century earlier, a failed revolt aboard the French slaver *Africain* in 1738 took the lives of the captain and one seaman.[94] The point is that slave rebels were motivated less by racial revenge than by the desire to gain and maintain their freedom. Rebel leaders controlled the understandable urge for retribution by individuals formerly enslaved and whose blood was now up.

A new day dawned on Tuesday, November 9, 1841, off the Abaco Islands in the Bahamas. More than 130 men, women, and children walked the decks of the *Creole* in freedom from American owners and traders for the first time.[95] Nineteen of them had risen against the crew and seized the ship. Four rebel leaders stewarded this liberty and its maintenance. Meanwhile, the crew and passengers were incarcerated in the ship's after hold.[96] This must have been the first time these people had been deprived of their individual liberty. They no doubt feared for their safety and perhaps even their lives. It must have been especially frightening for the youngsters Theophilus McCargo, the young nephew of one of the major traders, along with Captain Ensor's four-year-old daughter. They now faced the sort of uncertainty and potential dangers that so many young captives faced during the Coastal Passage.

The world was turned upside down; the times were out of joint. The critical question now was which would be the vessel's best direction to secure liberty sought by the rebels. The northern route meant possible encounters with US maritime vessels (merchant ships, warships, and the

[90] Taylor, *If We Must Die*, 139.
[91] Gomer Williams, *History of the Liverpool Privateers and Letters of Marque, with an Account of the Liverpool Slave Trade* (London: William Heinemann, 1897), 592; Taylor, *If We Must Die*, 104.
[92] Hall, *Africans in Colonial Louisiana*, 90.   [93] Rediker, *Amistad Rebellion*, 78.
[94] Robert Louis Stein, *The French Slave Trade in the Eighteenth Century: An Old Regime Business* (Madison: University of Wisconsin, 1979), 106.
[95] Taylor, *If We Must Die*, 125, refers interestingly to this type of liberation as a "sort of floating maroon colony."
[96] The captain and mate of the English slaver *Mary* were locked up in the cabin for twenty-seven days after slaves seized the ship in 1742. Taylor, *If We Must Die*, 128.

like) and proximity to American slavery's long coastline. The Caribbean route betokened an alternative maritime empire that had just legally abolished slavery but was by no means guaranteed to support armed insurrection aboard a merchant ship from another nation. The sun's rays pointed both ways.

6

"Their Determination to Quit the Vessel"

If you visit Nassau harbor today, your eyes will boggle at the sight of city-block-size cruise ships disgorging thousands of sun-and-fun tourists from the wealthy world searching for boutique bargains along Bay Street. You cannot miss Paradise Island – home to the Atlantis resort with rooms by the thousands, a massive gambling casino, and the location for an entertaining James Bond movie, *Casino Royale*. What you will seek in vain is an independent bookstore in the capital city. Perhaps the most worthwhile deal is the $5.00 admission fee charged by the Pompey Museum of Slavery and Emancipation to ponder its somber material, visual images, and written artifacts. There is no public marker, however, commemorating the dramatic course of events that occurred during November 1841 when an American slave ship pulled into the harbor after a maritime revolt and left several days later minus most of its human cargo.

The Bahamas part of the story of the *Creole* revolt has not been seriously researched. Most scholars report that the local British authorities freed the slaves.[1] This interpretation overlooks the actions of the

---

[1] In his letter to the US Secretary of State describing the *Creole* revolt, Consul Bacon wrote: "The other slaves [the non-rebels] were liberated through the interference of the authorities of the colony, with the exception of four or five who refused to accept their liberty at such a price and such a manner," Bacon to Webster, November 17, 1841, Dispatches from US Consul in Nassau, Roll 5, RG 59, T475, NARA. E. D. Adams concludes: "the slaves were given their liberty by British officials" in Nassau; see Adams, "Lord Ashburton and the Treaty of Washington," *The American Historical Review* 17, No. 4 (July 1912), 771. Philip M. Hamer refers to "her [GB] liberation of American slaves from the ship Creole"; see Hamer, "British Consuls and the Negro Seamen Acts, 1850 to 1860," *Journal of Southern History* 1, no. 2 (May 1935), 144. Wilbur D. Jones points to the *Creole* in Nassau, "where British authorities gave the slaves their freedom"; see Jones,

rebels, non-rebel captives, and local Bahamians.[2] It also overlooks relations among these groups that were essential to the liberation of the captives from the *Creole*. Indeed, the older approach skirts some key questions that are only answerable with a focus on these groups. Why did the rebels decide to point the vessel toward the Bahamas? What roles did local Bahamians play from the time the ship docked in the harbor to its departure more than a week later? What was the nature of their interactions with locals from Nassau and its outskirts? Both the British and American authorities failed to examine or question the imprisoned rebels, the liberated slaves, or the local residents. A careful examination of archival documents, with an eye toward descriptions and accounts of these peoples' actions and supplemented by a degree of historical imagination, centers on an alternative cast of characters in the historical drama of liberation in Nassau harbor and has important implications.[3]

The price of the former captives' new liberty was constant care. The rebel leaders issued orders on the ship. They left the sailing to the former chief mate. They kept beady eyes on the vessel's direction. Witness Zephaniah Gifford testified that Ruffin "watched the compass, to see we did not alter our course." He added that leaders Washington and Morris "threatened death" if the crew deceived the rebels or sought to change direction clandestinely. The rebels kept a "constant guard of the vessel, and threatening to throw

---

"The Influence of Slavery on the Webster-Ashburton Negotiations," *Journal of Southern History* 22, no. 1 (February 1956), 48. "Should the British Have Freed the Slaves?" is the title of chapter eight of Arthur T. Downey, *The Creole Affair: The Slave Rebellion That Led the U.S. and Great Britain to the Brink of War* (Lanham: Rowman and Littlefield, 2014). Johannes Postma reports that, after arresting the nineteen rebels, the British authorities "let the remaining fugitives go free"; see Postma, *Slave Revolts* (Westport: Greenwood Press, 2008), 83. In *From Rebellion to Revolution: Afro-American Slave Revolts in the Making of the Modern World* (Baton Rouge: Louisiana State University Press, 1979), Eugene D. Genovese writes: "Slaves aboard ships in the domestic slave trade rebelled and steered for Haiti or for the protection of the British" (6). Rebels on coastal slavers wanted liberty, not protection. The author's choice of language, however, exemplifies his hegemonic framework.

[2] Recent works by Rosanne Adderley and Anita Rupprecht also center them.

[3] The key documents include: the 1842 Senate Documents No. 51, twenty-seventh Congress, second Session, *Message from the President* (hereafter Sen. Doc. No. 51); "*Thomas McCargo v. The New Orleans Insurance Company*," in Merritt M. Robinson, *Reports of Cases Argued and Determined in the Supreme Court of Louisiana*, vol. 10, March 1 to June 20, 1845 (New Orleans: Samuel M. Stewart, 1845); and Dispatches from the US Consul in Nassau, Bahamas, Roll 5, January 9, 1840–December 28, 1841, RG 59, T475, NARA. As in my rendering of the shipboard revolt, particular attention has been paid to verbal exchanges reproduced in these documents in order to reveal the motivations and actions of rebels who neither testified nor left a written record.

deponent and the passengers over board, if they spoke to each other, excepting in the language they could understand." When Ruffin saw Gifford and Merritt writing the altitude and time on a slate, he ordered it rubbed out, for fear that the two were communicating in secret code.[4] Their caution was understandable. Why would they trust seamen who had recently supported their captivity? They had killed one man in the revolt and wounded several others including the captain. They might have known that rebels on the *Amistad* had been thwarted in their plans to return to West Africa through the machinations of a cunning pilot. This perfidious act had been widely reported by newspapers in New York and Connecticut, demonstrating how the Spanish slaver had ended up on a northern American shore leading to the rebels' capture and incarceration.[5]

Once the rebels had successfully secured the *Creole*, the pressing question was where they should go in order to protect their newly won liberties. There must have been much discussion by the rebels in the cabin that served as their headquarters while they freely partook of the ship's adequate food and drink supplies. The rebels ordered one of the passengers to fetch "four bottles of brandy, a jug of whiskey, and a demijohn [three to ten gallon bulbous-shaped bottle] of Madeira wine," and some apples and bread, which they probably enjoyed with great relish.[6] Where exactly were they on the high seas that warm night? None appear to have had maritime skills, so who would sail and steer the ship? Where could rebels with a price on their head sail to find freedom?[7] Gifford was brought into the cabin to explain the chart to the four rebel leaders: Blacksmith, Morris, Ruffin, and Washington. The former first officer showed them the chart and their approximate location. The sea chart would have revealed the proximate position of Abaco Island, located in Northwest Providence Channel, which guarded the entry to the important port at Nassau harbor in the Bahamas.[8]

---

[4] Gifford to Duncome & Burnside, deposition, November 9, 1841, Sen. Doc. No. 51, 31; New Orleans Protest, December 2, 1841, Sen. Doc. No. 51, 41; Gifford's testimony, "*Thomas McCargo v. The New Orleans Insurance Company*," 209.

[5] Marcus Rediker, *The Amistad Rebellion: An Atlantic Odyssey of Slavery and Freedom* (New York: Viking, 2012), 82, 86, 92, 257n44, 258, 70. The August 31, 1839, edition of the *New York Sun* reported the final movements of the *Amistad* "in a widely circulated and influential account" (92).

[6] Lietener to Bacon, deposition, November 15, 1841, Sen. Doc. No. 51, 27.

[7] Similar questions faced other slave ship rebels (Rediker, *Amistad Rebellion*, 80).

[8] Rosanne Marion Adderley, "*New Negroes from Africa*": *Slave Trade Abolition and Free African Settlement in the Nineteenth-Century Caribbean* (Bloomington: Indiana University Press, 2006), 24.

This archipelago of islands colonized by the British since the seventeenth century had recently become free soil since passage of the 1833 Abolition Act. Gifford subsequently provided ambivalent testimony on who was responsible for the rebels' eventual destination. In his deposition to British magistrates, he stated that "Madison Washington told deponent he wanted him to take them to a British port, and desired him to land them at Abaco." This order was backed up by Johnson's placement of "a musket to deponent's breast."[9] In later testimony, however, Gifford reported that all four rebels told him that "they wish to go to Abaco."[10] The "New Orleans Protest" confirmed that it was a collective decision. "Ben Blacksmith, D. Ruffin, and several other slaves, then said they wanted to go to the British islands; they did not want to go anywhere else but where Mr. Lumpkin's negroes went last year (alluding to the shipwreck of the schooner Hermosa on Abaco, last year, the taking of the slaves on board of that vessel, by the English wreckers to Nassau, in the island of New Providence.)"[11] Word had gotten out about slaves' liberation from a previous slave vessel by the British. The rebel leaders were aware that slaves from a coastal slaver had been liberated by the British after having run aground in the Bahamas; this helped determine their eventual destination because British waters offered them the best chance of securing their liberation from American slavery. They set sail at dawn.[12]

On the morning of Tuesday, November ninth, the *Creole* entered the mouth of Nassau harbor. Today's luxury liners would dwarf its 187 tons. The rebels controlled the ship and its weaponry. Washington came aft, collected all of the weapons, and ordered them thrown overboard.[13] The pistols and knives were jettisoned. The former chief mate assumed the rebels sought to hide their mutinous actions. Howard Jones thinks they disposed of their weapons to place themselves at the mercy of the

[9] Gifford to Duncome & Burnside, deposition, November 9, 1841, Sen. Doc. No. 51, 31; Gifford to Bacon, deposition, November 9, 1841, Sen. Doc. No. 51, 21.

[10] Gifford's testimony, "*Thomas McCargo* v. *The New Orleans Insurance Company*," 209.

[11] "New Orleans Protest," December 2, 1841, Sen. Doc. No 51, 40, 37.

[12] The *Creole* rebels' awareness of free soil in the British Caribbean played a critical role in their decision to head for Nassau. In contrast, the *Amistad* rebels spent more than a month in the Bahamas archipelago looking for water but never thought to approach Nassau where they might have obtained their liberty. This suggests that these Mende were either unaware of liberty's beacon or – more likely – were determined to head home to West African shores (Rediker, *Amistad Rebellion*, 83).

[13] Gifford's testimony, "*Thomas McCargo* v. *The New Orleans Insurance Company*," 209–210, 224.

FIGURE 6.1 The *Creole*'s rebellious passage, November 1841.
Cartographer: David Cox.

British authorities.[14] If the rebels had been asked, however, they would probably have responded that they wished to present a non-threatening appearance to the local authorities. What reception might they have encountered if they showed up unexpectedly in foreign waters armed to the teeth on a slave ship they had just seized? Indeed, the image of the *Amistad* – famously dubbed "the long, low black schooner" by the

---

[14] Howard Jones, "The Peculiar Institution and National Honor: The Case of the *Creole* Slave Revolt," *Civil War History* 21, no. 1 (March 1975), 31.

New York press – sailing the internal causeway of Long Island had recently caused considerable consternation among those who had seen the ship.[15] Besides, the rebels had little to fear from the British authorities. Past acts of maritime liberation demonstrated a not-unsympathetic attitude toward the cause of freedom. Why risk otherwise?

About one mile outside the harbor lighthouse, the black pilot and his all-black crew boarded the *Creole*.[16] Usually a seasoned seaman, the pilot guided ships into port based upon his knowledge of local tides, low-lying rocks, sand bars, seasonal weather, harbor protocols, and so forth. The British authorities often employed black pilots to steer ships and boats into colonial harbors. Gifford reported that, once aboard, the pilot and crew "mingled with the negroes, all being black."[17] This was probably the first time former American slaves encountered free black Bahamians. Their interactions were to play a vital role in the eventual liberation of former captives from the *Creole*.

About the same time, the quarantine boat came alongside the *Creole*. All visiting ships had to be checked for infectious diseases of people, animals, and plants before being allowed to enter the harbor. The former chief mate jumped aboard the returning craft and headed straight for the office of the US Consul, John F. Bacon. A former clerk to the New York senate for twenty-eight years, Bacon had been appointed to the consular role in Nassau in March of 1841.[18] Both Bacon and the chief mate proceeded to the house of the British governor of the Bahamas, Francis Cockburn. Cockburn was a former British Army officer who had seen military action in South America and on the Iberian Peninsula. Between 1811 and 1827, he had served as a military and colonial administrator in Canada, including during the War of 1812. From 1830 to 1837 he served as superintendent of British Honduras. A vacancy for the position of Governor of Bahamas arose with the death of Sir James Smyth in

---

[15] "The Long, Low Black Schooner," *New York Sun*, August 31, 1839 in Rediker, *Amistad Rebellion*, 92.

[16] Gifford's testimony, "*Thomas McCargo v. The New Orleans Insurance Company*," 210, 233.

[17] Ibid, 210.

[18] Franklin B. Hough, *The New York Civil List* (Albany: Weed, Parsons, and Company, 1858) 122–132; US Department of State, *Register of All Officers and Agents, Civil, Military, and Naval in the Service of the United States* (Washington, DC: J. & G. S. Gideon, 1843), 7; "John F. Bacon," Wikipedia, http://en.wikipedia.org/wiki/John_F._Bacon

1838. Cockburn applied for the position and began serving in the top colonial post during the summer of 1840.[19]

American Consul Bacon informed the recently appointed sixty-year-old colonial executive what had happened on board the *Creole* based on the account provided by Gifford. The US consul requested the governor "not to suffer any of the slaves on board to land *until further investigations can be made.*"[20] This request suggests a desire for the protection of slave property along with the fear that the rebels and others would jump ship without supervision. Consul Bacon's subsequent letter to US Secretary of State Daniel Webster reflects this concern: "Being apprehensive the slaves would soon all get on shore; and knowing, in that case, it would be deemed here, that, in regard to their freedom, no one would have a right to molest them, I immediately repaired with the mate, to the Government-house, and obtained an interview with his excellency the Governor, stated the circumstances, and requested him to take measures to protect the slaves from escaping on shore, and to have the murderers secured."[21] It is telling that the US consul not only knew that the slaves were determined to quit the vessel but that they would have to be restrained in order to prevent them from doing so. Governor Cockburn's response was to order "a military party on board of the said brig" with no impediment to the landing of the "white persons on board."[22] At this stage, the governor was mute on the other captives.

Major Cobbe of the Second West India Regiment immediately dispatched a company of twenty black privates, a black corporal, a black sergeant, and commanded by a white lieutenant to the *Creole*. In his subsequent deposition to the colonial Council at Nassau in April 1842, the regimental officer revealed that he ordered the soldiers' muskets be fully loaded both "from a fear that the negroes on board" might "resist" on seeing the approaching military guard, as well as to prevent any violence and to secure the ship. This was a sensible precaution in the aftermath of a slave ship revolt, although the former captives were visibly

[19] McKenna, Ed, "Cockburn, Sir Francis," *Dictionary of Canadian Biography*, vol. 9. Toronto: University of Toronto (1976), www.biographi.ca/en/bio.php?id_nbr=4357; "Francis Cockburn," Wikipedia, http://en.wikipedia.org/wiki/Francis_Cockburn.

[20] Bacon to Cockburn, November 9, 1842, Document A, Sen. Doc. No. 51, 5; "*Thomas McCargo v. The New Orleans Insurance Company*," 234. Original italics.

[21] Bacon to Webster, November 17, 1841, Sen. Doc. No. 51, 2. It also suggests Consul Bacon knew the captives were not content with their lot; otherwise, why worry about them leaving?

[22] Nesbitt to Bacon, November 9, 1841, Document B, Sen. Doc. No. 51, 5; *Thomas McCargo v. The New Orleans Insurance Company*, 234–235.

unarmed. Lieutenant Mends was instructed to prevent violence, to allow no one else aboard except the authorities, and not to permit any of the Negroes to land.[23] Once aboard, the military company separated the men and the women, bound the four rebel leaders, and confined them to the long boat. This was the largest boat on the ship and was used for provisioning, transporting water casks, and serving as a lifeboat whenever necessary.[24] In this particular case, it served as a floating wooden jail for rebel leaders, whose brief hours of liberty and command were now over. Those not involved in the revolt were guarded in the hold during nighttime but allowed on deck during the day.[25] The military unit remained on board until Friday, changing soldiers and officers every morning at 9:00 a.m.[26] Lieutenant Fitzgerald assumed command with a new company on Wednesday. Lieutenant Glubb and his company served on Thursday. Lieutenant Hill boarded with a new company on Friday.[27]

These rotating officers and soldiers aboard the *Creole* belonged to the Second West India Regiment. In 1795, the British Army created the West India Regiments (WIR).[28] Over the next thirteen years, the British government purchased 13,400 Africans for GBP 925,000 (more than GBP

---

[23] Cobbe's testimony, Nassau commission, April 1842, in "*Thomas McCargo v. The New Orleans Insurance Company*," 256; Bacon to Webster, November 30, 1841, Sen. Doc. No. 51, 3; Gifford's testimony, *Thomas McCargo v. The New Orleans Insurance Company*, 224. Gifford names this officer as Captain Mins. See Gifford's testimony, "*Thomas McCargo v. The New Orleans Insurance Company*," 210.

[24] Dean King, *A Sea of Words. A Lexicon and Companion for Patrick O'Brien's Seafaring Tales* (New York: Henry Holt. 1997), 274. For the fictional role of the longboat or yawl in the coastal West Africa slave trade, see Barry Unsworth, *Sacred Hunger* (New York: Norton, 1993), 190.

[25] *Thomas McCargo v. The New Orleans Insurance Company*, 242.

[26] Gifford's testimony, "*Thomas McCargo v. The New Orleans Insurance Company*," 210.

[27] The testimony of Lieutenants Mends, Glubb, Fitzgerald and Murray to Nassau Commission, in *Thomas McCargo v. The New Orleans Insurance Company*, 256; Attorney General Anderson's testimony, Nassau Commission, in "*Thomas McCargo v. The New Orleans Insurance Company*," 248. The ship's company referred to Fitzgerald as captain ("New Orleans Protest," December 2, 1842, Sen. Doc. No. 51, 42; *Thomas McCargo v. The New Orleans Insurance Company*, 242). They also state that Fitzgerald told Mary – one of the enslaved women – "how foolish they were, that they had not, when they rose, killed all the whites on board, and run the vessel ashore, and then they would have all been free, and there would have been no more trouble about it," "*Thomas McCargo v. The New Orleans Insurance Company*," 242.

[28] The classic work is Roger Norman Buckley's *Slaves in Redcoats: The British West India Regiments, 1795–1815* (New Haven: Yale University Press, 1979). For recent research on the social and political lives of these black soldiers designed to redirect our view of them away from imperial collaborators toward more social and cultural figures within an African Diaspora framework, see Marcus Weise, "A Social History of the West India Regiments, 1795-1838," (PhD diss., Howard University, 2017).

86 million in 2015). These WIRs provided one-third of all troops garrisoned in the British West Indies. In 1807, their status was changed to free men. In the following decades they continued to provide vital support for maintaining and enforcing British imperial control throughout the Caribbean and Atlantic world.[29] They also established links with enslaved and free people of African descent across the Caribbean, operated as social and cultural figures within the African Diaspora, and rebelled against their new military masters. Between 1795 and 1838, there were eleven general courts-martial concerning various forms of mutiny. In May 27, 1808, some fifty new recruits to the Second WIR rebelled during a drill at Fort Augusta, Jamaica. They killed Lieutenant Ellis and wounded Major Darley before being stopped by veteran members of the regiment. Seventeen rebels were killed and sixteen who tried to escape were captured and returned; six were executed and ten pardoned. What is striking is that this rebellion was motivated by the recruits' desire not to fight for the British government but to return to their West African homes and communities.[30] In early 1816, members of the same regiment protested against incorrect wages, poor rations, and inadequate clothing. They threatened to burn Nassau. In the subsequent inquiry, six soldiers faced prosecution. The investigation further revealed that liberated African women who were their partners had played a role in the public expression of grievances.[31]

Over the first two decades of its existence, the Second WIR drew African recruits from some twenty-three ethnic backgrounds including Chamba, Congo, and Coromantin. After serving in Jamaica, the Second WIR was transferred to Freetown, Sierra Leone, to combat ethnic conflict between the Assante and the Fante peoples with the British supporting the latter. The Second WIR also helped suppress transatlantic slave trading activities in West Africa. In May 1820, a slave dealer called Curtis captured and killed a crew member of the British frigate *Thistle*. The Second WIR supported the marines from the *Thistle*, located the trader's camp and destroyed it, and recovered the captured sailors.[32] The regiment was subsequently redeployed to the British West Indies. But it continued to attract African recruits.

According to an 1835 colonial report, thirty liberated Africans from the intercepted transatlantic Portuguese slaver *Hebe* chose to enlist in the Second WIR.[33] By the time the *Creole* entered Nassau harbor,

---

[29] Weise, "British West India Regiments," 8–9.   [30] Ibid, chap. 4, 123–128.
[31] Adderley, *"New Negroes from Africa,"* 137–140.   [32] Ibid, 54, 49, 70–71.
[33] Adderley, *"New Negroes from Africa,"* 57, 215.

the Second WIR in the Bahamas consisted of five hundred regular troops divided into four companies led by four captains.[34]

That Tuesday afternoon, November 9, 1941, Governor Cockburn met with his colonial Council. They summoned the US consul to appear before them and informed him of three decisions. The first was that "the courts of law here have no jurisdiction over the alleged offenses."[35] This would have included the Vice Admiralty Court, once mainly responsible for maritime disputes, but now a shadow of its former imperial grandeur.[36] Second, the accusation of the crime of murder required that "the parties implicated in so grave a charge should not be allowed to go at large." An investigation and examinations under oath should proceed with the accused parties "detained" until the British Foreign Secretary in Whitehall decided whether or not to deliver the accused into the hands of the American government.[37] Third, after the examinations had been conducted, all those aboard the ship *"not implicated in any of the offences alleged to have been committed on board of that vessel, must be released from further restraint."*[38] A detailed account of the entire affair was to be dispatched to the British minister in Washington. US Consul Bacon requested a written copy of the statement that was duly forwarded by the governor's secretary, C. R. Nesbitt.[39]

---

[34] New Orleans Protest, December 2, 1841, Sen. Doc. No. 51, 42; *Thomas McCargo v. The New Orleans Insurance Company*, 242–243. For an image of a soldier from the Second WIR in 1876, see the watercolor over pencil by Richard Simpkin in the online collection of the National Army Museum, London, England.

[35] Nesbitt to Bacon, November 9, 1841, Document C, Sen. Doc., No. 51, 6; "*Thomas McCargo v. The New Orleans Insurance Company*," 235.

[36] "Originating in the seventeenth century in response to needs to settle the ordinary maritime problems and disputes occurring from time-to-time in young colonies, they were again, by the middle of the nineteenth century, little more than shadowy relics, exercising the same occasional jurisdiction," Michael Craton, "Caribbean Vice Admiralty Courts and British Imperialism," in *Empire, Enslavement, and Freedom in the Caribbean* (Kingston: Ian Randle, 1997)116.

[37] Nesbitt to Bacon, November 9, 1841, Document 2, Sen. Doc. No. 51, 6; *Thomas McCargo v. The New Orleans Insurance Company*, 235.

[38] Ibid. Original italics.

[39] Ibid. Of this projected investigation and examination, George and Willene Hendrick write that Cockburn needed to appear "to be making an impartial investigation" because of recent British colonial abolition. See Hendrick and Hendrick, *The Creole Mutiny: A Tale of Revolt Aboard a Slave Ship* (Chicago: Ivan R. Dee, 2003), 97. This seems too cynical. From his head to his toes Governor Cockburn gives the impression of a colonial bureaucrat who adheres to instructions from London. What seems amazing is how he and his Council could hope to get to the bottom of the killing, maiming, and ship revolt without talking to the rebels.

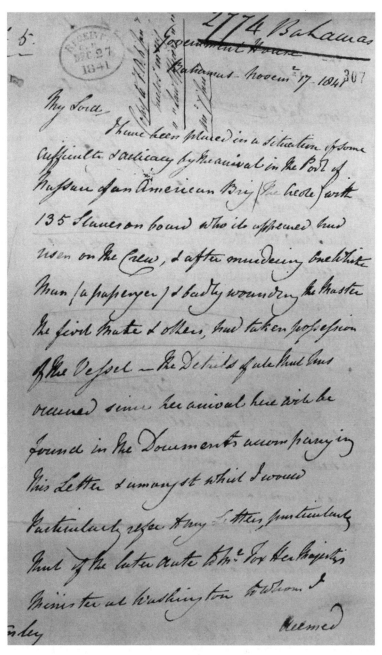

FIGURE 6.2 Governor Cockburn's letter on the ship revolt, Nassau, November 17, 1841.
Source: Aberdeen Papers, BL

The first two decisions probably met with the approbation of the US consul. The *Creole* was a US merchant ship engaged in legitimate commerce when slaves revolted and killed an American citizen. This demanded an official investigation into what had happened. The Council's last decision, however, must have disturbed him. If the majority of the slaves aboard the *Creole* were not to be detained by the British authorities, then it was probable that they would leave the vessel and seek their liberty ashore as he forewarned. This betokened the loss of valuable property of American citizens with little prospect of such chattel being recovered. There was a long tradition of such failed recoveries on land and sea stretching back to the American Revolution. It provided Bacon with a serious challenge in managing his official business. It also boded poorly for diplomatic relations between Washington and London. These relations were already tense with border incidents, territorial disputes, and British maritime aggression against transoceanic slave trading stretching back over several preceding decades.

Local colonial magistrates boarded the ship and questioned the officers and crew during the next three days. On Tuesday, November ninth, Police Magistrate (PM) Robert Duncome and Justice of the Peace (JP) J. J. Burnside, accompanied by US Consul Bacon, deposed Merritt and Gifford.[40] On Wednesday, November tenth, PM Duncome and JP Burnside interviewed Stevens, Curtis, and McCargo.[41] On Friday, November twelfth, they deposed Leidner.[42] It is unclear if any other depositions were taken from crew or passengers. None of the former captives were interviewed. The depositions abruptly halted on Friday morning. The exception was that of Captain Ensor. He could not be deposed because of the severity of his injuries. The wounded master was taken ashore after Bacon's first interview with the governor on the day of

---

[40] Merritt to Duncome & Burnside, November 9, 1841, Sen. Doc. No. 51, 28–29; Gifford to Duncome & Burnside, November 10, 1841, Sen. Doc. No. 51, 30–31; "New Orleans Protest," December 2, 1841, Sen. Doc. No. 51, 42; Bacon's testimony, "*Thomas McCargo* v. *The New Orleans Insurance Company*," 226. Zephaniah Gifford mistakenly states that these depositions were taken the next day. See Gifford's testimony, *Thomas McCargo* v. *The New Orleans Insurance Company*, 210.

[41] Stevens to Duncome & Burnside, deposition, November 10, 1841, Sen. Doc. No. 51, 31–33; Curtis to Duncome & Burnside, deposition, November 10, 1841, Sen. Doc. No. 51, 34; McCargo to Duncome & Burnside, deposition, November 10, 1841, Sen. Doc. No 51, 35; Gifford's testimony, "*Thomas McCargo* v. *The New Orleans Insurance Company*," 210.

[42] Leidner to Duncome & Burnside, deposition, November 12, 1841, Sen. Doc. No. 51, 36; Gifford's testimony, *Thomas McCargo* v. *The New Orleans Insurance Company*, 210.

arrival and he remained incapacitated. His was the last interview, nine days later.[43]

These official inquiries were aimed at finding out exactly who was responsible for the death of John Hewell, who caused the injuries to the officers and crew, and what had occurred during the uprising. The British authorities compromised their investigation, however, because they failed to depose any of the former captives. Even the four rebel leaders bound in the long boat, who were easily accessible for questioning, do not appear to have been consulted. This seems strange because there was no colonial law against soliciting such testimony. What did emerge during the questioning was the immediate identification of the other fifteen rebel slaves. They were subsequently arrested and detained – presumably in the hold – since the long boat would have been too small to hold all nineteen.

The increasing probability that former American slaves who were not identified as rebels would not be restrained by the British authorities prompted the US consul to help instigate an armed plot to seize the *Creole*. The plot's primary objective was to regain control of the brig and its slave cargo and to steer for American territorial waters. On the vessel's arrival in Nassau, Captain Woodside of the brig *Louisa* out of Portland, Maine, had boarded together with the US consul. He offered to use his crew to man the ship, "master the slaves," and steer the *Creole* to Indian Key, Florida. Located some four hundred miles from Nassau, Indian Key was usually home to an American warship. The US consul proposed using a crew from the *Congress*, which was lying dismasted in Nassau's harbor. Gifford agreed to assume mastership of the *Creole*. It was reported there were "frequent interviews" among Woodside, Bacon, and officers of the *Congress*. Both Bacon and Gifford tried to buy weapons from local Bahamians in Nassau, but were unsuccessful. One can only speculate as to why they failed: limited supply of arms? locals' refusal to co-operate with slave interests? The conspirators eventually obtained three muskets and cutlasses from the *Louisa*, nothing from the *Congress*, and a pair of horse-pistols owned by Captain Woodside.[44]

The attempt to seize the *Creole* began around 8:00 a.m. on Friday, November twelfth. Captain Woodside and his crew rowed a boat toward

[43] Ensor to Duncome & Burnside, deposition, November 18, 1841, Sen. Doc. No. 51, 30.

[44] "New Orleans Protest," December 2, 1841, Sen. Doc. No. 51, 44–45; *Thomas McCargo v. The New Orleans Insurance Company*," 246; Gifford's testimony, "*Thomas McCargo v. The New Orleans Insurance Company*," 213–214. The plot appears to have hatched soon after the US consul received the Colonial Council's decision not to interfere with the Negroes who were not involved in the rebellion.

the ship; they had muskets and cutlasses wrapped in the American flag concealed in the bottom of the boat. A Bahamian local, who was carefully monitoring the loading of the boat and its steering for the *Creole*, alerted the military guard on board ship. Upon approaching the vessel, the British officer of the Second WIR ordered the conspirators to: "Keep off, or I will fire into you." The military company lined up with loaded muskets and fixed bayonets pointed over the gunwale toward the conspirators. These black soldiers were under strict military orders to protect the ships and repel outsiders. It is not inconceivable, however, that fending off an attempt to return former American slaves to a condition of servitude met with their personal approbation. Captain Woodside was forced to retire and the attempt to seize the *Creole* and steer her to Florida waters and the safety of American jurisdiction fizzled out.[45]

This attempt to seize the coastal slaver by force raises several interesting points. The connivance of the consul with officers and seamen implicated the US government in the subsequent action. There was no advanced warning or deadline proposed to the local authorities but simply clandestine action overseen by a diplomatic official. Moreover, the *Creole* was an American merchant ship within British waters. Captain Woodside's actions might technically be construed as an illegal and illegitimate maritime attack and therefore piracy. Furthermore, if the attempted seizure had been successful, it probably would have resulted in several dead British subjects and American citizens, a ship steered to a US port minus its captain, and British territorial integrity compromised. In other words, a major altercation would have erupted. Finally, this attempt to seize the *Creole* was never mentioned in colonial dispatches to London nor was it ever referred to in subsequent correspondence between Washington and London.[46] This was probably less because it was deemed insignificant than because its mention would have compromised American claims.

On Friday, November twelfth, events reached their climax. The leaders of the revolt had been bound for three days, while the other fifteen rebels had been subsequently held on board ship. The rest of the captives had been cooped up on board without being able to leave the vessel. The local

---

[45] New Orleans Protest, December 2, 1841, Sen. Doc. No. 51, 44–45; "*Thomas McCargo v. The New Orleans Insurance Company*," 246; Gifford's testimony, "*Thomas McCargo v. The New Orleans Insurance Company*," 214.

[46] Captain Woodside made no mention of this attempted seizure in his deposition to Bacon, November 13, 1841, Sen. Doc. No. 51, 11–12. Perhaps he did not need to because "the arrangement was made under the control of the American consul" ("New Orleans Protest," December 2, 1841, Sen. Doc. No. 51, 44).

magistrates had nearly completed their investigations. The governor had promised not to restrain the movements of those not implicated in the rebellion once the inquiry had finished. An attempt to seize the *Creole* by armed force had been thwarted by an eagle-eyed Bahamian and by British troops. On accompanying the magistrates in their final business that morning, Bacon reported seeing "a large collection of persons on shore nearest the vessel, and many in boats." He was informed "the moment the troops should be withdrawn from the brig, an attempt would be made to board her with force." He requested the governor "do all he could to protect the vessel and cargo."[47] The governor's immediate response was incredulity. Consul Bacon was informed "that I cannot think it possible that any of her Majesty's subjects would act so improperly as to attempt to board, by force, the American brig Creole." Should it be attempted, he added, he was prepared to use "every authorized means for preventing it."[48] What is striking about his reply is not only its presumption of unquestioning loyalty by Bahamians to the British colonial government, but the implied threat that *any* attempt to seize the *Creole* by force by anyone would be swiftly dealt with.[49]

What followed was the liberation of the majority of the former captives from the *Creole*. The top legal office in the colony was that of attorney general. In the immediate aftermath of the British abolition of the slave trade in 1807, Attorney General William Wylly pursued, with mixed success, an aggressive campaign to liberate Africans from slave ships interdicted by the Royal Navy. This slaveholder was also seen as a gradual abolitionist who supported the end of the slave trade and the amelioration of slaves' conditions.[50] One of his successors was George Anderson, a career colonial official. Former attorney of the general court of the Bahamas in 1827, he served as attorney general of the colony from 1837 and joined the Executive Council in 1840.[51]

---

[47] Bacon to Cockburn, November 12, 1841, Document D, Sen. Doc. No. 51, 6; "*Thomas McCargo v. The New Orleans Insurance Company,*" 236.

[48] Cockburn to Bacon, November 12, 1841, Document E, Sen. Doc. No 51, 7; "*Thomas McCargo v. The New Orleans Insurance Company,*" 236.

[49] Consul Bacon gives the impression that this seizure was in response to imminent attacks by the locals although it had been planned a few days earlier. Bacon's testimony, *Thomas McCargo v. The New Orleans Insurance Company,* 228, 232–233.

[50] Adderley, "*New Negroes from Africa,*" 28–37.

[51] Anderson's testimony, Nassau Commission, April 1842, in *Thomas McCargo v. The New Orleans Insurance Company,* 250; Adam Bissett Thom, *The Upper Ten Thousand, An Alphabetical List* (London: Routledge, 1875), 10.

That Friday morning, Anderson boarded the *Creole* with several other local officials. He informed the nineteen rebels that they were to be incarcerated until word was received from London about their particular dispensation. He addressed the majority of those who had not been involved in the insurrection but who had been forced to stay on board that they were now at liberty to either stay put or leave the ship without interference from the local authorities. A flotilla of boats manned by local Bahamians surrounding the *Creole* proceeded to ferry the newly liberated people to the shore. It was reported: "Three or four of the persons shipped as slaves remained onboard, and those expressing their determination to return with the vessel to America." After the mass exodus, the rebels were transported to the city jail where they were incarcerated. The newly freed went to the police station "accompanied by between one and two thousand people," and registered their names with the local authorities. After years of enslavement in the American South, these people had finally gained their liberty in the British West Indies, although the rebels languished in jail awaiting their fate.[52]

These then are the bare facts of the captives' liberation from the *Creole* in Nassau harbor during the second week of November 1841. But American personnel and British officials disputed several points that were to further antagonize relations between Washington and London. The first disagreement concerned the number of boats that surrounded the *Creole* in Nassau harbor. According to the *Creole*'s crew, there were "about fifty boats lying around the brig, all filled with men from the shore, armed with clubs."[53] Captain Woodside described a "number of small boats" around the vessel "all filled with black people."[54] In contrast, Major Cobbe thought this to be a gross exaggeration. The number of boats, he reported, "'did not exceed five, if there were so many.'"[55] In other words, the American crew's larger number implied potential mischief; while the British officer's much smaller

[52] Anderson to Cockburn, November 13, 1841, Document G, Sen. Doc. No. 51, 10; "*Thomas McCargo v. The New Orleans Insurance Company*," 238–239; Bacon to Cockburn, November 14, 1841, Document F, in *Thomas McCargo v. The New Orleans Insurance Company*, 236–237; Bacon to Webster, November 30, 8141, Sen. Doc. No. 51, 4. In Frederick Douglass's 1853 novella, they marched "uttering the wildest shouts of exultation"; see Frederick Douglass, *The Heroic Slave*, in Ira Dworkin, ed., *Frederick Douglass: Narrative of the Life of Frederick Douglass, an American Slave* (New York: Penguin, 2014), 190.

[53] New Orleans Protest, December 2, 1841, Sen. Doc. No. 51, 42; Gifford's testimony, "*Thomas McCargo v. The New Orleans Insurance Company*," 211.

[54] Woodside to Bacon, deposition, November 13, 1841, Sen. Doc. No. 51, 11.

[55] Cobbe's testimony, Nassau Commission, April 1842, in *Thomas McCargo v. The New Orleans Insurance Company*, 256.

figure played down such threats and potential mischief by loyal colonial subjects. It is impossible to reconcile such a huge discrepancy. There were probably many more than five boats, however, because of extensive fishing activities by local Bahamians and Nassau harbor's activity as a vibrant Caribbean port.

The second dispute was over the precise words uttered by the attorney general to those assembled on the deck of the *Creole*. According to Anderson's own account, he informed the rebels that they were to be jailed and told the rest of the assembly: "As far as the authorities were concerned, all restrictions on their movements were removed." After his address, continued Anderson, passenger William Merritt "addressed the people who had been shipped as slaves, and told them they were at perfect liberty to go on shore if they pleased."[56] The officers and crew claimed to have heard rather differently. In the Nassau Protest, they stated: "as soon as the troops and criminals [sic] were paraded on the poop-deck, notice was given by the attorney general to the other slaves, that they were free, and could go ashore if they pleased."[57] In other words, it was the British official, not the US passenger, who told the former American slaves that they were now at liberty. Captain Gifford reported that, after addressing the nineteen rebels, Anderson informed the rest: "'My friends, you have all been detained on board of the Creole in the port of Nassau a short time to know who was most engaged in the murder of Mr. Hewell, and attempting to kill the captain, mate, and crew. We have ascertained that, and identified nineteen: and the rest of you are all free and at liberty to go ashore, and go where you please.'" Gifford said that he had protested against allowing the slaves to go ashore. The attorney general responded, he continued, with the following words: "'You had better not object to it; you had better let them go quietly ashore; if you object, I am afraid there will be blood shed.'"[58] Not surprisingly, the American crew substantiated the acting captain's account.[59] Merritt independently verified Gifford's account.[60] Captain Woodside told US Consul Bacon

---

[56] Anderson to Cockburn, November 13, 1841, Document G, Sen. Doc. No. 51, 10; "*Thomas McCargo v. The New Orleans Insurance Company*," 239.

[57] Nassau Protest, November 17, 1841, Sen. Doc. No. 51, 18.

[58] Gifford's testimony, "*Thomas McCargo v. The New Orleans Insurance Company*," 212; Gifford to Bacon, deposition, November 13, 1841, Sen. Doc. No. 51, 14.

[59] "New Orleans Protest," December 2, 1841, Sen. Doc. No 51, 43; "*Thomas McCargo v. The New Orleans Insurance Company*," 243–244.

[60] Merritt to Bacon, deposition, November 13, 1841, Sen. Doc. No. 51, 13; Merritt's testimony, "*Thomas McCargo v. The New Orleans Insurance Company*," 222.

that the attorney general had "said to the other slaves, 'Men, you are all free, you can go where you please,' or words of the same import."[61] In his testimony to the Council at Nassau several months later in April 1842, Attorney General Anderson admitted his unequivocal support for "the general emancipation of slaves."[62] But it is important to emphasize that this was only his personal preference. It seems unlikely that the highest-ranking jurist in the British colony would have told the former American slaves that they were simply free to go. Such an order would have exceeded the colonial Council's previous decision that all those not involved in the murder and insurrection simply "be released from further restraint."[63] His instruction was the logical consequence of a recently declared policy of imperial emancipation from London.

The third dispute concerns the potential role of violence. Many of the ship's company expressed fears for their safety from local Bahamians. Many seafarers carried weapons – knives, hooks, clubs – in their boats that they were only prevented from using by the orders of local authorities. Even without these weapons, the large number of boats surrounding the ship portended some sort of physical retribution. The former chief mate spoke for many when he stated that "he feared those in the launches and boats, when they come alongside, would commit some violence."[64] Former Second Officer Stevens told a policeman "he thought the crew and vessel ought to be protected after the troops were withdrawn."[65] The British authorities pooh-poohed the crew's trepidation. There were not that many boats and locals in the harbor. The occupants had been disarmed. There was an armed company of West Indian troops aboard to prevent any violence. The British authorities had everything under control.[66] It appears that the revolt had genuinely jolted the Americans while the British were firmly committed to a public display of colonial law and order.

The fourth point of contention concerned the control of British colonial authorities over local Bahamians in their boats. According to Gifford, the

[61] Woodside to Bacon, deposition, November 13, 1841, Sen. Doc. No. 51, 12.
[62] Anderson's testimony, Nassau Commission, April 1842, in *"Thomas McCargo v. The New Orleans Insurance Company,"* 250.
[63] Nesbitt to Bacon, November 9, 1841, Document C, Sen. Doc. No 51, 6; *"Thomas McCargo v. The New Orleans Insurance Company,"* 235.
[64] Gifford to Bacon, deposition, November 13, 1841, Sen. Doc. No. 51, 14.
[65] Stevens to Bacon, deposition, November 13, 1841, Sen. Doc. No. 51, 15.
[66] Cobbe's testimony, Nassau Commission, April 1842, in *"Thomas McCargo v. The New Orleans Insurance Company,"* 256–257; Anderson to Cockburn, November 13, 1841, Document G, Sen. Doc. No. 51, 9–10.

attorney general signaled the "musquito fleet to come alongside," after which "the boats made a general rush" to the brig.[67] Jacob Leidner reported that Anderson said: " 'Come alongside with your boats;' and he was speaking to the negroes in the boats around the Creole."[68] According to Merritt, it was JP Burnside and not Anderson who "made a signal for the boats to come alongside, beckoning with his hand."[69] According to Captain Woodside, it was neither Anderson nor Burnside but Police Inspector Pinder who gave the word: "Boats, you can come alongside."[70] Despite this confusion over who exactly issued the order to come alongside, all of the witnesses agreed that the British authorities were responsible for directing colonial subjects to carry out their orders. This view differs markedly from the view of the attorney general. He told the assembled boatmen to dispense with their weapons and that any violation of the peace would not be tolerated.[71] After his address on board, he vacated the *Creole*, during which time he witnessed the mass exodus from the ship without playing any further role.[72] Police Inspector Pinder later confirmed that the "passengers" exodus was "voluntary."[73] In short, the former captives left of their own volition aided by numerous local boatmen under the watchful eye of the local authorities.

In short, the Americans believed that the slaves from the *Creole* had been "liberated" by the local authorities. The ship's company was adamant: "If there had been no interference on the part of the legal authorities of Nassau, the slaves might have been safely brought to New Orleans. It was that interference which prevented aid from being rendered by the American sailors in Nassau, and caused the loss of the slaves to their owners."[74] Consul Bacon was no less certain about the role of interference even if he was unsure about its exact trajectory. The slaves could not have been freed without the role of the colonial authorities: ". . . whether the slaves were liberated with force, by a mob, after a knowledge of the existence of a mob had been brought to the knowledge of the governor

[67] Gifford's testimony, "*Thomas McCargo* v. *The New Orleans Insurance Company*," 212.
[68] Leidner's testimony, "*Thomas McCargo* v. *The New Orleans Insurance Company*," 221.
[69] Merritt's testimony, "*Thomas McCargo* v. *The New Orleans Insurance Company*," 222.
[70] Woodside to Bacon, deposition, November 13, 1841, Sen. Doc. No. 51, 12; "*Thomas McCargo* v. *The New Orleans Insurance Company*," 241.
[71] Anderson to Cockburn, November 13, 1841, Doc. G, Sen. Doc. No. 51, 10; "*Thomas McCargo* v. *The New Orleans Insurance Company*," 239.
[72] Ibid.
[73] Pinder's testimony, Nassau Commission, April 1842, in "*Thomas McCargo* v. *The New Orleans Insurance Company*," 254–255.
[74] New Orleans Protest, December 2, 1841, Sen. Doc. No. 51, 45.

and Council, or in a more quiet way, by persons deputed by them for that purpose."[75] In contrast, the British authorities insisted that the slaves on the *Creole* left of their own volition without any interference or even encouragement on their part. As the attorney general concluded in his dispatch to Governor Cockburn the day after the liberation occurred, their departure "was their own free and voluntary act, sanctioned by the express consent of the mate, and that neither myself nor any other of the authorities of the colony then on board interfered in the slightest manner to induce them to take that step."[76] The Americans were right to suspect the liberationist proclivities of British officials especially given the recent past of such actions on grounded US slavers together with the recent commitment to colonial emancipation. On the other hand, local colonial authorities were clearly following the letter of the law, albeit with a personal degree of enthusiasm against American slavery.

This Anglo-American dispute dominates the narrative of the liberation of former captives from the *Creole* in Nassau harbor.[77] It was to play an important role in defining contrasting notions of British antislavery and American slavery as we shall see in the following chapters. But a focus on the actions, behavior, and contacts between local Bahamians and American captives provides a very different narrative of liberation. While it is unfortunately true that neither captives nor Bahamians were interviewed, the documentary record is full of suggestive descriptions, accounts, and anecdotes that point to their historical agency during this significant moment of freedom. The actions and relations of American captives and black Bahamians provide us with a much more dynamic narrative of collective self-liberation in Nassau harbor that remains largely absent from historical accounts.

During the 1840s, the population of Nassau and its surroundings was estimated to have been between 12,000 and 13,000 blacks and from 3,000 to 4,000 whites.[78] Most of the whites originated from Britain, while most of the blacks were native-born Creoles. The exception was liberated Africans.

---

[75] Bacon to Webster, November 30, 1841, Sen. Doc. No. 51, 4.

[76] Anderson to Cockburn, November 13, 1841, Doc. G, Sen. Doc. No. 51, 10; "*Thomas McCargo v. The New Orleans Insurance Company*," 239. John Grant Anderson, the Receiver General & Treasurer of the colony, stated he was "positive as to Merritt giving the people the permission he has stated," Anderson's testimony, Nassau Commission, April 1842, in "*Thomas McCargo v. The New Orleans Insurance Company*," 255.

[77] Jervey and Huber, "*Creole* Affair," 204–205; Hendrick and Hendrick, *Creole Mutiny*, 105–106; Jones, "Case of Creole," 32–33; Downey, *Creole Affair*, 79–85.

[78] "New Orleans Protest," December 2, 1841, in "*Thomas McCargo v. The New Orleans Insurance Company*," 243.

Between 1811 and 1841 some 6,000 enslaved Africans liberated from trans-atlantic slavers by the Royal Navy were landed in the Bahamas.[79] In contrast to the older sugar mono-economy of Jamaica – and the newer sugar econo-mies of recently acquired Trinidad and Guiana in the late 1790s – the Bahamas was characterized by mixed agricultural, urban, and maritime economies, including fishing, trading, transportation, and coastal work throughout this massive archipelago. According to former slaveholder John Storr, Jr., a great many of the former slaves in the colony worked as fishermen or seamen engaged in commercial enterprise.[80] This was the maritime world entered into by the *Creole* in late 1841.

The black pilot and his crew played a vital role in the advent of the former captives' liberation from the *Creole* as demonstrated by the com-bination of archival analysis and comparative scholarship. Most ship pilots in New World slave societies were enslaved. They used their spe-cialized knowledge of hydrospace – or what one scholar usefully refers to as "green water" to distinguish ports, harbors, and coastal waters from "deep ocean" – to steer ships through treacherous inland waters, rocky terrain, coral reefs, and sandbars. They used their knowledge and skills during both wartime eruptions as well as in longer, quieter moments to chisel out spaces of freedom in the maritime Atlantic world.[81] It was black pilots who clandestinely steered the ship *Deep Nine* away from Jamaican slavery toward Haitian freedoms in 1817.[82]

---

[79] Adderley, *"New Negroes from Africa,"* 10, 45, 263n107.

[80] Adderley, *"New Negroes from Africa,"* 14; Michael Craton, "Hobbesian or Panglossian? The Two Extremes of Slave Conditions in the British West Indies, 1783–1834," in *Empire, Enslavement, and Freedom in the Caribbean* (Kingston: Ian Randle, 1997), 225–228; Storr's deposition to Board of Assistant Commissioners of Compensation at Nassau, July 31, 1834, in Jane Eva Baxter, "Negotiations for Compensations: Bahamian Slaveholders in 1834," Talk, forty-seventh Annual Conference, Association of Caribbean Historians, Nassau, Bahamas, May 17, 2015.

[81] Kevin Dawson, "The Cultural Geography of Enslaved Ship Pilots," in Jorge Canizares-Esquerra, Matt D. Childs, James Sidbury, eds., *The Black Urban Atlantic in the Age of the Slave Trade* (Philadelphia: University of Pennsylvania Press, 2013), 163–184, "green water" (164). For comparisons with slave pilots in Civil War coastal Georgia and North Carolina, as well as in the nineteenth-century North Atlantic, see Clarence Mohr, *On the Threshold of Freedom: Masters and Slaves in Civil War Georgia* (Athens: University of Georgia Press, 1986), 84, 289; David S. Cecelski, *The Waterman's Song: Slavery and Freedom in Maritime North Carolina* (Chapel Hill: University of North Carolina Press, 2001), 153–162; Jeffrey W. Bolster, *Black Jacks: African American Seamen in the Age of Sail* (Cambridge, Mass.: Harvard University Press, 1997), 18, 23, 79, 131–139, 137–143.

[82] Jeffrey R. Kerr-Ritchie, *Freedom's Seekers: Essays on Comparative Emancipation* (Baton Rouge: Louisiana State University Press, 2014), 68–69.

These pilots used their specialized knowledge to earn a living when freedom came. While the *Creole* moored in Nassau harbor, former First Mate Gifford reported that the pilot crew fraternized with the slaves, "mingled with the negroes, all being black."[83] The ship's company testified that one man claimed a female slave for himself. This might indicate the special entitlement of these respected maritime workers or it might just have been a personal liaison.[84] According to the same account, the pilot and his men "on coming aboard, mingled with the slaves, and told them they were free men; that they could go on shore, and never be carried away from there."[85] The pilot and crew further encouraged boats to surround the *Creole*. Passenger Stevens told Consul Bacon that he heard the black pilot say to the boatmen: "Come get this your business on board we want to commence ours," to which one replied "we won't be long, we are only waiting for some one from the shore."[86] During the evacuation of the former captives from the *Creole*, the black pilot reportedly shouted out to the British magistrates on board: "I wish you would hurry there. You have had your time, and we want ours."[87] This was local leadership from across the harbor waters.

Black troops also played their part in the liberation. These British soldiers were ordered by the local authorities to guard the ship. They were ordered to watch the rebels as well as the brig. This resulted in preventing an illegal seizure of the vessel. According to passenger Merritt, they were ordered not to "converse with the slaves." They obeyed the first day. "On the second day deponent [Gifford] saw the order was

---

[83] Gifford's testimony, "*Thomas McCargo v. The New Orleans Insurance Company*," 210.

[84] New Orleans Protest, Dec. 2, 1841, Sen. Doc. No. 51, 42.

[85] Ibid. Echoing earlier scholars like Julius Scott and Jeffrey Bolster, one scholar recently noted: "Pilots, mariners, and passengers exchanged colonial and overseas news"; see Dawson, "Enslaved Ship Pilots," 180.

[86] Stevens to Bacon, November 13, 1841, Dispatches, NARA.

[87] Gifford's testimony, "*Thomas McCargo v. The New Orleans Insurance Company*," 213; Merritt to Bacon, deposition, November 13, 1841, Sen. Doc. No. 51, 12. This notion of "our time" is expressed at other times in the British West Indies suggesting a meaningful moment of historical change for Caribbean people of African descent. In the summer of 1859, a rioter at Florence Hall estate in Westmoreland, Jamaica, shouted out "it is our time" against the lack of landholding and police enforcement of the status quo. See Thomas C. Holt, *The Problem of Freedom: Race, Labor, and Politics in Jamaica and Britain, 1832–1938* (Baltimore: John Hopkins University Press, 1992), 268. In May 1938, some demonstrators yelled out "This is black man day" against Chinese shopkeepers in a poor peoples' protest in Kingston, Jamaica. See Colin A. Palmer, *Freedom's Children: The 1938 Labor Rebellion and the Birth of Modern Jamaica* (Chapel Hill: University of North Carolina Press, 2014), 49.

not obeyed, that the soldiers were in constant contact with the slaves, and during the evening they were not placed as they had been, with no guard over the prisoners." Merritt complained to the lieutenant who shrugged it off replying: "If you will tell the sergeant he dared say he would have it attended to."[88] It would be useful to know the nature of this conversation. Without it, we can only speculate on the possibility of a racial politics of solidarity among people of African descent who shared a common condition of prior servitude and enslavement in North America and the British Atlantic.[89]

In addition to this racial solidarity, personal relationships were established between Second WIR troops and women of African descent. In 1825, the superintendent of British Honduras reported that some troops stationed in the colony had formed "conexions [*sic*] with the female part [of the enslaved population]; by whom many of them have families." He worried such relationships might undermine black soldiers' loyalty to the British Empire.[90] Several seamen reported personal relations between black soldiers and former captives on the *Creole*. Their concern was that such liaisons illustrated the loss of control of an American merchant vessel to a foreign entity.[91] A few years later, reports emerged of similar connections between WIR soldiers and enslaved women in Havana harbor, Cuba.[92] Without their own testimonies, we can never be certain as to the exact nature of these relationships. Were they acts of entitlement? Were they genuine? Based upon some recent research, it would appear that some of these relationships between soldiers and enslaved/free women were consensual, familial, and serious to the point that they concerned local officials because they offered the potential to undermine a soldier's obligation to serve King and Country.[93] The challenge, of course, is to reconstruct these personal relations through documents that are primarily concerned with the maintenance of colonial law and order.

---

[88] Merritt to Bacon, deposition, November 13, 1841, Sen. Doc. No. 51, 12.

[89] According to one historian, these troops "openly fraternized with the insurrectionists"; see Jonathan Levy, *Freaks of Fortune: The Emerging World of Capitalism and Risk in America* (Cambridge: Harvard University Press, 2012), 26.

[90] Weise, "British West India Regiments," 93–94.

[91] See Dispatches from US Consul in Nassau, RG 59, NARA.

[92] Rosanne Adderley, presentation at the American Historical Association, Atlanta, Georgia, January 2015.

[93] Weise, "British West India Regiments," chap. 3.

The local Bahamians were especially important actors in the drama. This was an island community full of maritime workers. Many brought their boats out around the foreign coastal slaver. Captain Woodside testified that the boats surrounding the *Creole* were "all filled with black people."[94] It is almost as if these boatmen were blockading the American slaver from leaving Nassau harbor. Without the foresight of one of these locals, the US plot to seize the *Creole* might have been successful. Some of these Nassau inhabitants carried weapons. They waited patiently (except for the pilot) before providing critical transport to ferry those who wanted to quit the ship and go ashore for their liberty.[95] Once the captives had transferred to the surrounding boats, "five cheers were given by those in the boats."[96] One scholar describes this maritime action as "mob action."[97] Perhaps a more suitable description would be freedom's flotilla.

This commitment was also evident among inhabitants on terra firma. One of the reasons why Captain Woodside and his confederates could not buy arms to seize the *Creole* was because Nassau locals (black and white) refused, saying: "There goes one of the damned pirates and slavers." On the Friday morning, the US consul received a note from a "respectable white person" informing him "the black servants in the service of the said person had gone to assist in liberating the slaves on board the Creole." On his way to the boat, Consul Bacon noticed "a number of females as well as males, on the front upper piazzas, with spy glasses directed towards the brig." But it was the collective power of the people on shore – much like boats in the harbor – that really played a significant role in the liberation. A mass of people – "mob on shore" according to the US consul – milled around the Governor's House during Bacon's visit to see Cockburn on Friday morning. Between 1,000 and 2,000 locals surrounded Police Inspector Pinder's office during the registration of the former captives. One can only imagine the sights, sounds, and joys of liberation as these newly freed people were jostled and clapped and cheered by thronging crowds all the way to the building.[98] In short,

94 Woodside to Bacon, deposition, November 13, 1841, Dispatches, RG 59, NARA.
95 Gifford's testimony, "*Thomas McCargo* v. *The New Orleans Insurance Company*," 210–213, 242.
96 Stevens to Bacon, deposition, November 13, 1841, Sen. Doc. No. 51, 16.
97 Jones, "Case of Creole," 31.
98 Bacon's testimony, "*Thomas McCargo* v. *The New Orleans Insurance Company*," 227–230. This "mob" blocked Bacon's path.

there was a powerful constituency of local opposition toward slavery that contributed toward liberation in Nassau.[99]

And what about those aboard the *Creole*? Liberation is usually described as something that was <u>done to</u> them rather than as a historical process in which they played an active role.[100] Many of them bided their time on board walking the deck during the day and not attempting to jump ship or challenge the military guard. Some of them interacted with the locals who came aboard as well as with the military company. But it was their immediate reaction to the words uttered by either Attorney General Anderson or passenger Merritt that speaks volumes. Upon being told that they were no longer confined to decks but could go where they pleased, "a shout almost immediately arose from among the colored persons." They seemed to Anderson, "with one voice to express their determination to quit the vessel."[101] The news that they were at liberty was information, "which they appeared to receive with great pleasure, and a general intimation of their intention to avail themselves of it."[102] According to Receiver General and Treasurer John Grant Anderson (no relation), it was not British officials who beckoned the ships but captives who called the boats alongside.[103] Lieutenant Hamilton reported the slaves positively "jumped and scrambled" to leave the ship.[104] Even Captain Woodside recalled, "In a few minutes most of the slaves had left the vessel."[105] Attorney General Anderson's last sight of "them crowding over her sides and getting into the boats"

---

[99] Rosanne Adderley points out that a large number of liberated Africans remained in and around Nassau. See Adderley, *"New Negroes from Africa,"* 31. Without concrete evidence, I can only speculate on their supportive role in the *Creole* liberation based on their own unique experience of being freed from transatlantic slavers.

[100] This is part of a traditional narrative of emancipation in the nineteenth-century Americas in which slaves were freed by noble individuals or benevolent governments. Despite vigorous scholarly refutation over the past few decades, it still surfaces during public commemorations such as the bicentennial of the abolition of the British slave trade in 2007, the bicentennial of Lincoln's birth in 2009, and the 150th anniversary of the Emancipation Proclamation in 2013. See Jeffrey R. Kerr-Ritchie, "Slaves' Supplicant and Slaves' Triumphant," and "Reflections on the Bicentennial" for critical evaluations of this myth of the Great Emancipator and its nation-building proclivities.

[101] Anderson's testimony, Nassau Commission, April 1842, in *"Thomas McCargo v. The New Orleans Insurance Company,"* 249.

[102] Anderson to Cockburn, November 13, 1841, Doc. G, Sen. Doc. No. 51, 10.

[103] John Grant Anderson's testimony, Nassau Commission, April 1842, in *"Thomas McCargo v. The New Orleans Insurance Company,"* 255.

[104] Lieutenant Hamilton's testimony, Nassau Commission, April 1842, in *"Thomas McCargo v. The New Orleans Insurance Company,"* 254.

[105] Woodside to Bacon, deposition, November 13, 1841, Sen. Doc. No. 51, 12.

feels like a genuine and accurate depiction of what people who saw liberty within their grasp would have done. Lewis, the enslaved steward of McCargo who had helped his former owner's nephew during the rebellion, was one of those who clambered over the vessel's side. It seems he preferred the uncertainties of individual freedom compared to the reality of domestic servitude.[106]

The collective role of local Bahamians and black Americans suggests an important alternative narrative to the existing historical scholarship on the *Creole's* liberation. The American crew testified: "Many of the negroes who were emancipated expressed a desire to go to New Orleans in the Creole, but were deterred from it, by reason of threats, which were made to sink the vessel, if she attempted to carry the slaves."[107] The lack of any supporting evidence suggests this was wishful thinking. Local Bahamians were neither docile subjects (British view) nor colonial pawns (American view), but historical actors who helped liberate their brethren. Indeed, this was the logical consequence of actions stretching back to post-revolutionary self-emancipators in Nassau with an old tradition of seeking independence and liberty. Black Americans were neither interfered with (American view), nor simply allowed to leave in orderly fashion (British view), but bided their time until the right opportunity presented itself. When it did, they seized the moment much like their predecessors either during poor weather conditions or the chaos of wartime conditions.

---

[106] McCargo to Bacon, deposition, November 10, 1841, Sen. Doc. No. 51, 26. According to shipping records, eighteen-year-old Lewis Carter was being transported by McCargo to New Orleans. See Appendix 3.

[107] "New Orleans Protest," December 2, 1841, Sen. Doc. No. 51, 43.

7

"Old Neighbors"

On Sunday evening, November 14, 1841, American Consul John Bacon penned a letter of "solemn protest" to the governor of the Bahamas against the "manner" of the slaves' liberation and all of the proceedings "on the part of Her Majesty's officers and subjects." These slaves, wrote Bacon, "were as much a portion of the cargo of the said brig, as the tobacco and other articles on board." Consequently, "her Majesty's government had not the right to interfere with, or control the officers of an American vessel." The consul ended his protest letter with the request that the governor permit the rebel slaves "be forwarded to the United States" in the *Creole*, where they would face trial for "murder and outrage."[1]

The consul's protest seems rather odd. It is unlikely that the governor would agree that the slaves were mere cargo, while the charge of local interference would not have met with his approbation given the careful deliberations and actions of the Council and Attorney General respectively. But to then follow these accusations with a request to return those suspected, after it had already been repeatedly made clear that they were to stay in the Nassau jail until London directed otherwise, was naïve, desperate, or both.

Governor Francis Cockburn was a little more diplomatic in his reply as one would expect given his high imperial perch. Drawing upon diplomacy's trusted cliché, he felt "somewhat disappointed" at the US consul's letter. The local authorities sought to "meet your views and wishes" as far

[1] Bacon to Cockburn, November 14, 1841, Doc. F, Sen. Doc. No. 51, 7–8; copied in "*Thomas McCargo* v. *The New Orleans Insurance Company*," 236–237.

as they were authorized, their intentions were "throughout made known," and did not call "forth any objections" on your behalf. Moreover, the US consul's account of the liberation did not concur with that of the attorney general's, a copy of whose account Cockburn enclosed for Bacon's edification. The rebels could not be extradited to the United States because of the Council's previous decision that they be examined and incarcerated until further instructions were received from London.[2]

Thus, the rebels stayed in jail, the former American slaves were at liberty as new colonial subjects, and the US consul failed to persuade British colonial officials to change their policies. But Bacon's points – slaves remained property belonging to Americans on the high seas, Her Majesty's Government had no right to interfere with a merchant ship, decisions like these resulting in the loss of property made London culpable – were to emerge as central planks in the American position in subsequent negotiations with the British government. Their more detailed exposition as well as contestation is examined at greater length in Chapter 8.

These contrasting positions quickly became entrenched. The Americans believed the slaves were chattel while the British believed they were not. This difference was further illustrated by two disputes over former captives' property and the sale of ship provisions.

Sometime over the weekend of November 13–14, 1841, the recently liberated captives visited the attorney general, requesting that the local authorities retrieve their property (clothes, blankets, bits and pieces) left aboard the *Creole*. On behalf of Bahamas Attorney General George Campbell Anderson, local attorney Thomas M. Mathews wrote to Captain Ensor demanding the return of the baggage belonging to fifty-four former slaves from the *Creole;* otherwise, legal proceedings would be instituted. Former First Officer Gifford received and responded to the letter because of the severity of Master Ensor's injuries. He knew of "no baggage on board belonging to the slaves . . . as he considered them cargo, and the property of their owners, and that if they had left anything on the brig it was the property also of their masters." He could have been quoting from Article 175 of the Louisiana Slave Code of 1824 which stipulated: "All that a slave possesses, belongs to his master; he possesses nothing of his own." Gifford then refused to allow the long boat to land the baggage.

---

[2] Cockburn to Bacon, November 15, 1841, Doc. G, Sen. Doc. No. 51, 8; copied in "*Thomas McCargo v. The New Orleans Insurance Company*," 237–238.

American Consul Bacon, however, advised against further obstruction because fifty-four law suits at a three-guinea fee apiece would be costly and probably a waste of time given the possibility of local, hostile juries. These would be "mostly composed of colored people." The customs officers brought their launch alongside and carried ashore all of the former slaves' baggage along with an unopened bale of blankets belonging to one of the passengers.[3]

The following day marked a week since the *Creole* had sailed into Nassau harbor. The brig had accrued expenses while it was lying up there. Captain Ensor proposed selling off the ship's stocks of barrels of beef, pork, and navy bread. These were no longer necessary because of the reduced "cargo," and there was a need to meet expenses. According to Consul Bacon, the local customs officer refused to allow the provisions to be landed, "unless the slaves which had been emancipated should be likewise entered as passengers." This condition was refused, and the provisions remained on board.[4]

---

[3] Nassau Protest, November 17, 1841, Sen. Doc. No. 51, 18–19; New Orleans Protest, December 2, 1841, Sen. Doc. No. 51, 44; copied in *"Thomas McCargo v. The New Orleans Insurance Company,"* 245; Gifford's testimony, *"Thomas McCargo v. The New Orleans Insurance Company,"* 215; Bacon's testimony, *"Thomas McCargo v. The New Orleans Insurance Company,"* 230–231; Louisiana Slave Code in Willie Lee Rose, ed., *A Documentary History of Slavery in North America* (Athens: University of Georgia Press, 1999), 176. For some influential studies of slaves' property notions, see Sidney Mintz, *Caribbean Transformations* (Baltimore: John Hopkins University Press, 1984); Ira Berlin & Philip D. Morgan, eds., *Cultivation and Culture: Labor and the Shaping of Slave Life in the Americas* (Charlottesville: University of Virginia Press, 1993); Dylan C. Penningroth, *The Claims of Kinfolk: African American Property and Community in the Nineteenth-Century South* (Chapel Hill: University of North Carolina Press, 2003). For local jurors' bias in seventeenth-century Gloustershire, England, see David Underdown, *Revel, Riot, & Rebellion: Popular Politics and Culture in England 1603–1660* (London: Oxford University Press, 1985), 111. For common jurors' favorable views on poachers in Staffordshire, England, see Douglas Hay, "Poaching and the Game Laws on Cannock Chase," in *Albion's Fatal Tree: Crime and Society in Eighteenth-Century England*, eds., Douglas Hay, Peter Linebaugh, John G. Rule, E.P. Thompson, and Cal Winslow (London: Pantheon Books, 1975), 211. For the problem of favorable bias toward police officers by secretive grand juries in Missouri and New York concerning the killings of Michael Brown and Eric Garner in 2014, see Patrik Jonsson, "In Wake of Eric Garner Case, Should Grand Jury System Be Reformed?" *Christian Science Monitor*, December 6, 2014, http://www.csmonitor.com/USA/Justice/2014/1206/In-wake-of-Eric-Garner-case-should-grand-jury-system-be-reformed-video

[4] New Orleans Protest, December 2, 1841, Sen. Doc. No. 51, 44; copied in *"Thomas McCargo v. The New Orleans Insurance Company,"* 245; Gifford's testimony, *"Thomas McCargo v. The New Orleans Insurance Company,"* 215–216; Bacon's testimony, *"Thomas McCargo v. The New Orleans Insurance Company,"* 231. Yet the title of

By the middle of the second week, there was not much more reason for the *Creole* to stay anchored in Nassau harbor. The rebels were incarcerated in the city jail and were not going to be returned. Those who had not been involved in the revolt were now at liberty ashore and would not be returned to American slavery. Five captives remained aboard. Gifford identified them as thirty-year-old Rachel Glover, thirteen-year-old Mary, two unnamed women, and a boy who was the son of one of the women.[5] The documents suggest Gifford was mistaken. Rachel Glover was twenty-four years old and was accompanied by her nine-year-old son Isah. Mary E. Scroggins was an eighteen-year-old female. The two other women remain anonymous.[6] These five people never left the vessel, with the two women remaining in the hold for the entire time. According to Gifford, "they did not wish such freedom as there was there; they preferred coming to their masters."[7] This refusal to leave the *Creole* has perplexed some writers.[8] Without their own words, we will never know why they acted the way they did. But there are some hints. Thomas McCargo was shipping Mary, Rachel, and Isah to New Orleans. These captives could well have left or have been joining family members. On the other hand, Wiley Glover was a twenty-two-year-old male who decided to take his chances in Nassau. Was he Rachel's partner or from the same plantation?[9]

Since Captain Ensor was too wounded to travel, Chief Mate Gifford assumed command of the *Creole*. On Wednesday, the new master was cleared by the Customs House to leave Nassau harbor. He was required to sign an

---

the 1842 Senate Executive Document read "In compliance with . . . and the liberation of the slaves who were passengers in the said vessel," Sen. Doc. No. 51, 1.

[5] "*Thomas McCargo v. The New Orleans Insurance Company*," 217; George and Willene Hendrick, *The Creole Mutiny: A Tale of Revolt Aboard a Slave Ship* (Chicago: Ivan R. Dee, 2003), 108.

[6] See Appendix 3; list of McCargo's nineteen slaves, docket No. 4408, NOPL.

[7] Gifford's testimony, "*Thomas McCargo v. The New Orleans Insurance Company*," 217.

[8] Hendrick and Hendrick, *Creole Mutiny*, 107. Anita Rupprecht refers to the "complications" of gender, but the vast majority of female captives opted for freedom. See Rupprecht, " 'All We Have Done, We Have Done for Freedom': The *Creole* Slave-Ship Revolt (1841) and the Revolutionary Atlantic," *Internationaal Instituut voor Sociale Geschiedenis*. vol. 58 (2013), 276. For an evocative treatment of such complications in the tragic story of fugitive Margaret Warner and the killing of her toddler daughter in the mid-western United States in 1856, see Nikki M. Taylor, *Driven Toward Madness: The Fugitive Slave Margaret Garner and Tragedy on the Ohio* (Athens: Ohio University Press, 2016).

[9] See Appendix 3.

oath – standard policy in the region – not to bring away "British subjects from the island," under penalty of $2,000 in US dollars and twelve months imprisonment.[10] This was an obvious reference to the former captives who were now de jure British subjects. Captain Gifford gained the services of two additional unnamed seamen and on Friday, November 19, the *Creole* departed Nassau harbor for New Orleans. The vessel arrived in the Crescent City on the second day of December 1841, minus its captain, one passenger, and captives.[11] What had begun as a typical coastwise slaving voyage had resulted in a series of remarkable events: a slave ship revolt; a week's stoppage in Nassau harbor; the incarceration of rebels; the self-liberation of the captives; and the transformation of former American slaves into British colonial subjects.

The day before the *Creole* left Nassau for New Orleans saw the departure of the schooner *Francis Cockburn* owned by Bahamas police inspector John Pinder. The British vessel was reported to have carried between "fifty to sixty colored people," including "between forty and fifty of whom were slaves from the Creole." The merchant ship headed for the British colony of Jamaica, more than 490 miles away to the southwest. Another vessel with former captives from the *Creole* was scheduled to leave on December 4.[12] According to an unsigned letter that appeared in the South Carolina newspaper *Charleston Courier* on December 9, 1841, these liberated slaves were unwelcome in the adjacent colony. Having arrived in Kingston, "with about 60 or 70 negroes . . . a portion of those taken into Nassau by the brig *Creole*," the schooner anchored in the harbor. The passengers, continues the letter, "were looked upon as a gang of murderers, and the inhabitants did not appear disposed to have anything to do with them."[13] The article was unclear on who exactly thought the arrivals were murderers. It provided no concrete evidence of local Jamaicans' reactions. The fact, furthermore, that the

---

[10] Gifford's testimony, "*Thomas McCargo* v. *The New Orleans Insurance Company*," 216.

[11] New Orleans Protest, December 2, 1841, Sen. Doc. No. 51, 46; Bacon to Webster, November 30, 1841, Sen. Doc. No. 51, 4; Bacon's testimony, "*Thomas McCargo* v. *The New Orleans Insurance Company*," 231. Captain Ensor recovered from his injuries by the end of the month and was fit to travel to New Orleans.

[12] "*Thomas McCargo* v. *The New Orleans Insurance Company*," 232, 245; Bacon to Webster, November 30, 1841, Sen. Doc. No. 51, 4. A bounty of $30 each was paid on their arrival.

[13] Reprinted in *Richmond Enquirer* January 1, 1842, in Hendrick and Hendrick, *Creole Mutiny*, 108–109.

so-called murderers were under guard in Nassau appears to have escaped the attention of the writer.[14]

In contrast to those at liberty in Jamaica, the rebels remained incarcerated. They were transferred from the *Creole*'s longboat to the Nassau jail.[15] British imperial loyalist Joseph Eve had constructed this imposing edifice of local stone reaching four stories high between 1798 and 1800 in Parliament Square in downtown Nassau. Today, this tall, striking building is painted in bright pink with green window shutters silhouetted by blue skies and a bright yellow sun and is home to the Nassau Public Library. But it once served as the city jail until its conversion in 1873. Its fortified architecture consisting of steep walls, small windows and doors, and tiny rooms belies its bookish transformation. Its basement is still referred to as the "dungeon."[16]

The city's first jail also functioned as a correctional workhouse. The kitchen, privy, and water well stood outside the main structure. The octagonal-shaped building consisted of a ground floor, four wards or cells for prisoners, and one ward for turnkeys (jailers). There was also a storeroom. The second and third floors were similar. Brick reinforced the upper floor, presumably for security reasons. The seven dungeons underground resembled the cells above. At the end of 1841, the jail housed sixty inmates, including two white males, forty-six black males, and twelve black females. They shared nineteen sleeping cells, four solitary cells, and the dungeons. They labored from sunrise to sunset with the male inmates working on the roads and female inmates working on the walls. They were allowed an hour for breakfast and one hour for lunch, which consisted of grits, bread, and fish. The whip was reportedly not used on the prisoners while solitary was reserved for those guilty of flagrant violations of rules and regulations.[17]

The *1842 Colonial Blue Book* for Nassau jail contains no references to the *Creole* rebels. But it is extremely likely that they were among the incarcerated black males. They were probably detained in the dungeon. It is likely that the rebels were on their best behavior because they awaited

---

[14] A search at the National Library of Jamaica in Kingston in local newspapers for reports of these ships arriving in Kingston from Nassau proved fruitless.

[15] A 1788 map of Nassau shows the old jail located at the corner of Bay Street and Prison Lane. See Michael Craton, *A History of the Bahamas* (London: Collins, 1962), 171.

[16] "Nassau Public Library," Bahamas National Library and Information Services, http://www .bahamaslibraries.org/index.php?option=com_content&view=article&id=580:nassau-pub lic-library-in-new-providence&Itemid=119

[17] "Gaols & Prisoners," *1841 Bahamas Blue Book*, 1841, 98–102, CO 27/39, TNA.

FIGURE 7.1 The public library that was once a jail, Nassau.
Source: Photograph by the author, May 2015.

the outcome of their fate. Even so, their confinement must have brought back recent memories of incarceration in Richmond and Norfolk before they were transported aboard the floating prison. Indeed, the rebels' real condition at this particular time was not unlike that of those captives

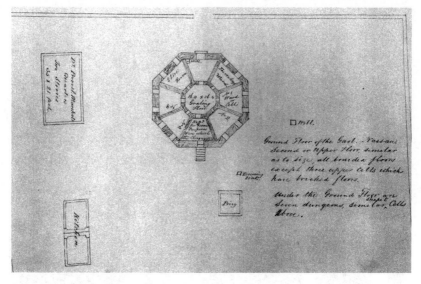

FIGURE 7.2 Plan of the jail in Nassau, 1842.
Source: Blue Book, Bahamas, 1842, Co 27/40, TNA.

successfully shipped to New Orleans who were imprisoned before being sold.[18]

In contrast to the celebrity status of the *Amistad* rebels who attracted thousands of temporary visitors to their New Haven jail,[19] the *Creole* rebels appear to have languished in relative obscurity. During their incarceration, George Grandy died from wounds sustained during the rebellion aboard the *Creole*. Adam Carnay also perished from what were described as "natural causes."[20] One wonders what these were. The *1842 Colonial Blue Book* does record the death of one male inmate, although the cause of death and his identity are not revealed.[21]

On January 31, 1842, British Colonial Secretary Lord Stanley wrote to Governor Cockburn informing him of the recent decision by the Law Lords on the *Creole* rebels. The British Empire's highest court concluded that:

---

[18] For comparison with the "transatlantic chain of incarceration" experienced by the *Amistad* rebels, see Marcus Rediker, *The Amistad Rebellion: An Atlantic Odyssey of Slavery and Freedom* (New York: Viking, 2012), 122.

[19] Rediker, *Amistad Rebellion*, chap. 4.

[20] Anderson's testimony, Nassau Commission, April 1842, in "*Thomas McCargo v. The New Orleans Insurance Company*," 250; Hendrick and Hendrick, *Creole Mutiny*, 9, 109.

[21] "Gaols & Prisoners," *1841 Bahamas Blue Book*, 1841, 98–102, CO 27/39, TNA.

The facts alledged [*sic*] do not bear out the charge of Piracy against the Negroes who compelled the crew of the 'Creole' to alter her course and take her into a British port, and that the offence committed by them not amounting to Piracy, and being committed by Foreigners on board a Foreign vessel, cannot be tried either by the Court of Commissioners constituted under Act 46, Geo 3, C., p 54 or by any other court of justice in that colony, or in any part of Her Majesty's dominions.[22]

In short, the rebels were not pirates, and their actions fell outside of the jurisdiction of the local colonial court. This was quite a punt up field! Having informed the governor of the court's ruling, the colonial secretary ended with expressing Her Majesty's Government's approbation for Cockburn's actions: "It affords me much pleasure to be enabled to convey to you the reassurances that HMG entirely approve of the course which you have taken in the difficult circumstances in which you were called upon to act on your own responsibility."[23] This official accolade must have warmed the cockles of the heart of the careerist colonial bureaucrat.

On April 16, 1842, a special session of the Court of Admiralty met in Nassau to decide the fate of the rebels.[24] Begun during the seventeenth century to adjudicate small maritime disputes, this judicial body blossomed into a major imperial conduit of power in the eighteenth century. During the early years of the nineteenth century, it appears to have played an important role in legal disputes concerning Spanish citizens' involvement in the Atlantic slave trade to Cuba. Chief Justice William Vesey Munnings even described the Bahamas as "'the Turnpike Road to the [slave] market of Cuba.'"[25] By mid-nineteenth century, however, it had reverted to its former shadowy past pattern of meeting only selectively. Its modus operandi was adjudicating cases dealing with British subjects or with those from foreign nations who had been detained under British law.[26] The consideration of charges against the *Creole* rebels caused one

---

[22] Lord Stanley to Governor Cockburn, January 31, 1842, RP6981/13, Aberdeen Papers, BL. See also Edward D. Jervey and C. Harold Huber, "The Creole Affair," *The Journal of Negro History* vol. 65, no. 3 (Summer 1980), 206. The *Amistad* rebels initially faced charges of piracy and murder but these were subsequently dropped. See Rediker, *Amistad Rebellion*, 131–132.

[23] Lord Stanley to Governor Cockburn, January 31, 1842, RP6981/13, Aberdeen Papers, BL.

[24] Governor Cockburn to Lord Aberdeen, April 5, 1842, Bahamas Ledger, Vol. 1, January to December 1842, page 125, CO 23/112, TNA.

[25] Rosanne Marion Adderley, *"New Negroes from Africa": Slave Trade Abolition and Free African Settlement in the Nineteenth-Century Caribbean* (Bloomington: Indiana University Press, 2006), 27.

[26] Michael Craton, "Caribbean Vice Admiralty Courts and British Imperialism," in *Empire, Enslavement, and Freedom in the Caribbean* (Kingston: Ian Randle, 1997), 104–116;

such occasional convocation. It is unclear why the local authorities waited so long to meet and adjudicate, especially since the colonial secretary had previously passed along the Law Lords decision to the governor. The Special Session met. The detained "Americans" were brought into court in custody. The attorney general on behalf of the US consul reported that the accused should be "committed by the court for trial for piracy." He proceeded to submit documents consisting of prior depositions taken from the *Creole* officers and crew by British officials in Nassau harbor. The court adjourned for at least an hour. The Chief Justice returned and

delivered the unanimous decision of the court that their [*sic*] being nothing detailed in the deposition which had been submitted which would in any way warrant the court in supposing that an act of piracy had been committed. The court did not feel justified in granting the application which had been made by the Att[orney] Gen[eral] at the insistence of the American Consul – and having stated this they/the parties who had been detained/ were discharged accordingly under the usual proclamation.

As a consequence of a lack of sufficient evidence, the judges liberated the surviving seventeen insurrectionists lodged in Nassau jail. The Chief Justice informed them: "It has pleased God to set you free from the bonds of slavery; may you hereafter lead the lives of good and faithful subjects of Her Majesty's Government." The governor wrote to the colonial secretary in London the following day informing him of the Nassau court's meeting, decision, and the acquittal of the rebels.[27]

The words of one of the Bahamas' leading jurists are noteworthy. Slave emancipation was divine inspiration – with the British as its overseers.[28]

Richard Huzzey, *Freedom Burning: Anti-Slavery and Empire in Victorian Britain* (Ithaca, NY: Cornell University Press, 2012), 46. For a map of Vice Admiralty Courts in the British Atlantic, see page 48 of Huzzey's book.

[27] Governor Cockburn to Lord Stanley, 17 April 1842, Bahamas Ledger, Vol. 1, January to December 1842, page 151, CO 23/112, TNA; Anderson's testimony, Nassau Commission, April 1842, in "*Thomas McCargo v. The New Orleans Insurance Company*," 250; Cockburn to Stanley, April 17, 1842; Hendrick and Hendrick, *Creole Mutiny*, 109–110; Jervey and Huber, "*Creole* Affair," 206.

[28] Compare to the following: "This result [of West Indian emancipation] was accomplished without the loss of a single life or the firing of a gun, or disturbance of any kind, simply by the silent operation of a law enacted some four thousand miles away, upon the other side of the wide and stormy Atlantic, by which all the enslaved Bahama [*sic*] negroes were changed from chattels into men, and became at once free citizens of that great empire which circles the world, and upon which the sun never sets." James H. Stark's *History of and Guide to the Bahama Islands* (Boston: Photo-Electrolyte Company, 1891), 193. The wittiest anti-colonial riposte to the author's final sentiment was that the reason why the sun never set on the empire was because God did not trust the British in the dark!

The new subjects were expected to be well behaved much like children or wards. This was clearly a response to some of the difficulties experienced in the transition from slavery to apprenticeship and emancipation in the British West Indies during the 1830s.[29] Most important, local imperial administrators demanded loyalty to the empire from these former rebels in exchange for the gift of emancipation that they had provided.

What happened to these new colonial subjects? According to one account, we shall never know these "stories written on water."[30] But the evocative metaphor is a poor substitute for robust research and historical analysis. Digging in the local archives reveals information about these former rebels and captives and their interactions and encounters with local Bahamians. Indeed, one of the central objectives of this chapter is to explain the meaning of colonial freedom uncovered through tracking regional encounters between the *Creole*'s newly freed, Bahamian Creoles, and liberated Africans.

The slave economy in the Bahamas was mixed. In 1815, it is estimated that there were four classes of enslaved workers: seamen, domestics, farm laborers, and plantation workers. On the eve of colonial abolition, there were about 2,250 slaves in New Providence of whom 1,182 were female and 1,068 were male. Some 47 percent were identified as domestics, 7 percent as tradesmen, and the work of 20 percent remains unclear. About 12 percent worked in the fields tending livestock and producing corn, potatoes, yams, fruit, okra, cassava, and onions. These unfree agricultural workers did not cultivate sugar or cotton. About 12 percent were mariners. A number of them would have been among the boatmen surrounding the *Creole* in Nassau harbor.[31]

Although the British legislated emancipation in 1833, the complete legal abolition of colonial slavery did not occur until 1838. Local slave-holders were compensated for the colony's 10,110 slaves. One of those who held the most was John Rolle who was paid for the loss of the lifetime labor of 376 slaves. With emancipation the estates were broken up and a new labor force was formed. This new labor force expanded through the influx of liberated Africans. It has been estimated that, between 1833 and

---

[29] Jeffrey R. Kerr-Ritchie, *Rites of August First: Emancipation in the Black Atlantic World* (Baton Rouge: Louisiana State University Press, 2007), chap. 1.

[30] Hendrick and Hendrick, *Creole Mutiny*, 110. Jonathan Levy also assumes the rebels and former captives disappeared from the historical record. See Levy, *Freaks of Fortune: The Emerging World of Capitalism and Risk in America* (Cambridge: Harvard University Press, 2012), 27.

[31] Michael Craton and Gail Saunders, *Islanders in the Stream: A History of the Bahamian People* vol. 1 (Athens, Ga.: University of Georgia Press, 1992), chap. 16.

1838, six ships deposited their human cargoes in Nassau.[32] This was the transitional world of former slavery and emerging emancipation entered into by former captives aboard the *Creole* in 1841.

The documents on the *Creole* used in Appendix 3 reveal particular work skills of captives. It is likely that this knowledge helped make freedom work. Lucy Beldin and Lucy French had washing and ironing skills. These probably helped them earn a living as they worked in exchange for cash or goods in local economies. George Butt was a blacksmith. His skills in the forge were probably much sought after by locals. Elizabeth Muerdough and Melvina Wilson were both seamstresses. Their skills with sewing, darning, and re-furbishing old clothes were no doubt useful as a means to earn a living.[33]

Moreover, the oral tradition throws remarkable light on a number of the *Creole* rebels and former captives and on what happened to them when freedom came. In 1970, prominent Bahamian archivist and historian Dr. Gail Saunders interviewed Arthur Fernandez.[34] He was born in the village of Gambier. Situated nine miles west of Nassau, Gambier (named after a prominent mid-eighteenth century British colonial official) was settled by liberated Africans – so-called "new Negroes" – during the 1830s. It was located on the coastline and consisted of no more than eight to ten houses built of wattle and daub, lime, stones and sand, with thatched roofs. The families farmed and fished and marketed their produce in nearby Nassau.[35] Mr. Fernandez recalled the story of the *Creole*. According to him, the "old Creole come in here by the crew on board the ship." They thought they were going to Surinam, "so they made a fuss aboard the boat and get a fight." They took over the boat, and made the shipmaster bring

---

[32] Craton, *History of the Bahamas*, chap. 18.

[33] See Appendix 3. Recent historical scholarship on slaves' knowledge challenges an older idea that enslaved Africans brought only their bodies and not their minds to work in the New World. See Judith Carney, *Black Rice: The African Origins of Rice Cultivation in the Americas* (Cambridge, MA: Harvard University Press, 2001); Frederick C. Knight, *Working the Diaspora: The Impact of African Labor on the Anglo-American World, 1650–1850* (New York, NY: New York University Press, 2010); Jorge Canizares-Esguerra, Matt Childs, James Sidbury, eds., *The Black Urban Atlantic in the Age of the Slave Trade* (Philadelphia, PA: University of Pennsylvania Press, 2013); Daniel B. Rood, *The Reinvention of Atlantic Slavery: Technology Labor, Race, and Capitalism in the Greater Caribbean* (New York, NY: Oxford University Press, 2017).

[34] Interview with Mr. Arthur Fernandez, Gambier Village, September 11, 1970, Gail Saunders, eighteen pages, Oral History Transcripts Collection, Department of Archives, Nassau, Bahamas.

[35] Gail Saunders, *Gambier Village: A Brief History* (UNESCO, Nassau, Bahamas, 2007), 7; Patrice Williams, *A Guide to African Villages in New Providence* (Nassau, Bahamas: Dept. of Archives, 1979), 13–14.

them to Nassau "because Nassau was free and the government took them of and he [the captain] couldn't compel them to stay."[36] Despite getting the destination wrong, the local villager accurately recalled the maritime revolt and the ship's voyage to the Bahamas.

Dr. Saunders asked the aged resident of Gambier if he was familiar with the names of the *Creole*'s slaves. These came from a list provided by Mrs. Greer who accompanied the historian. Many of the names of the former captives were unfamiliar to Mr. Fernandez. He could not recall the names of Reuben Knight, Dr. Ruffin, George Podlock [Portlock], Addison Tyler, America Woddice [Woodis], Sherman [Benjamin] Johnson, George Benton [Burton], Ivan Crawley, William [Williams] Jenkins, Phil[ip] Jones, Peter Smallwood, Walter Brown, and Horace Beverley.[37] It is possible these names were unfamiliar to Mr. Fernandez because the people did not settle in the village of Gambier. On the other hand, Mr. Fernandez was familiar with the names of many others from the *Creole* and where they settled. He said that Mr. Reid, Mr. [Peter] Smallwood, and Jordan [Jourdan] Phillips settled in Nassau. Mr. [Henry] White went to Lyford Cay. Andrew Moss stayed between Lyford Cay and Mount Pleasant. Richard Butler settled in the Outer Islands where he reared a son called Milo Butler. Willy [Wiley] Glover (shared surname with Rachel who had stayed on the *Creole*) went to Inagua. The interviewee recalled Pompey Garrison who did not settle in Gambier.[38]

The striking thing about these settlement patterns was their geographical spread across New Providence as well as the Outer Islands of the Bahamas. The Bahamas archipelago consists of some 29 islands, 661 cays, and 2,387 rocks, with a total land area of 4,404 square miles – about the same size as Jamaica or half that of Wales.[39] This points to the proximity of the colony as well as the dispersal of the new colonial subjects in search of free lives and greater security. We cannot overlook the importance of these former captives becoming islanders in the stream because of fear of possible repatriation back to American slavery.[40]

---

[36] Fernandez to Saunders, oral interview, 3.

[37] Ibid, 3–6. I have followed the original spelling of the names in the oral transcript. The names of Reuben Knight, Ivan Crawley, and Walter Brown are absent from the *Creole*'s shipping documents in Appendix 3.

[38] Ibid. Mr. Reid and Andrew Moss are also not listed in the documents.

[39] Craton, *History of Bahamas*, 11.

[40] One of the most memorable moments in Marcus Rediker's terrific historical documentary is an encounter between the film crew and local Mende villagers and the latter's fears of retribution from visiting whites because of their ancestor's successful rebellious actions. See *Ghosts of Amistad: In the Footsteps of the Rebels*, directed by Tony Buba (Pittsburgh, PA: University of Pittsburgh, 2014), DVD.

Mr. Fernandez recalled that one neighboring family, called Morris, traced their lineage back to *Creole* rebel leader Elijah Morris. After being released from the Nassau jail in April 1842, Morris settled in the village of Gambier. According to Mr. Fernandez, the Morris family was quite prolific because Elijah:

had two daughters and three sons, he had Alexander, and Elijah junior and Christianna, and Virginia children that he had, well, they have a few of them here now, but the most of them Morris went after they grow, they father died of, then grand-father died and then they daddy married and had these boys and girls, all of them trail back to America, and all all [sic] boys died save Alice and the two daughters, that Alexander had, and she died in America, all of them.[41]

These naming patterns for his children suggest that the past was not simply the past for Elijah. It is also revealing that many of the kin ended up returning to the United States, presumably long after the abolition of slavery in the 1860s. Mr. Fernandez recalled the old domestic ruins that were still standing. Elijah's son, Alexander, had about six children. He sold the place in 1923 to Herbert McKinney and died in 1928. According to the interviewee, the grandchildren did not recall their famous rebel grandfather Elijah Morris.[42] It also seems that Mr. Fernandez did not know him, although the families were close neighbors. "He used to go long together together [sic] lived right over here and grand-father and my daddy and them lived just next door." "They were old neighbors," he added.[43]

Along with settling in Gambier and raising a family, the former *Creole* rebel leader also became a landholder. Mr. Fernandez recollects he came out and bought "this place from the government."[44] According to Dr. Saunders, Morris obtained three land grants of five acres apiece in the village in 1859, 1864, and 1879.[45] The Crown Grants Land Index records the last of these three purchases.[46] On August 15, 1879, Morris visited the Registrar of Records in downtown Nassau and officially registered lots two and three in the village of Gambier for the fee of three pounds, two shillings, and ten pence (GBP 288 today). A copy of this deed was made on May 6, 1901. A plan of the village of Gambier shows at least three adjacent lots of five acres each belonging to Morris. This plan also shows the proximity of the Fernandez family, confirming they were neighbors.[47] Most important to the Morris family was that this acreage

[41] Fernandez to Saunders, oral interview, 7.   [42] Ibid, 8.   [43] Ibid.   [44] Ibid.
[45] Saunders, *Gambier Village*, 10.
[46] Registrar General's Department Index to Crown Grants, 1862–1944, Department of Archives, Nassau, Bahamas.
[47] Elijah Morris, land deed, August 15, 1879, Crown Grants, Book 9, page 225; Plan of the Village of Gambier, surveyed E. Aranha, December 1918, Produced by Survey and Mapping Section, Lands and Surveys Dept., P.O. Box 592, Nassau.

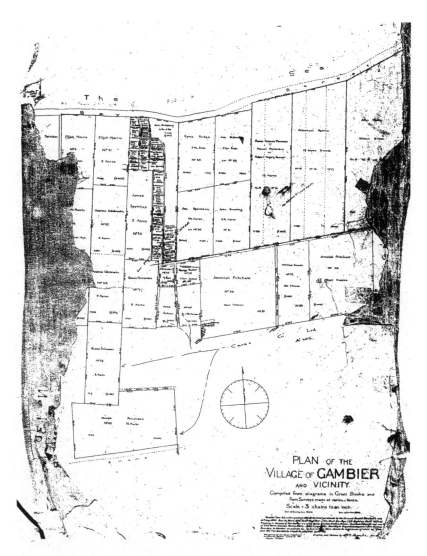

FIGURE 7.3 Plan of Gambier Village, New Providence Island, Bahamas, n.d. Note the proximity of the Morris and Fernandez households.
Source: Photographs, Department of Land and Surveys, Plans of Villages, Nassau, Bahamas National Archives.

bestowed a degree of independence vastly removed from the rebel's former dependent condition of enslavement to a Virginia trader.

What was village life like in post-emancipation New Providence? The village of Carmichael, named after a former British governor, stood

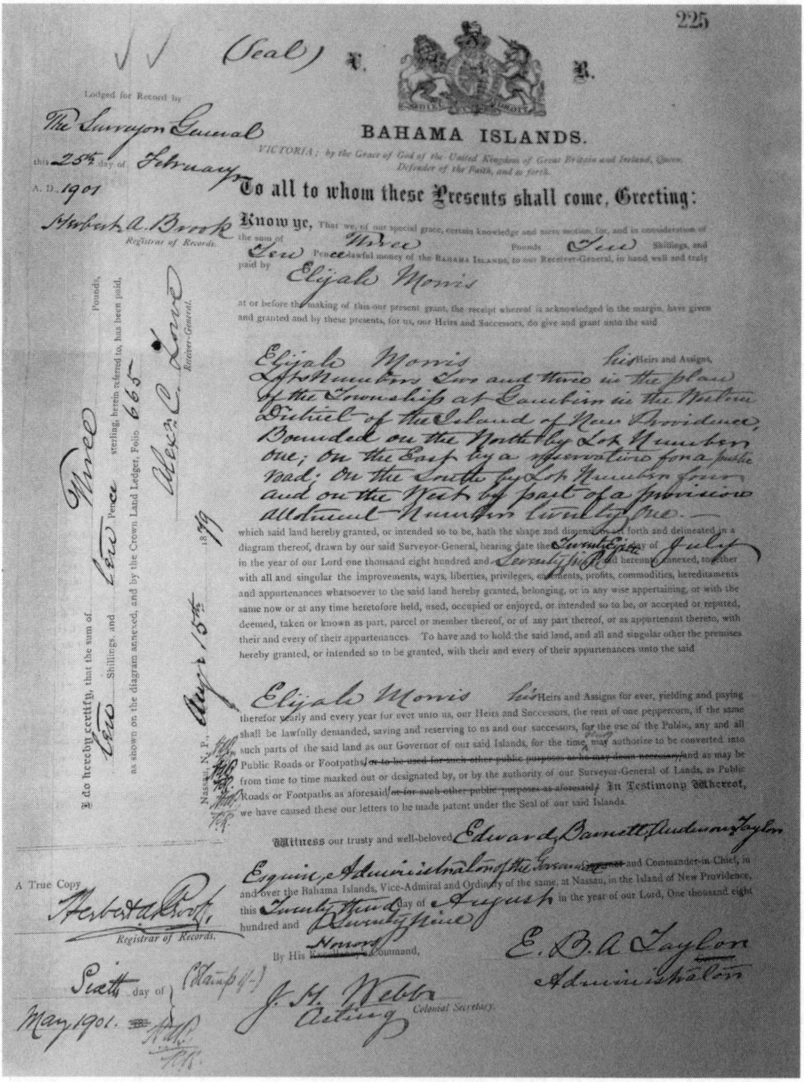

225

(Seal) V. R.

BAHAMA ISLANDS.

VICTORIA; by the Grace of God of the United Kingdom of Great Britain and Ireland, Queen, Defender of the Faith, and so forth.

Lodged for Record by The Surveyor General this 25th day of February A.D. 1901 Herbert A. Brook Registrar of Records.

To all to whom these Presents shall come, Greeting:

Know ye, That we, of our special grace, certain knowledge and mere motion, for, and in consideration of the sum of Three Pounds Ten Shillings, and Ten Pence lawful money of the Bahama Islands, to our Receiver-General, in hand well and truly paid by Elijah Morris at or before the making of this our present grant, the receipt whereof is acknowledged in the margin, have given and granted and by these presents, for us, our Heirs and Successors, do give and grant unto the said Elijah Morris his Heirs and Assigns, Lots Numbers Two and three in the plan of the Township at Gambier in the Western District of the Island of New Providence, Bounded on the North by Lot Number one; On the East by a reservation for a public road; On the South by Lot Number four and on the West by part of a provision allotment Number twenty one. which said land hereby granted, or intended so to be, hath the shape and dimensions set forth and delineated in a diagram thereof, drawn by our said Surveyor-General, bearing date the Twenty Eighth day of July in the year of our Lord one thousand eight hundred and Seventy Nine and hereunto annexed, together with all and singular the improvements, ways, liberties, privileges, easements, profits, commodities, hereditaments and appurtenances whatsoever to the said land hereby granted, belonging, or in any wise appertaining, or with the same now or at any time heretofore held, used, occupied or enjoyed, or intended so to be, or accepted or reputed, deemed, taken or known as part, parcel or member thereof, or of any part thereof, or as appurtenant thereto, with their and every of their appurtenances. To have and to hold the said land, and all and singular other the premises hereby granted, or intended so to be granted, with their and every of their appurtenances unto the said Elijah Morris his Heirs and Assigns for ever, yielding and paying therefor yearly and every year for ever unto us, our Heirs and Successors, the rent of one peppercorn, if the same shall be lawfully demanded, saving and reserving to us and our successors, for the use of the Public, any and all such parts of the said land as our Governor of our said Islands, for the time being may authorize to be converted into Public Roads or Footpaths ~~or to be used for such other public purposes as he may deem necessary~~ and as may be from time to time marked out or designated by, or by the authority of our Surveyor-General of Lands, as Public Roads or Footpaths as aforesaid ~~or for such other public purposes as aforesaid~~. **In Testimony Whereof,** we have caused these our letters to be made patent under the Seal of our said Islands.

Witness our trusty and well-beloved Edward Barnett Anderson Taylor Esquire, Administrator of the Government and Commander-in-Chief, in and over the Bahama Islands, Vice-Admiral and Ordinary of the same, at Nassau, in the Island of New Providence, this Twenty third day of August in the year of our Lord, One thousand eight hundred and Seventy Nine

By His Honor's Command,

J. H. Webb Acting Colonial Secretary.

E. B. A. Taylor Administrator

I do hereby certify, that the sum of Three Pounds, Ten Shillings, and Ten Pence sterling, herein referred to, has been paid, as shown on the diagram annexed, and by the Crown Land Ledger, Folio 665

Alex. C. Love Receiver-General.

Nassau, N.P., Augt 15th 1879

A True Copy Herbert A. Brook, Registrar of Records.

Sixth day of May 1901.

FIGURE 7.4 Elijah Morris's land grant, Gambier Village, August 23, 1879. Source: Index to Crown Grants, 1862–1944, Registrar General's Department, Nassau.

7 to 10 miles outside Nassau. It was settled in 1824 by a group of enslaved Africans liberated from transatlantic slavers by ships of the Royal Navy. The settlers engaged in subsistence farming and in road works under local

government supervision. In the years immediately following colonial abolition, local officials used public funds to provide religious and secular education to the liberated Africans. An Anglican minister and military doctor periodically visited and a teacher resided permanently in the village. Colonial Secretary Charles R. Nesbit sought to protect the settlers from white visitors. His official notice published in the November 26, 1836, edition of the *Royal Gazette* declared: "All Persons are hereby warned from trespassing upon the premises at Roslyn, Carmichael, the African Hospital, or any other settlement occupied by the liberated Africans."[48] The population of the village increased as a consequence of settling more liberated Africans during the late 1830s. Former American slaves from the *Creole* were to soon join them.[49]

In 1831, the governor of the Bahamas settled about 150 liberated Africans in their own village of Adelaide about 16 miles from Nassau in southwest New Providence. The village was named after the wife of British monarch William IV and was designed primarily to foster independent cultivation and living. In the governor's own descriptive words, "there is a small creek which abounds with fish; and after a certain length of time, partly by cultivating the ground & partly by fishing they will be able to take care of themselves."[50] He also authorized the Collector of Customs to "hire an overseer & a few intelligent free black people to remain with them for the present & instruct them in cultivating the ground." Historian Rosanne Adderley accurately summarizes the significance of this type of settlement for its "important dynamic of culturally and socially distinct newly arrived Africans beginning Caribbean lives with the opportunity to take some clues from the more long-standing black population."[51] At the same time, however, "civilizing practices" in the guise of school teachers and the Anglican Church were never far away. The November 11, 1835, edition of the *Bahama Argus* reported that the Infant school at Adelaide:

under the care of Miss Scott, is improving; the number of children attending is about 20. Some of them have learned the Alphabet, and are spelling words of 3

---

[48] *Royal Gazette*, November 26, 1836, in Michael Craton and Gail Saunders, *Islanders in the Stream: A History of the Bahamian People*, vol. 2. *From the Ending of Slavery to the Twenty-First Century* (Athens, Ga.: University of Georgia Press, 1998).

[49] Adderley, *"New Negroes from Africa,"* 53, 121, 253n33; Craton and Saunders, *Islanders in the Stream*, vol. 2, "liberated Africans" (8).

[50] Governor James Carmichael-Smyth to Lord Viscount Goderich, July 22, 1831, in Adderley, *"New Negroes from Africa,"* 56.

[51] Adderley, *"New Negroes from Africa,"* 56.

letters, are spending part of the day in reading, and attending to the various lessons that are taught; and part in learning to sew. When it is remembered that these children of African parents were growing up in ignorance of all that is useful and good, and to whom the English language was almost unknown, the [Adelaide Committee of the African Board] cannot but regard the establishment of School among them as one of the most valuable favors which they have received from the British nation.[52]

It is probable that several years later American-born children joined these African-born children in learning their letters, becoming literate, and gaining a formal education for the first time in their young lives.[53]

In 1831, the village of Gambier – named after a former colonial official – was begun on Crown land tracts. Resting about 9 miles from Nassau on the West Bay road, it was settled predominantly by liberated Africans. They were a long way from their birthplaces in West Africa, but had only briefly experienced slavery at sea. As one authority summarizes, they: "retained their ethnic identity and sense of community almost intact, and their livelihood was guaranteed by the ample stretches of unpatented land on which their people could squat and farm and by the nearby fishing grounds." The communal buildings included single-story churches and schools, the first stone building being for the police and jail. Many of the homes were no more than huts, and many were: "little better than collections of boards knocked together and thatched with palmetto straw, with just a bed, table and chair, and a few cooking utensils, by way of furniture."[54] Despite the humble surroundings, however, the family unit predominated. Numerous women marketed goods such as vegetables, fruits, shell work, straw hats, and market garden produce in downtown Nassau's main market. Produce from Gambier – and also Adelaide and Carmichael – was usually brought up to Nassau market either on a donkey cart or by shanks mare (walking) once or twice a week. Former captives from the *Creole* must have enjoyed what for them was this new way of life, especially Elijah Morris.[55]

Gail Saunders' fascinating interview with Mr. Fernandez, combined with land deed records, plans of villages, photographs, and a rich local

---

[52] *Bahama Argus*, November 11, 1835, in Craton and Saunders, *Islanders in the Stream*, vol. 2, 8.

[53] Adderley, *"New Negroes from Africa,"* 18, 56–57; Craton and Saunders, *Islanders in the Stream*, vol. 2, "British nation," 8.

[54] Ibid.

[55] Craton and Saunders, *Islanders in the Stream*, vol. 2, 8, 101–130, "fishing grounds" and "way of furniture" (103). The authors employ a vague adverb when they write that the liberated Africans "almost" retained their ethnic and communal identity. Did their short

Bahamian history, throws a spotlight on the post-emancipation village movement as well on those who gained their freedom from the *Creole* revolt. But many questions remain unanswered. Some of those who were liberated stayed close together, but why did so many branch off to different destinations? How did Morris obtain the funding to purchase land in the village of Gambier? We can assume that land was cheap and he earned enough from farming and fishing, but this is not certain. Most important, what precisely were the social interactions between these former captives born in the United States and newly liberated Africans? The villages of Gambier, Grant's Town, Bain's Town, Adelaide, and Fox Hill were all settled by Africans liberated from Atlantic slavers during the 1830s.[56] It is conceivable that some of these residents lined the shores, manned boats in Nassau harbor preventing the *Creole* from leaving the harbor, ferried the former captives to shore, and marched with them up to the police station for registration as new British subjects. Many of those who left the vessel ended up in these villages. Perhaps these former American captives found Africa while the liberated Africans found America in the Bahamas?[57]

The liberation of the former captives from the *Creole* in Nassau in late 1841 marked the end of chattel servitude for a small group of people. But it also signaled the culmination of a major diplomatic crisis between the United States and Great Britain. Ever since the seventeenth century, London ruled over a colonial slave empire in mainland North American and the Caribbean. Since the 1770s, this slave empire had been considerably diminished by the successful formation of the United States. By the 1830s, this Caribbean empire had been transformed into an antislavery empire committed to the prevention of slave trading and by extension to the monitoring of slave societies in Brazil, Cuba, and United States. It also opposed slave societies in general as a means to protect free labor in sugar plantation production. The one glaring exception, of course, was slave-produced cotton vital to Lancashire factories and the British economy.

experience with slavery at sea really make that much of a difference to them as individuals or as people? How to compare their ethnic/communal identity with those born into American slavery?

[56] Williams, *Guide to African Villages*, 13–20; Howard Johnson, *The Bahamas in Slavery and Freedom* (Kingston: Ian Randle, 1991), 38; Adderley, *"New Negroes from Africa,"* chap. 1.

[57] For some all-to-brief comments on former American slaves' settlements across the British Atlantic Empire – from veterans in Trinidad to self-emancipators in Nova Scotia to settlers in Sierra Leone – and their becoming new colonial subjects, see Kerr-Ritchie, *Rites of August First*, 46–47; Kerr-Ritchie, *Freedom's Seekers*, 49, 58, 135.

During the same decades, the United States was aggressively expanding across the continent establishing and consolidating a slave empire. Slavery's cotton production drove the American economy. A number of its political representatives were slaveholders who acted as major power brokers in the executive, legislative, and judicial branches of government. The abolition of the transatlantic slave trade, together with the failure to attract European immigrants to the region, ensured that this empire would only survive with the transplanting of hundreds of thousands of enslaved people from the upper South to the lower South states. This entailed a Coastal Passage that juxtaposed expanding slave shores with free shores. The *Creole* revolt catapulted this dangerous proximity to the forefront of Anglo-American disagreement.

8

"A New State of Things"

On a hot Saturday evening in early August 1842, a number of dignitaries sat down to a sumptuous dinner at Swann House, American Secretary of State Daniel Webster's lavish mansion on H Street in Washington, DC. The guests included President John Tyler and his cabinet, British Special Envoy Lord Ashburton, British minister to Washington Henry Fox, commissioners from the states of Maine and Massachusetts, and several American senators. They met to celebrate the recent signing of the Webster-Ashburton Treaty on August 9. Secretary Webster raised his glass to "Queen Victoria! Long may she continue to reign over a prosperous and happy people." Lord Ashburton replied with the toast: "The President! Perpetuity to the institutions of the United States." President Tyler followed with: "The Commissioners! Blessed are the peace makers." Lord Ashburton expressed a "strong regard for his kinsmen on this side of the Atlantic," together with a wish to "see removed all causes of dispute between them and his countrymen at home." He concluded with an expression of confidence in the settlement of "all those controversies."[1]

The sense of relief in that stuffy dining room must have been palpable. The Webster-Ashburton Treaty settled several outstanding issues between Washington and London concerning disputed northeastern boundaries, the final suppression of the African slave trade, and extradition of fugitive criminals from justice. These "controversies" had been exacerbated by maritime tensions over the liberation of human cargoes from American

---

[1] *Richmond Enquirer*, August 12, 1842. America's peculiar institution was probably not included in Lord Ashburton's toast.

coastal slavers in British Caribbean ports culminating in the *Creole* revolt. The assumption that the 1842 treaty ended these maritime differences, however, is inaccurate.[2] The treaty never mentioned the *Creole* revolt and Anglo-American maritime clashes. Rather, its importance lay in preceding diplomatic exchanges revealing fundamental differences over slave trading, property rights, and maritime territorial sovereignty between two competing empires. Indeed, what marks the Webster-Ashburton Treaty is not that it settled the *Creole* case or that it successfully prevented a third Anglo-American conflict as claimed by some scholars, but rather that it crystalized an ongoing clash between a republican slave state and a colonial abolitionist state that remained unresolved.[3]

On January 11, 1842, US Senator John C. Calhoun of South Carolina issued a strongly worded resolution condemning local British interference with an American merchant ship and its human cargo. In response, President Tyler provided the Senate with letters from US Consul Bacon together with depositions from the *Creole*'s officers and crew. These documents clearly demonstrated that the local authorities in Nassau had interfered with the American merchant vessel and that the slave rebels, the purported murderers, and the rest of the slaves had been released with the full approbation of the British government.[4] This was unsatisfactory to Senator Calhoun who on Thursday February 3, 1842, rose in the upper chamber to condemn the Tyler administration for its failure to demand the "surrender of the murderers," even though the chief executive had been "in full possession of the facts" for more than a month. The Senate leader "believed our right to demand the surrender of the murderers clear, beyond doubt, and that, if the case was fairly stated, the British government would be compelled, from a sense of justice, to yield to our demand." There "was nothing more clear," the South Carolinian continued:

---

[2] "The case [*Creole*] would in time be settled diplomatically by Secretary of State Daniel Webster, assisted by the British, as part of his treaty negotiations with Lord Ashburton," Sean Wilenz, *The Rise of American Democracy: Jefferson to Lincoln* (New York: W. W. Norton, 2005), 556.

[3] E. D. Adams, "Lord Ashburton and the Treaty of Washington," *The American Historical Review* vol. 17, no. 4 (July 1912), 766, notes "a real danger of war," while Arthur T. Downey, *The Creole Affair: The Slave Rebellion That Led the U.S. and Great Britain to the Brink of War* (Lanham: Rowman and Littlefield, 2014), vii, maintains the treaty "was significant in deflecting the potential for a third US-UK war."

[4] Tyler to US Senate, January 19, 1842, Sen. Doc. No 51, 1842, 1.

than that according to the laws of nations, a vessel on the ocean is regarded as a portion of the territory of the State to which she belongs, and more emphatically so, if possible, in a coasting voyage; and that if forced into a friendly port by an unavoidable necessity, she loses none of the rights that belong to her on the ocean.[5]

By boarding the *Creole* and assuming control of the criminals rather than aiding the ship's crew to convey them to one of "our ports," the British acted against these "admitted principles." The senator's claim was unequivocal: any vessel and its property remained under the jurisdiction of the laws of the state with which it was registered – in this case the *Creole* and its human cargo – within any territorial waters.[6]

Senator Calhoun was only mouthing the indignation of his fellow Southern slaveholders concerning the protection of their sacred property rights. Secretary Webster responded to them by instructing Edward Everett, the US minister in London, to lodge an official protest with the British government and to request security against all future likely actions. The British Foreign Office (FO) formally acknowledged his note. At the same time, the FO commended the actions taken by Governor Francis Cockburn and others over the *Creole* altercation.[7]

Meanwhile, advocates of British colonial abolition defended their new imperial policy. In late January 1842, British Foreign Secretary Lord Aberdeen passed along dispatches and enclosures from the Bahamas about the *Creole* to members of Britain's highest court requesting that they rule on its key issues. The Law Lords identified six questions requiring resolution. Were the slave rebels liable? Were they "answerable" to an American court? Was Her Majesty's Government (HMG) required to "deliver up" these rebels under international law? Were the local authorities in the Bahamas in breach of international or British laws? Was the US consul accurate in his assertions of the principles of law? Could the customs officials at Nassau lawfully grant the *Creole* clearance with a cargo of slaves?[8]

After a few days deliberation, the venerable jurists responded to the British government's request, and provided answers to their own set of six

---

[5] *Congressional Globe*, 27th Congress, 2nd Session, December 6, 1841 to August 31, 1842, in Jervey and Huber, "Creole Affair," 205.

[6] *Congressional Globe*, 27th Congress, 2nd Session, December 6, 1841 to August 31, 1842, 203; Edward D. Jervey and C. Harold Huber, "The Creole Affair," *The Journal of Negro History* vol. 65, no. 3 (Summer 1980), 205.

[7] Adams, "Lord Ashburton," 774.

[8] Dodson, Pollock, Follett to Stanley, January 29, 1842, enclosed in Stanley to Cockburn, January 31, 1842, Reserve Photocopy (hereafter RP) 6981/13, Aberdeen Papers, BL.

questions. First, the slave rebels were not liable either in "that Colony or [any] other part of the Queen's dominions." In other words, Britain's antislavery empire was as extensive and far-reaching as Senator Calhoun's American empire of slavery. Moreover, the rebels were not pirates because their "sole objective" was to compel the American crew to take them "to some Port where they might obtain their Freedom." Second, an American court was responsible for adjudicating an offense on an American ship perpetrated against an American citizen. John Howell had been killed on a merchant ship and locating the perpetrator/s remained the responsibility of that nation's judicial authorities. Third, HMG was not bound to "deliver up the persons in question" because "there is not at present any subsisting Treaty." American slaveholders had previously sought to use an 1833 Anglo-Canadian extradition act for returning escaped criminals as a means of repatriating fugitive slaves from Canada but this had proved unsuccessful. Fourth, local authorities had acted without "variance" of international and British laws. This was a direct refutation of claims of "interference" by Senator Calhoun and Consul Bacon. Fifth, the US consul's letter labored under a misapprehension because "the Slaves were not liberated by the British authorities," but allowed to move unimpeded. Finally, the customs officials in Nassau could have cleared the vessel for passage to New Orleans, but it was not their "duty" to determine whether the slaves were returning to America "of their own free will or otherwise." This last decision was probably shaped by the liberation of slaves from the *Comet* in 1830 in which customs officers were judged to have acted improperly. After careful review of "various conflicting authorities," and "an anxious consideration of this important subject," the Law Lords concluded "that in our Judgment the British Government cannot legally direct the delivery up of the persons now in custody in the Bahamas to the Authorities of the United States." Two days after writing this letter, the British colonial secretary Lord Stanley informed Bahamas Governor Cockburn of the legal decision upholding his actions.[9]

These contrasting positions between American slavery and British antislavery fueled a major diplomatic crisis. On January 12, 1842, Governor Cockburn anxiously wrote Sir Charles Adams: "I have not as yet received any answer from Mr. Fox, H[er] M[ajesty's] Minister in Washington, on the subject of what occurred here in respect to the American Brig *Creole* and the slaves on board at the time she anchored

---

[9] Dodson, Pollock, Follett to Stanley, January 29, 1842, enclosed in Stanley to Cockburn, January 31, 1842, RP 6981/13, Aberdeen Papers, BL.

in the port of Nassau." The Governor still awaited a response to "my application for a vessel of war being sent to this place."[10] In early February 1842, British Secretary Aberdeen informed British Envoy Ashburton "that we still hear nothing of the Creole; but we shall be prepared."[11] On March 1, Everett, the American minister to England, presented British Secretary Aberdeen with a note stating that British soldiers and officials had been requested aboard the *Creole* by the commanding officer and the US consul "to arrest the mutineers and to prevent the slaves from landing." "Their presence," US Minister Everett protested, "for any opposite purpose, was not asked, and therefore not lawful."[12] Two days later, British Secretary Aberdeen wrote to British Envoy Ashburton informing him of US Minister Everett's protest. Curious though the case was, he wrote, HMG "are fortunately left without any option as to the course of the government." The Law Lords in the House of Lords had "all agreed in declaring that the trial, or delivery to the United States of the accused persons, would be contrary to law. This unanimity precludes all possibility of doubt with respect to our conduct." At the same time, British Foreign Secretary Aberdeen cautioned, "we must do the best we can to put the matter on a right footing, and to obviate irritation and resentment."[13] The reasons to obviate difficulties were primarily economic and political. The United States imported some 15 percent of Britain's total exports while Britain imported about 50 percent of America's cotton crop.[14] The young republic was also the most powerful empire in the western hemisphere, with a very long border with British Canada.[15]

[10] Governor Cockburn to Sir Charles Adams, January 12, 1842, Bahamas Ledger, vol. 1, January to December 1842, page 19, CO 23/112, TNA.

[11] Aberdeen to Ashburton, February 9, 1842, folder 21, Add MS 43123, Aberdeen Papers, BL.

[12] Jervey and Huber, "Creole Affair," 206.

[13] Aberdeen to Ashburton, March 3, 1842, folder 59–61, Add MS 43123, Aberdeen Papers, BL.

[14] Thomas A. Bailey, *A Diplomatic History of the American People* (New York: Appleton-Century-Crofts, Inc. 1955), 213; Gavin Wright, *Slavery and American Economic Development* (Baton Rouge: Louisiana State University Press, 2006), 91–93; John Mack Faragher, Mari Jo Buhle, Daniel Czitrom, and Susan H. Armitage, *Out of Many: A History of the American People*. 4th ed. vol. 1 (Upper Saddle River, N.J.: Prentice Hall, 2005), 313; Sven Beckert, *Empire of Cotton: A Global History* (New York: Alfred A. Knopf, 2014), chap. 5.

[15] Downey's *Creole Affair* ignores these political and economic connections, but their extensiveness undermines the author's thesis of imminent military conflict between the two nations. It is like arguing for a military showdown between China and the United

It is conceivable that Secretary Aberdeen recognized that his advice to Special Envoy Lord Ashburton in Washington was inadequate. On April 1, 1842, the British Foreign Secretary wrote a private dispatch titled "The Case of the Creole." It was sent by an FO clerk to Envoy Lord Ashburton to replace an original dispatch sent in early February. The clerk asked Envoy Lord Ashburton to return the "cancelled Dispatch to Lord Aberdeen by a safe opportunity."[16] This dispatch deserves close analysis because it represents one of the most lucid expressions of official British antislavery policy on the high seas during this new era that remains buried in the archive.

This dispatch from HMG in London to its special envoy en route to Washington makes several key points specifically about the *Creole* revolt as well as broader policy concerns of the British antislavery state. To begin with, the *Creole* was "a case of the greatest importance as to the principles and consequences involved in it." Secretary Aberdeen believed it would be "the chief ground of complaint and difficulty"[17] by the Americans and that US Minister Everett concurred. This consensus by high-ranking diplomats on both sides challenges the view that the *Creole* revolt was incidental and only a minor irritant in Anglo-American relations.[18]

Moreover, the channel circling the Cape of Florida "is the great highway of the sea" between the Atlantic and the Mississippi. Its daily trade was immense – much like the commerce traversing the southern Downs between the eastern and western counties of England where people and merchandise moved to and fro between Kent and Sussex counties in eastern England and Devon and Cornwall counties in the west of the country. Besides being "the great artery" for legitimate trade, this sea channel was also "the chief passage for the slaves conveyed from the Breeding states of

---

States over control of the South China Sea or southern Asia while at the same time overlooking entrenched economic interests linking the two powerhouses. But historian Thomas Heinrich reminds me that economic ties between Germany and Britain did not prevent both powers going to war in August 1914.

[16] On the "general" nature of the mission, see Aberdeen to Ashburton, February 8, 1842, in Adams, "Lord Ashburton," 766; Aberdeen to Ashburton, April 1, 1842, RP 6981/13, Aberdeen Papers, BL.

[17] Aberdeen to Ashburton, April 1, 1842, RP 6981/13, Aberdeen Papers, BL.

[18] Ibid; Adams, "Lord Ashburton,"; Bailey, *Diplomatic History*, chap.14; Alan Brinkley, *The Unfinished Nation: A Concise History of the American People* vol. 1: To 1877 (New York: McGraw Hill, 1993), 267. Wilbur D. Jones, "The Influence of Slavery on the Webster-Ashburton Negotiations," *Journal of Southern History* vol. 22, no. 1 (Feb. 1956), 58, argues the *Creole* case "poisoned the atmosphere." Alexander Deconde, *A History of American Foreign Policy* (New York: Charles Scribner, 1963), 157–158, says it added to "martial fever" in the United States.

Virginia to Louisiana."[19] The Secretary's distinction between legal and illegal trading was becoming central to British colonial antislavery, although it had little relevance for the United States for whom slavery and coastal slave trading were both legitimate endeavors.[20]

Furthermore, the recent passage of British colonial abolition had resulted in "a new state of things." Unlike the past, there were now juxtaposed a "slave shore on one side and a free shore on the other." These free shores consisted of "small Rocky islands" with little value beyond wartime resources.[21] These islands had served as military and strategic bases in the British Empire for centuries. More recently, commerce had begun to flourish in the maritime channels between these colonies and the United States. Now, colonial abolition was proximate to the chief passage for slave trading. There had not been an issue "while both shores were in slavery." But now, British free shores "form so many Decoys for any American slaves," that can catch a few white men unawares and "claim their freedom in a British port."[22] This was the new state of things.[23]

In addition, the *Creole* was a "specimen" of all of these cases. There had been others and they would "be increasing" for "every instance of impunity provokes to them repetition." It appears "that the slaves in their deliberations referred to former successful experiments [*Comet, Hermosa,* etc.]" which would only encourage further cases.[24] The British Foreign Secretary clearly understood that "repetition" was not only an issue for American slaveholders and their representatives in Washington, but also for local colonial officials as well as their masters in London.

Having stated the case, the British Foreign Secretary called for a "remedy." This new "state of things" required America "to turn over

---

[19] Aberdeen to Ashburton, April 1, 1842, RP 6981/13, Aberdeen Papers, BL.

[20] For the complexities of post-emancipation free trade in the British Empire, see Richard Huzzey, *Freedom Burning: Anti-Slavery and Empire in Victorian Britain* (Ithaca, NY: Cornell University Press, 2012), chap. 5. For the transition from illegal (slaves) to legal (palm oil) commercial exchange at the local level in West Africa, see Robin Law, *Ouidah: The Social History of a West African Slaving 'Port' 1792–1892* (Athens: Ohio University Press, 2004), chap. 6.

[21] Aberdeen to Ashburton, April 1, 1842, RP 6981/13, Aberdeen Papers, BL. [22] Ibid.

[23] It is noteworthy that the British minister recognized that slaves seized opportunities for freedom in contrast to American politicians like Calhoun for whom slave fugitives were outlaws and slave rebels aboard the *Creole* murderers who needed to be brought to justice. The difference, however, was less moral than territorial.

[24] Aberdeen to Ashburton, April 1, 1842, RP 6981/13, Aberdeen Papers, BL.

a new leaf," and Britain "to act our part." Before outlining what these were, it should be emphasized that this was the language of détente rather than war.

American Minister Everett had made several suggestions but they were all "untenable" in Secretary Aberdeen's opinion. For one thing, the British official could not pursue "any thing to weaken the principle that a man of whatever color once on our shores cannot have his liberty questioned, and in this respect the Rocks of the Bahamas must have the same privilege as our own Shores."[25] This principle of inviolate free soil was the logical consequence of the 1772 legal ruling in the Somerset case and upheld in recent Law Lords' opinions regarding several American coastal slavers entering British territorial waters during the 1830s leading up the latest example of the *Creole*.

Foreign Secretary Aberdeen recognized the need for a "treaty for reciprocal extradition" between the two nations when murder was committed. Although this was largely irrelevant for coastal slavers that entered British colonial ports due to poor weather conditions, the problem was that "the same scene occurs," attended by "much false swearing as to the complicity of our authorities in the escape of all the slaves." The familiarity of the scenario must have been deeply disturbing to the British minister.

The escape of slaves from American slavers must be a "thorn in the side of the Southern states," and thus produce "hostility" toward Great Britain even in "general questions" pertaining to the two nations. Southern states were "entitled to have their real grievances considered," rather than every case "provoked by general declamations against the horrors of slavery." This was an "act of good neighborhood."[26] It was also the only instance when Lord Aberdeen acknowledged US sectional differences.

In the face of all of these challenges, Secretary Aberdeen proposed the following "practical scheme." When American ships entered British waters, they deserved legal protection and all communication should be prohibited except "through the Consul."[27] Moreover, if any slaves found their way on shore, "we cannot suffer them to be recovered by their master." These policies would be restricted to the Bahamas, Bermuda, and vessels traveling between American ports. The British official concluded that his aim was to state his view of the case and its possible remedy

---

[25] Aberdeen to Ashburton, April 1, 1842, RP 6981/13, Aberdeen Papers, BL.   [26] Ibid.
[27] What this otherwise reasonable suggestion overlooks, however, was duplicitous behavior exemplified by US Consul Bacon's support for the seizure of the *Creole*.

with "the strong opinion that we should be prepared to do <u>something</u>."[28] Britain's antislavery policy was sacrosanct, the Americans had legitimate concerns, and these differences required resolution.

This important dispatch would have been among the diplomatic papers awaiting British Envoy Lord Ashburton when he arrived in Washington, DC, on April 4, 1842. The fifty-four-gun frigate *Warspite* manned by 500 sailors that transported the special envoy was an impressive symbol of British maritime power. The winds were less impressed, though, blowing the vessel off course from its original destination of New York City and forcing it into Annapolis two days earlier.[29] Less than two weeks later, a special session of the Vice Admiralty Court at Nassau met to decide the fate of the *Creole* rebels who had been incarcerated in the city jail on Parliament Square since November 12, 1841. Based upon insufficient evidence, the court discharged them. The following day, Governor Cockburn informed London of the court's decision.

This liberation of the slave rebels, together with the emancipation of the other captives, was unacceptable to the US government. It demanded a guarantee that the British government produce some type of security against future occurrences. Secretary Aberdeen recognized the reasonable nature of this request in his long dispatch quoted above. But he informed his special envoy Ashburton in late May 1842 that the existing law made it "impossible to give any positive security against a repetition of the same kind of proceeding." Whether due to poor weather or forcible circumstance, i.e., slave rebellion, "the slaves must at once be free," whenever they ended up in British jurisdiction. "In a British port, we could not place them at the mercy of the American Consul for an hour," he explained, because this would mean their return to bondage. In short, "if the slaves bring a vessel into an English port, I do not see how we can again consign them to slavery, however we might be disposed to deal with them as mutineers."[30] The attorney general of the Bahamas had made a similar point before the Nassau inquiry a month earlier. He held that "as slavery is abolished throughout the British dominions, the moment a vessel comes into a British port with slaves on board, to whatever nation such vessel may belong, and however imperious the necessity may have been which

---

[28] Aberdeen to Ashburton, April 1, 1842, RP 6981/13, Aberdeen Papers, BL.

[29] "Foreign News by the Steamer Acadia," *Richmond Enquirer*, March 22, 1842; Adams, "Lord Ashburton," 770; Jervey and Huber, "*Creole* Affair," 207; Downey, *Creole Affair*, 114–115.

[30] Aberdeen to Ashburton, May 26, 1842, folder 112–13, Add MS 43123, Aberdeen Papers, BL.

drove her into such port, such slaves became immediately entitled to the protection of British laws, and that the right of their owners to treat and deal with them as slaves, ceases."[31]

The *Creole* revolt raised several other pressing maritime matters. First, there was the issue of security through the Bahamas Channel. This was a busy seaway of legitimate and slave trades. More recently, it had become split between slavery and freedom's shores. Secretary Aberdeen suggested that if "the Americans must send a slave cargo along the coast, why not give it convoy by one of their own vessels."[32] Second, there was the issue of the extradition of the slave rebels or "mutineers." The Law Lords had already ruled that they were not pirates. Secretary Aberdeen had already expressed his reservations about returning slaves to slavery even if they were considered "mutineers." In early June, the British Foreign Secretary was even more adamant about the impossibility of the extradition of the so-called mutineers. Any treaty could not include mutiny and revolt without reference to cases like the *Creole*. All men on board ship were required to be obedient. But the attempt "of slaves to recover their freedom would scarcely be considered as any violation of that law which, for the good of all, is supposed to exist in these cases; and in no case do I think that our authorities would recognize it as mutiny or revolt. Any treaty of this kind will require an Act of Parliament to carry it into effect; and I doubt much if with such a provision as this, it would meet with the necessary assent of the two houses."[33] Such approbation was further unlikely in the face of the Law Lords' recent ruling, together with popular antislavery constituencies who would refuse to support such legislation.[34]

The third issue concerned suppression of the transatlantic slave trade. Britain's key strategic objectives included the consolidation of antislavery policy as well as buttressing imperial control of the high seas. In contrast, Washington's objective was to extract the perennial thorn of Britain's right of search of their merchant marine. The key stumbling block was the right of British impressment of American seamen examined in Chapter 1.

---

[31] Anderson's testimony, Nassau commission, April 1842, in Merritt M. Robinson, *Reports of Cases Argued and Determined in the Supreme Court of Louisiana*, vol. 10, (March 1 to June 20, 1845. New Orleans: Samuel M. Stewart, 1845), 251.

[32] Aberdeen to Ashburton, May 26, 1842, folder 112–13, Add MS 43123, Aberdeen Papers, BL.

[33] Aberdeen to Ashburton, June 3, 1842, folder 122–3, Add MS 43123, Aberdeen Papers, BL.

[34] For popular antislavery, see Jones, "Influence of Slavery," 49; Huzzey, *Freedom Burning*, chap. 2.

British Foreign Secretary Aberdeen reminded Envoy Lord Ashburton of the importance of coming to an agreement over the "subject of impressement [*sic*] . . . But the subject is one of much delicacy in this country, and although publick feeling may be a good deal modified, there is still much excitement connected with it. It is our <u>Droit de Visite [right of search]</u>."[35] The compromise was to make such visits less oppressive. The Duke of Wellington, former successful military commander and Tory prime minister, insisted on a distinction: "Which is not the Right of Search, but the Right to verify the national character of a Vessel, which shows the colors of the U. States." His suggestion was mutual verification:

And the Commander thereon ought to be required to deliver to the Commander of the vessel detained, a copy under the official signature of the entry on his log in respect to the cause of the detention. Such an arrangement would at all events facilitate enquiry, and ensure satisfaction, and might put an end to dissension on the subject.[36]

Envoy Ashburton's suggestion was that US observers be allowed on board British ships to oversee interference with slave ships carrying an American flag. Things remained at an impasse because the United States would not accept the right of visit of her ships in peacetime, and Britain would not end its policy of impressment.[37]

The impression from much of the historical literature on the *Creole* revolt was that the dispute was eventually settled due to the diplomatic skills of the two key protagonists.[38] Regardless of the particular skills of the negotiators, however, maritime disputes between the two nations did not end in the summer of 1842.

August 1, 1842, marked the ninth year of the legal passage of the Slavery Abolition Act. The event was commemorated in towns and cities across Massachusetts and New York. Prominent white abolitionists like

---

[35] Aberdeen to Ashburton, July 18, 1842, folder 148–149, Add MS 43123, Aberdeen Papers, BL.

[36] Duke of Wellington Memorandum, February 8, 1842, folder 23–30, Add MS 43123, Aberdeen Papers, BL.

[37] Jones, "Influence of Slavery," 55; Huzzey, *Freedom Burning*, chap 3. Transatlantic slavers from Spain, Brazil, France, and elsewhere frequently flew the American flag because the United States was the only major maritime power not to sign a slave trade treaty with Britain.

[38] E. D. Adams lists the following terms to describe the British envoy: "conciliatory," "master hand," "independent," "skill[ful]," and "tactfully." He concludes Lord Ashburton "accomplished his mission with distinguished success" (781) and "proved himself an accomplished diplomatist, courteous, patient, considerate, and above all, just" (782). Adams, "Lord Ashburton."

William E. Channing, William Jay, and Wendell Phillips, together with well-known black abolitionists like Charles L. Remond and John R. Hilton, addressed large crowds of racially mixed citizens for the dual purpose of celebrating the glories of British colonial abolition as well as mobilizing against the brutalities of American slavery.[39] That same day, US Secretary of State Daniel Webster sat down in his Washington office and penned a long letter to British Envoy Ashburton. It deserves detailed scrutiny because it provides one of most eloquent expressions of the official American position on the protection of property rights and the law of nations.[40]

The US Secretary began by expressing his regret that the envoy was not empowered to provide for "the better security of vessels of the United States" when passing between the United States and the Bahamas. This was a subject of "great importance" and had to be addressed right now.[41]

"Several cases," he continued, had arisen over the last few years in which slaves had been liberated from ships traveling in these lanes and that compensation had been received for some and not for others. President Tyler thought that both countries' interests would best be served if future recurrences were "prevented."

The British envoy was no doubt aware of the case of the *Creole* in which "persons" rose upon the "lawful authority" of the vessel and "committed murder." The US Secretary of State was cognizant of the "difference of opinion" over whether or not the colonial authorities liberated the slaves, but that was not his concern. It was his purpose to obtain "some practical means of giving security to the coasting trade of the United States, against unlawful annoyance and interruption, along this part of their shore." The Secretary pointed out the nature of the channel between Florida and the Bahamas and its vital importance to commerce linking the Atlantic states with those in the Gulf and Mississippi. This was a region whose commercial importance to the nation paralleled that of the southern counties in Great Britain. The Secretary was mute on the proximity of slavery and freedom's shores that was the major cause of the conflict.[42]

---

[39] Kerr-Ritchie, *Rites of August First*, chap. 2 and 3.
[40] Webster to Ashburton, August 1, 1842, RP 6981/13, Aberdeen Papers, BL. This important letter is usefully reproduced as Appendix III in Downey, *Creole Affair*, 185–192. The author characterizes it as a "brilliant lawyer's brief" (123). Adams, "Lord Ashburton," 778, only observes Webster's request that colonial officials be instructed to "safeguard" the rights of US citizens.
[41] Webster to Ashburton, August 1, 1842, RP 6981/13, Aberdeen Papers, BL.   [42] Ibid.

Furthermore, slavery existed by the laws of southern states as well as "under guarantee of the Constitution of the United States." Slaves were often on board as "hands," "servants," and cargo from port to port. (The massive extent of coastal trading makes the US Secretary's comparison a trifle disingenuous.) When poor weather or "unlawful force" brought these vessels into port, the American authorities expected "faithful and exact observance" of the "law of nations."[43] The rest of Secretary Webster's letter was primarily concerned with an explication of this law of nations or "comity" and how it must serve as the basis of future relations between the two countries.[44]

This law of nations exempted any ship driven into port through "disasters of the sea" or "unlawful force" from "interference." A vessel "beyond the distance of a marine league from the shore, is regarded as part of the territory of the nation to which she belongs, and subjected, exclusively, to the jurisdiction of that nation." These laws operate even if a ship is "forced out of her voluntary course." Indeed, the Secretary states, it "is natural to consider vessels of a nation as parts of its territory though at sea, as the state retains its jurisdiction over them; and, according to the commonly-received custom, this jurisdiction is preserved over the vessels, even in parts of the sea subject to a foreign dominion."[45]

Although vessels must obey the "laws of the place" while in foreign ports, the law of nations: "show that enlightened nations, in modern times, do clearly hold, that the jurisdiction and law of a nation accompany her ships, not only over the high seas, but into ports and harbors, or wheresoever else they may be water borne, for the general purpose of governing and regulating the rights, duties, and obligations of those on board thereof, and that, to the extent of the exercise of this jurisdiction, they are considered as parts of the territory of the nation herself."[46] One can imagine both President Tyler and Senator Calhoun nodding in agreement to this expression of the inviolate nature of slavery's property rights on the high seas.[47]

---

[43] Ibid.

[44] I count nine references to "comity" and "law of nations" in Secretary Webster's August 1 letter.

[45] Ibid. Did this mean that South Carolina violated British maritime rights after imprisoning free black sailors after 1822?

[46] Webster to Ashburton, August 1, 1842, RP 6981/13, Aberdeen Papers, BL.

[47] Secretary Webster supported slavery's property rights because he served at the pleasure of Virginia-slaveholding President Tyler. He also needed southern slaveholders' support should he run for the highest public office in the land.

Lord Ashburton, Secretary Webster argued, must be aware that merchant vessels fell under their own national jurisdiction according to the "comity of the law of nations, and the practice of modern times." The US Secretary of State further pointed out that according to English law, "no sooner does a slave reach the shores of England than he is free." This was true, but English law may not "enter where the jurisdiction of another nation is acknowledged to exist." While English ports were open to foreign ships for trade, they bring "with them the jurisdiction of their own Government and the protection of its laws."[48] And then Secretary Webster expressed the heart of the matter:

If, therefore, vessels of the United States, pursuing lawful voyages, from port to port, along their own shore, are driven by stress of weather, or carried by unlawful force [i.e. *Creole*], into English ports, the Government of the United States cannot consent that the local authorities in those ports shall take advantage of such misfortunes, and enter them, for the purpose of interfering with the condition of persons or things on board, as established by their own laws. If slaves, the property of citizens of the United States, escape into the British territories, it is not expected that they will be restored. In that case, the territorial jurisdiction of England will have become exclusive over them, and must decide their condition. *But slaves lying on board of American vessels, lying in British waters, are not within the exclusive jurisdiction of England; or under the exclusive operation of English law* [italics added].[49]

The American government, continued Secretary Webster, was of the opinion that vessels through duress or "wrongful violence," "ought to receive all assistance necessary to enable them to resume that direct course; and that interference and molestation, by the local authority, where the whole voyage is lawful, both in act, and in intent, is ground for just and grave complaint." The US Secretary of State concluded with a practical suggestion and a future concern. If British Envoy Ashburton had no authority for making a treaty, perhaps instructions might be directed toward local officials in the Caribbean islands "to regulate their conduct" so as to remove grounds for any future complaints. "It would be with the most profound regret," warned Secretary Webster, "that the President should seem that whilst it is now hoped so many other subjects of difference may be harmoniously adjusted, nothing should be done in regard to this dangerous source of future collisions."[50]

---

[48] Webster to Ashburton, August 1, 1842, RP 6981/13, Aberdeen Papers, BL.   [49] Ibid.
[50] Ibid.

This detailed letter by Secretary Webster provides an important summary of the nation's position on the maritime rights of merchant vessels, the supremacy of original jurisdiction for US vessels, and the principle of comity. It was unlikely, however, to persuade Envoy Ashburton in Washington, as well as the British government in London. The implication of slave liberation through local interference had already been repeatedly denied and explained away by various British jurists and government officials in London and the colonies. Moreover, Secretary Webster must have been aware – even if he did not say so outright – that the principle of comity and American slaves' struggle for liberation were incompatible. Finally, Secretary Webster's repetitive evocation of the "laws of civilized nations" rubs awkwardly against both nations' long histories of trading human beings, the creation and reproduction of brutal slave colonies and societies, and prolonged attempts to dehumanize people of African descent.

Five days later, Lord Ashburton penned a reply to Secretary Webster. He agreed that it was a subject of "great importance." But he had departed London with no instructions regarding the case and consequently believed that "the question had better be treated in London." The *Creole* was a difficult case because it not only raised questions of national and international law but "public feeling is sensitively alive to everything connected with it." This is why he thought the matter best left to London. He assured the US Secretary on their mutual agreement on general principles: "You admit that if slaves, the property of American citizens, escape into British territories, it is not expected that they will be restored; and you may be well assured that there is no wish on our part that they should reach our shores, or that British possessions should be used as decoys for the violators of the laws of a friendly neighbor." The moral limitations of British antislavery policy could not be expressed more cogently.

Yet, the British envoy explained, the US Secretary had advanced some propositions with regard to vessels passing through channel and jurisdiction of local authorities "which rather surprise and startle me." He warned against governments establishing "false precedents and principles" through diplomatic intercourse. What was better was "future prevention of such occurrences." In that spirit, Lord Ashburton proposed "that instructions shall be given to the Governors of her majesty's colonies to the southern borders of the United States to execute their own laws with careful attention to the wish of their Government to maintain good neighborhood, and that there shall be no officious interference with

American vessels driven by accident or by violence into these ports."
It was, concluded the British envoy, his earnest desire that the president
receive his "suggestion" as contributory toward "my work of reconcilia-
tion and friendship."[51]

Secretary Webster wrote back two days later. The president, he stated,
would have preferred a "formal treaty" to establish the better security of
American vessels. But the chief executive would rely on "principles of
public law" as well as "your Lordship's engagement that instructions" be
delivered to colonial governors. President Tyler, however, was still hopeful of a treaty that would remove "all cause of complaint connected with
this subject."[52]

The Webster-Ashburton Treaty was signed the next day. It settled
many of the key differences that had bedeviled Anglo-American relations
for decades concerning the *Caroline* affair, northeastern boundary disputes, and so forth.[53] But it had little to say about other pressing issues.
The Americans failed to obtain British consent for the prevention of ship
impressments.[54] There was no final settlement for the suppression of the
Atlantic slave trade beyond agreement for joint patrols of the West
African coastline that resulted in limited American participation.[55]
Moreover, although the British agreed to the extradition of fugitive criminals between the United States and Canada, this did not include cross-
border fugitive slaves.[56] Article X on the rendition of criminals would
have made the person/s guilty of killing John Hewell liable but not the
rebels nor captives who walked to freedom.[57]

---

[51] Ashburton to Webster, August 6, 1842, in Downey, *Creole Affair* 192–195. The author
characterizes this response as being "strange" without any further explanation (123).
Adams, "Lord Ashburton," 779, merely notes that Ashburton thought the "question
better dealt with in London."

[52] Webster to Ashburton, August 8, 1842, in Downey, *Creole Affair*, 195–196.

[53] The Webster-Ashburton Treaty 1842 and Associated Documents, The Avalon Project,
Yale Law School, http://avalon.law.yale.edu/subject_menus/br1842m.asp; Bemis,
Diplomatic History, chap. 15; Bailey, *Diplomatic History*, 220–221; DeConde,
American Foreign Policy, 160–162.

[54] Bailey, *Diplomatic History*, 224.

[55] DeConde, *American Foreign Policy*, 160; Bailey, *Diplomatic History*, 222; Wilbur Jones,
"Influence of Slavery"; Howard Jones, "Case of *Creole*."

[56] Kerr-Ritchie, *Rites of August First*, 125; Wilbur Jones, "Influence of Slavery," 52; Bailey,
Diplomatic History, 223; DeConde, *American Foreign Policy*, 160. This outcome was
hardly surprising since it would have required the British authorities to turn over the
Creole rebels.

[57] The Webster-Ashburton Treaty 1842 and Associated Documents, The Avalon Project,
Yale Law School, http://avalon.law.yale.edu/subject_menus/br1842m.asp; Downey,
Creole Affair, 127; Adams, "Lord Ashburton,"779.

Most important, the *Creole* revolt was not mentioned in the treaty and was left to informal diplomatic notes. In his reply to Webster's letter, Envoy Ashburton promised the US Secretary that British colonial officials would not engage in "officious interference" if American vessels were forced into British ports due to poor weather.[58] Of course, this was not admission that they had always done so in the past. On August 8, 1842 Secretary Webster acknowledged Envoy Ashburton's note of the 6th in reply to Webster's of August 1st over "stipulation for the better security of American vessels, driven by accident or carried by force, into the British West India Ports." President Tyler desired the implementation of principles of public law, together with the instructions to British colonial governors: "to maintain good neighborhood; and that there shall be no officious interference with American vessels, driven by accident or by violence, into those ports." The President also hoped that HMG would remove, by stipulation, treaty, and otherwise, "all cause of complaint connected with this subject."[59] The same day the treaty was signed, Special Envoy Lord Ashburton informed British Foreign Secretary Aberdeen: "My great plague was the *Creole* and you will see how I have at last disposed of it."[60] This was not much to show for the enormous amount of differences between the two nations. Moreover, ship revolt due to "former successful experiments" and voyage deviation as a consequence of poor weather threatened that the "same scene occurs" between a "slave shore" and a "free shore." After all, the *Creole* ended up in Nassau not because of poor weather but because of enslaved people's desire to obtain freedom in what they believed to be free territorial waters. The issue of compensation to American slaveholders for slaves liberated by the British in the *Enterprize*, *Hermoza*, and *Creole* remained unresolved. The fundamental clash between expansionist empires embarked on divergent paths exceeded the reasonable and capable exertions of British and American diplomats.

---

[58] Wilbur Jones, "Influence of Slavery," 53; Bailey, *Diplomatic History*, 224; DeConde, *American Foreign Policy*, 161; Jervey and Huber, "*Creole* Affair," 207.

[59] Tyler to Webster, August 7, 1842, RP 6981/13, Aberdeen Papers, BL; Webster to Ashburton, August 8, 1842, RP 6981/13, Aberdeen Papers, BL; Ashburton to Aberdeen, August 9, 1842, folder 154–155, Add MS 43123, Aberdeen Papers, BL.

[60] Ashburton to Aberdeen, August 9 1842, folder 154–155, Add MS 43123, Aberdeen Papers, BL. Elsewhere, he acknowledged the *Creole* revolt had "proved the most difficult of all the topics with which he had attempted to deal." See Ashburton to Aberdeen, August 13, 1842, in Adams, "Lord Ashburton," 779.

9

"Property Rights" versus "Rights of Man"

On December 2, 1841, the *Creole* entered the New Orleans harbor.[1] Its tobacco cargo was intact, but there were only five captives on board of more than 130 captives who had embarked from the Chesapeake Bay. The captain was not present, so the vessel was under the command of the first officer. One of the passengers was missing. What had happened at sea? The *Creole* crew lodged an official protest before the New Orleans Notary Public, where the details of the ship's dramatic story emerged.

Over the course of the following year, the *Creole* revolt crystalized key differences over the question of rights. For many southerners and defenders of slavery, it represented a flagrant violation of basic rights of property as well as international agreements regarding the protection of such property on the high seas. In contrast, many northerners argued that the ship rebellion represented a successful struggle for natural rights and that any protection of the unnatural rights of slavery was only of a local jurisdiction. This polarity is quite familiar to antebellum historians especially specialists in Civil War causation. But what made the argument over the *Creole* different was that it transcended sectional rivalries because of British involvement. British people rallied against the extension of property rights in man while the British state sought to extend slave abolition across the continent in self-declared republics like Texas. In other words, there were transnational dimensions to the fallout over the *Creole* revolt that are easily overlooked if we just focus on sectional rivalries.

Newspaper editors led the southern charge. Upon learning what happened aboard the Virginia slaver, the New Orleans press immediately

---

[1] *Le Courrier de la Louisiane,* December 2, 1841, New Orleans.

condemned the egregious attack.[2] One reported this "shocking and horrible revolt at sea."[3] Another referred to this "shocking outrage committed on board the brig *Creole*" in which "mutiny and massacre" had occurred.[4] It was "mutiny and murder" that headlined the narrative of the *Creole* elsewhere.

The slave rebels were clearly culpable for mutiny and murder. But responsibility for their freedom and the loss of all those other captives lay squarely with the British. The refusal of local authorities to deliver the "wretches" only served to add "another item to the dark catalog of outrages upon American rights committed by the English government."[5] That "insolent and intolerable meddler, John Bull," fumed one editorial, "must be held responsible. And should he persist in his outrageous course, there can be no other alternative left, but for the American Eagle to make such a noise about his ears, as will awake him from his [famed?] security, considerably lighten the British exchequer, arrest the practical proceedings of fanatics [abolitionists] on both sides of the water, and punish the hypocrites whose end and aim is the destruction of southern prosperity – American liberty and independence."[6]

If the British continued such behavior and refused to defend American property rights, some New Orleans newspapers proposed unleashing the dogs of war. One editor warned: "If Great Britain will not listen to the voice of reason, resort must be had in another of bringing her to her senses, and a just perception of the law of nations."[7] This affair, opined another, "is the cap sheaf of British aggression upon the American rights." "If it be not promptly discountenanced, and simple reparation immediately made by her Majesty's Government, there can be but one course for the United

[2] William Joseph Poole, Jr., "The Creole Case," M.A. thesis, Louisiana State University, Baton Rouge, 1970, chap. 3.

[3] *Bee*, December 3, 1841, New Orleans.

[4] *Commercial Bulletin*, December 3, 1841, New Orleans.

[5] *Bee*, December 3, 1841, New Orleans.

[6] Editorial, *Courrier*, December 3, 1841, New Orleans. The December 3, 1841, edition of the New Orleans *Daily Picayune* reported slaves at Nassau "acknowledged" being advised by an English Baptist minister named Bourne aged around forty who had once resided in Nassau but "had absconded, leaving his family" and resettled in Norfolk. We have reason to be skeptical of this claim since the slaves were not interviewed and the extensive documentary record on the *Creole* revolt contains no references to such a character. We can reasonably assume, however, that this was yet another piece of "evidence" with which to stab the ubiquitous British meddler. Besides, it supports the proslavery idea that slaves were incapable of revolting without the help of outsiders. Recall the same fake generalizations about black activists during the 1950s and 1960s Civil Rights Movement.

[7] *Commercial Bulletin*, December 3, 1841, New Orleans.

States to pursue – a course that the pride, honor, and dignity of the nation will sternly demand the execution of."[8] On December 22, 1841, Louisiana senator Alexander Barrow drew the attention of his fellow senators to the case of the *Formosa* the previous year in which Mr. Templeman's slave property had been seized by "persons dressed up in the uniform of British soldiers [West India Regiment soldiers]" resulting in "the liberation of the slaves." The owner had sued the insurance company for liable. He "was satisfied that this subject might involve the question of peace or war between this country and Great Britain."[9] In other words, some newspaper editors in New Orleans warned of military action unless the British government atoned for its role in slaves' liberation in the *Creole* and prohibited all such future actions.[10]

Although the Old Dominion did not threaten armed conflict, it was no less assertive regarding the protection of its citizen's property rights. Under the sensationalist headline "MUTINY AND MURDER" – which would no doubt have met with the approbation of Rupert Murdoch's tabloid and profitable Fox News Channel today – Richmond's leading newspapers reproduced the short narrative of this "shocking and horrible revolt at sea."[11]

More sober was their statement of opposition toward Britain's right of search of American merchant vessels. If we "admit the claim which Great Britain sets up," wrote the *Richmond Enquirer*, "we should have to submit to numerous invasions and indignities against the flag of our country." There were three trenchant reasons for refusing such a claim. First, the "right of search belongs to a state of war and not of peace." The *Creole* was a merchant ship engaged in a peaceful enterprise. This was also the point made by US Secretary Webster. Second, the British officer who boarded a ship would not only "disregard our flag" but also "examine our papers" without justification. Constitutional rights in the aftermath of the successful War of Independence against the British had been established to prevent this eventuality, but these were now being undermined at sea. Third, the claim to search would be extended to all seven

---

[8] *New Orleans Advertiser* copied in *The Northern Star and Leeds General Advertiser*, January 15, 1842, Leeds, England.

[9] *Congressional Globe*, 27th Congress, 2nd Session, 11, "Seizure of American Property," 47–48; Granville Hicks, "Dr. Channing and the Creole Case," *American Historical Review*, vol. 37, no. 3 (April 1932), 518.

[10] Arthur Downey's case for a potential third Anglo-American war in his *Creole Affair* book might have been strengthened by unearthing these press references.

[11] *Richmond Whig*, December 17, 1841, Richmond, VA.

nations that had adhered to the antislavery convention. This would mean that a vessel could be searched by the British, then the French, "and finally it might be subjected to the infamy of being searched by a black Haytian Crew," because Haiti was a treaty signatory.[12] Not only was Haiti a major concern due to its successful revolution inspiring other slaves and free blacks but the Haitian state with its federal employees was in a position to interfere with US property rights and to turn racial etiquette upside down. The editorial quoted previous diplomatic correspondence between the US Minister to England Andrew Stevenson and British Foreign Secretary Lord Palmerston in 1837 concerning shipwrecked vessels in which the latter had declared "that it is the intention of her Majesty's Government to adhere to its determination of not only refusing all compensation to the owners of the slaves on board '*The Enterprise*,' but for any other slaves belonging to Citizens of the U.S., who may *hereafter, under any circumstance whatever*, be brought within the dominions and jurisdiction of the British Crown." The editor added: "The outrageous case of the Creole will, however, bring up the question again."[13]

These protests in Virginia were not limited to newspaper editorials. At 7:00 p.m. on Thursday, January 26, 1842, a meeting of Richmond citizens was held at the Exchange Hotel. Mayor General Lambert chaired the meeting and Mr. H. L. Brooke served as secretary. The gathering expressed their complaints and solutions in classic American republican style. The preamble stated that the "People of Virginia" having "as a free and independent State, absolute right of property in, and sole dominion over their slaves," been "assailed by those whose constitutional duty it was to protect it." This opening was followed by ten resolutions, a number of which directly concerned the protection of the rights of property from foreign interference. Virginians resolved they "will never submit to any other people or nation, the questions of their right of property." The gathering further resolved that the US flag "should be a protection and guarantee of safety of the persons and property under it." The Richmond citizenry also resolved that "the aggressive policy of [the] British government, and their Colonial authorities upon the rights of property, especially in the recent case of the *Creole*, sailing from our own port, and thrown by mutiny of the slaves on board thereof, and the murder of its passengers into the port of Nassau, calls loudly for remonstrance and redress." This preamble and resolutions were twice read and

[12] *Richmond Enquirer*, December 18, 1841.   [13] Ibid.

"unanimously adopted." It was also reported that the "Captain of the Creole" was present at the meeting.[14] (See Appendix 4.)

It is obvious why Richmond and New Orleans would take the lead protesting the so-called assault on property rights by the British government and its colonial authorities. But other southern states also expressed their desire for the protection of property rights in slaves from interfering parties. Alabama was a burgeoning new slave state whose bustling port of Mobile transported captives westward to New Orleans and eastward to Pensacola in a vibrant coastal trade in the Gulf.[15] One of the state's leading newspapers, *The Mobile Register and Journal*, protested that the "right to protect slaves who have killed their masters, and run into British islands with a stolen vessel, is but another form of the principle already announced by the British government: that her own statutes abolishing slavery, control the law of nations, and [illegible] of the pale of comity, not to say the justice due to civilized nations." Previous ships like the *Comet*, *Encomium*, *Enterprise*, and *Hermosa* had run into British ports and had their slaves removed, with compensation in some cases and not in others. The US Senate had recently ruled: "Vessels on the high seas, are as exclusively under the jurisdiction of the State to which their flag belongs as if a part of the domain." And now, added the Alabama newspaper, "comes this dreadful tragedy of the *Creole* . . . The alarming consequences to this quarter of the Union," explained the editorial, "of seeing a harbor opened in the neighboring islands where runaways, mutineers, and murderers will be received by an alien sovereign demands an immediate [issue?] to the diplomacy long pending."[16]

The much older state of South Carolina was equally condemnatory of recent British actions. Its distrust of British merchant ships had resulted in a serious breach during the early 1820s over the imprisonment of black seamen as discussed in Chapter 1. The Palmetto State was also engaged in the movement of captives from Charleston to New Orleans in the southeast Atlantic and Gulf coastal trade as examined in Chapter 2. On December 13, 1841, the *Charleston Mercury* reprinted from New

---

[14] "Adjourned Meeting of the Citizens of Richmond" *Richmond Enquirer*, January 29, 1842, Richmond, VA. Captain Robert Ensor had recovered sufficiently from his wounds to return from Nassau to his home city.

[15] Examination of the Coastal Passage in the Gulf would make a great dissertation topic

[16] *Mobile Register & Journal* copied in New Orleans *Commercial Bulletin*, December 9, 1841. This fear of a magnet for slave runaways makes nonsense of the proslavery notion of slave contentment: If they were that happy, then no amount of enticement would move them.

Orleans newspapers "some account of this new outrage by British colonial authorities on American property." An additional source purported that the attorney general boarded the vessel, "expounded" the law of British emancipation to the slaves, and informed them they were "now free to go where they pleased."[17] Several days later, the venerable senator from the Palmetto State weighed in on the question of the most extreme option for dealing with this latest British infraction. John C. Calhoun regretted "so much had been said about war with Great Britain." His own opinion was that "with proper conduct," there was "little danger of immediate conflict" on our part. But, he added, "if there should be a war, it would be because this country wanted a due foresight to secure common respect" because of previous failures to "arrest the aggressions and innovations of that power."[18]

If the *Creole* revolt further stimulated southern states' defense of property rights, it only served to bolster insistence on the sanctity of rights of man. Politicians, jurists, abolitionists, and antislavery advocates were equally vociferous. William Goodell, the leader of the recently formed Liberty Party defined by an antislavery political platform, remarked favorably on the calendar day coincidence of the ship revolt and the martyrdom of Ohio abolitionist newspaper editor Elijah Lovejoy four years previously. Elizur Wright, editor of the abolitionist New York newspaper the *Emancipator*, believed the revolt was God's work.[19] But it was a stubborn Ohio Congressman and a blue-blooded New York jurist who provided some of the most trenchant arguments for universal rights.

Born in Pennsylvania in 1795, Joshua Reed Giddings moved with his parents to New York and Ohio where he received a common-school education. After serving in the Second Anglo-American War on the side of slave traders like Woolfolk and Franklin against the British, he taught school, studied law, and was elected to the state House of Representatives in 1826. He soon fell into the orbit of Congressman Elisha Whittlesey and was elected to the 25th Congress after the vacancy caused by the resignation of his mentor in 1838. At the same time, he gravitated toward political abolitionism, the leadership of John Quincy Adams, and

---

[17] *Charleston Mercury*, December 14, 1841, copied in *Richmond Enquirer*, December 18, 1841.
[18] *Congressional Globe*, 27th Congress, 2nd Session, 11, 47–48, "Seizure of American Property."
[19] Sean Wilentz, *The Rise of American Democracy: Jefferson to Lincoln* (New York: W. W. Norton, 2005), 556.

a small group of antislavery Whigs headquartered at Mrs. Ann Spriggs' convivial boarding house opposite the Capitol.[20]

In 1836, the US Congress voted to stop airing discussion and debate of antislavery petitions by implementation of a formal gag rule in the House and an informal one in the Senate. Radical Whig congressmen like Adams and Giddings repeatedly introduced these petitions after which they were tabled. One petition in late January 1842 reportedly requested the recall of the US consul from Nassau "in relation to the mutineers of the *Creole*." In response to this repeated failure to consider these antislavery petitions, Adams presented a petition calling for Union dissolution after which he faced censure. Virginia congressman Henry A. Wise claimed that Adams was working with British authorities to undermine and abolish American slavery. Fellow Whig Giddings and others defended the seasoned anti-slavery warrior. In early February, the censure resolution was tabled as was the petition calling for disunion. Adams remained, but Giddings took a political path that he could claim as his own.[21]

On March 21, 1842, Ohio Congressman Giddings rose in the House of Representatives to introduce nine resolutions.[22] The first one recognized that prior to the US Constitution, each of the "several States" had "full and exclusive jurisdiction over the subject of slavery" and the power to "continue or abolish." This was a clear recognition of states' rights over the institution of slavery and of contrasting local approaches prior to 1789. The second resolution stated that the "aforesaid powers" were retained by the states after adoption of the Constitution. Both of these resolutions would have been agreed to by southern states. The third resolution stated that maritime commerce and navigation was the domain of the federal government. This was undoubtedly less palatable to southern slave states. Did not Maryland, Virginia, South Carolina, Alabama,

---

[20] US House of Representatives, "Giddings, Joshua Reed" http://history.house.gov/People/Listing/G/GIDDINGS,-Joshua-Reed-(G000167)/; Wilentz, *Rise of American Democracy*, 550–551, 556; James B. Stewart, *Holy Warriors: The Abolitionists and American Slavery* (New York: Hill and Wang, 1976), 85–86. James Stewart's *Joshua R. Giddings and the Tactics of Radical Politics* (Cleveland: Case-Western Reserve University Press, 1970) is excellent.

[21] Arthur T. Downey, *The Creole Affair: The Slave Rebellion That Led the U.S. and Great Britain to the Brink of War* (Lanham: Rowman and Littlefield, 2014), 96–97; Wilentz, *Rise of American Democracy*, chap. 18; Michael F. Holt, *The Rise and Fall of the American Whig Party: Jacksonian Politics and the Onset of the Civil War* (New York: Oxford University Press, 1999), 44, 155.

[22] *Congressional Globe*, 27th Congress, 2nd Session, March 21, 1842, 342. All subsequent quotations related to Giddings's resolutions come from this source.

and Louisiana have jurisdiction over their coastal trade in slaves? The fourth resolution was where the Ohio representative began to sketch out the major differences between property rights and natural rights. Slavery, he reminded his colleagues, was "an abridgment of the natural rights of man." It could only exist "by force of positive municipal law," and was confined to its own "territorial jurisdiction." In other words, slavery was local not national or international. This territorial and judicial limitation was spelled out in the fifth resolution. When an American merchant ship left the state and entered onto the high seas, "the persons on board cease to be subject to the slave laws of such a State." The most recent example was described in the next resolution. When the brig *Creole* left Virginia, "the slave laws of that State ceased to have jurisdiction over the persons on board of said brig, and such persons became amenable only to the laws of the U.S." This was a clear refutation of maritime states' rights propounded by southern newspaper editors, Virginia citizens, Senator Calhoun, and others. In the seventh resolution, the Ohio representative stated that the "persons" on the vessel were "preserving their natural rights of personal liberty," and were thus guilty of no legal violations or liable to punishment. (A more accurate term than "preserving" would have been "regaining.") The next resolution stated that all attempts to "regain possession of or to re-enslave, said persons" were unconstitutional and dishonorable. This was an indictment – intentional or otherwise – of Captain Woodside's attempt to seize the *Creole* in Nassau harbor supported by US Consul Bacon. The final resolution considered that the "coastwise slave trade" was "subversive of the rights and injurious to the feelings and the interests of the free States," was unauthorized by Congress, and "prejudicial to our national character."[23] (**See Appendix 5.**)

While the senior Whig Adams had escaped censure, his younger antislavery accomplice was less fortunate. Representative Giddings's opponents demanded an instant vote on a motion to censure him for broaching

---

[23] *Congressional Globe*, 27th Congress, 2nd Session, March 21, 1842, 342. Arthur Downey summarizes that Giddings's Resolutions upheld "the right of the slaves to go free." Downey, *Creole Affair*, 97–98, quote on 97. Sean Wilentz concludes they asserted "the laws of slavery had no effect outside of the southern states," and that the *Creole* rebels "were fully justified in their violent strike for freedom," Wilentz, *Rise of American Democracy*, 556. See also Stewart, *Joshua R. Giddings*. Michael Holt's massive narrative of the rise and fall of the Whig party is oddly mute on this important moment in party history. I also prefer to view Giddings, Adams, Wilson, and others as radicals rather than "extreme antislavery Whigs." Holt, *American Whig Party*, 44, 319.

the topic in general and specifically for advocating that slavery was a local institution outside of the purview of the federal government's protection. The vote carried 125 to 69. Giddings strolled over to Adams, shook his hand, resigned his seat, and returned home. In a special election in Ohio's sixteenth congressional district held in April 1842, Giddings was returned by 7,469 votes to 393 votes for a mocking Democrat. He soon returned to the Capitol to resume his antislavery crusade.[24]

It is clear that Giddings's resolutions helped cement his place in the pantheon of political antislavery heroes. He also succeeded in promoting antislavery agitation. What is harder to gauge is the impact of his resolutions on broader audiences. Most obviously, his constituents supported his antislavery rhetoric in Congress. Part of that concerned the importance of the rights of man over property rights in slaves. Moreover, it was clear that during early 1842, the *Creole* revolt provided one of the most powerful and compelling recent examples of the successful struggle for human rights over the sanctity of property rights. Indeed, the affirmation of the right of slaves to rebel and resist as illustrated by the *Creole* was perhaps the most incendiary statement that northern abolitionists could make toward their fellow Americans in southern states. Arguments for natural rights, the rights to resist slavery through violence, and the limited reach of slave states' rights in Giddings's resolutions caused anger and resentment when they were read in southern newspapers.[25]

If Congress was Giddings's chosen battlefield, it was civil society in which his fellow antislavery adherent operated. William Jay, son of the statesman and jurist John Jay, was born in New York in 1789. After graduating from Yale, he pursed legal studies until poor eyesight intervened. He became drawn toward philanthropic causes including Christian Evangelicalism, pacifism, and antislavery. In December 1833, he was one of sixty-two abolitionists who founded the American Antislavery Society in Philadelphia; he went on to write its constitution and to become its corresponding secretary. His abolitionism was of a conservative cast that ultimately led to his leaving, in 1840, the organization he helped found. Although he opposed interference with slavery in the states where it existed and (unlike Giddings) did not support armed struggle against

---

[24] Wilentz, *Rise of American Democracy*, 557; Downey, *Creole Affair*, 99–101; Eric Foner, *Free Soil, Free Labor, Free Men: The Ideology of the Republican Party before the Civil War* (New York: Oxford University Press, 1970), 82; Stewart, *Joshua R. Giddings*.

[25] "Twenty-Seventh Congress—2nd Session," *Richmond Enquirer*, March 24, 1842. Note that Virginia readers would have come across the Ohio congressman's resolutions in their states' leading newspaper and no doubt fumed – much to the delight of the editor!

slavery, he did share the Ohio Congressman's belief in the natural rights of man. This commitment he elaborated on quietly and eloquently in his short and powerful pamphlet *The Creole Case and Mr. Webster's Dispatch.*[26]

Published by the New York American located at 47 William Street, New York, the pamphlet ran thirty-nine pages. Its objective "was to arouse more general attention to the portentous issue" of war for the "protection, and extension of Slavery."[27] It was divided into two sections. The first part reproduced Secretary Webster's letter of instruction to minister Everett dated January 29, 1842. It briefly narrates the "serious occurrence" of the *Creole* revolt, the liberation of the slaves due to "interference of the Colonial authorities," and the alternative "course" that the local authorities should have taken based upon the comity of nations. The US Secretary was adamant that the "persons" on the *Creole* were only passing between US ports "within the reach of English authority only for the moment, and this only through force and violence."[28] Moreover, the minister's task was to communicate the two most important points. First, the modern world had wrought civilized states that were independent of each other and whose communication required adherence to the "doctrine of non-interference of any with the domestic concerns of others." Second, the United States and England differ "in the forms of their Government and their laws respecting personal servitude," and that without mutual respect, "the peace of the two countries" was endangered.[29]

The second part consists of Jay's rebuttal of Webster's arguments anchored in the antislavery advocate's assertion of the unacceptability of America's slave empire as well as the sanctity of the natural rights of man. "Here we have," Jay asks in feigned shocked terms, "the Federal government putting forth and pledging all of its powers to protect slavery," not in the US or a marine league from the coast but "on the high seas, and even in a harbor of a nation, that does not acknowledge slavery."[30] In other words, writes the pacifist Jay, the question raised by the US Secretary's dispatch is "Peace or War for the extension and security of the domestic slave trade."[31] This was literally the American empire at sea.

---

[26] Stewart, *Holy Warriors*, 50, 69, 113. For analysis of Jay's earlier pamphlet *A View of the Action of the Federal Government, in Behalf of Slavery* published in 1839, see Downey, *Creole Affair*, 24–6.

[27] William Jay, *The Creole Case, and Mr. Webster's Dispatch: With the Comments of the New York American* (New York: New York American, 1842), iii–iv.

[28] Ibid, 9.   [29] Ibid, 10.   [30] Ibid, 12.   [31] Ibid.

Moreover, much of the discussion on the subject of American rights, British laws, the comity of nations, and so forth ignored "the slaves themselves."[32] Of course people consent to the laws of their own country by coming or remaining within that nation's legal jurisdiction. But Jay insists accurately that the slaves never consented to these laws: "They have been brought within its jurisdiction by force, and by force alone. Therefore, when they find themselves or place themselves beyond its jurisdiction, they are no longer subject to that law."[33] And then came the New Yorker's key statements: "Once out of American jurisdiction, American law cannot be applied to them as slaves; the only law that can be applied is the universal law of nature."[34] And elsewhere: "What shall we say of the attempt to determine the case of human beings, with souls immortal as our own – with like hopes, feelings, passions, capacities and responsibilities – by the law applicable to certain bales of goods?"[35] (In other words, boxes of tobacco and human beings were not the same cargo on the *Creole*.) Jay's summary was brief and concise. Comity does not require "the surrender of the self-emancipated slaves of the *Creole*." Neither local law nor federal law could "be deemed of force on the high seas." Diplomacy and policy could not reverse England's law of free soil stretching back to the 1770s and forward to the 1840s. Finally, the "revolted slaves of the Creole" were "neither mutineers or murderers."[36] Few documents written during the early 1840s so powerfully expressed the rights of man in opposition to the rights of property in man.

Eleven years earlier, the British government had demonstrated unequivocally its legal opposition to property rights in man. Its 1833 Slavery Abolition Act liberated around three-quarters of a million slaves in the West Indies, implemented an apprenticeship system designed to transform masters and slaves into employers and employees in a capital-labor free market economy supervised by Stipendiary Magistrates, and provided GBP 20 million to former slaveholders. The measure was depicted by London as a glorious gift of freedom to the slaves. In actuality, it was recognition of the increasing breakdown of colonial slave management illustrated by several recent rebellions in 1816 Barbados, 1823 Demerara (now Guyana), and 1831–1832 Jamaica. This last upheaval was the most

---

[32] Ibid, 21.
[33] Ibid. This is precisely what the rebels sought to do by steering the *Creole* toward free water and soil.
[34] Ibid.   [35] Ibid, 28.   [36] Ibid, 37–38.

extensive in the long history of the British West Indies involving around 60,000 slaves and resulting in the deaths of more than 500 of them. The legislation was met with joyful enthusiasm by those about to be freed who celebrated the end of the long night of slavery in chapel service, processions, fetes, and dinners on plantations and in villages and towns throughout the colonies. The system of apprenticeship, however, proved less glorious as former masters refused to act as wage-paying employers while former slaves often saw little difference between the new apprentice-ship setup and the old institution of chattel slavery. In 1838, the entire system was abolished and more than two centuries of British colonial slavery were brought to an end.[37]

West Indian emancipation was also celebrated in the United States. Every first day of August – the day the abolition law came into effect in 1834 – white and black abolitionists would organize meetings to both commemorate this glorious day and mobilize local communities to both challenge and eventually terminate the system of American slavery.[38] On the same day that Secretary Webster penned his long letter to Lord Ashburton on the rights of property and the principle of comity, West Indies emancipation commemorations were being held across northern states. Several speakers addressed the issues of the rights of man, the rights of slave states beyond their boundaries, and British emancipation in commemorative speeches on August 1, 1842. In Lenox, Massachusetts, William Ellery Channing spoke of slavery as an "intolerable wrong" because it "deprives men of Freedom." "Nature cries aloud for Freedom," said the prominent Unitarian theologian, "as our proper good, our birthright, and our end, and resents nothing so much as its loss."[39] "Has he not human powers, human rights?" asked Dr. Channing rhetorically concerning the slave.[40] Moreover, Dr. Channing called on Americans to "deprecate all political action on slavery, except for one end, and this end, is to release the free states from all connection with this oppressive institution, to sever slavery wholly from the National Government, to make it exclusively the concern of the States in which it exists."[41] In other words, the federal government would not be able to

---

[37] J. R. Kerr-Ritchie, *Rites of August First: Emancipation in the Black Atlantic World* (Baton Rouge: Louisiana State University Press, 2007), chap. 1.

[38] Ibid, chaps. 2 and 3.

[39] William E. Channing, *Dr. Channing's Last Address, Delivered at Lenox, on the First of August, 1842, The Anniversary of Emancipation in the British West Indies* (Boston: Oliver Johnson, 1842), 8.

[40] Ibid, 12.   [41] Ibid, 21.

protect the property rights of slaveholders and traders beyond Virginia, Louisiana, and other slave-holding states. Although unstated, this was clearly opposite to the argument of Calhoun, Webster, Tyler, and others that property rights in man had unlimited jurisdiction.

In Boston, Massachusetts, William Cooper Nell – twenty-six years old and a founding member of the American Anti-Slavery Society and the Massachusetts Antislavery Society – carefully narrated the stages of British abolition to a packed, mixed audience at the Belknap Street Church in Boston. The prominent black American abolitionist began his address by returning to the early 1770s and James Somerset "who was liberated from the grasp of a man-stealer by the decision of the Judiciary in his favor, by whom it was declared that as soon as a slave sets his foot on British soil, he is free."[42] In Newark, New Jersey, James W. C. Pennington – self-emancipator, abolitionist, and Congregationalist minister – took great pleasure in describing the current state of British antislavery and its significance for American slaves. The "territory of the United States," he proclaimed to his audience in Newark, New Jersey, "is bounded on the northeast and north by the British provinces, which serve as so many cities of refuge to which hundreds of southern pieces of property find their way; flying from the *claws of the devouring Eagle* to the JAWS OF THE PROTECTING LION!!"[43] The latest demonstration of this principle in action was the liberation of the *Creole* captives in the West Indies.

Why, it is reasonable to question, were there so few references to the *Creole* revolt in these West Indian emancipation speeches, especially given its recent notoriety? I think there are two likely explanations. To begin with, the emphasis of much of these speeches was on the peaceful nature of emancipation in the British West Indies. William Jay quoted Sir Lionel Smith, Governor of Barbados and Jamaica between 1833 and 1839, on the "good order, decorum, and gratitude" of the people when freedom came on August 1, 1834.[44] Dr. Channing reminded his listeners at the Lennox commemoration that, since emancipation "not a report has reached us of murder perpetrated by a colored man on the white population."[45] The "lesson of this day," he continued, "is the safety of

---

[42] "First of August in Boston," *Liberator*, August 19, 1842, Boston.
[43] Rev. James W. C. Pennington, *An Address Delivered at Newark, N.J. at the First Anniversary of West India Emancipation, August 1, 1839* (Newark: Aaron Guest, 1839), 7–8. Original italics and capitals.
[44] William Jay, *The Progress and Results of Emancipation in the English West Indies* (New York: Wiley & Putnam, 1842), 24.
[45] Channing, *Last Address*, 14.

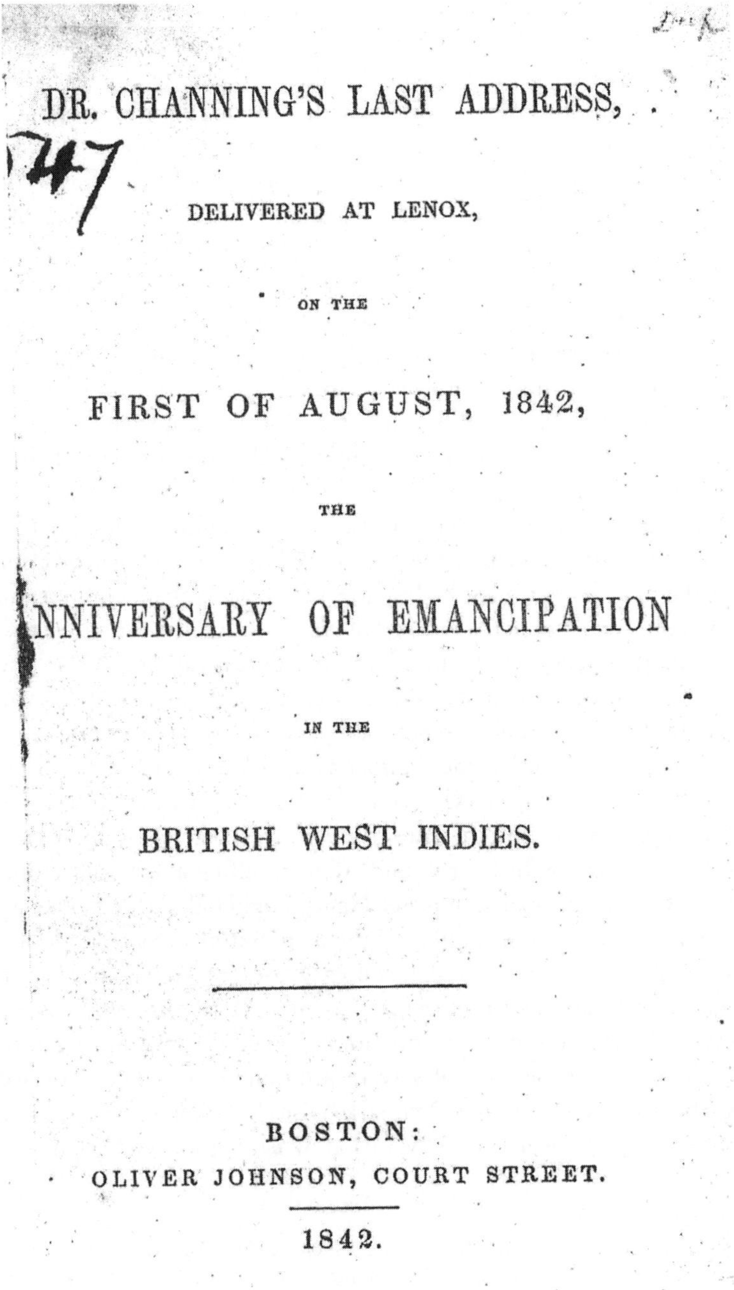

DR. CHANNING'S LAST ADDRESS,

DELIVERED AT LENOX,

ON THE

FIRST OF AUGUST, 1842,

THE

ANNIVERSARY OF EMANCIPATION

IN THE

BRITISH WEST INDIES.

BOSTON:

OLIVER JOHNSON, COURT STREET.

1842.

FIGURE 9.1 *Dr. Channing's Last Address*, Lenox, Massachusetts, August 1, 1842.

Emancipation."[46] West Indies emancipation had not wrought "insurrection and murder," explained the great patrician abolitionist from
Massachusetts, Wendell Phillips.[47] In other words, the bloody nature of
the path toward liberty exemplified by the *Creole* revolt went against the
peaceful nature of legal abolition in the British Caribbean.

This peaceful abolition process in the British colonies, furthermore,
served as a useful model for emancipation in the United States.
"We hope," lectured William Jay, in the "home of our fathers, justice
will triumph not by insurrection among the slaves – but by the righteous
efforts" of those around them.[48] Dr. Channing could "recommend no
crusade against slavery, no use of physical or legislative power for its
destruction, no irruption into the South to tamper with the slave, or to
repeal or resist the laws."[49] In other words, American emancipation was
to be modeled on the mighty experiment of abolition in the British West
Indies.

That being said, times changed. Born enslaved in Tennessee in 1816,
Josiah Jones self-emancipated and relocated to Chatham, Upper Canada.
Over the next few decades, he became a farmer, Baptist church member,
and volunteer soldier in the local community. In August 1842, twenty-six-
year-old Jones delivered the keynote address at the West Indian
Emancipation Day commemoration held in Chatham, British Canada.[50]
He wished that John Bull, the national personification of Britain, "would
roar in the East, and that the thunder of his voice might be heard by the
tigers of the south, for then would they burst in sunder their prison house,
and sweep with the bosom of destruction, the enemies of liberty and of
humanity."[51] One year later in mid-August, self-emancipator, abolitionist, and Congregationalist minister Henry Highland Garnet spoke at the
National Negro Convention assembled in Buffalo, New York. In his
"Address to the Slaves of the United States of America," Reverend
Garnet demanded his "Brethren, arise, arise. Strike for your lives and
liberties. Now is the day and the hour. Let every slave throughout the
land do this, and the days of slavery are numbered." Their rise would
resemble "noble men" like Denmark Vesey, Nathaniel Turner, Joseph
Cinque of the *Amistad*, and "Madison Washington, that bright star of

---

[46] Ibid, 21.
[47] Wendell Phillips, "Freedom's Jubilee," *Herald of Freedom*, August 5, 1842, Concord.
[48] Jay, *Progress and Results*, 39.   [49] Channing, *Last Address*, 23.
[50] C. Peter Ripley, ed., *The Black Abolitionist Papers*, vol. 2 *Canada 1830–1865* (Chapel
Hill: University of North Carolina Press, 1985), 95.
[51] *Chatham Journal*, August 6, 1842, in Ripley, ed., *Black Abolitionist Papers* vol. 2, 95–96.

freedom" along with "Nineteen [who] struck for liberty or death."[52] These early calls for armed struggle against American slavery were to fall on more fertile ground during the 1850s in the context of the 1850 Fugitive Slave Act, the 1854 Kansas-Nebraska Act, the 1857 *Dred Scott* decision, John Brown's raid on Harper's Ferry in 1859, and so forth. This was much more fertile soil for the sort of armed insurrection exemplified by the *Creole* rebels. In his 1857 August 1 address at Canandaigua in upstate New York, former slave and renowned abolitionist Frederick Douglass reminded his antislavery audience of English poet Lord Byron's immortal line: "Who would be free, themselves must strike the first blow." He then read out a roll call of heroic resisters: Margaret Garner, who killed her infant "to save it from the hell of our Christian Slavery," fugitive William Thomas, who preferred drowning to "submission to the hell hounds" pursuing him, William Parker and his "noble band of fifteen" who fought against kidnappers "with prayers and pistols," Joseph Cinque's "burning protest against slavery" on the deck of the *Amistad*, and "Madison Washington who struck down his oppressor on the deck of the Creole," who is more worthy to be remembered than the colored man who shot [British marine major John] Pitcaren [Pitcairn] at Bunker Hill."[53]

The *Creole* revolt also stoked support for natural rights over property rights in Great Britain. All of the historical literature on the *Creole* revolt restricts commentary on the British side to the various doings of colonial officials in the Caribbean, government politicians in London, and Lord Ashburton's special mission to Washington. But preliminary research into the British press during this period suggests that editors together with ordinary men and women were not only aware of the maritime revolt but drew upon it to make statements concerning human rights, the limitation of slave property rights, and other antislavery principles.[54]

---

[52] Henry Highland Garnet, "Address to the Slaves of the United States of America," in Richard Newman, Patrick Rael, Phillip Lapsansky, eds., *Pamphlets of Protest: An Anthology of Early African American Protest Literature, 1790–1860* (New York: Routledge, 2001), 160–164, "are numbered," "noble men," "star of freedom," "liberty or death" (164). After debate, the address failed to be adopted by the convention. It was subsequently published in 1848 together with David Walker's *Appeal*. Ibid, 156.

[53] Frederick Douglass, "West India Emancipation Delivered at Canandaigua, Aug. 4," in John Blassingame, ed., *The Frederick Douglass Papers*, Series 1, Speeches, Debates, and Interviews, vol. 3. (New Haven: Yale University Press, 1985), 202–206.

[54] A subject search "Creole" for British newspapers between January 1, 1840 and January 1, 1843, turned up 112 references, some of which probably do not relate to the maritime

There were two major ways the British public was informed of the *Creole* revolt. Several newspapers narrated the story of the rebellion, the killing of John Hewell, the imprisonment of the rebels, the release of the other slaves, and the American consul's protest. These details were taken from New Orleans newspapers and published in the British press under familiar subheadings "Mutiny and Murder" and "Case of the Brig *Creole.*"[55] The other means was through the personal report of Captain J. R. Crosbie of the brig *Elizabeth* who arrived at Liverpool from Nassau and reported the *Creole* revolt, the US consul's protest, and the vessel's subsequent embarkation for New Orleans. His account was posted in the Liverpool Underwriters rooms and reproduced in several Scottish, Irish, and English newspapers.[56]

These press accounts engaged some of the broader issues presented by the *Creole* revolt and its crisis-ridden role in Anglo-American relations. On the one hand, some newspaper editors professed support for Lord Ashburton's mission to solve Anglo-American tensions. The *Hampshire Advertiser & Salisbury Guardian* commented on Lord Ashburton's mission as being difficult already, but the *Creole* was an even "more difficult subject." The American press was "outrageous" at the lack of respect for the flag, and "indifference to the rights of owners of slaves." Since England declared free all who set foot on her soil, then Ashburton had to settle a "vexatio quaestio." In response to questions about Ashburton's qualifications, the newspaper observed that his American connections, manner, and business sense made him the "fittest man in this kingdom" for facing these "delicate negotiations."[57]

Other newspapers, however, were less concerned about resolving Anglo-American conflict and more interested in drawing upon the *Creole* revolt to condemn the failure of the United States to acknowledge human rights. The *North Devon Journal* regretfully reported Mr. Calhoun's resolution on the *Creole* and its unanimous resolution.

revolt (Kate McMahon, email message to author, July 11, 2017). Shout out to Kate for sending me twelve digital newspaper articles.

55 *Cork Examiner*, January 17, 1842, Cork, Ireland; *Hampshire Advertiser*, January 15, 1842, Southampton, England; *The Morning Post*, January 13, 1842, London, England; *The Northern Star and Leeds General Advertiser*, January 15, 1842, Leeds, England.

56 *Caledonian Mercury Edinburgh*, December 27, 1841, Edinburgh; *Cork Examiner*, December 29, 1841; *Devizes and Wiltshire Gazette*, January 20, 1842; *Freeman's Journal and Daily Commercial Advertiser*, December 27, 1841, Dublin, Ireland; *Belfast News-Letter*, December 28, 1841, Belfast, Ireland; *The Standard*, December 25, 1841, London, England.

57 *Hampshire Advertiser & Salisbury Guardian*, January 15, 1842.

It was a pity that Kentucky Whig senator Henry Clay went along "in the various absurdities and gross misrepresentations." The debate on Senator Calhoun's resolution exhibited the "most remarkable instance of disguised shame on the part of these pretended men of freedom."[58] The *Devizes and Wiltshire Gazette* was even more adamant. After narrating the "facts" of the Creole revolt concisely and accurately, it lectured the Americans on the rights of man. When "liberated creatures" were left the option of returning to the brig or "remain under British protection, free men, in a free country," they "remained one and all." (This was not strictly accurate.) American folk had become "clamorous" on the subject, calling for compensation and punishment. This was "preposterous" since "the moment a slave touches our soil he is free." The local authorities had decided the slaves were uninvolved hence "much at liberty," while the culprits were sent to trial. Those standard legal authorities Puffendorf and Vattel were invoked to prove that slavery was only a positive law in contra to the natural law of liberty. But the "strongest point" was the English law that the air was too pure for slaves to breath in "commencing with the famous case of Somersett" in 1772 and ending with that of Lord Stowell's verdict on the "Grace" case in 1827. As to the culprits, their "act is to be regretted, but it may not be condemned." Let those who denounce it put themselves in position of slaves "and then question themselves as to its legality."[59]

Of course, these British editors and newspaper readers quickly forgot the hypocrisy of a nation that played a vital role in the making of New World slavery, reaped the material rewards of centuries of unrequited toil that contributed to its becoming a global power, only to turn around and not only proceed to lecture other nations on the moral impropriety, backwardness, and economic inefficiency of the slave system, but to continue

---

[58] Editor, "Important from America" *North Devon Journal*, February 10, 1842, Barnstaple, England.

[59] "America – Slavery – The Rights of Man," *Devizes and Wiltshire Gazette* January 20, 1842. Grace, an enslaved domestic in the Allan household, spent 1822–1823 with Mrs. Allan in England before returning to Antigua. She sued for liberty based upon temporary residence in England drawing upon the 1772 Somerset decision. The verdict went with the claimant John Allan and Grace's appeal was denied since "in England no dominion, authority, or coercion can be exercised over such person, yet on her return to her place of birth and servitude, the right to exercise such dominion revives." Temporary freedom on free soil did not mean its continuation once returned to slave soil. " The Slave, Grace," in Helen Tunnicliffe Catterall, ed., *Judicial Cases Concerning American Slavery and the Negro* vol. 1 (Washington, DC: Carnegie Institution, 1926), 179–193 (quote on 179).

to benefit from that so-called "inefficient" system's provision of slave-based cotton from southern plantations.[60]

Eighteen months prior to the *Creole* revolt, the US Supreme Court had ruled in the legal case of the *Amistad* rebellion that the African rebels had exercised the "right of human beings" to gain their liberation.[61] The captives aboard the *Creole* did the same – but not according to southern newspapers that were quick to draw comparisons. The difference between the *Amistad* and the *Creole* was that in the former, the slave trade was "forbidden" by Spanish law, but in the latter slaves were transported "under the flag and according to the laws of this Union."[62] The *Mobile Register and Journal* rejected the comparison because "the Amistad negroes were not held to service lawfully in the country under whose flag they sailed, when they seized the vessel and brought her into American waters." In contrast, the *Creole* Negroes were free "by force of the local law into which they brought themselves by felony against the law of their own sovereign."[63]

In contrast to this southern position, northern antislavery adherents thought the comparison compelling. In his 1842 pamphlet, William Jay referenced the decision in the *Amistad* case, "so similar in many respects to that of the *Creole*." These slave rebels were demanded by Spain under a treaty between that country and the United States and not under "the comity of nations." This was the condition under which they gained their freedom. Although the language of the dispatch – "mutineers and murders" – resembled that in the *Creole* revolt, the law of nations "reached them not."[64] More generally, Jay's own argument that the *Creole* captives were not bound to

---

[60] I have not come across British newspaper editorials defending slaveholder property rights during this time. This is hardly surprising. But that is not say that there were not proslavery sentiments expressed in pamphlets and articles. One only has to recall the mild, tolerant, and humane sentiments of Scottish writer Thomas Carlyle on the post-abolition West Indies expressed in his *Occasional Discourse on the Negro Question* published in 1849!

[61] Howard Jones, *Mutiny on the Amistad: The Saga of a Slave Revolt and Its Impact on American Abolition, Law, and Diplomacy* (New York: Oxford University Press, 1987), 188–194; Marcus Rediker, *The Amistad Rebellion: An Atlantic Odyssey of Slavery and Freedom* (New York: Viking, 2012), 184–193.

[62] *Commercial Bulletin*, December 4, 1841, New Orleans.

[63] *Mobile Register and Journal* copied in New Orleans *Commercial Bulletin*, December 9, 1841.

[64] Jay, *Creole Case*, 14.

American laws because they were not citizens was equally applicable to slaves aboard the *Amistad* who were not bound to Spanish laws.[65]

Mexico, part of New Spain, was bound to the laws of Madrid until its military struggle for national independence succeeded in 1821. Eight years later, America's new nation abolished the institution of slavery after more than two hundred and fifty years. Enslaved Indians and Africans had worked the silver mines, plantations, households, and urban economies of New Spain. Enslaved Africans escaped to create their own *palenques* (settlements). In 1608, for instance, some 500 self-emancipators lived in one such settlement near Veracruz.[66] The cost of enslaved labor, together with high mortality rates, and the difficulties of supply resulted in the gradual demise of the institution of slavery in Mexico. At the time of independence, there were about 3,000 slaves living mostly in the coastal areas of Veracruz, Acapulco, and elsewhere. On October 13, 1824 the Mexican government ended the slave trade. On September 15, 1829 President Vincente Guerrero proclaimed the abolition of slavery from the federal palace. His first decree – "Slavery is forever abolished in the republic" – was motivated by several factors including the "anniversary of our independence," the passage of "an act of national justice and beneficence," the increase of "more public tranquility," and the "aggrandizement of the republic."[67]

The advent of abolition in Mexico, however, was a little bit more complicated than the law's language suggested. At the time of the declaration of independence, there were some 2,240 *Tejanos* (Spanish-speaking) residents in Texas. This northern province of Mexico served as a buffer zone between the center of the new republic and Comanche raiders. As such, it granted Connecticut-born lead businessman Moses Austin 18,000 square miles within the territory of Texas. Austin died soon thereafter, but the new settlement attracted southern slaveholders and slaves. By 1830, there were 7,000 Americans who outnumbered the 4,000 *Tejanos* in the province. And cotton was king. By the early 1830s, the

[65] Sean Wilentz judged the two ship revolts as "eerily similar" although the parallel is unclear. Wilentz, *Rise of American Democracy*, 555.

[66] Colin Palmer, *Slaves of the White God: Blacks in Mexico, 1570–1650* (New York: Cambridge University Press, 1976).

[67] John Lynch, *The Spanish American Revolutions, 1808–1826* (London: W. W. Norton, 1973), 332; Randolph B. Campbell, *An Empire for Slavery: The Peculiar Institution in Texas* (Baton Rouge: Louisiana State University Press, 1989), 25–29; " Decree of Abolition of Slavery in Mexico," in Junius Rodriguez, ed., *Encyclopedia of Emancipation and Abolition in the Transatlantic World* (Armonk, NY: Sharpe, 2007), 689.

settlement was sending $500,000 of goods, mainly slave-grown cotton, to New Orleans.[68] Mexico ended slavery in its nation to stop the transformation of the northern province, which was being populated by incoming southern American slaveholders and their slaves, into a slave society.

Texas's colonial period between 1821 and 1835 inextricably linked white southern settlement with slaveholding. Stephen J. Austin initially proposed land distribution based upon individual households and fifty acres per slave. Josiah Bell moved his family and three slaves. Jared E. Groce transported ninety slaves from Georgia in early 1822 and established the Bernado plantation on the Brazos River. Although Mexican politicians disapproved of this settlement policy of bringing in slaves, they did not impede it. As historian Randolph B. Campbell summarizes, Mexican leaders found it "extremely difficult to choose between the revolutionary ideal of liberty and the practical need to protect property interests and encourage settlement of their nation." By the early 1830s, founding father Stephen Austin's conclusion that "Texas *must be* a slave country" had become a reality on the ground. Slavery gained a foothold during the colonial era for two major reasons. The first southern American settlers brought their human property with them. These enslaved people usually marched westward with slaveholders rather than being transported by ship like those aboard the *Creole*. Moreover, the settlement of Texas by slaveholders was a practical necessity since without them there would have been no colony.[69]

Conflict between Mexico's desire to retain control over its northern province and incoming southern immigrants who desired their own independent state resulted in military conflict breaking out in the fall of 1835. After the crushing defeat of the Texans at the Alamo and the subsequent defeat of Mexican general and President Antonio Lopez de Santa Anna at the San Jacinto River in April 1836 America's newest republic was born. Its southern border with Mexico was fixed at the Rio Grande. On August 4, 1837 the Lone Star State petitioned the US Congress for annexation to the Union, but was unsuccessful. On October 12, 1838 the new republic withdrew its offer of annexation by the United States. Instead, it sought international recognition. This

---

[68] John Mack Faragher, Mari Jo Buhle, Daniel Czitrom, and Susan H. Armitage, eds., *Out of Many: A History of the American People*, 4th ed., vol. 1 (Upper Saddle River, NJ: Prentice Hall, 2005), chap. 14; Campbell, *Empire of Slavery*, chaps. 2 and 3.

[69] Campbell, *Empire of Slavery*, chap. 1, "their nation" (15), "slave country" (3).

came from Washington in 1837, Paris in 1839, and London the following year.[70]

There were two major reasons why the United States refused Texas's offer for annexation. The first was that it would have opened up the intractable slavery question in American politics. The second was what historian Michael Holt dubs the "northern Whigs anti-Texas assault." John Quincy Adams, Joshua Giddings, Seth M. Gates, and William Slade expended much energy opposing annexation because it would mean the expansion of slavery. This opposition toward the extension of slavery expressed in the aftermath of the *Creole* revolt was a continuation rather than abatement or pause in the radical Whig agenda. In April 1844, the Ohio Congressman's response to Texas annexation came straight out of his 1842 resolutions against the extension of slavery beyond state borders: "The great question of slavery or liberty. Will we extend slavery or will we promote Liberty & Freedom?"[71]

Southerners who supported annexation wanted it for the opposite reasons. The incorporation of Texas would mean more real estate for subsequent settlement and the expansion of the Slave South. This would bring more political power to the Slave South in the federal legislature. And, it would mean greater security for slaveholding interests as well as the region as a whole. President John Tyler, a slaveholding Virginian, agreed. He supported annexation because of its enhancement of territory, slaveholding, and regional protection. But he also shared southern slaveholders' fears of British interference in Texas, especially the movement toward abolition of slavery.[72]

As *Rebellious Passage* has tried to make clear, there was a long history of British interference in the affairs of the United States in general and in the American South in particular stretching back to the Revolutionary Era.[73] The anxiety, therefore, that this former colonial ruler and now self-declared antislavery state with global power would not be concerned with the future of slavery in the Republic of Texas was not entirely without

---

[70] Faragher, Buhle, Czitrom, Armitage, *Out of Many*, chap. 14; Arthur M. Schlesinger, Jr., ed., *The Almanac of American History* (New York: Barnes and Noble, 2004), 235, 237.

[71] Holt, *American Whig Party*, 168–169, "anti-Texas assault," "Liberty & Freedom," (169).

[72] Ibid.

[73] This is the place to acknowledge the writing of this book during a backdrop of scandalous headlines concerning Russian "interference" in US elections during 2016. The historical eras and actions are obviously different, but whether or not there are similar practices of interference or parallel paranoia about outsider actions, the contemporary issue should help readers appreciate how it could have been so significant in the past.

merit. President John Tyler sent special envoy Duff Green to London to inquire into the nature of British plans toward the new Republic of Texas. The newspaper editor and Calhoun supporter wrote back to the new American Secretary of State, Abel P. Upshur, informing him that the British government was going to provide the Republic of Texas with funds to compensate slaveholders in exchange for emancipation. This would result in the creation of a large, new, free territory on the southwest border of the United States. This would also mean proximity to free soil and a location for fugitive slaves who were already crossing into post-emancipation Mexico. Duff Green's claim was persuasive enough for the president and his foreign secretary.[74]

New Secretary of State Abel P. Upshur remained convinced that British abolition was a strategy designed for global commercial domination. He wrote Senator Calhoun that Britain was "determined to abolish slavery throughout the American continent," and was pursing specific policies – such as ending slavery in Texas – as a means to fulfill this goal.[75] His tenure proved ephemeral because of a shocking explosion aboard the American warship *Princeton* during an official visit on February 28, 1844 that claimed his life and those of seven others.[76]

His successor wasted little time in presenting the annexation of Texas as being in the best interests of the Slave South. On April 12, 1844 Secretary of State John C. Calhoun signed a treaty that would bring Texas into the Union as a territory. A week later, he wrote a letter to the British minister, Richard Pakenham. In his haste for political office, this blue blood had departed Trinity College Dublin – that citadel of English Protestantism – without his degree and entered the Foreign Office. In 1835, he was made minister plenipotentiary to the United Mexican States. Over the next several years, he sought to persuade the Mexican republic to adhere to a British anti-slave trade agreement through a policy of the right of search of Mexican merchant ships. He succeeded with a treaty in 1841. In December 1843, Pakenham was appointed minister

---

[74] Holt, *American Whig Party*,170; Wilentz, *Rise of American Democracy*, 561; William W. Freehling, *The Road to Disunion: Secessionists at Bay, 1776–1854* (New York: Oxford University Press, 1990), 385–386; Jeffrey R. Kerr-Ritchie, *Freedom's Seekers: Essays on Comparative Emancipation* (Baton Rouge: Louisiana State University Press, 2014), 22–27.

[75] Don E. Fehrenbacher, *The Slaveholding Republic: An Account of the United States Government's Relations to Slavery* (New York: Oxford University Press, 2005), 121.

[76] Wilentz, *Rise of American Democracy*, 566; Freehling, *Road to Disunion*, 407.

plenipotentiary to the United States. It was in his Washington office that he read Secretary Calhoun's letter.[77]

Unsurprisingly, the US foreign secretary began diplomatically. While expressing the president's "pleasure" at Lord Aberdeen's "disavowal . . . to disturb the tranquility of the slaveholding States," he was concerned at the "avowal" that Great Britain "is constantly exerting herself to procure the general abolition of slavery throughout the world." Of even "deeper concern" to the president, wrote Secretary Calhoun, was "the avowal of Lord Aberdeen of the desire of Great Britain to see slavery abolished in Texas," and was endeavoring, "through her diplomacy, to accomplish it, by making the abolition of slavery one of the conditions on which Mexico should acknowledge her independence." This was followed by the secretary's avowal of the unmitigated failure of emancipation wherever it had occurred. In "all instances in which the States have changed the former relation between the two races," he claimed, "the condition of the African, instead of being improved, has become worse. They have been invariably sunk into vice and pauperism, accompanied by the bodily and mental inflictions incident thereto—deafness, blindness, insanity, and idiocy—to a degree without example; while, in all other States which have retained the ancient relation between them, they have improved greatly in every respect—in number, comfort, intelligence, and morals." Despite the realities of post-emancipation successes in Haiti and the British West Indies as well as northern American states, Secretary Calhoun continued his anti-abolition leitmotif that should Great Britain "succeed in accomplishing, in the United States, what she avows to be her desire and the object of her constant exertions to effect throughout the world, so far from being wise or humane, she would involve in the greatest calamity the whole country, and especially the race which it is the avowed object of her exertions to benefit."[78] The Secretary sent a copy of the letter to the US Senate, after which it was passed over to the press as was its author's original intent.[79]

This so-called Pakenham letter is familiar to historians of antebellum politics and sectional rivalry. Sean Wilentz describes it as "notorious" and its publication "a master stroke" of polarizing national politics during

---

[77] Charles Alexander Harris, "Pakenham, Richard" in *Dictionary of National Biography*, 1885–1900, vol. 43, https://en.wikisource.org/wiki/Pakenham,_Richard_(DNB00)

[78] "John C. Calhoun Letter to Richard Pakenham, April 18, 1844," *Econospeak*, http://econospeak.blogspot.com/p/mr.html

[79] Wilentz, *Rise of American Democracy*, 567.

a presidential election year.[80] Michael Holt refers to it as "famous" because its writer changed the Slave South's previous stance by asserting "annexation as a proslavery measure."[81] William Freehling depicts that "infamous Calhoun document" that was the logical consequence of "Calhoun's pet panacea – finding the right issue to educate Southerners out of both parties and into a southern convention."[82] While all three views differ, they remain united in situating the South Carolina slaveholder at the heart of the matter – namely contribution toward sectionalism leading to the American Civil War.

This focus on John Calhoun's lust for the American presidency, sectional divisions, and the roots of civil war causation, however, tends to downplay the broader theater of political conflict over slavery and emancipation across borders and between new republics and old colonial powers. American slavery was being surrounded by free soil. There were Caribbean spaces of freedom with Haiti (1804) and British West Indies (1833). There were North American spaces of freedom in British Canada and the Republic of Mexico (1829). Fugitive slaves who crossed borders voted with their feet against property rights in man. Meanwhile, American slavery was growing in southern states like Mississippi (1817), Alabama (1818), Missouri (1821), and Arkansas (1836) through the US slave trade and the Coastal Passage. It was also being buttressed by the creation of a new slaveholding republic on its southwest frontier in which natural rights were for white immigrants only. There were also expanding western spaces of freedom in Michigan (1837), Iowa (1846), Wisconsin (1848), and California (1850). The battle between property rights in man versus natural rights was not simply restricted to the United States, but swept across northern and central parts of the Americas.

This chapter seeks to expand our understanding of the *Creole* revolt and its implications. In general terms, it surveys the various ways in which American newspapers and politicians used the *Creole* revolt to make conflicting statements about the rights of property, sovereign domain, and human rights. Specifically, it illustrates how maritime slaves' liberation revealed sectional differences between southern slaveholders for whom property rights in slaves were sacrosanct and state laws protected those rights beyond state and national borders versus northern antislavery proponents dedicated to universal rights and the principle that slave laws

---

[80] Ibid, 567.   [81] Holt, *American Whig Party*, 171.
[82] Freehling, *Road to Disunion*, chaps. 22 and 23. "Calhoun document," 408, "southern convention," 390.

had no jurisdiction outside southern states. It goes further than the familiar sectional divide, however, by unearthing the transnational dimensions of this rich debate through examinations of British West Indian emancipation celebrations in northern US cities, British newspaper accounts of the *Creole* revolt and support for human over property rights, and the transatlantic dimensions of Mexican independence and abolition together with Texas independence and annexation. If there were broader spatial aspects to these arguments than usually allowed for, this was no less true of the legal proceedings pursued in dusty New Orleans courtrooms regarding liability for the *Creole* revolt.

10

Causa Proxima, Non Remota, Spectatur

Having examined the fiery maritime revolt, the captives' self-liberation and hope-filled resettlement in the Caribbean, and the sweeping transatlantic clash over property and human rights, we now turn to the more arcane aspect of this remarkable story. From December 1841 through March 1845, slave traders and insurance companies battled over culpability and liability for the loss of human cargoes in Louisiana courts. The traders had contracted as risk against loss and insisted they be reimbursed because the slaves had been freed by British interference. Their claim was supported by British actions in several recent maritime cases and during the Anglo-American wars. In contrast, representatives for the insurance companies argued that their clients were not responsible because the loss was caused by slave mutiny, a contingency that was not part of the original contract. The debate rolled through the lower and upper courts of Louisiana for forty months at the same time that the politics of slavery stalked the legislative halls of the United States, the Royal Navy scoured the Atlantic and Caribbean seas seeking out illegal slave traders, and former captives were enjoying the fruits of freedom as new colonial subjects in the Caribbean.

This consequence of the *Creole* rebellion has drawn some attention but limited analysis.[1] There are several possible explanations. The legal

---

[1] Edward D. Jervey and C. Harold Huber, "The Creole Affair," *The Journal of Negro History* vol. 65, no. 3 (Summer 1980), 207–208; George Hendrick and Willene Hendrick, *The Creole Mutiny: A Tale of Revolt Aboard a Slave Ship* (Chicago: Ivan R. Dee, 2003), 116–120; Eli N. Evans, *Judah P. Benjamin: The Jewish Confederate* (New York: Free Press, 1988), 37–39; Arthur T. Downey, *The Creole Affair: The Slave Rebellion That Led the U.S. and Great Britain to the Brink of War* (Lanham: Rowman and Littlefield, 2014),

process was complex. The report of the proceedings in the lower and upper courts is full of arcane language, legal precedent, technical jargon, ambiguities, and outright errors.[2] Moreover, a prolonged legal suit in dusty chambers seems dull compared to the blood and guts of slave rebellion on the high seas. It might also be because of the exacting demands of careful and systematic research required to unravel the arguments, rebuttals, counter-arguments, and so forth. Whatever the precise reason, we cannot ignore the *Creole* insurance dispute, sidestep detailed analysis of arguments on behalf of traders and insurers, or overlook what the legal process reveals about the maritime revolt and broader questions concerning the role of commercial insurance in America's coastal slave trade.

The insurance dispute over the *Creole* revolt demands our full attention for several reasons. The business of insuring slaves has often taken a back-step to studies of the slave trade, yet it was implicit in the activities of owners, traders, and companies from the eighteenth century onward. Capital investment and underwriting its risk marched arm in arm. Maritime insurance was an international business that transcended local and national borders. Moreover, the insurance dispute over the *Creole* revolt reveals the mysteries of maritime insurance. It further illustrates the extent to which the law was complicit in slaveholding, along with the reduction of human beings to the cash nexus. On the other hand, this dispute highlights the humanity of the slaves because owners and traders felt the need to assume risk against revolt and loss. As we shall see, the need to insure against the loss of valuable property exempting the potential of slave revolt reveals that the owners and insurers were cognizant of the agency of those who were legally defined as chattel. Most important, the legal dispute over the *Creole* revolt illustrates the maturation of maritime insurance of trading slaves in the commercial marketplace. The forty-month legal disputation in Louisiana between late 1841 and early 1845 provides a treasure trove of maritime insurance law in Great Britain and the

---

133–139; Jonathan Levy, *Freaks of Fortune: The Emerging World of Capitalism and Risk in America* (Cambridge: Harvard University Press, 2012), 49–57. This amounts to twenty-two pages that focus mainly on the 1845 Louisiana Supreme Court session.

[2] It is not quite as bad as the everlasting legal suit of Jarndyce and Jarndyce at the Court of Chancery in Charles Dickens' *Bleak House* published about a decade later in 1852–1853.

United States and the evolution of this important financial industry from the late eighteenth through mid-nineteenth centuries.[3]

Most ships trading in enslaved Africans in the Atlantic were insured internationally. The business of underwriting capital risk began in Antwerp, Belgium, and spread to Amsterdam in the Netherlands, to London, England, and to Paris, France, and then to smaller slave-trading ports by the late eighteenth century. Insurance premiums on French slavers ranged from 7 percent during peacetime to 35 percent during international crises. The slave ships of La Rochelle, France, were often insured elsewhere in Nantes, France, Amsterdam, the free city of Hamburg in Hanover, and London, England. The insurer Duvivier of La Rochelle made enough profit to become a slave ship trader. Hayley and Hopkins, a London marine insurance company, offered premiums on British slave ships to Jamaica ranging from 8 to 10 percent during the early 1770s. English companies often insured slave ships in the American mainland colonies. By the Revolutionary era, insurers were springing up in Philadelphia, Pennsylvania; and Boston, Massachusetts; and elsewhere.[4]

The coastal town of Newport in the colony of Rhode Island was an especially lucrative spot for slave trading and insurance companies. According to custom records, from fifteen to twenty-two slavers cleared the port annually for West African shores between 1763 and 1774. Historians of the city's slave trading business estimate sales of 40,000 Africans between 1761 and 1775. This profitable business demanded insurance against potential damages. The Newport Insurance Company, the Bristol Insurance Company, and the Mount Hope Insurance Company underwrote many of these transatlantic slavers. The de Wolf family were maritime slavers who founded Mount Hope to meet a growing need. Samuel and William Vernon were prominent traders, insurers, and

---

[3] For the growth of the insurance business and its impact on religion and magic as a means to alleviate "the incidence of human misfortune" in early modern England, see Keith Thomas, *Religion and the Decline of Magic: Studies in Popular Beliefs in Sixteenth and Seventeenth Century England* (New York: Oxford University Press, 1971), 651–654.

[4] Hugh Thomas, *The Slave Trade: The Story of the Atlantic Slave Trade* (New York: Simon & Schuster, 1997), 312; Elizabeth Donnan, ed., *Documents Illustrative of the History of the Slave Trade to America*, Vol. 4, *The Border Colonies and Southern Colonies* (Washington: Carnegie Institution of Washington, 1935), 229. George Hayley was a London alderman, Member of Parliament, and brother-in-law to London radical journalist and parliamentarian John Wilkes. His business interests in New England included insuring slave ships for the Brown family of Rhode Island. See Amanda Bowie Moniz, "A Radical Shrew in America: Mary Wilkes Haley and Celebrity in Early America," Common Place, 2008, http://common-place.org/book/a-radical-shrew-in-america/.

resellers of risk to London underwriters. Interestingly, prominent Newport merchant and slaver Aaron Lopez contracted with London marine insurer Hayley and Hopkins. Premiums were high, ranging from 5 to 25 percent depending on conditions, cargoes, and the market. But these were more than offset by the tremendous profits to be made from trading in human cargoes.[5]

The underwriting of slave ships was a necessity because of what maritime insurers described as the "perils of the sea." Potential hazards faced by ships, masters, and crews included fire, shipwreck, piracy, capture, arrests, barratry or fraud by the captain and crew against owners or insurers, jettison, and attacks from men-of-war from other nations. These were considered "extraordinary" perils rather than ordinary maritime challenges such as wear and tear of rigging, destruction by rats and mice, and so forth. One of the risks that insurers refused to underwrite was contagion of human cargoes from disease. If they did, the ship's master might be tempted to ignore its spread and subsequently claim insurance liability.[6]

Liability for slave ship revolts was one of the maritime perils that underwriters often refused to assume. "The insurers [are] free from any Loss or damage that may happen from the Insurrection of the Negroes" was one clause in the insurance policy on the *Fly* dated October 9, 1788.[7] This refusal by insurance companies to assume liability for maritime rebellions was more frequent than reported in most Atlantic slave trade studies. It was a peril of the sea understood by contemporary shippers, investors, and others. From the late eighteenth century onward it was probably buried by Anglo-American abolitionist rhetoric on victimization

---

[5] Elaine F. Crane, "'The First Wheel of Commerce': Newport, Rhode Island and the Slave Trade, 1760–1776," *Slavery and Abolition* vol. 1 (1980), 178–198; Thomas, *Slave Trade*, 312; Jonathan Ira Levy, "The Ways of Providence: Capitalism, Risk, and Freedom in America, 1841–1935," vol. 1, PhD dissertation, University of Chicago: Chicago, IL, 2008, 43–44. For a fictional account of the insurance of the slaver *Liverpool Merchant*, see Barry Unsworth, *Sacred Hunger* (New York: Norton, 1993), 274.

[6] James D. B. De Bow, "Art. I.—Marine Insurance," *Debow's Review* vol. II, no. 1 (July 1846), 16; Daniel P. Mannix and Malcolm Cowley, *Black Cargoes: A History of the Atlantic Slave Trade* (London, Penguin, 1976), 111.
In Charles Dicken's novel *Dombey and Son*, London shipping manager Mr. Carker reminds Captain Cuttle of the reason for maritime insurance: "You must have begun very early on your day's allowance [rum measure], if you don't remember that there are hazards in all voyages, whether by sea or land" (508).

[7] Emma Christopher, *Slave Ship Sailors and Their Captive Cargoes, 1730–1807* (New York: Cambridge University Press, 2006), 183n64.

that ignored or downplayed slave ship revolts that ill-befitted their anti-slave trade campaign, and has only reappeared in recent scholarship.

Slave trading was such a lucrative business, however, that insurance companies could not refuse to underwrite revolt altogether. In early August 1774, one ship's master requested insurance against slave insurrection. Twelve years later, a court ordered an insurance company to pay up after a maritime insurrection, indicating that revolt was part of the original policy.[8] But the standard means of insuring against ship revolt was to provide limited liability in those cases in which a certain amount (usually 5 percent) of Africans died. In other words, the company would be responsible for the losses of any slaves over a certain percentage in recognition of the fact that ships' captains would seek to limit the number of African deaths for pecuniary motives.[9] In 1776, an insurance policy for a Rhode Island slaver stated in rather opaque terms: "Wresk of Mortality and Insurrection of 220 slaves, Value 9000 Ste'[rlin]g at 5 per cent is P[e]r Month = 37.10s." In other words, the slaver was transporting 220 captives worth a combined total of GBP 9,000. The insurer would be liable for any losses <u>after</u> GBP 450 (or 5 percent of the total worth of the slaves) in the event of either the slaves' death or rebellion. The slave ship owners paid GBP 37.10 shillings per month to cover the risk.[10] In 1792–1793, the slaver *Lumbey* was insured for GBP 1,200 and the slaves were insured for GBP 1,800. The policy included a clause stating that "if there was a loss of slaves by insurrection exceeding 5 per cent, that loss was to be covered by the policy."[11] In 1794, Lloyds of London issued a policy to Fermin de Taster and Company on the slaver *Guipurzcoa* with the ship valued at GBP 3,500 and the slaves at GBP 45 each. The premium amounted to twenty guineas "per cent" and a marginal clause stipulated that the London insurer was "Free from particular average by insurrection under 5 percent." It is not clear how many slaves were on board, but if there were 200 slaves and they revolted, then Lloyds would be liable for any amount exceeding GBP 450. In other words, one captive's value (GPB 45) multiplied by

---

[8] Harvey Wish, "American Slave Insurrections before 1861," *The Journal of Negro History*, vol. 22, no. 3 (July 1937), 302–303.

[9] Eric Robert Taylor, *If We Must Die: Shipboard Insurrections in the Era of the Atlantic Slave Trade* (Baton Rouge: Louisiana State University Press, 2006), 165.

[10] Wish, "American Slave Insurrections," 302.

[11] Christopher, *Slave Ship Sailors*, 183n64.

200 equals GBP 9,000; 5 percent of GPB 9,000 equals GPB 450. Lloyds would be liable for any loss in excess of GPB 450.[12]

The authors of this traditional history of Lloyds published in 1932 refer to this insurance policy as somewhat "curious," even though the insurance of transatlantic slavers represented business as usual. As historian Eric Williams pointed out in *Capitalism and Slavery* published twelve years later: "Lloyds, like other insurance companies, insured slaves and slave ships, and was vitally interested in legal decisions as to what constituted 'natural death' and 'perils of the sea.'"[13] But the company's historians follow with the astonishing claim that the "abolition of the slave trade is indeed very largely due to Lloyds." To paraphrase Williams's famous quip that laudatory studies of British abolition sound like the colonial slave trade was invented in order to abolish it, it would seem that Lloyds of London invented the slave trade insurance policy in order to take credit for its abolition!

To understand the mechanics of maritime insurance a little better, let's examine two legal cases of insurance liability concerning slave ships during a formative period. The first concerns two insurrections aboard the English slaver *Wasp* in 1783. In the first rebellion, women captives seized Captain Richard Bowen and tried to heave him overboard. Twelve slaves died of their injuries and a hunger strike. In the second revolt, which also failed, fifty-five slaves died of several causes, including "bruises, swallowing salt water, chagrins at disappointment, and abstinence."[14] The original insurance policy contained a clause in which the underwriters assumed risk for deaths as a consequence of rebellion beyond 10 percent of the slaves' total monetary worth. At the subsequent trial, Captain Bowen testified that some slaves were shot, some died by falling through the hatchway, and others died after the rebellion from injuries, "disappointment," and "abstinence." The insurance company paid for those who were killed during the revolt. The plaintiff insisted that the

---

[12] Frank Worsley and Glyn Griffith, *The Romance of Lloyds: From Coffee House to Palace* (New York: Hillman-Curl, 1937), 47. Begun as a small coffee house on Tower Street in the City of London, Lloyds branched out to become the major maritime insurer in the English Atlantic slave trade until abolition. For the role of London's coffee house in the development of early capitalism's "bourgeois rationality," see Robin Blackburn, *The Making of New World Slavery: From the Baroque to the Modern, 1492–1800* (London: Verso, 1997), 270–271.

[13] Eric Williams, *Capitalism and Slavery* (London: Andre Deutsch, 1964), 104.

[14] Taylor, *If We Must Die*, 204; Marcus Rediker, *The Slave Ship: A Human History* (New York: Viking, 2007), 288, 293, 295 – the last two pages incorrectly place the *Wasp* revolt in 1785.

underwriters were also responsible for those slaves who died in the aftermath of the rebellion. The jury decided in favor of the insurance company
because the slave revolt clause covered immediate deaths only. Those
slaves who died after the revolt were not covered and therefore the underwriters were not culpable.[15]

The other legal case of insurance liability involved the English slaver
Zong. In late 1781, this vessel overshot its Jamaica destination and ran
short of water. Captain Luke Collingwood ordered 133 African slaves be
thrown overboard in order to preserve water for the rest of the slaves so
that they would be market-ready. The ship's owners took the insurers to
court claiming costs for the jettisoned slaves under the familiar rule of
legitimate cargo. In March 1783, the case was heard in the Guildhall,
London, with a jury deciding that the insurers were liable for the loss of
132 slaves (one survived). The underwriters requested a retrial. On
May 21–22, 1783, the Court of the King's Bench met in Westminster
Hall, London, to decide on a retrial of the original case. Lord Chief Justice
William Murray Mansfield, one of the three judges, opened the case with
the simple statement: "This is the case of a Policy of Insurance upon the
ship the *Zong*." The ship's owners, represented by Solicitor General John
Lee and his assistant Mr. Chambres, argued that the dearth of water
entailed the killing of the slaves as a "necessity." The insurers' lawyers
consisting of Messrs. Davenport, Pigot, and Heywood and advised by
prominent antislavery activist Granville Sharpe objected to what they
depicted as a fraud designed to make the insurers liable for a loss-
making voyage. The legal team argued that there was no "such necessity
as could justify such a very extraordinary transaction." Indeed, their
argument in favor of the underwriters went beyond maritime insurance.
Mr. Pigot stated "that as long as any water remained to be divided, these
men [slaves] were as much entitled to their share as the captain, or any
other man whatever." This claim for the universal rights of man leaps out
in a simple case concerning a policy of insurance on a slave ship.[16] We will
encounter a similar standout claim concerning the human right to rebel

---

[15] Taylor, *If We Must Die*, 166. The captain's terminology of "disappointment" and
"abstinence" signifies the deep meaning of liberty to these rebels.

[16] James Walvin, *The Zong* (New Haven: Yale University Press, 2011), 1–2, chap. 8;
Simon Schama, *Rough Crossings: The Slaves, the British, and the American Revolution*
(New York: Harper Collins, 2006), 157–161, 166–169; Adam Hochschild, *Bury the
Chains: Prophets and Rebels in the Fight to Free an Empire's Slaves* (Boston: Mariner,
2005), 79–82.

FIGURE 10.1 Africans thrown overboard from a Brazilian slave ship, 1832.
Source: *Liberator*, January 7, 1832.

against tyranny in the *Creole* insurance case more than six decades later in New Orleans.

According to the most recent historian of the *Zong* atrocity, there is no evidence of a retrial.[17] But the horror of the mass murder helped galvanize British public opinion against the Atlantic slave trade leading to its eventual legal abolition in 1807.[18] More immediately for our purposes, it revealed Lord Mansfield to be the "big daddy" of maritime insurance law. William Murray was born into the Scottish nobility and attended Westminster School and then Christ Church, Oxford University. He served as Lord Chief Justice, the highest jurist in the Empire, for more

[17] Walvin, *Zong*, 155. [18] Walvin, *Zong*, chaps. 9 and 10.

than a generation between 1755 and 1788.[19] Apart from modernizing an antiquated legal system, his main field was commercial law especially insurance. This interest no doubt reflected the burgeoning business of the era. By the late eighteenth century, British maritime insurance covered around GBP 100 million worth of goods. This massive commercial expansion helps explain Lord Mansfield's desire to make the law as lucid and accessible as possible.[20] It also explains his reluctance to interfere with the massive economic profits culled from British colonial slavery. This conservative approach was displayed in his 1772 decision to merely prevent the owner of James Somerset from taking his personal slave back to Jamaica rather than abolishing slavery on British soil altogether.[21] It also shaped his understanding of maritime insurance that underwriters could only be liable for losses they had insured against rather than "indirect losses."[22] Not only did the shadow of this distinguished British jurist hang over subsequent legal disputes over maritime insurance, but the principle of limited liability for insurance companies was to shape the final verdict over the legal case of insurance liability concerning the *Creole* decades later and thousands of miles away in a southern US court.

In 1839, the Louisiana legislature created the Commercial Court of New Orleans (CCNO). It held concurrent jurisdiction with the Orleans Parish Court and the First Judicial District Court, but was exempted from dealing with prolonged lawsuits concerning land, slave ownership, domestic relations, tort suits, or eminent domain expropriations. The new court was probably created in order to meet the bustling city's large and growing number of commercial suits that were clogging the existing courts. The state legislature's objective was to resolve commercial disputes in order to encourage economic growth. More than 80 percent of

---

[19] One gets a sense of his jurisprudence from the following wry comment by historian Edward P. Thompson: "Lord Mansfield pronounced that the real issue was not the legality or illegality of the coneys [rabbit burrows], but 'whether the commoner can do himself justice,' and it was his decided view that the commoner might not. It was perhaps fortunate for commoners' rights that Lord Mansfield never sat in judgment upon fences." E. P. Thompson, *Customs in Common: Studies in Traditional Popular Culture* (New York: The New Press, 1993), 118. See also pages 112 and 139 for the jurist's caution and conservatism, an approach easily transferred from rural to maritime matters.

[20] Walvin, *Zong*, 123–125; Schama, *Rough Crossings*, 32–34.

[21] Walvin, *Zong*, chap. 7; Schama, *Rough Crossings*, 44–45; Hochschild, *Bury the Chains*, 48–53. The continuation of slavery in England was exemplified not only by newspaper advertisements for self-emancipators but also by the attendance of enslaved boy George to South Carolinian Henry Laurens who was incarcerated in the Tower of London in 1781. Schama, *Rough Crossings*, 137.

[22] Walvin, *Zong*, 125.

the new court's business dealt with financial instruments, debts for merchandise, and debts for services. The state Supreme Court fielded appeals from the new court.[23]

The CCNO was the venue for litigation by slave traders against insurance companies for the loss of their human cargoes as a consequence of the *Creole* revolt. Charles Watts, a local businessman and former judge, presided over the lower court during the insurance dispute. Between mid-December 1841 and early January 1842, Edward Lockett, Charles Hatcher and Jason Andrews, Sherman Johnson, John Hagan, and Thomas McCargo sued the Fireman's Insurance Company of New Orleans (FICNO), the Merchant's Insurance Company of New Orleans (MICNO), the Ocean Insurance Company (OIC), and the New Orleans Insurance Company (NOIC) in seven lawsuits. Three of the insurance companies hired legal representatives F. B. Conrad, Thomas Slidell and Judah Benjamin. Conrad and Slidell were both prominent in the state's legal business. According to *Gibson's Guide*, an attorney-at-law called Conrad resided at Exchange Place over the post office building. Thomas Slidell became US attorney for the Eastern District of Louisiana in 1837 and seven years later was elected to the state senate.[24]

The third legal representative proved to be the standout counsel. Judah P. Benjamin was born in the Danish slave colony of St. Croix in 1811.[25] His family migrated to Savannah, Georgia, after which they relocated to Wilmington and Fayetteville in North Carolina. After attending Yale College, in 1831 Benjamin moved to New Orleans where he studied law and was admitted to the state bar in 1832. He served two years as state legislator between 1842 and 1844. *Gibson's Guide* lists his office as on the upper floor of 15 Exchange Place in New Orleans. He purchased the *Belle Chasse* plantation in Plaquemines Parish about nine miles outside of New Orleans. There he built one of the "best plantation homes" in the state. He also owned between 140 and 161 slaves. His plantation, it was later reported, was "noted for its humaneness," with one observer claiming that former slaves held "none but kindly memories and romantic legends

---

[23] New Orleans Public Library, City Archives, http://nutrias.org/inv/commct.htm. The CCNO was terminated in 1845, with pending cases transferred to the newly created Fourth District Court.

[24] Downey, *Creole Affair*, 134; *Gibson's Guide and Directory of the State of Louisiana and the Cities of New Orleans and Lafayette* (New Orleans: John Gibson, 1838), 47.

[25] For a pioneering account of the making of colonial slavery in the Danish West Indies, see Neville A. T. Hall, *Slave Society in the Danish West Indies: St. Thomas, St. John and St. Croix*, ed., Barry W. Higman (Mona, Jam.: University of West Indies Press, 1992).

of the days of glory of the old place."²⁶ One early biographer described Benjamin's personality as neat, courteous, calm, collected, and forcible, He spoke rapidly in mellifluous tones, was concise, bilingual in French and English, admired and liked. He was a southern Whig with a readiness of mind who was a leading light in New Orleans.²⁷ The insurance companies banked on this gifted legal team, although their investment initially went unrewarded.

Unfortunately, records of the filing, proceedings, and outcome of these seven legal suits are scattered and sporadic, making it hard to provide an exact narrative.²⁸ On December 15, 1841, Edward Lockett's lawyers filed suit against MICNO. On January 17, 1843, Judge Watts approved the jury decision of awarding $9,333 with 5 percent interest from March 1842 until the amount plus court costs was paid to the plaintiff.²⁹ They also filed suit against the OIC for the loss of twenty-six human cargoes worth $20,000. In March 1843, the jury awarded Lockett the losses plus interest and court costs.³⁰

The following day, counsel representing Charles Hatcher and Jason Andrews sued the OIC for eight human cargoes valued at $3,300. Judge Watts summoned the insurer to the CCNO to answer the claim. On June 15, 1842, both plaintiffs appear to have transferred their claims in a notarized document before public notary William Christy, although the recipient remains unclear.³¹

---

²⁶ "Benjamin, Judah Philip, (1811-1884)," Biographical Directory of the United States Congress, http://bioguide.congress.gov/scripts/biodisplay.pl?index=b000365; Eli N. Evans, *Judah P. Benjamin: The Jewish Confederate* (New York: Free Press, 1988), 32–33 "old place"; Pierce Butler, *Judah P. Benjamin* (Philadelphia: G. W. Jacobs, 1907), 62; Frederick Bancroft, *Slave-Trading in the Old South* (Baltimore: J. H. Furst, 1931), 325–326, "plantation homes" (161); Downey, *Creole Affair*, 134; *Gibson's Guide and Directory*, 18. Many of the interviews with former slaves by WPA workers during the 1930s depict harsher slave experiences far removed from such romantic legends.

²⁷ Butler, *Benjamin*, 43–45. Southern Whig Benjamin no doubt disagreed with the anti-slavery actions of his party's northern colleague, Joshua Giddings.

²⁸ The documents – often difficult to read – are randomly spread over one microfilm reel at the New Orleans Public Library (NOPL), among court records in Box 256 at the University of New Orleans (UNO), and scattered as loose papers in Box 106 at the Amistad Research Center (ARC).

²⁹ Docket No. 4410 *Edward Lockett v. The Merchants Insurance Company of New Orleans*, 1841 microfilm, NOPL. The docket number is the CCNO's.

³⁰ Docket No. 4411 *Edward Lockett v. The Fireman's Insurance Company of New Orleans*, 1841 microfilm, NOPL.

³¹ Docket No. 4413, *Andrews and Hatcher v. The Ocean Insurance Company*, 1841 microfilm, NOPL.

On January 19, 1842, two shippers of human cargoes aboard the *Creole* filed claims in the CCNO. Sherman Johnson had insured twenty-three human cargoes with the OIC. John Hagan had insured nine human cargoes valued at $6,500 with the same assurer. Lawyers Conrad, Slidell, and Benjamin answered the claims. They proved unsuccessful and the property owners were awarded compensation.[32] The most complete documentation we have on these lower court proceedings concerns the two lawsuits instituted by slave trader Thomas McCargo. Two weeks after the *Creole* arrived in New Orleans minus most of its human cargoes, McCargo filed a claim against the MICNO to recover losses on nineteen human cargoes. His lawyers' contention was that slave revolt caused the vessel to deviate to the Bahamas. While there, representatives of "her Majesty the Queen of England and Ireland" seized his slaves. He claimed he had already informed the insurance company of his loss and made full abandonment of his former property. He asked the court to order the MICNO to pay him $15,200 with 5 percent interest given as compensation for the loss. On January 7, 1843, the jury delivered its verdict compensating the plaintiff for his losses.[33]

That same day, McCargo's lawyers filed a claim that the NOIC owed him $20,800 with interest accrued at 5 percent annually. According to the opening brief, McCargo had insured twenty-six slaves worth $800 each for transportation to New Orleans for a paid premium.[34] After an "affray and disobedience of about nineteen slaves," the vessel went to Nassau where "public authorities and other agents of Her Majesty" subsequently "interfered with said slaves, captured, seized, and detained, and emancipated them, whereby the said slaves were all totally lost by the risks insured against in said policy." They were not lost by "their own elopement, insurrection, or natural death." Since the loss, McCargo had informed the NOIC, made proof of his loss, abandoned his claim to the slaves, "and demands payment of the value thereof, as fixed by the policy." Legal counsel on behalf of the NOIC denied all of the charges

[32] Docket No. 4414, *Sherman Johnson v. The Ocean Insurance Company*; Docket No. 4419 *John Hagan v. The Ocean Insurance Company*, 1841 microfilm, NOPL.

[33] Docket No. 4408 *Thomas McCargo v. Merchants Insurance Company of New Orleans*, 1841 microfilm, NOPL; Thomas McCargo, Petition 20884135, RSPP, http://library.uncg.edu/slavery/petitions/details.aspx?pid=16043

[34] The case is the most complete record of the seven lawsuits filed in the CCNO and is reproduced in "*Thomas McCargo v. The New Orleans Insurance Company*," in Merritt M. Robinson, *Reports of Cases Argued and Determined in the Supreme Court of Louisiana*, Vol. 10, March 1 to June 20, 1845 (New Orleans: Samuel M. Stewart, 1845), 202–258.

except the making of the contract. They specifically denied that the plaintiff "had complied with the warranties" for which he was responsible. The original insurance policy was introduced as evidence.[35]

The lawyers' argument on behalf of McCargo was that the British authorities had liberated their client's slaves and that this act had made the NOIC liable because it had agreed to cover any loss from "foreign interference" as stipulated in the original contract. Their key witness was Chief Mate Zephaniah Gifford, who had served thirteen years at sea, was wounded in the rebellion, and sailed the *Creole* to New Orleans as acting master because Captain Ensor was incapacitated. Broadly speaking, Gifford's deposition to the Court consisted of a detailed narrative of the *Creole*'s voyage, the slave revolt and steering for Nassau, the actions of local Bahamians as well as those of the colonial authorities, the abortive attempt to seize the vessel, the arrest and incarceration of the rebels, the liberation of the rest of the slaves, and the ship's journey to New Orleans with only five of the original number of slaves.[36]

More specifically, the acting captain's testimony consistently supported the argument that it was British interference that led to the liberation of the slaves thus making the insurance company liable for the monetary loss. Mr. Gifford insisted that the vessel "was well manned, and prepared with everything for carrying slaves," that "every precaution was taken to prevent insubordination on the part of the negroes," and that he saw "nothing like insubordination among the negroes" until the riot.[37] This evidence served to counter the charge that the unseaworthy nature of the coastal slaver, together with its unpreparedness, had contributed to the loss of its slaves thus making the ship, crew, and anyone else but the NOIC liable. Once the *Creole* reached Nassau, he explained, local authorities took control of the ship. The soldiers "took and kept entire possession of the vessel," while "the English officers had control of the vessel."[38] "If Captain Woodside and his men had been permitted," testified Gifford, "they would have been in sufficient force to take the brig to

---

[35] Docket No. 4409 *Thomas McCargo v. New Orleans Insurance Company*, 1841 microfilm, NOPL; "*Thomas McCargo v. The New Orleans Insurance Company*," 202–205. McCargo had written to the NOIC on December 6, 1841, informing them of his official "abandonment" of his slave property. They acknowledged receiving his letter on December 8, 1841.

[36] "*Thomas McCargo v. The New Orleans Insurance Company*," 206–218.

[37] "*Thomas McCargo v. The New Orleans Insurance Company*," 206, 216.

[38] "*Thomas McCargo v. The New Orleans Insurance Company*," 210, 211.

Indian Key, with the remaining slaves."[39] The central plank of this argument for British interference was Gifford's recollection of Attorney General Anderson's address to the non-rebels that they were now "all free and at liberty to go ashore, and go where you please."[40] In short, Gifford maintained, "If there had been no interference of the English authorities, the negroes would have been brought to New Orleans certainly. That interference has caused the loss of the negroes."[41] This was the key argument on behalf of the plaintiff making the NOIC liable for the loss of trader McCargo's slave property valued at more than $20,000.

Under cross-examination by the defense counsel on behalf of the NOIC, Mr. Gifford testified that after the insurrection, the nineteen rebels controlled the ship, and there was not a moment when he and the crew could have regained control. He also stated that he steered the vessel toward Nassau because this was the direction the rebels wished to go. He was adamant concerning the loss of control over the vessel: "The officers and crew of the *Creole*, from the moment that the insurrection occurred, were in a situation in which they could do nothing under Heaven, by which they could have brought the vessel to New Orleans."[42] This is interesting evidence because it confirms the integrity of the slave revolt and its complete success. The depiction of the ship's company as victims seems a trifle perverse, but such were the demands of defense counsel.

Mr. Gifford's evidence was corroborated "in thema" by other witnesses for the plaintiff, including passengers Leidner, Merritt, McCargo, and seamen Stevens, Curtis, and Foxwell. They confirmed that the British authorities controlled the *Creole*, liberated those slaves not involved in the rebellion, and encouraged boats manned by Nassau locals to transport the liberated to shore. Their testimony only differed on the British attorney general's address to the non-rebels aboard the *Creole* and his precise wording.[43]

Next up was John F. Bacon who testified on behalf of the plaintiff. The former US consul to the Bahamas insisted that the liberation of the *Creole* slaves was primarily due to the interference of the British

---

[39] "*Thomas McCargo v. The New Orleans Insurance Company*," 214. It is doubtful that poorly paid and outnumbered seamen were a match for rebel slaves with a thirst for freedom who faced the gallows for killing a slave overseer.

[40] "*Thomas McCargo v. The New Orleans Insurance Company*," 212.

[41] "*Thomas McCargo v. The New Orleans Insurance Company*," 214.

[42] "*Thomas McCargo v. The New Orleans Insurance Company*," 218–220.

[43] "*Thomas McCargo v. The New Orleans Insurance Company*," 221–224.

authorities and their usage of native Bahamians to carry out their policy. "I am confident," he concluded his extensive testimony, "that the interference of the authorities at Nassau was the sole and only cause of their liberation, no volition on the subject being permitted to the officers and crew of the brig."[44]

The more intriguing aspect of his testimony, however, concerns the issue of the correct status of the slaves aboard the *Creole*. At a meeting with Bahamas governor Cockburn on the morning of the liberation of those slaves who had not rebelled, US Consul Bacon noted that the British official "introduced the subject of the slaves being *passengers*, and contended strenuously that he so considered them, and the Council agreed with him that they must be treated as passengers; while I contended that they were slaves, and, under the circumstances, as much a portion of the cargo as the tobacco on board."[45] The local authorities, in choosing such language, were guilty of interference because of a well-established protocol of maritime insurance that recognized slaves as human cargoes.[46]

The defense counsel representing the NOIC proceeded to cross-examine the former US official. Was the first interference by the British authorities "not solicited by yourself?" Yes, replied Consul Bacon, although the pilot boarded the vessel outside the harbor. If no military guard were present, would the slaves not have gone ashore anyway? John Bacon could not say, but an "attempt" would have been made to prevent them from leaving. Were you not informed by the authorities, asked the lawyers on behalf of the NOIC, that they would arrest the rebels, but "would not interfere" with the others going ashore? Yes, answered Bacon. The *Creole* was under whose control when she entered Nassau harbor? The pilot, but she was bought to the harbor "by the directions of the mutineers." John Bacon added that he did not believe "they had gained their freedom . . . before landing on the island."[47] Again, the US consul's argument for local interference conveniently ignored certain realities. The captives were de facto free once they had secured the ship.

[44] "*Thomas McCargo* v. *The New Orleans Insurance Company*," 232. Consul Bacon served in Nassau until November 27, 1841. Timothy Darling replaced him as US consul for the Bahamas three weeks later. It is possible that his departure was related to his handling of the aftermath of the *Creole* revolt. Darling to Webster, December 18, 1841, Dispatches from US Consul in Nassau, RG 59, T475, Roll 5, NARA; US Dept. of State, *Register of the Officers*, 7, https://books.google.com.br/books?id=YVoFAAAAM AAJ&pg=PA7&hl=pt-BR#v=onepage&q&f=false

[45] "*Thomas McCargo* v. *The New Orleans Insurance Company*," 229.

[46] Walvin, *Zong*, 2.

[47] "*Thomas McCargo* v. *The New Orleans Insurance Company*," 233–234.

The success of their insurrection was demonstrated by their choice of destination. The decision to sail to the Bahamas was taken to secure this freedom. The majority of captives chose to leave the vessel by walking off the ship into waiting boats steered by local Bahamians. And, the recent policy of British colonial abolition implemented by local officials con-firmed rather than inaugurated their liberty.

In his testimony, Mr. Bacon referred to several documents from himself and the British authorities written between November 9 and 15, 1841. These were alphabetized A through G and were used to support the plaintiff's argument that the human cargoes were liberated as a consequence of foreign interference. The problem for the plaintiff was that the documents largely refuted the argument for British interference: the US consul initially requested local assistance; the colonial authorities arrested the rebels and awaited instructions from London; the colonial authorities further stated they would not interfere with the movements of non-rebels; they had nothing to do with negroes quitting the vessel or landing; and the negroes left of their own free will with non-interference by the authorities.[48]

Captain Robert Ensor was then examined on behalf of the plaintiff. But "having being disabled by his wounds" sustained during the revolt, fol-lowed by a night atop the vessel in rough weather and lacking immediate attention, he was bedridden while the *Creole* was moored in Nassau. Consequently, the plaintiff's lawyers believed "his evidence is unimportant."[49] This lack of participation at the trial concerning critical events affecting his vessel must have been hard for the veteran shipmaster.

Turning from the testimony of live witnesses, the plaintiff's counsel offered written evidence from Senate Document No. 51 published in early 1842.[50] They considered this documentary evidence crucial because they proceeded to return to it to support the argument that the NOIC was liable because of losses accrued through foreign interference. Captain Woodside was not present because he was "a seafaring man," so they drew on his deposition to the US Consul Bacon that many boats sur-rounded the vessel, that the mate and crew were "intimidated," and that the British authorities – especially the attorney general – were always in control of events.[51]

---

[48] "*Thomas McCargo v. The New Orleans Insurance Company,*" 234–239.
[49] "*Thomas McCargo v. The New Orleans Insurance Company,*" 235–236.
[50] "*Thomas McCargo v. The New Orleans Insurance Company,*" 237–40.
[51] "*Thomas McCargo v. The New Orleans Insurance Company,*" 240–241. His absence was also convenient because it meant he was unavailable for cross-examination on the illegal, abortive, and piratical attempt to seize the *Creole* anchored in a British port.

The plaintiff's counsel also subjoined the New Orleans Protest signed by the *Creole's* crew and passengers on December 7, 1841, which overwhelmingly supported the view that it was foreign interference that led to loss of slaves through encouragement of locals, liberation of slaves, and prevention of the American crew from retaking the slaves. The British guard took possession of the vessel and all of the slaves. Fifty boats surrounded the vessel, armed with clubs, and were subject to the order of the attorney general. Anderson had said to those assembled on the ship: "You are free and at liberty to go onshore and wherever you please." Many of the males and all of the female slaves would have come to New Orleans but for this colonial interference. "That many of the negroes who were emancipated expressed a desire to go to New Orleans in the Creole, but were deterred from it, by reason of threats, which were made to sink the vessel, if she attempted to carry the slaves." This so-called "desire" amounted to speculation since the view that those enslaved aboard the *Creole* wished to travel on to New Orleans was unsubstantiated by written evidence and eyewitness reports. In short, the New Orleans Protest concludes that it was foreign inference that prevented slaves from going to New Orleans, prevented aid from the crew, and caused the slaveholders to lose their property. "It was that interference [the British company guarding the *Creole* stopped Captain Woodside's seizure attempt] which prevented aid from being rendered by the American sailors in Nassau, and caused the loss of the slaves to their owners."[52]

It was now the turn of defense counsel on behalf of the NOIC and their rebuttal of this major charge of foreign interference. They were at a certain disadvantage. The lawyers had no witnesses because the rebels and former captives were enjoying liberty in the Bahamas and Jamaica. Richard Butler was on the Outer Islands and Elijah Morris was settling in the village of Gambier in New Providence. Consequently the defense attorneys would only have been able to cross-examine witnesses from the other side. Their most important witnesses were unavailable: The five slaves who stayed on the *Creole* and came to New Orleans could not testify in a Louisiana court, while British colonial officials were unlikely to bother showing up in a New Orleans courtroom. Consequently, the defendant's lawyers introduced evidence taken by the Nassau Commission in the Bahamas

---

[52] *"Thomas McCargo v. The New Orleans Insurance Company,"* 242–247; "It was that interference," 247.

in April 1842. It is unclear how they obtained this evidence.[53] It included a deposition from Attorney General Anderson supporting the view that local authorities did not interfere with the slaves. He had no instructions to "interfere" between himself and the slaves. In his address to the non-rebels, he stated that all restrictions on their movements were removed. It was the passenger Merritt, he testified, who said they could depart or remain on board.[54]

The defendants' lawyers next introduced the testimony of other witnesses from the Nassau Commission that substantiated Attorney General Anderson's evidence that the Negroes who left the vessel did so voluntarily and without encouragement from civil or military authorities thus further contradicting the New Orleans Protest statement. Lieutenant Hamilton stated that it was passenger Merritt, not the attorney general, who granted permission to the non-rebels to go ashore, that the blacks "scrambled" on the boats as fast as they could, and that the "four or five" who stayed behind were not prevented by the other blacks. Inspector Pinder confirmed the evidence that they left "of their own voluntary act" and that this was sanctioned by the "mates." Sergeant Dalzell confirmed Anderson's telling the slaves they were free to go. Surveyor-General of the Bahamas Burnside further corroborated the evidence of the deponents. Receiver General and Treasurer John Grant Anderson confirmed that it was Merritt, not the attorney general, who granted slaves permission to leave ship. Five lieutenants of the 2nd West India Regiment (2nd WIR) confirmed the testimony of the other colonial officers. Major Cobbe of the same regiment testified he had strict orders not to interfere but only to prevent violence, and that the slaves that went on to New Orleans did not hide but were clearly visible on deck.[55] After this testimony was presented, Gifford, T. J. D. McCargo, and Stevens were re-examined by the plaintiff's counsel basically refuting the testimony of these British officials by stating that it was the attorney general who gave slaves permission to leave not Merritt.[56]

After hearing arguments and evidence from both sides, local jurors found the New Orleans Insurance Company liable for the losses of the

---

53 The 1845 court record merely states: "*This evidence [Attorney General's] and that of the other witnesses for defendants was taken under a commission at Nassau in April, 1842" ("*Thomas McCargo v. The New Orleans Insurance Company,*" 247). I found no documentary record of these proceedings in the archives in Nassau and London.
54 "*Thomas McCargo v. The New Orleans Insurance Company,*" 247–253.
55 "*Thomas McCargo v. The New Orleans Insurance Company,*" 253–256.
56 "*Thomas McCargo v. The New Orleans Insurance Company,*" 257–258.

slaves aboard the *Creole* and awarded $18,400 to the plaintiff Thomas McCargo. This award was $2,400 less than the sum of $20,800 that he had sued for. The jury deducted $800 for one of the slaves who stayed with the *Creole* ("who reached New Orleans in safety" according to the report) and another $1,600 as half the value of four of the plaintiff's slaves who were rebels, the jury having decided the loss should be split between the insurers and the owner.[57] This was a victory for slaveholding interests, although it proved ephemeral. More important, these lower court trials in New Orleans – much like the earlier high court case over the *Zong* in London – were a powerful reminder that human cargoes were simply dollars and cents.

Louisiana's Supreme Court is currently located on 400 Royal Street in Vieux Carré, New Orleans. Numerous palatial windows dot the imposing white marble structure flanked by two circular wings. The front of the building boasts a stone image of a pelican in a circle underneath a feather and a ball. There is an imposing statue of prominent state jurist Edward Douglass White bearing a law book under his left arm. The magnificence of the building testifies to the importance of the rule of law in the state of Louisiana in much the same way that contemporary visitors to Government House in Nassau cannot fail to be impressed by its imperial splendor.

A short judiciary article in Louisiana's revised constitution of 1812 created the Supreme Court. It seated three to five judges appointed by the governor to serve on good behavior. It had appellate jurisdiction only. The court was required to sit in New Orleans and Opelousas, some 138 miles northward. Named after indigenous people, the latter is now home to zydeco music, the Louisiana African American Heritage Trial, and sundry food spices. As a consequence of the state constitutional convention of 1844, the court was redesigned. It now consisted of a chief justice and three associate justices appointed by the governor for eight-year terms. Its former narrow jurisdiction was expanded to cover law, criminal cases, and civil municipal suits. It usually met in New Orleans between November and August at Government House along the river.[58]

---

[57] "*Thomas McCargo v. The New Orleans Insurance Company*," 258–259; Downey, *Creole Affair*, 136. The court record's word choice of "safety" is a reminder of the documentary bias against slaves. The former captives were now at liberty in safety outside of the slaveholding republic!

[58] "Louisiana Supreme Court History," Louisiana Supreme Court, http://www.lasc.org/about_the_court/history.asp; Downey, *Creole Affair*, 134.

The leading jurist of the Louisiana Supreme Court was Henry Adams Bullard. Born in Pepperell, Massachusetts, in 1788, he attended Harvard University, after which he studied law in Boston and Philadelphia, and was admitted to the bar around 1812. He relocated to Louisiana, where he served as a district judge and legislator in the 22nd and 23rd US Congresses. In 1834, Bullard was elected to the Louisiana Supreme Court, where he served as judge and chief justice for twelve years.[59] It was his court that was to settle the insurance dispute over the *Creole* revolt in 1845.

The NOIC chose its lead counsel wisely. Attorney Benjamin had represented the insurer and other companies in the cases before the CCNO. Although he proved unsuccessful, his forte was the higher court. By 1834, he had co-authored a summation of numerous cases before the state Supreme Court and these had become very influential in legal circles. Between 1839 and 1844, he reportedly presented fifty-five cases before the court, most of which he won.[60]

In March 1845, the Louisiana Supreme Court under Chief Justice Bullard heard the appeal of *Thomas McCargo* v. *The New Orleans Insurance Company*. Counsel Benjamin led the insurance company's appeal and was assisted by Conrad and Slidell. Their major argument was that the NOIC was not liable for the loss of the slaves because the contract's written clause included a warranty "by the assured free from elopement, insurrection, and natural death."[61]

The NOIC's defense team made eight specific points to support this contention. First, the risk never commenced because the slaves of the plaintiff did not board at Norfolk but at Richmond. The policy provided insurance only for transportation of the slaves from Norfolk to New Orleans.[62] They next argued that the insurers should be discharged because the vessel was not deemed seaworthy.[63] It was unarmed, poorly policed, and overcrowded for its "nature and purpose," thus violating basic insurance law. The ship's logbook recorded there were 186 slaves on board, but the plaintiff's lawyers stated there were 135 slaves. The defense team quoted an Act of Congress passed March 2, 1819, limiting two

[59] "Bullard, Henry Adams, (1788–1851)," *Biographical Directory of the U.S. Congress*, h ttp://bioguide.congress.gov/scripts/biodisplay.pl?index=B001049

[60] Evans, *Benjamin*, 28.

[61] "*Thomas McCargo* v. *The New Orleans Insurance Company*," 259; the defense appeal is reproduced on pages 259–286.

[62] "*Thomas McCargo* v. *The New Orleans Insurance Company*," 259.

[63] "*Thomas McCargo* v. *The New Orleans Insurance Company*," 259–261.

passengers to every five tons per vessel. Although this law did not apply to coastwise slavers, the defense team asked: "Will this court be disposed to recognize one standard of humanity for the white man, and another for the negro?" The unseaworthy nature of the vessel violated one "of the great and wholesome principles of insurance law." Although the plaintiff's counsel switched from reason to usage, this was unacceptable to defense counsel because it offended the requirements of safety demanded aboard a slave ship. This concern for decent conditions aboard a vessel engaged in the inhumane business of forcibly transporting people seems contradictory to the modern reader.[64]

The defense counsel's third point was that slave insurrection "put an end to the risk."[65] This occurrence was covered in the policy and went against what the "assured warranted the underwriters." The plaintiff counsels' position was that slave-owners did not provide a warranty.[66] The appellants' lawyers drew upon British jurist Lord Mansfield's ruling in *Hore* v. *Whitmore* "that an irresistible force, *though one of the perils insured against,* would not excuse a non-compliance with a warranty."[67] "In this case there is insurance against British interference, with a warranty by the assured that his slaves shall not mutiny. They do mutiny, and carry the vessel within British jurisdiction. Of what value is the warranty to defendants, if they are held to be liable for the direct consequences of the very contingency against which they were warranted." The defense counsel concluded that the "palpable meaning of the contract is, we will assure you against British interference, but you must warrant that your slaves will not expose us to that interference by a mutiny."[68]

Their fourth point was that the plaintiff's "slaves were lost by the excepted risk; i.e., by the insurrection; and have not been recovered to the present hour. The mutiny then was the proximate cause of the loss, even if a British interference to aid the slaves on their arrival at Nassau were clearly proved."[69] Although slave revolt was not a mutiny as previously argued, this 1845 legal interpretation of what happened aboard the *Creole* is essentially accurate. Indeed, defense counsel's skepticism

---

64 "*Thomas McCargo* v. *The New Orleans Insurance Company*," 260; Downey, *Creole Affair*, 136–137. For a similar claim by the insurer's legal team in the 1783 *Zong* case, see Walvin, *Zong*, 147.
65 "*Thomas McCargo* v. *The New Orleans Insurance Company*," 261–264.
66 "*Thomas McCargo* v. *The New Orleans Insurance Company*," 263–264.
67 "*Thomas McCargo* v. *The New Orleans Insurance Company*," 264. Italics in original.
68 Ibid.   69 "*Thomas McCargo* v. *The New Orleans Insurance Company*," 264–265.

about British interference being disputable further supports the point that it was the captives' own actions that led to their liberation.

Lawyers Benjamin, Conrad, and Slidell's fifth point consisted of a prolonged discussion over the responsibility for insurrection and its consequences: Was it the underwriters' or the slave trader's?[70] Amidst the rather tedious legal jargon, however, was a remarkable declaration by the NOIC's court representatives. Roman, French, and Louisiana laws stated that the slaveholder was responsible for the "wrong doing of his slave."[71] They drew on Article 180 of the 1824 Louisiana slave code: "The master shall be answerable for all the damages occasioned by an offence or quasi-offence committed by his slave, independent of the punishment inflicted on the slaves."[72] Unless underwriters assumed the risk, the owner was responsible for the insurrection and consequent deviation of the vessel from its original destination of New Orleans. Moreover, argued defense counsel, the slave was prone to rebellion because he was "ever ready to conquer his liberty."[73] One can just imagine Counsel Benjamin's mellifluous tones reverberating around the state's high court:

Will any one deny that the bloody and disastrous insurrection of the Creole was the result of the inherent qualities of the slaves themselves, roused not only by their condition of servitude, but stimulated by the removal from their friends and their homes, for the purpose of sale by their owners in an unknown land, and encouraged by the lax discipline of the vessel, the numerical weakness of the whites, and the proximity of a British province.[74]

Although liberation struggles rarely succeed without the shedding of blood, and the liberation of the captives as a consequence of the *Creole* revolt was not exactly a disaster, nonetheless the defense team's focus on the origins of the revolt facilitated by shipboard conditions was largely accurate. Indeed, it is quite striking to encounter such a clear articulation of the reasons for a slave rebellion expressed in the courtroom of a slave society.[75]

---

[70] "*Thomas McCargo v. The New Orleans Insurance Company*," 265–72.

[71] "*Thomas McCargo v. The New Orleans Insurance Company*," 265.

[72] Ibid. See also Louisiana Slave Code of 1824 in Willie Lee Rose, ed., *A Documentary History of Slavery in North America* (Athens: University of Georgia Press, 1999), 176.

[73] "*Thomas McCargo v. The New Orleans Insurance Company*," 266.   [74] Ibid.

[75] In Hendrick and Hendrick, *Creole Mutiny*, 120, the authors state these words suggest Benjamin had "qualified sympathy for the slaves' longing for freedom." It is more likely that the NOIC lawyers selected "slave mutiny" because this contingency was not covered by the insurance contract and would thus absolve their client. Evans, *Benjamin*, 37–39, makes the same point. Of course, the defense's argument and language does raise the question of

The defense team's fifth point consisted of a detailed account of a 1778 French tribunal decision concerning the brig *Le Compte d'Estaing*. This transatlantic French slave trader mastered by Captain Jean Jacques Olivier experienced a slave revolt off the Guinea coast in West Africa. The slaves were emboldened to act because of a ship's crew weakened by disease and enervating climatic conditions. A number of the rebels died during the revolt and afterward from their wounds. What costs were the underwriters responsible for? The defense counsel drew on maritime insurance authority Lord Mansfield who thought that those rebels who died either during the revolt or as a consequence of injuries sustained during the revolt "were to be paid for" by the assurer, but that those who died through fasting or despondency did so because of the failure of the revolt "were not to be paid for."[76] The British jurist's long reach into the Anglo-Atlantic world of maritime insurance was demonstrated by defense attorney Benjamin's usage of him to bolster his argument that "underwriters are not liable for losses by the mutiny or insurrection of the slaves, unless by the positive provisions of the policy they, the underwriters, have taken upon themselves that risk."[77]

The sixth point was central to the defense counsel's argument: "It has been contended," they claimed, "that the insurrection was only the remote, and that British interference was the proximate cause of the loss. It will hereafter be shown that the slaves were not lost by 'foreign interference,' the risk expressly assumed by the underwriters; that, on the contrary, if the policy was not extinguished by the insurrection and deviation, still the slaves *voluntarily* left the vessel at Nassau, thus accomplishing the sole object of their going there, and that the underwriters are protected by the clause that the company is not liable for 'elopement.'"[78] In other words, the slaves' actions – not interference by the British authorities – led to the slave traders' property loss. The assurer had assumed the risk for the latter but not for the former.

This crucial distinction was supported by illustrations from barratry and insurance law. In the legal case *Vallejo* v. *Wheeler*, goods aboard the vessel *Thomas and Mathew* scheduled to sail from London to Seville, Spain, were damaged as a consequence of a deviation in course for

what the slaveholding lawyer really thought of the "inherent qualities" of all of those people on his *Belle Chasse* plantation whose liberty he was withholding.
[76] "*Thomas McCargo* v. *The New Orleans Insurance Company*," 271.
[77] "*Thomas McCargo* v. *The New Orleans Insurance Company*," 270.
[78] "*Thomas McCargo* v. *The New Orleans Insurance Company*," 272. Italics in original.

purposes of smuggling by the ship's captain. Lord Mansfield ruled: "this smuggling voyage was barratry in the master."[79] The *causa proxima, non remota, spectatur* – the insurance principle that the proximate cause of the loss, and not that which is remote – was quoted from *McGowan* v. *The New England Insurance Company* as well as from several other cases.[80] The court, based upon these cases, will accept "that the voyage was gone, and all recourse under the policy lost, when the slaves took possession of the vessel, and changed her destination."[81] This is precisely what happened as a consequence of the *Creole* revolt.

In their concluding point, the defense team turned to occurrences at Nassau to determine whether slaves were lost to "foreign interference" that was insured for, or "elopement" of slaves assumed by the plaintiff.[82] Liberation due to "foreign interference" or disregard for comity was something against which insurance could not be made.[83] Slavery was not a natural but positive condition according to local, municipal, and national laws extending to a nation's ships. But such slavery had "no force or binding effect *beyond* the jurisdiction of such a nation."[84] This was an astonishing legal rebuttal of America's diplomatic position expressed so eloquently by federal officials in Nassau, Washington, and London. The NOIC's lawyers drew upon a list of official communications between the United States and Great Britain concerning "certain outrages" pursued on the ships *Hermosa*, the *Comet*, the *Encomium*, and the *Enterprise*, all American vessels driven into British ports by poor weather, boarded by British authorities, followed by "active interference to set slaves free," actions that if continued afforded a "justest cause of war for this nation."[85]

Moreover, the team referred to letters in 1837 from US Secretary of State John Forsyth to Andrew Stevenson, US minister to Great Britain and

---

[79] "*Thomas McCargo v. The New Orleans Insurance Company,*" 273.

[80] "*Thomas McCargo v. The New Orleans Insurance Company,*" 275. English philosopher Sir Francis Bacon is thought to have codified the principle in 1597. See Levy, *Freaks of Fortune*, 52.

[81] "*Thomas McCargo v. The New Orleans Insurance Company,*" 276. The defense counsel's penultimate point rejected the plaintiff's claim that slaves were pirates and that the insurance company was liable for loss due to piracy. Ibid, 277; Downey, *Creole Affair*, 137.

[82] "*Thomas McCargo v. The New Orleans Insurance Company,*" 277–286.

[83] "*Thomas McCargo v. The New Orleans Insurance Company,*" 279.

[84] Ibid. Italics added.

[85] "*Thomas McCargo v. The New Orleans Insurance Company,*" 281; Downey, *Creole Affair*, 137.

Virginia slaveholder, and the latter's letter to British foreign secretary Lord Palmerston pointing out the "absurdities of these pretentions."[86] While admitting the "fullest extent of these doctrines," defense counsel denied "their application to the case of the Creole."[87] "In the case of the *Creole*, the blacks brought the whites captive into Nassau, on board of a vessel captured in a successful revolt. In all the other cases, the whites brought submissive slaves into Nassau on their own vessels."[88] "The freedom was acquired by their *escape* from slavery into a free country. The *means* of escape cannot affect the consequences resulting from it."[89] There was now an extradition treaty, the Webster-Ashburton Treat of August 1842, which had not been in place during the *Creole* revolt. The only issue is the law of nations: If blacks reached British shores under white control, then they are slaves, but if they reached there under black control, then they are free. In the lawyers' own words, if "the blacks reach there under the control of the whites, and as their slaves, so to consider them; but if the blacks reach there uncontrolled by any master, and apparently released from any restraint on the part of whites, to consider them as free."[90] This was a rather incendiary conclusion to arrive at in a southern slave society in which enslaved people had repeatedly self-liberated during the US slave trade and two prior Anglo-American wars.

Messrs. Peyton and I. W. Smith spoke "contra" on behalf of the plaintiff Thomas McCargo.[91] Their central argument was that without British interference, the slaves aboard the *Creole* would not have gained their freedom, and that this contingency was covered in the insurance policy, thus making the company liable. Their rebuttal was framed in nine supporting points to bolster this contention and to undermine the case of defense counsel Benjamin et al. that slave liberation was the consequence of insurrection thus making it the liability of the slave-owner, not the insurance company.

To begin with, argued the lawyers on behalf of the New Orleans slave trader, the vessel was in strict compliance "with every usage" and "the brig was fitted for carrying the slaves."[92] There was no difference between the *Creole*'s voyage in November 1841 and its previous coastwise slave operations. Moreover, congressional legislation in 1820 was not

---

[86] "*Thomas McCargo v. The New Orleans Insurance Company*," 281.   [87] Ibid.
[88] "*Thomas McCargo v. The New Orleans Insurance Company*," 282.   [89] Ibid.
[90] "*Thomas McCargo v. The New Orleans Insurance Company*," 283.
[91] The plaintiff lawyers' rebuttal is reproduced in "*Thomas McCargo v. The New Orleans Insurance Company*, 286–312.
[92] "*Thomas McCargo v. The New Orleans Insurance Company*," 286–288.

applicable because it "applies only to voyages from a foreign country, and leaves vessels making voyages coastwise [including slavers] to carry as many passengers as they choose."[93] The plaintiff lawyers' language of "passengers" would not have impressed their slave trader client who preferred the term slaves.

The plaintiff counsels' next three points basically challenged defense counsel's claims of warranty and insurrection.[94] It was now their turn to evoke the eminent Lord Mansfield. In the legal case of *De Hahn* v. *Hartley*, a Liverpool ship carrying arms was captured off West Africa when it carried more seamen than when it was originally insured. Lord Mansfield had supported the warranty in this case.[95] Moreover, the defense counsel "have attempted, but most signally failed, we apprehend, to prove that the insurrection severed the tie of slavery which bound the slaves to their owners, and changed their condition to that of free men."[96] They failed to show that the voyage was prevented by "excepted perils" of natural death (none), elopement (no desertion), leaving only insurrection. The plaintiff's counsel referred to the case of *James* v. *Schmoll* and a policy on 225 slaves that exempted the insurer, in case of mutiny, from loss of less than 10 percent. A slave revolt off the African coast was suppressed with nineteen rebel slaves killed. The insurer paid for those who died. There were thirty-six slaves who died subsequently from other means. But Lord Mansfield ruled they did not die from the "mutiny" and so the insurer was not liable for them, nor liable for the surviving slaves whose value depreciated.[97] In *Green* v. *Elmslie*, the plaintiff claimed for loss of perils of sea. The ship was driven by a gale to France where it was captured. Lord Kenyon, who succeeded Lord Mansfield as chief justice in 1788 and served as Britain's senior jurist for fourteen years, held that the loss was not due to sea perils because if it had been driven elsewhere it could have been safe. "May we," argued Peyton and Smith, "not say on the same principle, that the loss was not the consequence of the insurrection, because if the brig had been driven elsewhere, the slaves would not have been emancipated, and thus placed beyond the reach of their

---

93 "*Thomas McCargo v. The New Orleans Insurance Company*," 287.
94 "*Thomas McCargo v. The New Orleans Insurance Company*," 288–296. This section of the report on the 1845 high court session is ambiguous and error-strewn without apparent reason.
95 "*Thomas McCargo v. The New Orleans Insurance Company*," 291.
96 "*Thomas McCargo v. The New Orleans Insurance Company*," 292. The point is introduced as "Plaintiff's counsel" but this must be an error in the record.
97 "*Thomas McCargo v. The New Orleans Insurance Company*," 294.

owners?"[98] What their rebuttal overlooked, of course, was that it was slave revolt, not extreme weather, that drove the *Creole* to the Bahamas and that its anchorage in Nassau harbor secured – rather than gained – the former captives' existing liberty.

Their fifth point refuted defense counsel's claim that the "mutiny" was caused by the vessel's deviation from New Orleans thus relieving the insurance company of liability.[99] The rebels, insisted Peyton and Smith, were pirates who had stolen the ship: "The running off with the brig was, on the part of the nineteen culprits, an act for which the insurer would be responsible, as an act of pirates, thieves, etc. within the printed clause of the policy."[100] The plaintiff's advocates then followed with English and American common laws broadly defining pirates and acts of piracy. The problem with their contention, of course, was that the *Creole* slaves were not pirates but human beings deprived of their natural rights through positive laws in Virginia and Louisiana buttressed by federal legislative power. The plaintiff counsel's sixth point was simply a run-on from their previous point that the warranty did not make the slave-owner responsible for the loss of the slaves.

Their seventh point challenged defense counsel's contention that slave rebellion caused the vessel's deviation, thus releasing the insurers.[101] They quoted the contract clause authorizing deviation from "usual cases." In fact, "overwhelming necessity" caused the deviation: "the menaces and demands of the criminals, with drawn knives – the eminent danger of loss of life compelled the officers" to take the vessel to Nassau. The events at Nassau were not under the "control" of officers and the "plaintiff is not responsible." (The stark contrast between the plaintiff lawyers' "criminals" and the "inherent qualities" of freedom's seekers depicted by defense counsel illustrates the primacy of cleverness over moral truth in the courtroom.) The defense further contended that deviation was caused by excepted risk thus voiding the policy and supported their claim with several decisions that were either misunderstood or inapplicable. Indeed, argued Peyton and Smith, defense counsel quoted Judge Radcliff's remarks in the case of *Roget* v. *Thruston* accurately except they "were *obiter dicta* entirely, made forty years ago, when

---

[98] Ibid; "Kenyon, Lloyd Kenyon, 1st Baron," *Encyclopedia Britannica*, 15, 11th ed. https://archive.org/stream/encyclopaediabri15chisrich#page/748/mode/2up

[99] "*Thomas McCargo* v. *The New Orleans Insurance Company*," 296–298.

[100] "*Thomas McCargo* v. *The New Orleans Insurance Company*," 296.

[101] "*Thomas McCargo* v. *The New Orleans Insurance Company*," 299–300.

insurance law was in its infancy."[102] This point by the counsel for the plaintiff – together with the collation of numerous supporting and contending legal cases drawn on by both sides – is a useful reminder of the broader dimensions of the dispute over the *Creole* revolt. This insurance dispute was not simply an isolated case, but reflected the maturation of maritime insurance law across the nineteenth-century Anglo-Atlantic world.[103]

James D. B. De Bow, the prominent southern journal editor and future federal census enumerator, illustrated this development in an interesting article on marine insurance published in his influential monthly journal *De Bow's Review*. It opened with some basic definitions of insurance and policies. The first major section explained the absence of insurance law during antiquity and its subsequent takeoff in busy commercial ports of thirteenth-century Italy and eventual spread to seventeenth-century England and France. During the last two centuries, wrote the editor, marine insurance made "great head" in commercial jurisprudence. This was probably an exaggeration since many of the treatises, legal cases, and authorities concerning maritime underwriting emerged during the mid-to-late eighteenth century coterminous with the bustling transatlantic slave trade. The article's second section turned to some of the technicalities of the business, including forms of policy, contractual obligations, what was insurable versus what was not allowed, the nature of risk, and so forth.[104]

The southern editor's essay also wished to examine fire and life insurance but ran out of space. Nonetheless, what De Bow wrote represented an unabashed celebration of the commercial enterprise of maritime insurance. Its premise was that this business was "one of the noblest creations of human genius." It was "beautiful" in its endeavor, pervasive across societies, and contributed to the "moral and political condition of human

---

[102] "*Thomas McCargo v. The New Orleans Insurance Company,*" 299.

[103] For a snapshot, compare the depth of maritime law in the 1840s *Creole* case to its thinness in the *Zong* case in the 1780s.

[104] J. D. B. De Bow, "Art. I.—Marine Insurance," *DeBow's Review* vol. II, no. 1 (July 1846), 2–21. The Medici family began as merchant bankers in fifteenth-century Florence and helped establish maritime insurance. Jerry Brotten, *The Renaissance: A Very Short Introduction* (New York: Oxford University Press, 2006), 27. John Dickens, father to the great Victorian novelist, contributed articles on marine insurance to *The British Press* during the late 1820s. See Peter Ackroyd, *Dickens* (London: Sinclair-Stevenson, 1990), 113. The character of John Podsnap in Dickens' last completed novel *Our Mutual Friend* published in 1864–1865 is a disappointment because his commercial world is small and his success in the marine insurance business escapes the usual stinging rebuke expected from English fiction's finest satirist of institutional corruption.

society." This veneration helps explain the importance of the insurance industry to the local economy of New Orleans – something of which Chief Justice Bullard could not have been oblivious. What this hagiography on commerce ignored, of course, was the brutality of trading human beings, the role of maritime insurance in securing fortunes by depriving people of their natural human rights, and the expansiveness of this cruel and exploitative business across Atlantic empires. Perhaps this oversight was deliberate. *McCargo v. New Orleans Insurance Company* ran more than 150 pages in the Louisiana Annual Reports published in 1845 and is by far the longest entry, yet it does not merit a single mention in De Bow's extensive article on maritime insurance published the next year.[105]

The plaintiff's counsel's eighth point was the longest by far and contained the heart of their rebuttal in its succinct opening statement: "The loss was occasioned by British interference."[106] The plaintiff's slaves were carried into Nassau by piracy. The shippers still held the rights in slaves at sea: "The laws of the United States protected the rights of the owners, at the time of the departure of the brig from the limits of Virginia. Those laws followed the brig and her cargo upon the voyage."[107] The lawyers for the slave trader were issuing an important statement on American slavery's imperial reach beyond landed borders that had already been endorsed by the federal government and repeated by southern editors, politicians, and supporters of property rights in man. (See Chapter 9.) The plaintiff drew on numerous sources to support the view that slaveholders were American citizens with property that had been stolen by pirates. Moreover, the attorney general of the Bahamas "testifies that the slaves on board an American vessel, sailing from one port to another, and driven by necessity or force into a British port, become free, and that the right of the owners ceases."[108] This was an important point because it supported the plaintiff's case for British interference; it was also an important reminder of the maritime reach of British colonial abolition. These doctrines applied to the *Creole* slaves, and "they were liberated by the interference of the British authorities."[109] The American witnesses all testified that "but for the British interference," the *Creole* and its slaves would have continued on to New Orleans. The plaintiff's counsel drew on several cases to show how insurance companies were only culpable for

[105] De Bow, "Marine Insurance."
[106] "*Thomas McCargo v. The New Orleans Insurance Company*," 301–311.
[107] "*Thomas McCargo v. The New Orleans Insurance Company*," 301.
[108] "*Thomas McCargo v. The New Orleans Insurance Company*," 301–302.   [109] Ibid.

losses for immediate rather than circumspect causes. As Lord Ellenborough – member of Parliament, attorney general, and Lord Chief Justice from 1802 to 1818 – put it in the law suit *Powell v. Gudgeon,* *"causa proxima, non remota spectatur."* The case of *Forder v. Christie* succinctly described the liability: *"The risk insured against must be the effective cause of the loss, in order to charge the underwriters."*[110] Ergo, the effective cause of the loss was British interference.[111]

Having listened carefully to the defense counsel's case on behalf of the insurance company followed by the plaintiff counsel's rebuttal for the slave trader, Louisiana's chief justice responded.[112] Since the several cases involved the same voyage, and all of the slaves insured "were lost at the same time and by the same disaster," they were lumped together. The decision in one case would stand equally for the rest.[113] His opening question was: "What risks did the insurers assume?" In this case and three others, the policy stated that the insurers were "warranted free from elopement, *insurrection,* and natural death." In *Lockett v. Firemen's Insurance Company*, the terms were that "the insurers are not liable for suicide, *mutiny,* natural death, or desertion." In the other two cases, the company was not liable for "suicide, desertion, or natural death."[114] In common parlance, briefs, witness statements, and official correspondence, there was little difference between "mutiny" and "insurrection." The only difference was that mutiny is clearly an "excepted risk," and in the others whether a "technical warranty" or intended to exempt the insurers from risk of insurrection.[115] Chief Justice Bullard viewed the

---

[110] *"Thomas McCargo v. The New Orleans Insurance Company,"* 308 (italics in original). Thomas Law, the British jurist's brother, settled in the United States in 1793 and married Eliza Custis, granddaughter of Martha Washington. The British jurist's eldest son, also named Edward Law, served as Governor-General of India between 1842 and 1844. "Edward Law, 1st Baron of Ellenborough," Wikipedia, https://en.wikipedia.org/wiki/Edward_Law,_1st_Baron_Ellenborough

[111] The plaintiff counsel's final point reiterates the importance of primary cause by stating that even if the *Creole*'s crew were negligent it was not the leading reason – that would be foreign interference. *"Thomas McCargo v. The New Orleans Insurance Company,"* 311–312.

[112] Chief Justice Bullard's response is reproduced in *"Thomas McCargo v. The New Orleans Insurance Company,"* 312–332, and summarized in Downey, *Creole Affair,* 138–139.

[113] *"Thomas McCargo v. The New Orleans Insurance Company,"* 312. Bullard's "disaster," of course, was the former captives' liberty.

[114] *"Thomas McCargo v. The New Orleans Insurance Company,"* 312–313, italics in original.

[115] *"Thomas McCargo v. The New Orleans Insurance Company,"* 313.

terms of the policy as not creating a warranty, "but as only exempting the insurers from any liability on account of losses which might be sustained in consequence of a mutiny, or insurrection on board." All the cases fell into two categories: (a) those where underwriters assumed risk of loss from insurrection and (b) those exempted from that loss. "The great question, therefore, upon the merits, which this case, and the others of the same class present," Chief Justice Bullard summarized, was "whether the loss of the slaves was caused by insurrection, or by illegal and unauthorized interference on the part of the authorities of Nassau."[116]

Louisiana's top jurist followed with a succinct narrative of the *Creole* revolt marked by some telling emphases. He observed that the "brig was taken into Nassau by the slaves, in this state of successful revolt."[117] This was accurate. Moreover, the vessel's eventual destination was the consequence of a triumphant revolt: "The insurrection had been entirely successful, the master badly wounded, one passenger killed, and the mate and crew compelled to deviate from the course of the voyage."[118] The mutineers "felt so secure" they threw arms overboard and relied on future safety from "their physical superiority, and upon the sympathies of the people of the Bahamas, or the direct interference of the local authorities."[119] The chief justice's interpretation contrasts markedly with that of the *Creole*'s acting skipper Zephaniah Gifford who had testified that the rebels simply threw themselves on the mercy of the British authorities.

Chief Justice Bullard then turned to the laws and comity of nations. He drew upon US Secretary of State Webster's August 1, 1842, letter to Lord Ashburton stating that "local law does not supersede the laws of the country to which the vessel belongs," and the British diplomat's message that HMG desired "good neighborhood, and that there shall be no officious interference with American vessels driven by accident, or by violence into those ports."[120] This was an unequivocal declaration of the rights of slave property and its extended reach by Louisiana's highest court, although the chief justice's reference to the diplomatic exchange of 1842 appears a little odd since later on he dismisses it as being irrelevant to the case.

[116] "*Thomas McCargo v. The New Orleans Insurance Company,*" 314.
[117] "*Thomas McCargo v. The New Orleans Insurance Company,*" 315.
[118] "*Thomas McCargo v. The New Orleans Insurance Company,*" 316.   [119] Ibid.
[120] "*Thomas McCargo v. The New Orleans Insurance Company,*" 317–318.

The state jurist proceeded to narrate the slaves' liberation in Nassau harbor; that was also marked with some key emphases.[121] He did not agree with defense counsel that the slaves were free because of the insurrection and sailing into Nassau, but insisted they were "still as slaves while on board, though in a state of insurrection."[122] This tortuous logic illustrates the sanctity of property rights in a southern slave society.[123] Moreover, correspondence between the US consul and the governor of the Bahamas shows that the latter interfered at the request of the former "singling out and confining the guilty," with "no further restraint" upon the others.[124] He drew particular attention to the attorney general having informed persons on the vessel that "*as far as the authorities of the island were concerned, all restrictions on their movements were removed.*"[125] The chief justice concluded his narrative with four facts. There was "no violence" and no one from ashore or the boats "boarded or attempted to board" the ship. The four slaves who remained on board ship were "not disturbed, nor interfered with." No member of the ship's crew ever demonstrated "any authority" over the slaves' movement. Only the rebels were taken ashore with the "consent of all concerned."[126] The chief justice's facts appear irrefutable – except that the rebels would not have been happy being marched ashore in chains; five, not four, captives remained on board; and Captain Woodside and his co-conspirators attempted an illegal seizure of the *Creole* with armed intent.

The key question in the legal dispute over the *Creole* revolt, then, was what was the cause of the loss? Was it insurrection or mutiny? Was it interference by authorities at Nassau? Was it foreign interference?

---

[121] "*Thomas McCargo v. The New Orleans Insurance Company,*" 318–326.

[122] "*Thomas McCargo v. The New Orleans Insurance Company,*" 318.

[123] This was exemplified by the Louisiana Supreme Court's judgment in the appeal of *Francois v. Jacinto Lobrano* reproduced in Robinson, *Reports of Cases Argued,* 450–452, 566. Francois, an enslaved man sold several times over, sued for his freedom because he claimed to have already reimbursed his first owner and subsequent masters in exchange for his freedom. His continued enslavement resulted in his running away repeatedly. Lobrano stuck him in jail to serve on the city chain gang. The lower court found for the defendant and Francois appealed the decision to the high court. The judges affirmed the original decision explaining that a "slave cannot become partially free, nor can he, until legally and absolutely emancipated, own any property, without the consent of the master." This denial of slaves' property also supports the contention of Chief Mate Gifford and US Consul Bacon in November 1841 that slaves aboard the *Creole* could not own property because they were property themselves.

[124] "*Thomas McCargo v. The New Orleans Insurance Company,*" 320.

[125] "*Thomas McCargo v. The New Orleans Insurance Company,*" 324. Italics in original.

[126] "*Thomas McCargo v. The New Orleans Insurance Company,*" 326.

The latter was a diplomatic issue that was not the court's concern, and had already been dealt with in 1842. "Our only inquiry," explained Bullard, was "whether that interference, such as it is shown by the evidence before us, was the proximate, efficient cause of the loss according to the settled principles of the law of insurance."[127] He reviewed two cases to demonstrate the significance of *causa proxima, non remota spectatur* in maritime insurance cases.[128] Drawing from these cases, he made the sort of lucid distinction that would have met with the approbation of Lord Mansfield. "The emancipation of the slaves," he stated, "was the immediate and natural consequence of the insurrection, and of the running of the vessel upon the British shores by the mutineers."[129] Louisiana's senior jurist asked if "abortive attempt," and "public prejudice of the place," and "persuasive influence," were perils against which the plaintiff was insured and the cause of the loss. The case was not about the conduct of local authorities or the extent of popular support for slaves, "but whether their acts and interference were, according to the law of insurance, the cause which prevented the property insured from arriving at the port of destination."[130]

After briefing the case, narrating what happened aboard the *Creole*, and stripping the debate down to its bare essentials, Chief Justice Bullard delivered his decision: "We conclude that the insurrection of the slaves was the cause of breaking up the voyage and prevented that part of the cargo, which consisted of the slaves, from reaching the port of New Orleans; and consequently, that the defendants are not liable on the policy in this case." The judgment of the lower court was reversed and the higher court found for the NOIC with costs in both courts.[131]

Judge Bullard's ruling in *McCargo v. The New Orleans Insurance Company* paved the way for adjudicating the other six insurance cases concerning the *Creole* revolt.[132] In *James Andrews and another v. The Ocean Insurance Company*, there was an action to recover $3,300 insurance on eight slaves in the lower court. The facts were the same as in the *McCargo* case but the verdict and judgment went for the

---

[127] "*Thomas McCargo v. The New Orleans Insurance Company*," 327.
[128] "*Thomas McCargo v. The New Orleans Insurance Company*," 327–328. The two cases reviewed were *Potter v. The Ocean Insurance Company* and *Schieffelin v. The New York Insurance Company.*
[129] "*Thomas McCargo v. The New Orleans Insurance Company*," 329.
[130] "*Thomas McCargo v. The New Orleans Insurance Company*," 330–331.
[131] "*Thomas McCargo v. The New Orleans Insurance Company*," 332.
[132] "*Thomas McCargo v. The New Orleans Insurance Company*," 332–354.

defendants. C. M. Jones and Mr. Roselius appealed on behalf of the slave-owners to the higher court while Conrad, Slidell, and Benjamin represented the insurance company. The chief justice affirmed the lower court judgment with costs for the same reasons as the primary case.[133]

The case of *Edward Lockett v. The Fireman's Insurance Company of New Orleans* represented an action to recover $20,000 on twenty-six slaves liberated from the *Creole*. A written clause was inserted into the insurance contract: "The assurers are not liable for suicide, mutiny, natural death, or desertion; but to take the risk of interference by foreign governments or their agents." The jury had ruled in favor of the defendant at the lower court trial. Mr. Peyton, I. W. Smith, and Mr. Eustis tended the plaintiff's appeal, while Messrs. Lockett, Micou, and Hunt defended the insurance company. The appellant's lawyers understandably questioned the usage of the word "mutiny" because it "applied to occurrences on ship-board, to the crew and subordinate officers." Slaves, they stated correctly, "are incapable of committing a mutiny." Chief Justice Bullard, however, had already insisted on the similarity of mutiny and insurrection in the *McCargo* case and affirmed the lower court judgment with costs for the same reasons as the first case.[134]

In the case of *John Hagan v. The Ocean Insurance Company*, the slave merchant launched suit against the company to recover $6,500 on nine slaves. The contract was similar to the one in the *McCargo* case. The verdict went against him. The plaintiff Hagan appealed with the same legal team. Chief Justice Bullard affirmed the lower court judgment for the same reasons as the *McCargo* case.[135] In *Sherman Johnson v. The Ocean Insurance Company*, there was an action to recover $15,000 on twenty-three slaves. It too was the same policy as in the *McCargo* case. The defendants won. The plaintiff appealed using the same lawyers. The lower court judgment was affirmed for the same reasons as the *McCargo* case.[136]

In *Edward Lockett v. The Merchants Insurance Company of New Orleans*, there was an action to recover $10,000 for fifteen slaves. In the lower court, the verdict and judgment went for the plaintiff for $9,333.33 minus $666.66 for one of the five slaves who stayed aboard the *Creole* and landed in New Orleans. The same three lawyers led the appeal on behalf of

[133] "*Thomas McCargo v. The New Orleans Insurance Company*," 332.
[134] "*Thomas McCargo v. The New Orleans Insurance Company*," 332–333.
[135] "*Thomas McCargo v. The New Orleans Insurance Company*," 333.
[136] "*Thomas McCargo v. The New Orleans Insurance Company*," 334.

the defendants. They argued that the "vessel deviated," thus releasing their insurance company client. The plaintiff's lawyers argued there was no deviation but that vessel "stoppages were necessary." Chief Justice Bullard ruled against voyage deviation, refused to interfere with the verdict and judgment of the jury, and affirmed the original lower court judgment in favor of Lockett.[137]

In *Thomas McCargo* v. *The Merchants Insurance Company of New* Orleans, the New Orleans trader sought to recover $15,200 on nineteen slaves from the *Creole*. The verdict and judgment in the lower court trial went for the plaintiff for $14,400, minus $800 for one slave who reached New Orleans. The same lawyers appealed on behalf of the insurance company. They argued that the loss was caused by "mutiny or insurrection." The defendants assumed the risk. The plaintiff was entitled to recover and the lower court judgment was affirmed.[138] A legal action that had begun in mid-December 1841 was finally concluded four years later in early February 1845. The insurance companies were the clear winners in the courts, besting the slave traders in five of the seven cases.

The final act in this high court drama was the defendants' lawyers' petition for the rehearing of the McCargo and Lockett cases against the MICNO. They wished to reverse the two decisions against the insurance company. Mr. Benjamin et al. argued for the difference between America's coastal trade and the Atlantic slave trade. But the chief justice rejected the argument, upheld the original judgment in both cases, and refused a rehearing.[139]

During their presentation before the Louisiana Supreme Court, the defense counsel quoted an observation, made by Judge Joseph Story, who served on the US Supreme Court between 1811 and 1845, that the maritime insurance business required the application "of sound common sense and practical reasoning" over "abstractions and refined distinctions."[140] A careful examination of the legal record concerning the insurance dispute over the *Creole* revolt proves its application in New Orleans. The law was a sensible avenue to settle the affairs of commerce. Slave traders knew that the transportation of human cargo was a risky business. Consequently, they transferred the risk by insuring their slaves with insurance companies. Louisiana's lower court ruled in

---

[137] "*Thomas McCargo* v. *The New Orleans Insurance Company*," 339–348.
[138] "*Thomas McCargo* v. *The New Orleans Insurance Company*," 335–338.
[139] "*Thomas McCargo* v. *The New Orleans Insurance Company*," 349–354.
[140] "*Thomas McCargo* v. *The New Orleans Insurance Company*," 277.

their favor but this was largely overturned in the higher court. The risk was eventually borne by most of the slave traders. It was all the outcome of sound sense and reason.

But this insurance dispute over a successful slave ship revolt also raised some thorny issues that contradicted the practical operation of a slave society. What are we to make of the fact that twelve local jurors from New Orleans agreed with local and Virginia slave traders against Louisiana insurance companies in a lower court? How are we to reconcile defense counsel's claim that sailors and slaves were of the same human stock in a society ruled by the chattel principle? If the rule of law in a slave society was about sending the right message for the purpose of social control, especially where rebels occasionally killed slave-owners and their agents, what are we to do with defense counsel's argument endorsed by the chief justice's ruling that the loss of the slaves aboard the *Creole* was due to a slave revolt *that had been successful*? Did not the outcome of the *Creole* revolt threaten just as much "contagion" as British colonial abolition, Nat Turner's rebellion, and the Haitian Revolution? Did not the successful relocation of slaves from slave to free soil negate the safety of proximate borders at sea as well as on land? According to one biographer, this successful legal defense guaranteed Benjamin's future as a successful commercial lawyer and spread his name across the Union.[141] However his well-compensated personal triumph rested on an argument for natural human rights that directly contradicted the laws and premises of a slave society defined by the chattel principle. The insurance dispute was assuredly marked by common sense and practical reason, but human society is usually more complex.

[141] Butler, *Benjamin*, 40–44.

"Full and Final Settlement"

On a typical cold and gray February morning in London in 1853, representatives from the United States and Great Britain concluded a convention.[1] The charge of the Adjustment Claims Commission (ACC) was the "settlement of outstanding claims of the citizens of either country against the other." Both sides agreed to a series of measures designed to adjust and settle all claims dating back to the peace treaty of Ghent in December 1814 that had ended the two-year military conflict between the two nations. All of the claims were to be adjudicated by two commissioners representing each country. Nathaniel Gookin Upham served on behalf of the United States. Born in 1801, he came from a long line of New Englanders stretching back to 1635. After graduating from Dartmouth College in 1816, Upham turned to the business of law and moved to Concord, New Hampshire, where he spent most of his life. He served as Associate Justice of the New Hampshire Supreme Court between 1833 and 1843, after which he presided over the Concord Railroad. Historical and biographical pursuits distracted him from his poor health.[2] Edmund Grimani Hornby represented British interest. Born in

---

[1] This analysis of the Adjustment Claims Commission (ACC) between 1853 and 1855 draws from the US Congress, Senate, Executive Document 103, 34th Congress, 1st Session *Message of the President of the United States* (Washington 1856), hereafter Sen. Doc. No. 103, 1856. It further rests on several useful memorials and supporting documents, located in the Creole Affair Collection at the Amistad Research Center (ARC), from shippers who lost their human property as a consequence of the *Creole* revolt and were required to provide supporting documentation.

[2] "Nathaniel Gookin Upham," Wikipedia, http://en.wikipedia.org/wiki/Nathaniel_Gookin_Upham. This Wikipedia entry mistakenly limits the ACC's activities to resolving disputed land claims.

1825 in Yorkshire to an Italian mother and trained as a lawyer, Commissioner Hornby proved to be quite the prodigy. At twenty-eight years of age, he was selected for the commission. At thirty-two, he was made judge of the British Supreme Consular Court at Constantinople. He was knighted five years later.[3]

Proceedings began at No. 9, Wellington Chambers, Lancaster Place, London, on September 15, 1853. The address is situated in an interesting part of Britain's capital city. Directly southward is Waterloo Bridge, made of granite and with nine arches, which was first opened in 1809. In the same year as the *Creole* revolt, it was the venue for the accidental death of American daredevil Samuel Gilbert Scott whose balancing act went horribly awry, resulting in his hanging.[4] To the northeast stood the imposing neoclassical Somerset House whose three-century history up until that point included serving as a royal residence, a royal art gallery, Admiralty headquarters for the Royal Navy, and registration office for births, deaths, and marriages.[5] These rather colorful surroundings contrast with the more prosaic business of settling outstanding financial claims.

On October 31, 1853 the commissioners appointed an arbitrator in the event of disagreement between the two representatives. Joshua Bates was their choice. Born in Massachusetts in 1788, he became a successful merchant and banker. In 1828 Bates was made financier and senior partner in Baring Brothers and Company of London, the leading banking house in Great Britain and the world. This was due to the retirement of Alexander Baring Ashburton who went on to serve as Britain's special envoy to sort out Anglo-American difficulties in 1842. Mr. Bates specialized in trade with Russia and Calcutta and acquired an unrivaled knowledge of American business and businessmen. He was described as "pawky, dour, charmless," with a dry tone and taciturn.[6] American

---

[3] "Edmund Grimani Hornby," Wikipedia, http://en.wikipedia.org/wiki/Edmund_Grimani _Hornby.

[4] "Waterloo Bridge," Wikipedia, https://en.wikipedia.org/wiki/Waterloo_Bridge.

[5] "Somerset House," Wikipedia, https://en.wikipedia.org/wiki/Somerset_House.

[6] "Baring Family," *Encyclopedia Britannica*, http://www.britannica.com/EBchecked/topic/ 53302/Baring-family#ref212753; Ron Chernow, *The House of Morgan: An American Banking Dynasty and the Rise of Modern Finance* (New York: Grove Press, 1990), 3, 5, 6, 19; Philip Ziegler, *The Sixth Great Power: A History of One of the Greatest of All Banking Families, The House of Barings, 1762–1929* (New York: Alfred Knopf, 1988), 93, 112, 122–123. It was John Baring – Alexander Baring's father – who had overseen the Louisiana Purchase in 1803 virtually doubling the United States' land size and securing the territorial expansion of the slaveholding republic. The global financial power of this

Commissioner Upham believed Bates's "long residence in England in that position and his great success" had given him standing and character "that should impact full confidence to the claimants of both countries, as well as to the governments themselves, in the intelligence, integrity, and impartiality of his decisions."[7]

General John A. Thomas of New York, acting as agent on behalf of American citizens, presented forty claims against the British government. James Hannen representing British citizens entered seventy-five claims against the American government. These two agents presented their combined 115 cases before the two commissioners between September 1853 and the end of 1854. Commissioners Upham and Hornby were responsible for adjudicating these claims. Those cases they were unable to decide would be passed onto umpire Bates. Many claims were dismissed, usually because they were deemed outside the commission's remit. By January 15, 1855, the commission's business had been completed. Nineteen British parties were awarded $277,102.88, more than $7.8 million in today's money. One was an old war claim: The Hudson Bay Company was paid $3,182.21. Others concerned maritime disputes. John Lidgett, owner of the ship *Albion,* was paid $20,000, while George Buckham, owner of the brig *Lady Shaw Stewart,* received $6,000. Twelve American parties received $329,734.16, more than $9.3 million today. Maritime issues predominated: Nine of the twelve parties concerned ship-related issues at sea. Settlement of two cases, the *Jones* and the *Creole,* accounted for more than 63 percent of the payout to the American claimants.[8] By July 1855, the ACC concluded that all cases had been "fully and finally settled." All financial claims between the United States and Great Britain for the first half of the nineteenth century had been taken care of with the UK government paying a greater amount than the US government. These financial agreements, however, did not succeed in terminating maritime disputes between the two nations.

The two commissioners were presented with a vast array of claims for compensation. These involved: land disputes in Florida, Maine, and

firm was famously expressed by the Duc de Richelieu in 1818: "There are six great powers in Europe: England, France, Prussia, Austria, Russia and Baring Brothers."

[7] Upham to Hornby, October 31, 1853, ACC, Sen. Doc. No. 103, 1856, 457–458; "Joshua Bates, Financier," Wikipedia, http://en.wikipedia.org/wiki/Joshua_Bates_%28financier%29. This Wikipedia entry inaccurately restricts the actions of the ACC to settling the claims of American citizens from the War of 1812.

[8] ACC, Sen. Doc. No. 103, 1856, 78–79. These payouts were often made to more than one claimant.

Vermont; the smuggling of merchandise; improper taxation claims; false arrests; destruction of goods and property during the Mexican War; default payments on state bonds, and so forth.[9] There were also American slaveholders' claims for restitution for fugitive slaves who had gravitated toward British lines with the prospect of liberty during the Second Anglo-American War. On March 4, 1854 John McClure and other slave-owners claimed for slaves "alleged to be owned by citizens of the United States in Florida," when it was under Spanish control, who had "escaped from Florida to Cumberland Island and were taken away by the British authorities at the close of war of 1815."[10] This was the same island that Rear Admiral George Cockburn had once defended as "governed by the laws of Great Britain [and] I do not conceive it to be within my power *forcibly* to send back any [enslaved] individuals."[11] The claim was disallowed because of want of jurisdiction and prior adjustment at a previous convention.

Many of the cases before the ACC, however, involved maritime disputes over property rights and contested borders. In 1843, the US schooner *Washington* was fishing in the Bay of Fundy when she was seized by a British revenue cruiser *Julia*, taken to Nova Scotia, and charged with violating an 1818 fisheries treaty between the two nations. The vessel's owners claimed damages of $4,121. The commissioners could not agree on the case – was it British maritime interference or had the American fishermen abrogated agreed-upon borders – so it was turned over to the umpire. Mr. Bates ruled that the owners were owed $3,000 because the area in question was one in which "no nation can have the right to sovereignty," and the claim was deemed "excessive."[12] This was very different language compared to official US claims for extensive slave states' maritime rights beyond the nation's coastline and into the northern Caribbean after the *Creole* revolt. Impressment – that perennial British thorn in the side of the Americans – was also the subject of dispute. Agent Thomas presented the claim of the brig *Brookline* for the removal of a deserter from the Royal Navy.[13] The US representative also brought a claim on behalf of the *John A. Robb* for the removal of a sailor by a British cruiser. Although the right to board was "disavowed," the case

---

[9] Ibid, 15–77. Details of these cases are discussed later in this chapter. [10] Ibid, 51–52.
[11] Jeremy Black, *Slavery: A New Global History* (Philadelphia, PA: Running Press, 2011), 152.
[12] ACC, Sen. Doc. No. 103, 1856, 170–186. [13] Ibid, 32, 34.

was dismissed because the sailor was in dispute with the captain and had departed with his consent.[14]

Of particular note were disputes involving American merchant ships and their interception by British vessels for possible involvement in illegal slave trading. In late 1840, the barque *Jones* under Captain Gilbert traded goods to central African ports before entering St. Helena in the South Atlantic where she was seized by HMS *Dolphin* commanded by Lieutenant Littlehales and charged with being in British waters without papers and therefore without "national character," and for being "engaged in and equipped for the slave trade." The vessel was taken to Sierra Leone for trial where the court decided it was not trading in slaves and that it did have the correct papers. The vessel was nevertheless auctioned. The owners P. J. Farham and Co. of Salem, Massachusetts, sought "full remuneration" for the lost vessel. American Commissioner Upham argued that the lack of papers did not constitute an offence, there was no probable cause for boarding the ship, and it was unjust to remove the vessel to another jurisdiction. British Commissioner Hornby disagreed. He argued that there were discrepancies with the papers, the *Jones* was engaged in slave trading because "letters, irons, spare plank, and articles used for slave food were found" aboard the vessel, and the ship had been moved because St. Helena did not maintain a Vice-Admiralty Court which was the appropriate venue.[15]

As a result of this disagreement between the commissioners, the case was sent to the adjudicator. After short deliberation, umpire Bates awarded $96,720 – more than $2.7 million today – to the owners for the loss of their vessel and cargo. Captain James Gilbert received $1,863. Chief Mate Ebenezer Symonds was granted $842. F. Sexton was given $1,200. The total payout amounted to $100,625 (more than $2.8 million) or 20,747 pounds, 8 shillings, 5 pence (more than GBP 2.1 million today). The British government kept the money from the sale of the brig and cargo as well as the silver coin left with the Vice-Admiralty Court.[16] This was the second largest payout by the British government to American claimants by the ACC. It concerned a maritime dispute over slave trading and the legality of its policing. It also demonstrated the transatlantic

---

[14] Ibid, 53
[15] ACC, 83–119, "trade" "remuneration" 84, "found" 113. See also 21, 27, 29, 30, 31, 32, 43, 50, and 79.
[16] Ibid, 119.

dimensions of imperial antislavery as well as the right of search as an infringement of national sovereignty.

On July 5, 1854 American agent Thomas presented the claim of the brig *Volusia* on behalf of owners John W. Disney and John Graham for "seizure and condemnation" by the British steamer *Rattler* en route from Rio de Janeiro, Brazil, for being a suspected slaver. The commissioners disagreed on the case and passed it on to the umpire who disallowed the claim.[17] On August 2, 1854, the US agent made a claim for the brig *Cyrus* on behalf of owner Peter C. Dumas for "seizure and detention" by the British warship *Alert* for being engaged in the slave trade off the West African coast. On November 25, the commissioners disallowed the claim.[18] The schooner *Levin Lank* owned by James Sullivan was sold to foreign owners on the coast of Africa by its owner and lessee. The US vessel was seized and condemned at St. Helena for engaging in the slave trade business. The owners' claim was disallowed.[19] Most of these cases were dismissed by the commission no doubt much to the chagrin of those whose property was lost or damaged. But the major point is that all of these disputes illustrate the extent of the maritime clash between American slavery and British antislavery across the Atlantic world after the legal abolition of transatlantic trading in 1807 and 1808.

On March 14, 1854 agent Thomas presented the case of the US brig *Enterprize*. Joseph W. Neal and several other slave-owners claimed compensation for the liberation of slaves by British authorities after the coastal slaver had been driven into Bermuda by bad weather. Further papers were filed on June 19. The commissioners heard the case on May 23 and 24. A not-unexpected disagreement between the commissioners brought the case before the umpire on October 19 and 21. On Saturday, December 23, 1854 Mr. Bates ruled that an infraction had been committed and awarded $16,000 – about $453,000 today – to the Augusta Insurance Banking Company and $33,000 ($933,000) to the Charleston Marine Insurance Company. The assurers were to receive the payments because they had already compensated the slave-owners.[20]

The case of the *Hermoza* followed the same timeline as the *Enterprize* before the commission and also ended up before the umpire. In his summary of the vessel's voyage and wreckage in the Bahamas, Mr. Bates

---

[17] Ibid, 34, 42, 43, 44, 51.   [18] Ibid, 36, 42, 50.   [19] Ibid, 50.
[20] Ibid, 26, 30, 31, 33, 38, 40, 45, and 57; Arthur T. Downey, *The Creole Affair: The Slave Rebellion That Led the U.S. and Great Britain to the Brink of War* (Lanham: Rowman and Littlefield, 2014), 144.

reported that despite Captain Chattin's correct conduct supported by the actions of US Consul Bacon, British magistrates backed by well-armed soldiers "took forcible possession of said vessels and the slaves were transported in boats" to the shore where "they were set free" against the "urgent remonstrances" of the master and consul. The ship's captain only required "aid and assistance" from one friendly nation to another. Instead, the local authorities ignored comity and liberated the slaves. The adjudicator awarded $16,000 ($453,000) split evenly between the Louisiana State Marine and Fire Insurance Company and the New Orleans Insurance Company who had already compensated the owners.[21]

On March 14, 1854 agent Thomas presented papers on behalf of Edward Lockett and other shippers on the *Creole* from the November 1841 voyage. He filed further papers on May 23. The case was heard on June 3 and submitted. Further claims were submitted on June 10 and 14. On September 26, the two commissioners disagreed on the allowance of the claim and the case was referred to the umpire. Mr. Bates heard it on October 19 through October 21. In his summation, the umpire provided a brief narrative of the *Creole* revolt from the ship's initial voyage to the liberation of the slaves. His language is vivid. The slaves were responsible for "murdering" a passenger. These "mutineers" forced steerage for Nassau. The vessel was surrounded by a large number of boats "filled with colored persons armed with bludgeons," while a "vast concourse of people collected on the shore." During the whole time local government officials were aboard the ship, "they encouraged the insubordination of the slaves." In short, the slaves rebelled and local officials facilitated their escape.[22]

Umpire Bates's inaccurate interpretation of the *Creole* revolt shaped his summation and verdict. Although slavery was "odious" and "contrary to the principles of justice and humanity," it was legal and not contrary to the laws of nations. The adjudicator followed an older distinction traceable to the venerable English jurist Lord Mansfield in the case of James Somerset in 1772: "[T]he state of slavery is of such a nature that it is incapable of being introduced on any reasons, moral or political, but only by positive law, which preserves its force long after the reasons, occasions and time itself from whence it was created, is erased from memory. It is so odious that nothing can be suffered to support it, but positive law."[23] The *Creole* was pursuing legitimate commerce protected by US laws as

[21] Ibid, 26, 31–33, 38, 40, 45, 47, 57, 78, 238–241; Downey, *Creole Affair*, 145.
[22] Ibid, 26, 31–33, 38, 40, 52, 242–244; Downey, *Creole Affair*, 145.
[23] Black, *Brief History of Slavery*, 157.

well as by the laws of nations. The role of the British authorities should have been to "keep the mutineers in custody" and nothing else. The rest of the slaves were under the control of the US crew and they should have received protection under the law of nations. Instead, they were "forcibly taken from the custody of master of the Creole, and lost to the claimants." In short, the "conduct of the authorities at Nassau was in violation of the established law of nations," and the claimants were justly entitled to compensation. On Tuesday, January 9, 1855, Umpire Bates made the following awards: $23,140 – about $654,000 today – to William H. Goodwin and Thomas McCargo; $22,250 ($629,000) to Edward Lockett; $20,470 ($579,000) to George H. Apperson and Sherman Johnson; $8,000 ($226,000) – to John Hagun [Hagan]; $5,874 ($166,000) to James Andrews; and $2,136 ($60,400) to P. Rotchford. One John Pemberton, liquidator of the Merchants' Insurance Company of New Orleans, was awarded $28,460 ($805,000) for two claims. The total amount paid by the British government to those who lost their human property on the *Creole* amounted to $110,330 – more than $3.1 million today.[24] It is unclear how the umpire arrived at some of these sums. But this compensation package was the largest handout paid by the British government to American claimants at the ACC and illustrates the importance of maritime disputes and their eventual adjudication in Anglo-American relations. One week later, No. 9 Wellington Chambers closed its doors.

This Anglo-American agreement during the early 1850s was significant for three key reasons. Most obviously, it settled outstanding disputes concerning lost property and financial claims. The *Creole* slave-owners, who were awarded payment in the lower court of Louisiana in 1843 only to have these rescinded by the upper court in 1845, were finally compensated for the value of their lost cargoes. Moreover, disputes that had dogged relations between the United States and Great Britain for nearly four decades were now settled once and for all.

But the agreement held broader significance. Fierce controversies during the late 1830s and early 1840s had been smoothed over by diplomatic dealing between Secretary Webster and Envoy Ashburton. A decade later, these issues were finally resolved in a quiet, upscale residential square in the heart of central London. Why then? What made the early 1850s more conducive to financial adjudication – especially by the British government – over the early 1840s? I would argue there were three key reasons. First, entrenched economic ties between the two nations, especially in

[24] Ibid, 32, 33, 47, 52, 78, 244–245; Downey, *Creole Affair*, 146.

terms of the global economy in which southern plantation cotton kept British factory spindles running, kept both nations at the negotiating table. As already noted, plantation cotton accounted for nearly 60 percent of all US exports in 1860. In the United Kingdom, cotton exports from textile factories accounted for nearly 40 percent of all British exports.[25] Second, both nations had illegalized the Atlantic slave trade and were committed to its eradication as illustrated by their joint policing actions against maritime trading in West Africa. Third, Britain respected the hemispheric power of the slaveholding republic, while America was aware of Britain's global maritime power. This made such agreements increasingly viable. It explains why compensation claims that had been dismissed by British Law Lords during the late 1830s were met in the early 1850s. Economic and diplomatic bonds were stronger; while the pressure of the times – British colonial abolition and US merchant ships' repeated losses of human cargoes – no longer weighed like a nightmare on the brain of the living.[26]

The rebellious passage and captives' self-liberation occurred in November 1841. The maritime rebels were eventually freed five months later in April 1842. Four months thereafter, Washington and London settled a number of conflicting issues, including an understanding concerning US coastal slavers and antislavery actions by British colonial officials. The dispute over liability between slave-owners and insurance companies began in December 1841 and was settled in February 1845. The diplomatic dispute over compensation claims from 1812 through the 1840s – including those pertaining to the *Creole* revolt – was eventually settled in 1855. So we can agree that this vessel's extraordinary chronology ran about fifteen years from initial voyage and shipboard revolt to financial settlement.

But as *Rebellious Passage* has tried to argue, we can only make sense of this important historical event within broader chronological and spatial dimensions of clashing empires, the operation of the coastal passage, the

---

[25] Tristram Hunt, *The Frock-Coated Communist: The Revolutionary Life of Friedrich Engels* (London: Allen Lane, 2009), 190; Sven Beckert, *Empire of Cotton: A Global History* (New York: Alfred A. Knopf, 2014), 73.

[26] I am paraphrasing Marx's famous metaphor describing the rise of Louis Bonaparte, the nephew of Napoleon, as the consequence of the tradition of past generations. Karl Marx, *The 18th Brumaire of Louis Bonaparte* (New York, International Publishers, 1984), 15. The 1850s did not carry the political baggage of the 1830s when US coastal slavers kept losing human cargoes in British ports due to foul weather or ship revolt with London either providing or not providing compensation.

maturation of maritime law, and traditions of slave agency and resistance. In contrast to the actual *Creole* revolt itself, many of these issues both preceded and continued beyond timeframes of a month or a decade and a half.

Slave ships continued human trading beyond American borders. During the final decade of the coastal passage, the inter-provincial trade in Brazil took off as hundreds of thousands of enslaved Africans were transported from the declining sugar regions of the northeast to the dynamic coffee valleys of the southwest provinces, either overland or via slave ships along the coast. In 1857, the *Jornal do Commercio* described the awful conditions of ninety slaves who had been shipped from Maranhao to Recife: "The deck of the steamer appeared like one of those coming from the coast of Africa, loaded with human flesh: we saw one unhappy child combating with death, and others miserably naked."[27] British officials even reported that American slavers sailing from New York to Rio de Janeiro continued to transport enslaved Africans from one Brazilian port to another during the mid-1870s.[28] The extent of US slave ships – and/or Spanish and Brazilian ships flying under American colors – has yet to be thoroughly researched by historians. It was not to end until Brazil's abolition of the inter-provincial slave trade by state legislatures in 1881.[29]

There is some evidence of maritime revolt. In 1844, the American slaver *Kentucky* sailed from Rio de Janeiro to Mozambique and obtained around 500 human captives. The morning after leaving the southeast African coast, British seamen William Page reported "the negroes rose upon the officers and crew," "got their irons off," and broke into the females' department and the forecastle. The captain and crew quickly armed and began firing, suppressing the revolt within half an hour. The perpetrators were "hung, shot, and thrown overboard."[30] During the late summer of 1861, Africans revolted once their ship left Cuba for Baltimore because of the fear of becoming

---

[27] Robert Conrad, *The Destruction of Slavery in Brazil, 1850–1888* (Malabar, FL: Krieger Publishing Company, 1993), 36.

[28] Gerald Horne, *Race to Revolution: The United States and Cuba during Slavery and Jim Crow* (New York: Monthly Review Press, 2014), 11.

[29] Conrad, *Destruction of Slavery*, 33; Robert Edgar Conrad, ed., *Children of God's Fire: A Documentary History of Black Slavery in Brazil* (University Park: Pennsylvania State University Press, 1994), 432.

[30] Page to US consul in Rio de Janeiro, in Conrad, *Children of God's Fire*, 39–42. This testimony details the horrific treatment meted out to the rebels.

enslaved in the United States.[31] Only systematic research through official diplomatic dispatches as well as Brazilian newspapers will reveal the extent of such rebellion against maritime trading.

The liberation of captives from slave vessels in British Caribbean ports also continued unabated. In 1853, the *Paraguay* docked in Kingston, Jamaica. H. A. Handy and William Lewis, slaves from Charleston, South Carolina, were liberated. Local authorities refused to hand them over.[32] Two years later, in May 1855, the brig *Young America* under Captain Samuel Rogers sailing from Baltimore docked at Savanna-la-Mar, Westmoreland Parish, Jamaica. It was rumored that the vessel carried a captive called John Anderson, a twenty-five-year-old hired slave from Baltimore. A crowd, some 300-strong, gathered to liberate Anderson. Since the wharves gates were shut, locals launched rowboats – much like the *Creole* rescue – and ferried Anderson ashore where he was put in custody. After a brief court session the next day, he was liberated. Robert Monroe Harrison, proud Virginian and long-term US consul in Kingston since 1832, protested in ritual terms. His "knowledge of the character of the inhabitants of the West Indian colonies, and more specifically of this Island, who are more hostile to us than any other class of people I have met," led him to conclude pessimistically that "the abduction of black or coloured persons from our vessels will never cease unless our Government address England on the subject in terms not to be mistaken."[33] Although these actions were taken by local Jamaicans rather than carried out under the auspices of British colonial officials, the liberation of Anderson resurrected the specter of tension between the two governments over the sanctity of property rights and the clash between slave and anti-slave empires. It also illustrated the continuation of Americans of African origin gaining liberty in foreign waters.[34]

---

[31] Horne, *Race to Revolution*, 12.
[32] Richard Blackett, *Making Freedom: The Underground Railroad and the Politics of Slavery* (Chapel Hill: University of North Carolina Press, 2013), 24.
[33] Ibid, 22–30, "mistaken" 30; Henry Barkly to Lord John Russell, 20 June, 1855, Jamaica Ledger 1855, pp. 530–531, CO 137/326, TNA; *New York Times*, 20 July 1855.
[34] Was there a radical tradition of popular discontent in Westmoreland Parish, Jamaica? Four years after Anderson's rescue, settlers on Florence Hall estate were jailed for trespass after which a crowd of several hundred supporters liberated them. In an ensuing melee, two women were killed and several wounded. Emily Jackson and Samuel Sutherland set light to the police station while the crowd marched around. In May 1938, workers on the Frome sugar estate rebelled against unfair remuneration for tedious and backbreaking labor tasks. They were supported by hundreds of unemployed workers whose hopes of paid employment were soon dashed. See Thomas Holt, *Black over White: Negro Political Leadership in South Carolina during Reconstruction* (Urbana: University of Illinois Press,

Sometime during early 1856, the local authorities in St. John's, Antigua, boarded the US merchant ship *Loango* and removed "a coloured man named John Ross, who alleged that he was a fugitive." Lord John Russell requested the Law Lords provide an opinion for colonial governors on interference with American shipping. After reviewing the documents, they decided that the "liberation of the alleged slave" by the local officers "was an abuse of their authority and a proceeding that which though it may be excused on account of the motive which led to it, cannot possibly be justified." On the more general issue of slaves being transshipped in British water, however, the Court was unequivocal: "All slaves found within the British territorial jurisdiction should be liberated; and the vessels, and free persons used for keeping them in slavery, if found in British territory acting as slave-owners or 'slavers,' should be detained in custody, and instantly delivered up to the nearest British authority, to be dealt with according to law under the advice of the Crown lawyers."[35]

And free and enslaved blacks continued to liberate ships from slavery. In June 1861, the schooner *S. J. Waring* from New York en route to South America was captured by Confederates and steered toward Charleston. William Tillman, a free black seaman and steward, was appropriated as new property and informed he would be sold into slavery upon arrival in South Carolina. Once night arrived, Tillman took a hatchet, killed two officers, and wounded another, before driving the rest of the crew below decks. He reversed the vessel's course and five days later sailed into New York City harbor with his freedom intact. The *New York Tribune* reported: "To this colored man was the nation indebted for the first vindication of its honor on the sea."[36]

Robert Smalls lived and worked as a domestic slave on a plantation near Beaufort, South Carolina, until the American Civil War. After the

---

1979), 276, 384–385; Colin A. Palmer, *Freedom's Children: The 1938 Labor Rebellion and the Birth of Modern Jamaica* (Chapel Hill: University of North Carolina Press, 2014), 33–40. At an academic conference marking the 150th commemoration of the Morant Bay Rebellion held at the University of the West Indies at Mona, Jamaica, in October 2015, Professor Swithin Wilmot's opening address referred to this local rebellious tradition in Savannah-la-Mar.

[35] J. D. Harding, Richard Bethell, William Atherton to Lord John Russell, April 28, 1856, in Baron Arnold and Duncan McNair, "Slavery and the Slave Trade," in *International Law Opinions* (London: Cambridge University Press, 1956), 89–92. It is not entirely clear why the Law Lords would have written to Lord Russell since he had vacated the position of Secretary of State for the Colonies the previous July.

[36] James M. McPherson, *The Negro's Civil War: How American Negroes Felt and Acted during the War for the Union* (New York: Vintage, 1965), 154.

conflict broke out, Smalls worked several semi-skilled and unskilled jobs around Charleston harbor. Like many hundreds of thousands of slaves, he used the military and political struggle to escape from slavery. Smalls served as pilot and his brother John worked as assistant pilot and sailor aboard the *Planter*, a light-draught, high-pressure, side-wheel steamer used to transport military supplies and freight for the Confederate States of America war effort. On Monday evening, May 12, 1862 the families of Robert and John went aboard. Between 3:00 and 4:00 the following morning, the Smalls and fifteen other slaves steered the steamer out of Charleston harbor. The knowledgeable pilot gave the required whistles of two long and one short at Fort Sumter, thus escaping detection before cutting through an inland waterway and encountering a Union ship. The new masters ran up a bed sheet and the federal flag, cheered the Union, and reached Hilton Head in the evening where they handed over the ship's cargo of artillery as well as the *Planter* to astonished Union authorities. Smalls was reported to have quipped: "I thought the *Planter* might be of use to Uncle Abe."[37] Although the context and circumstances were very different from that of the *Creole* revolt twenty-one years previously, both vessels' seizures represented a collective effort, inverted the ships' intended purpose, aimed for freedom's shore, and ultimately proved successful.[38]

America's coastal slave trade underwent de facto cessation by the end of 1861 as a consequence of the successful Union blockade of southern ports. Three years later, this maritime slave-trading business was legally terminated after operations stretching back more than five decades.

---

[37] Smalls fought in numerous other engagements and went on to serve in the South Carolina House of Representatives between 1868 and 1870 and in the state Senate between 1870 and 1875. He served five terms in the US House of Representatives between 1875 and 1887. He became a tax collector for the port of Beaufort, died in 1915, and was interred in the Tabernacle Baptist Church Cemetery. See Thomas Wentworth Higginson, *Army Life in a Black Regiment* (New York: Collier Books, 1972), 33, 80; McPherson, *Negro's Civil War*, 154–157; Willie Lee Rose, *Rehearsal for Reconstruction: The Port Royal Experiment* (New York: Oxford University Press, 1964), 149–150; Holt, *Black over White*, 47–48; Eric Foner, *Freedom's Lawmakers: A Directory of Black Officeholders During Reconstruction* (Baton Rouge: Louisiana State University Press, 1993), 198; Leonard L. Richards, *Who Freed the Slaves? The Fight Over the Thirteenth Amendment* (Chicago: University of Chicago Press, 2015), 92; "Smalls Robert," US House of Representatives, History, Art and Archives, http://history.house.gov/Peopl e/Detail/21764.

[38] This inversion also occurred on land. Prince Rivers took his owner's horse and rode from behind enemy lines in Edgefield, South Carolina, to enlist in the Union army. See Holt, *Black over White*, 48.

On July 2, 1864 Section Nine of an act for appropriations to the US government repealed the 1807 legislation regulating maritime commerce in human beings, concluding that the "coastwise slave trade is prohibited forever."[39] Its termination was followed by the outlawing of slavery through ratification of the Thirteenth Amendment to the US Constitution on December 18, 1865.

There is little doubt that the Webster-Ashburton Treaty of 1842 resolved many of the existing diplomatic difficulties between the two nations. But it would be incorrect to assume that tensions – even the potential of military conflict – ceased altogether. The joint occupation of Oregon Country led to a divide in which President James K. Polk threatened war against Britain unless the United States controlled all of the land south of the latitude line 54 degrees 40 minutes which would serve as the border between Russian Alaska and British Canada. In 1846, the dispute was eventually settled with the forty-ninth parallel serving as the border between the slaveholding republic and the antislavery empire.[40] This dispute is usually shelved under American westward expansion; yet it should not be forgotten that three nations were engaged in conquering and occupying disputed territory.

During the opening year of the American Civil War, the Confederate States of America sought diplomatic recognition from Europe. The newest nation in the Americas dispatched James Murray Mason of Virginia and John Slidell of Louisiana to London and Paris respectively. Slidell was Judah Benjamin's law partner in New Orleans and had co-defended the insurance companies during the *Creole* trial. In Havana, Cuba, they boarded the British merchant ship *Trent*. On November 8, 1861, precisely two decades after the *Creole* revolt, the American warship *San Jacinto* mastered by Charles Wilkes stopped the British ship, boarded it, and removed the two southern commissioners. This was quite a reversal of the usual pattern of British ships boarding American merchant vessels. Outrage at this illegal action toward a neutral ship led to threats of war. Henry Adams wrote his brother from London: "This nation means to make war ... A few weeks may see us ... on our way home." But the affair was eventually settled with Foreign Secretary William Steward

---

[39] Charles H. Wesley, "Manifests of Slave Shipments along the Waterways, 1808–1864," *The Journal of Negro History*, vol. 27, no. 2 (April 1942), 174.

[40] John Mack Faragher, Mari Jo Buhle, Daniel Czitrom, and Susan H. Armitage, *Out of Many: A History of the American People*, 4th ed. vol. 1 (Upper Saddle River, NJ: Prentice Hall, 2005), 406–410.

acknowledging that Captain Wilkes had erred and the two commissioners were liberated to make their way to Europe.[41] This famous incident is usually examined as to whether or not Great Britain would have gone to war with the United States over the issue and whether or not this would have weakened the Union cause. But the key issue of impressment – usually decisions by British captains to board American vessels uninvited – has a long history as we have seen, and most assuredly did not cease after the *Creole* rebellion.

This maritime dispute between Washington and London stretching over decades was finally resolved as a consequence of the advent of the American Civil War and the absence of slaveholding politicians in the national legislative body. In 1862, the Republican-controlled legislature and presidency finally acquiesced to Britain's right of search of suspected slavers during peacetime. It is probable that Washington disliked this measure but agreed to it to help weaken the slaveholding Confederate States of America in order to win the war and bring back the secessionist states. In contrast, the newest republic still adhered to the illegality of British boarding but proved even less capable of preventing it. Moreover, the Coastal Passage was no longer functioning because of a successful federal navy embargo of the southern states. This embargo helped transform the US Navy. In 1860, this military branch contained ninety ships, of which forty-two were in commission and mostly stationed abroad. Under Gideon Welles, Secretary of the Navy in Lincoln's cabinet, the US Navy increased to 700 vessels by the war's end. Only the Royal Navy boasted greater maritime power globally.[42]

Maritime clashes, however, continued in less well-known locales. One historian has recently unearthed evidence of a British captain who was accused of abusing black sailors in the port of Darien, Georgia, in 1871. Louis Jackson, a local African-American official in McIntosh County with links to powerful black state senator Tunis Campbell's political machine, called for the arrest of the skipper. Ignoring the protests of the local British consul, armed blacks and a black constable arrested the master and took him into custody. It is not clear what the outcome of this dispute was, but it suggests that maritime skirmishes between the United States and Great

---

[41] David Herbert Donald, Jean Harvey Baker, Michael F. Holt, *The Civil War and Reconstruction* (New York: Norton, 2001), 314–317.
[42] William E. Gienapp & Eruca L. Gienapp, eds., *The Civil War Diary of Gideon Welles, Lincoln's Secretary of the Navy* (Urbana: University of Illinois Press, 2014).

Britain were not over.[43] Fast forward to the First World War, and President Woodrow Wilson's earliest messages of assertions of America's maritime rights against interference by both British as well as German shipping.[44]

Slave-owners and insurance companies continued to battle over maritime slave compensation. On November 25, 1852, Henry M. Summers insured five of his slaves with the United States Insurance Annuity and Trust Company of Philadelphia for one year. The five people enslaved were: twenty-year-old Thomas Bass; eighteen-year-old William Brooks; twenty-year-old Henry Carter; twenty-one-year-old Townley Johnson; and seventeen-year-old William Lee. All were tobacco warehouse workers. In early November 1853, Johnson went overboard from the steamer *Emperor* and was presumed lost in the Mississippi River. The insurance company refused to pay the $800 liability for Johnson. The Philadelphia insurance business insisted that the slaves were insured as tobacco workers, but Summers's usage of them in more dangerous work on sugar plantations exceeded the remit of the policy. The slave-owner sued the company in the Fourth District Court of New Orleans on January 5, 1857 and won. The insurance company appealed. The Louisiana Supreme Court affirmed the lower court judgment and Summers was compensated for the loss of his tobacco worker.[45]

If ideological representations about slaves and slavery both preceded as well as informed ways in which the *Creole* revolt was presented, then it should come as no surprise that these presentations continued. A decade later, visiting African-American artist and antislavery activist William Wells Brown treated crowds in London, Newcastle, and Scotland to

---

[43] Gregory Mixon, *Show Thyself a Man: Georgia State Troops, Colored, 1865–1905* (Gainesville: University Press of Florida, 2016), 48–49.

[44] J. M. Roberts, *Europe 1880–1945* (London, Longman, 1967), 286. According to the *Central Intelligence Agency World Factbook*, one of the outstanding transnational issues with the Bahamas today concerns the alignment of the northern axis of the potential maritime boundary.

[45] Henry M. Summers to the Fourth District Court of New Orleans, January 5, 1857, Petition 20885724, http://library.uncg.edu/slavery/petitions/details.aspx?pid=16481, RSPP. Johnson might have jumped to freedom or survived if he fell overboard. Robert Ellett, formerly enslaved in Virginia, recalled: "I was in the mouth of the Mississippi at Orleans on the Zephyr, a 3,676 ton [sic] ship. I fell overboard and went under the ship, but I saved myself by swimming out from under the ship and swam up to the surface on the other side." Ellett to Anderson, December 25, 1937, in Charles L. Purdue Jr., Thomas E. Barden, Robert K. Phillips, eds., *Weevils in the Wheat: Interviews with Virginia Ex-Slaves* (Charlottesville: University of Virginia Press, 1976), 87–88.

panoramic views of the *Creole*.[46] In opposition to this antislavery depiction was the defense of slavery. Loyal slaves shuffle across the pages of Margaret Mitchell's 1930s novel *Gone with the Wind* – later turned into a blockbuster Hollywood movie – in which happiness and contentment reigned supreme in that lost plantation world of noble whites and pitiful blacks until the terrible conflagration of the 1860s destroyed this halcyon world. "As slaves they received generally good care and as slaves they were happy." There was "no record of any single case in the state in which freedmen resorted to violence to avenge wrongs suffered under slavery." These quotes – and there are many others on slaves' docility, humility, and contentment – populate Vernon's Wharton's *Negro in Mississippi* first published in 1947.[47] The troublesome role of interfering outsiders spouted by southern white elites against any challenge to their power from congressional Reconstruction in the 1870s to the Populists' rebellion in the 1890s through the Civil Rights Movement in the 1960s to mobilizing for the Democratic Party in the 1980s to union organizing in the region today can be traced back to those meddlesome British.

Images of the freedom fighter and the heroic slave also sowed deep roots. The pantheon of heroes created by the abolitionist movement paved the way for representations of William Tillman and Robert Smalls. More recently, scholars have resurrected this pantheon of black heroes in their depiction of slave ship rebels in general as well as the *Creole* rebels in particular.[48] Their readers are academics and interested members of the

---

[46] William Wells Brown, *A Description of William Wells Brown's Original Panoramic Views of the Scenes in the Life of an American Slave, from His Birth in Slavery to His Death or His Escape to His First Home of Freedom on British Soil* (London: Charles Gilpin, 1850); William Edward Farrison, *William Wells Brown: Author and Reformer* (Chicago: University of Chicago Press, 1969), 173–176; Ezra Greenspan, *William Wells Brown: An African American Life* (New York: Norton, 2014), 239–245.

[47] Vernon Lane Wharton, *The Negro in Mississippi, 1865–1890* (New York: Harper & Row, 1965), 13, 50. It was also, oddly enough, pioneering in its attention to the post-emancipation life, politics, and labor of formerly enslaved people.

[48] Vincent Harding, *There Is A River: The Black Struggle for Freedom in America* (New York: Vintage Books, 1983), 13; Edward D. Jervey and C. Harold Huber, "The Creole Affair." *The Journal of Negro History* vol. 65, no. 3 (Summer 1980), 197; George Hendrick and Willene Hendrick, *The Creole Mutiny: A Tale of Revolt aboard a Slave Ship* (Chicago: Ivan R. Dee, 2003). In describing mass murder on the vessel *Zong*, Peter Fryer refers to the last ten victims who were thrown overboard as "pulling away from their captors [who] chose to die as heroes." Peter Fryer, *Staying Power: The History of Black People in Britain* (London: Pluto, 1984), 128. This is classic celebratory history of course, but we must not forget that Fryer's book was one of the earliest narrative histories of black people in Britain, a pitiful historiography that denied agency to people of African descent.

public for whom black freedom fighters remain important in a history that has generally ignored, made pathological, or criminalized resistance to oppression. Some academics have recently questioned such heroic depictions as simplistic and not true to the complexity of the historical record. A more productive approach would be to ask not only why black heroes are still considered necessary, but also why the posing of "complexities" remains a fruitful pathway to success in academia. In the words of former British communist Peter Fryer: "Robbed in the past of all they had, from their freedom to their very names, Afro-Americans have made up their minds never to be robbed again – and no longer to tolerate the pillage of their history by ignorant and superficial white writers out for fame and gain."[49] The writing of this history by white and black historians today grants neither riches nor a seat at the table with the gods, but it can build lucrative careers, help land prestigious book contracts, and establish professional reputations, all without bothering about tackling the legacies of slavery, racism, and colonialism that continue to negatively impact the lives of people of African descent in today's world.

[49] Fryer, *Staying Power*, xi.

Epilogue

Rebellious Passage has tried to meet several aims. It has sought to reveal the maritime dimensions of the US slave trade. This book adds to a growing awareness of this understudied aspect of an otherwise flourishing scholarly topic. Furthermore, it traces certain important continuities such as the expansion– rather than rupture – of maritime trading as well as a tradition of slave ship revolt that transcends region and century. Moreover, it presents a history of connections of people, ideas, and spaces that challenge national narratives usually informed by Whig notions of the inevitability of things always improving and progressing. Finally, it offers an example of history from the bottom up in which the actions of ordinary people shook nations and empires.

It is up to the ken of the reader to decide whether these objectives were met. It is the author's task to show what was historically significant about the *Creole* revolt. Most obviously, a small group of captives gained their freedom as a consequence of a successful slave ship revolt led by rebels whose gamble to head for colonial free soil paid off. This act of human liberation contributed to the sectional crisis over slavery that led to the American Civil War and ultimately to the termination of a major economic and political institution. To pursue a watery metaphor: The rebellious passage was a ripple among thousands of antislavery actions that became a tide that eventually washed away an oppressive regime that had marked the American republic for generations.

Moreover, the *Creole* revolt – together with Haitian independence, British colonial abolition, and the *Amistad* rebellion – contributed to the destabilization of the coastal passage. This argument is suggested by different bits of evidence, none of which are conclusive, but which collectively are intriguing. To begin with, some contemporaries pointed to the danger of shipping slaves southward because of potential interference from British authorities. Recalling his coastal passage from Baltimore to New Orleans, captive William Grose observed that nothing "especial occurred except on one occasion, when, after some thick weather, the ship came near an English island: the captain then hurried us all below and closed the hatches. After passing the island, we had liberty to come up again."[1] Visitor Ethan Andrews spoke with slave trader Joseph W. Neal, owner of slaves aboard the *Enterprise* who were liberated in Bermuda in 1835. The trader expected to recoup some of his losses through settlement of an insurance claim, but wrote off the rest. "But why don't you go there and claim them?" asked a bystander. "Because," said Neal, "A NIGGER IS JUST AS FREE THERE, AND STANDS JUST AS GOOD A CHANCE IN THEIR COURTS AS A WHITE MAN."[2] Speaking on behalf of slaveholders, Kentucky Senator Henry Clay reported that the *Creole* had been carried to Nassau by "an act of mutiny and murder," and if the British authorities sanctioned "the enormity" of the crime, then "Americans would be virtually denied the benefits of the coastwise trade of their own country, because their vessels could not proceed in safety from one port to another *with slaves on board.*"[3]

Moreover, an older historiography on the US slave trade hints at the decline of the maritime business by the 1850s. Ulrich Phillips suggests that one anonymous firm switched to overland trading because of the potential hazards at sea.[4] Frederick Bancroft estimates that a "greater portion of the interstate trade from the old States is supposed to have gone coastwise in the 'thirties than in the 'fifties."[5] Charles Wesley argues that the annexation of Texas, the discovery of gold in California, and the reduced number

---

[1] William Grose in Benjamin Drew, *A North-Side View of Slavery. The Refugee or the Narratives of Fugitive Slaves in Canada. Related by Themselves, with an Account of the History and Condition of the Colored Population of Upper Canada* (Boston: J.P. Jewett and Company, 1856), 82–84, "up again" 84.

[2] Ethan Andrews, *Slavery and the Domestic Slave Trade in the United States* (Boston: Light & Stearns, 1836), 145–146, capitals in original; Frederic Bancroft, *Slave-Trading in the Old South* (Baltimore: J. H. Furst, 1931), 278–279; Wendell H. Stephenson, *Isaac Franklin: Slave Trader and Planter from the Old South* (Baton Rouge: Louisiana State University Press, 1938), 52.

[3] John R. Spears, *The American Slave Trade: An Account of Its Origin, Growth, and Suppression* (New York: Charles Scribner, 1900), 181.

[4] Ulrich B. Phillips, *American Negro Slavery: A Survey of the Supply, Employment and Control of Negro Labor As Determined by the Plantation Regime* (Baton Rouge: Louisiana State University Press, 1966,) 195.

[5] Bancroft, *Slave-Trading*, 276–277.

of ship manifests demonstrates the decline of the coastal passage by the early 1850s.[6] Only a thorough examination of all US ship manifests for 1807 to 1864 will reveal the extent to which this decline was real or just a scholarly impression.

The numerical reduction in slave ship voyages constitutes a third piece of evidence. In particular, there were fewer coastal passages during the 1840s compared to the 1830s according to some ship manifest records. Between 1835 and 1845, twenty-five slavers arrived inbound to Mobile from Baltimore. Only eight came after 1841. Between 1837 and 1843, fourteen slave ships left Norfolk and Portsmouth for Mobile, of which only three departed after 1841.[7] In other words, the *Creole* slave revolt, its success, and a history of British complicity in securing captives' liberty rendered the coastal passage an increasingly dangerous means of transporting human chattel. Indeed, one reliable scholar finds "very few" ship manifests after 1852.[8] This was during the height of the US slave trade. It is not at all clear why this would have been the case given the obvious advantages – shortness of passage, lower cost, better survival rates – of coastwise transportation compared to prolonged, expensive, and physically demanding overland coffles.

Let's not overdo it. There do not appear to have been increased preventative measures on coastal slavers during the 1840s. And the coastal passage continued. On March 29, 1842 the *Creole* embarked from Richmond with seventeen captives shipped by Robert Lumpkin of Richmond to John Mitchell of Alabama, arriving a month later on April 25 in New Orleans. Thomas Nelson signed off in Richmond, and G. Brent Bayly passed the ship in New Orleans harbor. All appeared to be business as usual. But the coastal slaver had a new skipper, Alexander Riddell. The number of captives was considerably reduced compared to previous slaving voyages. And the *Creole* did not survive the year. It appears that the vessel never fully recovered from the ship revolt.[9]

---

[6] Charles H. Wesley, "Manifests of Slave Shipments along the Waterways, 1808–1864," *The Journal of Negro History*, vol. 27, no. 2 (April 1942), 172–173.

[7] "RG 36, US Customs Service, Slave Manifests – Mobile, Alabama Inward (By Owner Name)," National Archives at Atlanta, Georgia, www.archives.gov/atlanta/finding-aids/rg36_slave_mobileinw_owner.html

[8] Wesley, "Manifests of Slave Shipments," 173.

[9] Robert Lumpkin (owner), Alexander Riddell (master), Thomas Nelson (collector), Manifest of the *Creole*, March 29, 1842, *Slave Manifests of Coastwise Vessels Filed at New Orleans, Louisiana, 1807–1860*, Microfilm Serial: M1895, Microfilm Roll: 9, NARA. A search for Alexander Riddell in the federal census records proved unsuccessful.

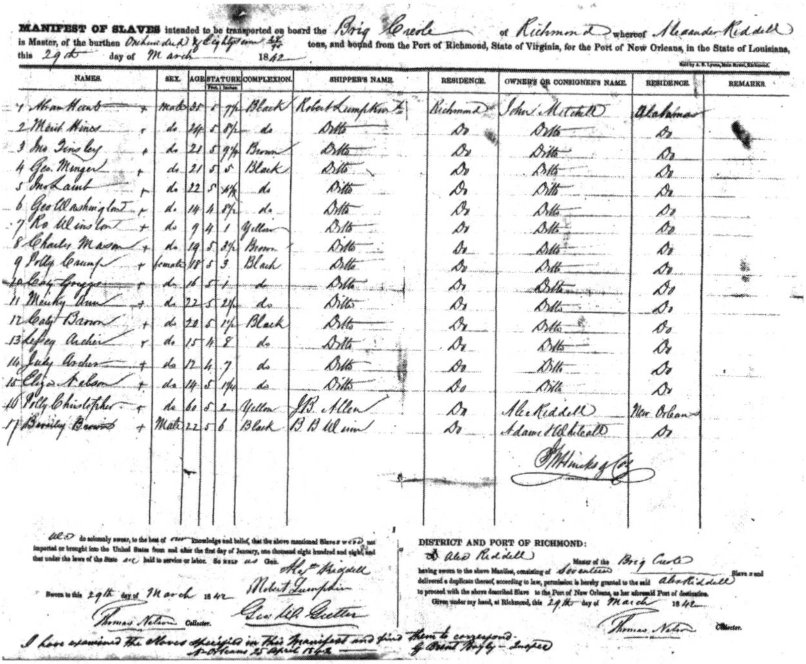

MANIFEST OF SLAVES intended to be transported on board the Brig Creole of Richmond whereof Alexander Riddell is Master, of the burthen One hundred & Eighty seven $\frac{47}{95}$ tons, and bound from the Port of Richmond, State of Virginia, for the Port of New Orleans, in the State of Louisiana, this 29th day of March 1842

NAMES.		SEX.	AGE	STATURE Feet	STATURE Inches	COMPLEXION.	SHIPPER'S NAME.	RESIDENCE.	OWNER'S OR CONSIGNEE'S NAME.	RESIDENCE.	REMARKS.
1 Abram Hunt	+	Male	35	5	7½	Black	Robert Lumpkin Jr.	Richmond	John Mitchell	Alabama	
2 Merit Hines	+	do	24	5	8½	do	Ditto	Do	Ditto	Do	
3 Jno Tinsley	+	do	21	5	9¼	Brown	Ditto	Do	Ditto	Do	
4 Geo. Minger	+	do	21	5	5	Black	Ditto	Do	Ditto	Do	
5 Jno Laimb	+	do	22	5	4½	do	Ditto	Do	Ditto	Do	
6 Geo Washington	+	do	14	4	8½	do	Ditto	Do	Ditto	Do	
7 Ro Winston	+	do	9	4	1	Yellow	Ditto	Do	Ditto	Do	
8 Charles Mason	+	do	19	5	3½	Brown	Ditto	Do	Ditto	Do	
9 Polly Camp	+	female	18	5	3	Black	Ditto	Do	Ditto	Do	
10 ~~Lucy Griggs~~	+	do	16	5	1	do	Ditto	Do	Ditto	Do	
11 Minky Ann	+	do	22	5	2½	do	Ditto	Do	Ditto	Do	
12 Caty Brown	+	do	20	5	1½	Black	Ditto	Do	Ditto	Do	
13 Lesey Archer	+	do	15	4	8	do	Ditto	Do	Ditto	Do	
14 Judy Archer	+	do	12	4	7	do	Ditto	Do	Ditto	Do	
15 Eliza Nelson	+	do	14	5	1¼	do	Ditto	Do	Ditto	Do	
16 Polly Christopher	+	do	60	5	2	Yellow	J.B. Allen	Do	Alex Riddell	New Orleans	
17 Berilley Brown	+	Male	22	5	6	Black	B. B. Wm	Do	Adam Whitcall	Do	

P.W. Hicks & Co.

We do solemnly swear, to the best of our knowledge and belief, that the above mentioned Slaves were not imported or brought into the United States from and after the first day of January, one thousand eight hundred and eight, and that under the laws of the State are held to service or labor. So help us God.

Alexr Riddell
Robert Lumpkin
Geo. W. [illegible]

Sworn to this 29th day of March 1842
Thomas Nelson Collector.

DISTRICT AND PORT OF RICHMOND:
Alex Riddell Master of the Brig Creole having sworn to the above Manifest, consisting of Seventeen Slaves and delivered a duplicate thereof, according to law, permission is hereby granted to the said Alex Riddell to proceed with the above described Slave to the Port of New Orleans, as her aforesaid Port of destination.
Given under my hand, at Richmond, this 29th day of March 1842

Thomas Nelson Collector.

I have examined the slaves specified in this Manifest and find them to correspond.
N. Orleans 25 April 1842 [illegible] – Inspec

FIGURE E.1 Ship manifest for the *Creole*, Richmond, March 29, 1842. Source: *Slave Manifests of Coastwise Vessels Filed At New Orleans, Louisiana, 1807–1860*, Microfilm M1895, Roll 9, RG 36, NARA.

Most important, the passage of British colonial emancipation during the mid-1830s increased the risk of American slavers being driven toward British free soil, where captives could gain their liberty and traders and owners could lose their investments and profits in the Coastal Passage through the Bahamas Channel and Northern Caribbean. Moreover, successful slave ship revolts like the *Amistad* in 1839 and the *Creole* in 1841 raised the prospect of future maritime revolts. In short, the combination of antislavery practices in the Caribbean in proximity to American slave trading, together with ruinous as well as potential slave ship revolts, negatively impacted the Coastal Passage.[10]

10 In Frederick Douglass's 1853 novella *The Heroic Slave*, old sea salt Jack Williams expresses his shame "to have the idea go abroad, that a ship load of slaves can't be safely taken from Richmond to New Orleans." His bravado was not necessarily fictional. See Frederick Douglass, *The Heroic Slave*, in Ira Dworkin, ed., *Frederick Douglass: Narrative of the Life of Frederick Douglass, an American Slave* (New York: Penguin, 2014), 184.

Along with successful liberation and a destabilized coastal trade, the *Creole* revolt proved to be one of the most successful slave rebellions in the history of American slavery. Some have characterized it as "perhaps the only successful slave revolt and the largest in American history."[11] But what to do with the counter claim by another historian that the slave rebellion in 1811 New Orleans was "America's Largest Slave Revolt?"[12] They cannot both be right. In actuality, both are wrong because the largest slave rebellion in American history was what one quiet scholar once dubbed the "Great American Slave Rebellion," one in which the system of southern slavery and its federal protection was systematically undermined by fugitive slave escapes, the withdrawal of labor on southern plantations and farms, laboring for federal forces, and fighting and dying for the Union cause.[13]

Moreover, African-American captives' attainment of freedom in a British colony has always made the *Creole* an awkward fit with the idea of "progress" in the American historical narrative. These rebels and captives were not trying to live up to the ideals of the US nation; rather they turned their back on the iniquities of the deprivation of liberty. Nor were they simply "refugees" – an inaccurate way to characterize self-emancipators to British Canada, Mexico, England, and the Caribbean – that unfortunately still carries resonance in much historical literature. For all of these people, Canaan represented free soil beyond national borders.

The *Creole* revolt was also significant because it was probably one of the last times that the prospect of armed conflict between Washington and London was mooted. The United States and Great Britain went to war twice between the 1770s and 1812–1814. Over the next thirty years, the occasional killing of each other's citizens was accompanied by passionate disputes and threats of war. They clashed over Oregon during the mid-1840s. There was war talk over the *Trent* affair during the American Civil War. But war for political ends by another means, as Carl von Clausewitz

---

[11] "Seagraver" from Dinwiddie County, Virginia, Message Board, Ancestry.com http://bo ards.ancestry.com/thread.aspx?mv=flat&m=1&p=surnames.mccargo

[12] The full title of Daniel Rasmussen's book is *American Uprising: The Untold Story of America's Largest Slave Revolt* (New York: Harper, 2011).

[13] Robert F. Engs, "The Great American Slave Rebellion," unpublished lecture, University of Georgia, February 13, 1987. This paper was requested for a collection edited by Gabor Boritt for Oxford University Press for which the author was given an advance. The editor rejected the final product deeming it to be too radical. Dr. Engs kept the money! For the full story, see Robert F. Engs, "Who Freed the Slaves and Does It Matter: An Adventure in the Politics of Race and History," ASALH presentation, Charlotte, NC, October 6, 2007, unpublished manuscript in author's possession.

famously instructed us, was no longer plausible by mid-century. Both nations were tied economically through white gold and economic development. Great Britain was a global empire, while the United States was the most powerful nation in the New World. This was the historical era, I would argue, that rendered military conflict between the two nations obsolete. Subsequent wars in the twentieth century brought these two nations closer together in fighting European fascism, totalitarianism, communism, Arab dictators, radical jihadists, and now Russian expansionism. On the other hand, the passing of the imperial baton from London to Washington during the 1950s and 1960s has wrought severe problems globally, including a set of disastrous policies toward the Arab-speaking world and Islam during the opening decades of the twenty-first century.

But perhaps the most long-lasting significance of the *Creole* revolt is not to be found in nation-state relations or as prologue to sectional crisis or even colonial freedom versus republican slavery, but in border crossings away from national tyrannies. In our world, refugees continue to cross national boundaries in order to escape death and persecution as tragically exemplified by the Syrian diaspora over the last decade. Modern slaves flee to new countries in which bondage is not tolerated because it is justly considered a crime against humanity. The human quest for liberty links these modern efforts with the past actions of the *Creole* rebels. This tradition will continue until all forms of human persecution and exploitation no longer make such dangerous journeys necessary.

Far removed from the sweeping verdict of the historian were the outcomes of the lives of the dramatis personae after the shipboard rebellion. The slave traders experienced mixed fortunes. New Orleans trader Thomas McCargo continued his activities. On January 11, 1842 he exchanged twenty-year-old Hannah for twenty-five-year-old John with Alonzo Demolino Alexander of East New Orleans. On January 20, he sold twenty-year-old Michael and nineteen-year-old Aaron to Garrigan Flackjack of Opelousas for $1,650. Six days later, he sold fifteen-year-old Sarah Tomkins to Adolphe Landry for $625. On February 4, he sold fifteen-year-old Henry to Josephine Wallace for $650. On St. Valentine's Day, he sold Adson Newton and Simon Fernstall, both nineteen years old, for $1,500 to Ramon Martinez of Assumption Parish, Louisiana.[14] McCargo was also the joint awardee of more than $23,000

---

[14] Acts No. 27, 60, 74, 93, 126, Edward Barnet, Public Notary, January to February 1842, New Orleans Notarial Archives (NONA).

from the ACC in 1855.[15] But according to a recent message posting on
a prominent genealogical site, he "lost everything" as a result of the *Creole*
rebellion and was forced to "put up everything" to meet his debts.
The same source reports his death in 1851.[16]

Richmond trader Robert Lumpkin ended up deriving considerable
profit from buying, jailing, and transporting captives. According to the
1850 census, he cohabited with another slave trader and owned real estate
worth $9,521.[17] His establishment – aptly called "the Devil's half acre" –
was located three blocks from the Capitol building. He is also reputed to
have married and had a child with an enslaved woman called Mary whom
he had formerly purchased. Hours after the fall of Richmond
in April 1865, a large crowd of United States Colored Troops and local
residents assembled on Broad Street outside Lumpkin's jail, singing
*"Slavery chain done broke at last! Broke at last! Broke at last! Slavery
chain done broke at last! Gonna praise God 'til I die."* A year later,
Lumpkin died leaving his property to Mary and their child. In 1867,
Mary Lumpkin sold the land to a Baptist minister; later it became part
of Virginia Union University. Today, it is crossed by Interstate 95 and
serves as a student car park.[18]

Trader George W. Apperson appears to have relocated to the state
capital sometime after the *Creole* rebellion. In 1850, the forty-seven-
year-old was listed as sharing a household with forty-four-year-old
Robert Lumpkin and twenty-three-year-old John Starke in the city of
Richmond. The latter's occupation was that of clerk, while Apperson
and Lumpkin were identified as slave traders. Over the next decade,
Apperson operated a private jail in the city's notorious Birch Alley.

---

[15] US Congress, Senate, Executive Document 103, 34th Congress, 1st Session *Message of
the President of the United States* (Washington 1856), 32, 33, 47, 52, 78, 244–245;
Arthur T. Downey, *The Creole Affair: The Slave Rebellion That Led the U.S. and Great
Britain to the Brink of War)* Lanham: Rowman and Littlefield, 2014), 146.

[16] Thomas McCargo, Halifax County, c.1840, http://boards.ancestry.com/thread.aspx?m
v=flat&m=1&p=surnames.mccargo. I failed to locate him in federal census records.

[17] Robert Lumpkin, Henrico County, 1850 US Census. Thanks to Kate McMahon for
assistance.

[18] "Lumpkin's Jail," Wikipedia, https://en.wikipedia.org/wiki/Lumpkin%27s_jail; Anonymous, "Preliminary History of the Lumpkin's Jail Property," www.richmondgov.com/Com
missionSlaveTrail/documents/historyLumpkinJail.pdf; Steven Deyle, *Carry Me Back:
The Domestic Slave Trade in American Life* (New York: Oxford University Press, 2005),
267; Elizabeth Kambourian, "Slave Traders in Richmond," *Richmond Times-Dispatch*,
Feb. 24, 2014 www.richmond.com/slave-traders-in-richmond/table_52a32a98-9d56-11e3-
806a-0017a43b2370.html; Matthew R. Laird, "Lumpkin's Jail," Encyclopedia Virginia, w
ww.encyclopediavirginia.org/Lumpkin_s_Jail#).

In 1860 he was listed as living with thirty-five-year-old Louisa (presumably his wife), seventeen-year-old Leonard and fourteen-year-old Tarquinia (children). According to Troy Valos at Norfolk Public Library, Apperson had once cohabited with an African-American woman and they had two daughters. Both daughters grew up and also had children. The slave trader's grandson became a medical doctor who practiced in Richmond.[19]

Bacon Tait ended up becoming very wealthy as a consequence of his slave-trading activities at his business located on 17th and Broad Streets in Richmond. According to the 1850 federal census, he owned real estate worth $130,000. At some point, he struck up a relationship with Courtney Fountain, a free black woman from Alexandria, who was thirty-five years old in 1842. During the 1850s, he split his time between Richmond and Salem, Massachusetts. Most remarkably, Tait presented Courtney as his housekeeper in Virginia but as his legal wife in Massachusetts. They were to have four children. The move north no doubt was inspired by the 1843 repeal on interracial marriage in Massachusetts as well as the benefits to a free black woman of living in a free society. By 1860, only Bacon Tait's name appeared in the Massachusetts census. On May 31, 1871 Courtney died of inflammatory rheumatism in Salem. Two weeks later, Bacon died of old age and "softening of the brain." The bulk of his property – more than $100,000 – went to his twins Constance and Bacon C., available once they turned twenty-one years of age. In 1874, Tait's jail was auctioned and turned into tobacco warehouses. His body lies in Hollywood Cemetery, the same resting place as that of former US president John Tyler.[20]

John Hagan, long-term cotton merchant and slave trader in New Orleans since the 1820s, had an interesting final inning. After his loss of property due to the *Creole* revolt, he continued to trade slaves. On January 6, 1842 he sold fifteen-year-old Elsey to Charles Darby for $700. On January 17, he sold twenty-year-old Ben Bryan and eighteen-year-old Sam Herron to the unforgettably named Livain Bourgeois of

---

[19] Henrico County, 1850 US census; Henrico County, 1860 US census. Thanks to Troy Vallos for emailing 1850 federal census materials, email, July 19, 2017. See also Elizabeth Kambourian, "Slave Traders in Richmond," *Richmond Times-Dispatch*, February 24, 2014 www.richmond.com/slave-traders-in-richmond/table_52a32a98-9d56-11e3-806a-0017a43b2370.html

[20] Hank Trent, *The Secret Life of Bacon Tait, a White Slave Trader Married to a Free Woman of Color* (Baton Rouge: Louisiana State University Press, 2017), 114–172. It was not until 1967 that prohibition against interracial marriage ended in the United States.

St. James Parish for $1,637.50. The following day, Hagan was back in front of local notary Edward Barnet to settle a dispute. On June 5 of the previous year, he had sold twenty-seven-year-old Jack Harrard to Norbert Cropper of Iberville for $1,400. The price was unusually high because Jack was sold as a brickmaker and plasterer. After several months, however, the buyer claimed that Jack lacked these skills, Hagan returned $275 to the buyer, and Jack stayed with Cropper.[21]

At some point, John Hagan purchased Lucy Ann Cheatam and the two began a personal relationship. On May 10, 1856 Hagan filed suit in the Fifth District Court of New Orleans for the freedom of twenty-six-year-old Lucy Ann Cheatam and her two children, Frederika (Dolly) and William Lowndes. The petitioner vouches that Lucy et al. were mortgage-free, of "good character," with no past criminal record. His petition was granted less than two weeks later on May 23.[22] The merchant's mind became focused on Lucy, her children, and their future freedom during that spring and summer. Seventeen days after his successful petition was granted, Hagan went before New Orleans Judge P. H. Morgan to arrange for the disposition of his "property, monies, stock, slaves" after his death. His first wish was that his slave "Lucy Ann Cheatham and her daughter Dolly, or any other children Lucy may have, be immediately emancipated, and all expenses paid out of my estate." He then turned to his family outside of the household. He bequeathed $40,000 and 102 shares in the Citizens Bank Stocks of New Orleans to his mother, $10,000 to his sister, $15,000 to his niece, $5,000 to his nephew, and $10,000 to his brother. John Hagan further bequeathed $10,000, together with residential property on Esplanade Street, to Lucy's children and $5,000 for their maintenance. The balance of his estate, which amounted to $80,000, he left to his brother Alexander. He appointed notary Edward Barnet, who had overseen numerous slave transactions over the years, and his brother Alexander to be his executors.[23] John Hagan died soon thereafter and the executers implemented the will.[24] In 1861, John R. Hobson built twin

---

[21] Acts No. 11, 49, 53, Edward Barnet, Public Notary, January to February 1842, NONA. See also Acts No. 83 and 99 for other notarized transactions by Hagan for the year.

[22] John Hagan, Petition No. 20885631, May 1856, RSPP, http://library.uncg.edu/slavery/petitions/details.aspx?pid=8822

[23] John Hagan to P. H. Morgan, filing 10362, June 9, 1856, Orleans Parish, Louisiana, Wills and Probate Records, 1756–1984, 367. The New Orleans merchant's disposition of $175,000 to recipients suggests an enormously profitable life as a cotton factor and slave trader.

[24] Ibid, p. 368. Hagan revoked his previous will made on August 15, 1855.

two-story Greek Revival plastered brick semi-detached town houses at 529 and 533 Esplanade Avenue, New Orleans, for free woman of color Lucy Cheatam who sometimes signed as Lucy Hagan.[25] Her life, together with the lives of Courtney Fountain, Louisa Apperson, Mary Lumpkin and all of their children, illustrates some of the complicated dimensions of gender, freedom, property, and families in an antebellum slave society.

We know little about what happened to other *Creole* traders. Lancaster, Denby and Company was listed separately in a prominent Richmond directory, suggesting a break-up at some point during the early 1840s.[26]

Edward Lockett's action to recover $20,000 from the Fireman's Insurance Company of New Orleans for twenty-six captives transported aboard the *Creole* failed at the lower and superior courts in New Orleans, as we have seen. But his quest for compensation continued. On June 22, 1855 Lockett together with Henry Johnson and James Berret filed a lawsuit in the Circuit Court of DC. They had previously contracted with John Pemberton – liquidator of the MICNO that had insured slaves on the *Creole* – to reclaim damages from the British government. On January 9, 1855 umpire Bates of the Anglo-American Commission awarded $12,460 to Pemberton as a first claim and $16,000 for a second claim. The three petitioners – Lockett, Johnson, and Berret – had paid all of the court expenses. Pemberton's final claim, however, proved fraudulent. The three petitioners believed he had already received the first payment and wanted the DC Circuit Court to prevent him from receiving the second payment. Their petition was granted, but reversed on appeal. The uncompensated Lockett disappears from the historical record.[27]

Government officials involved in the *Creole* revolt also experienced mixed fortunes. Sir Francis Cockburn went on to serve as Governor and

---

[25] Friends of the Cabildo, *New Orleans Architecture*, vol. 4, *The Creole Faubourgs* (Gretna, La.: Pelican, 2002), 133. This local history also contains a picture of the property on Esplanade. See also Loren Schweninger, "Property Owning Free African-American Women in the South, 1800 to 1870," in Darlene Clark Hine, Wilma King, and Linda Reed, eds., *"We Specialize in the Wholly Impossible": A Reader in Black Women's History* (New York: Carlson, 1995), 262–263.

[26] *Ellyson's Business Directory and Almanac for the Year 1845* (Richmond: H. K. Ellyson, 1845).

[27] Edward Lockett, Henry Johnson, James Berret, Petition to the Circuit Court of District of Columbia, June 22, 1855, Petition 20485503, RSPP, http://library.iouncg.edu/slavery/petitions/details.aspx?pid=4413; "Adjustment of Claims," Sen. Doc. No. 103, 1856, 52; Arthur T. Downey, *The Creole Affair: The Slave Rebellion That Led the U.S. and Great Britain to the Brink of War* (Lanham: Rowman and Littlefield, 2014), 146–148.

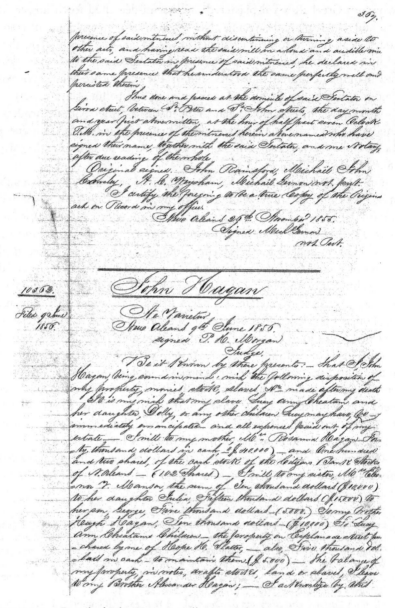

FIGURE E.2   Detail of John Hagan's will, New Orleans, June 9, 1856.
Source: Orleans Parish, Louisiana, Wills and Probate Records, 1756–1984.

Commander-in-Chief of the Bahamas until 1844. Between 1846 and

1860, he was promoted from Major General to General. He died at East Cliff, Dover, in 1868, at the ripe old age of eighty-eight. Cockburn Island in Ontario, Canada, and Cockburn Town on San Salvador Island, Bahamas, are living testament to his colonial endeavors.[28]

American consul John Bacon vacated his post at Nassau in November 1841. His departure was probably due to his inept actions in response to the *Creole* revolt. In 1844, Bacon became deputy treasurer of New York State. The Bahamas appear, however, to have held a magnetic lure that he found irresistible. He was reappointed US consul to Nassau in 1846 under Democratic president James K. Polk and served until 1850. On Monday April 7, 1851 the Nassau press announced the marriage of John R. Bacon, son of John F. Bacon, of Albany, New York, to Jane Mary, third daughter of the late John M. Lockhart at Ragged Island; the Rev. W. H. Strombom presided. Bacon senior assumed the consulship for a third time in 1853, serving for three years before his final resignation from public office in 1856. He died in the Bahamas four years later on February 25, 1860, at age seventy-one.[29]

Ten months after his diplomatic success with the 1842 treaty, Secretary Webster resigned as a consequence of financial difficulties and a disagreement with President Tyler over the annexation of Texas to the American republic. Webster returned to his former post, serving from July 1850 through October 1852 during the presidency of Millard Fillmore. In this second term, he opposed American filibustering expeditions to seize Cuba and expand the slaveholding empire. On September 3, 1850, for example, he contacted numerous marshals, district attorneys, and collectors, telling them to keep alert for possible invasions of Cuba from New York and New Orleans. His death while serving in public office

---

[28] Ed McKenna, "Cockburn, Sir Francis," Dictionary of Canadian Biography, v.9, http://www.biographi.ca/en/bio.php?id_nbr=4357; Francis Cockburn, https://en.wikipedia.org/wiki/Francis_Cockburn; "Sir Francis Cockburn (1780–1868) – Canada, Belize, Bahamas and Dover," The Dover Historian, Posted February 11, 2017, https://doverhistorian.com/2017/02/11/sir-francis-cockburn-canada-belize-bahamas-and-dover/; Downey, *Creole Affair*, 161.

[29] "John F. Bacon," Wikipedia, http://en.wikipedia.org/wiki/John_F._Bacon; Sharyn Thompson, *Marriage, Birth and Death Notices from Newspapers of the Bahamas* (Off Island: Tallahassee, FL., 2002), 106–107; US Consular Officials in the Bahamas, PoliticalGraveyard.com, http://politicalgraveyard.com/geo/ZZ/BI-consuls.html Downey, *Creole Affair*, 159–160. I searched for Bacon's burial record in Thompson's *Marriage, Birth, and Death Notices*, the Christ Church Cathedral Memorial Plaque and Tombstone book, and St. Mathews' Cemetery & Eastern Burial Ground book in the Bahamas National Archives, but had no luck.

seems appropriate, although he never landed the jewel of the presidency that he desired.[30]

Lord Aberdeen continued to serve as British Foreign Secretary under the Tory administration of Sir Robert Peel until 1846. These were the most productive years of his public service. The slings and arrows of outrageous fortune, however, filled the final fourteen years of Aberdeen's life. In 1852, he became the Tory choice for Prime Minister leading a coalition government of Peelites, Whigs, Radicals, and Irish representatives. Three years later, he resigned after a parliamentary vote of no confidence in his leadership during the murderous debacle of the Crimean War. He is buried in the family vault at Stanmore, England.[31]

The 1842 treaty represented the pinnacle of Lord Ashburton's public career. He returned to Britain to dabble in trustee affairs at the British Museum and the National Gallery, those architectural glories of the Victorian age. He also provided occasional commentary on government policy from his perch as peer before passing away on May 12, 1848, at the stately English home, Longleat, northwest Wiltshire, at the age of seventy-four. He truly lived the family motto *Virtus in Arduis*.[32]

After the death of the British peer, the Baring firm continued to function as a family enterprise with sons and grandsons serving as bankers and public servants in the United Kingdom and throughout the empire. After lending large sums of money to the Argentine government, which subsequently defaulted on its loans, there was a general financial crisis in England. The Bank of England and other leading banks bailed out the company, assuming its liabilities of GBP 21 million. Barings was reorganized as a joint stock company, repaid the debt eventually, and became investment advisor to the royal family. By the mid-1980s, Barings remained a family business: great-great-great-great grandson John served as chair, great-great-great grandson Nicholas was deputy chair, and five of

---

[30] "Biographies of the Secretaries of State: Daniel Webster (1782–1852)," US Department of State, Office of the Historian, https://history.state.gov/departmenthistory/people/web ster-daniel; Gerald Horne, *Race to Revolution: The United States and Cuba during Slavery and Jim Crow* (New York: Monthly Review Press, 2014), 86.

[31] "Aberdeen, George Hamilton Gordon, 4th Earl of," *1911 Encyclopedia Britannica*, vol. 1, Wikisource, http://en.wikisource.org/wiki/1911_Encyclop%C3%A6dia_Britanni ca/Aberdeen,_George_Hamilton_Gordon,_4th_Earl_of; "George Hamilton Gordon Earl of Aberdeen," Gov.UK, Past Prime Ministers, www.gov.uk/government/history/past-prime-ministers/george-hamilton-gordon-earl-of-aberdeen

[32] "Ashburton, Baron (UK 1835)," Cracroft's Peerage, www.cracroftspeerage.co.uk/onlin e/content/ashburton1835.htm; "Alexander Baring, 1st Baron Ashburton," Wikipedia, http://en.wikipedia.org/wiki/Alexander_Baring,_1st_Baron_Ashburton.

eight board members were kin. In 1985, the firm boasted a balance sheet of GBP 2.7 billion, but was becoming dwarfed by other British merchant banks. In 1995, it declared bankruptcy because an employee lost GBP 1.5 billion speculating on unauthorized futures and options trading. Barings was taken over by a Dutch financial company, ending the oldest merchant banking business in the City of London.[33]

After briefly serving as secretary of state due to Upshur's spectacular demise, South Carolinian John C. Calhoun returned to lead the US Senate. Much like Webster, he spent the rest of his years in public service and in pursuit of the greatest prize in American politics. During debates over what became known as the 1850 Compromise, before succumbing to tuberculosis, he advocated states' rights against federal interference. This was a continuation of his argument for the sovereign rights of states regarding slavery expressed in the aftermath of the *Creole* revolt.

Ohio Congressman Joshua Giddings' defense of slave rights to rebel and opposition toward the extension of slavery expressed in the aftermath of the *Creole* revolt continued as part of the radical Whig agenda. In early 1844, he opposed the annexation of Texas because it would expand slavery beyond state borders.[34] A few years later in 1852, Giddings supported a monument to commemorate fugitive slave William Smith who was killed while resisting arrest. Smith deserved a "suitable mausoleum" because he lost his life "while defending his inalienable right to freedom against a gang of piratical men stealers who dared pollute the soil of Pennsylvania." At an 1855 August First celebration in Buxton, Maine, the Ohio Congressman "instructed the audience with rich historical facts of freedom, from their source in England a century ago, down to the present auspicious hour."[35] After helping to establish the new Republican Party, Giddings eventually retired from Congress. President

[33] "Baring Family: British Merchants," *Encyclopedia Britannica*, www.britannica.com/topic/Baring-family#ref212751; Philip Ziegler, *The Sixth Great Power: A History of One of the Greatest of All Banking Families, The House of Barings, 1762–1929* (New York: Alfred Knopf, 1988), 362–363. But old ways continue. In order to conduct research in the firm's business records in London, one must first obtain a reference of good standing. This disqualifies most professors, of course.

[34] Michael F. Holt, *The Rise and Fall of the American Whig Party: Jacksonian Politics and the Onset of the Civil War* (New York: Oxford University Press, 1999), 169.

[35] R. J. M. Blackett, *Making Freedom: The Underground Railroad and the Politics of Slavery* (Chapel Hill: University of North Carolina Press, 2013), 45–46 "soil of Pennsylvania"; "First of August Celebration," *Liberator*, August 17, 1855 "auspicious hour"; "Giddings, Joshua Reed," US House of Representatives, History, Art & Archives, http://history.house.gov/People/Listing/G/GIDDINGS,-Joshua-Reed-(G000167)/.

Lincoln appointed him US General Consul to Canada in 1861 where he served until his death in 1864. In 1990, Giddings's former congressional district was eliminated through redistricting and renumbered as the tenth district. From 1996 through 2012, radical democrat Dennis J. Kucinich served as its representative linking him to his nineteenth-century predecessor.[36]

The fates were kind to the legal authorities concerned with the *Creole* revolt. Five years after ruling on the insurance dispute in the *Creole* revolt, Judge Bullard entered the Louisiana legislature. That same year, Charles M. Conrad resigned his seat, and Bullard entered the thirty-first US Congress as a Whig and served from December 5 through to March 3 1851. He died in New Orleans on April 17, 1851, at the age of sixty-three. He was originally interred at Girod Street Cemetery, a Protestant cemetery established in 1822. After years of neglect, the remains of white Americans were removed to Hope Mausoleum and those of black Americans went to Providence Memorial Park. The original cemetery now serves as a car park for employees and consumers at a local shopping mall.[37]

The lead counsel for the New Orleans insurance companies was to enjoy a peripatetic life post his 1845 courtroom success. Judah Benjamin went on to become a Louisiana senator from 1853 through 1861, after which he withdrew from federal service once his state seceded from the Union. He landed prestigious public office posts in the breakaway nation, serving as Secretary of War followed by Secretary of State. After the failure to establish a new nation, Benjamin moved to Great Britain where he studied law at Lincoln's Inn and was admitted into the ranks of barristers. After a decade of legal and public work, Benjamin retired and moved across the English Channel to Paris, where he died on May 6, 1884 at seventy-three years of age. He was buried in 1884 at *Cimetière du La Père Lachaise* in Paris under the name of "Philippe Benjamin" in the family plot of the Boursignac family, in-laws of his daughter. In 1938, the Paris chapter of Daughters of Confederacy provided an inscription that identified him in an almost anonymous grave.[38]

[36] "Ohio's 10th Congressional District," Wikipedia, https://en.wikipedia.org/wiki/Ohio%27s_10th_congressional_district

[37] "Bullard, Henry Adams, (1788–1851), Biographical Directory of the United States Congress, http://bioguide.congress.gov/scripts/biodisplay.pl?index=B001049

[38] "Benjamin, Judah Philip Benjamin (1811–1884), Biographical Directory of the United States Congress, http://bioguide.congress.gov/scripts/biodisplay.pl?index=b000365; Eli N. Evans, *Judah P. Benjamin: The Jewish Confederate* (New York: Free Press, 1988), 299.

FIGURE E.3 Judah Benjamin's tombstone, Cimetière du Père Lachaise, Paris.
Photograph by the author, June 2018.

In 1853–1854, Samuel Packwood acquired his *Belle Chasse* plantation
for nearly $168,000. According to an 1859 inventory of the sugar estate,
there were fifty-five enslaved males appraised at $54,450 ($1.6 million
today) or almost $1,000 each ($29,400). Packwood did not live long to
enjoy his plush new property but passed away in 1860. The property was
auctioned for $250,000 in 1860. It is likely that the estate's unfree workers

gained their de facto liberty with the coming of Union troops and the passage of the Emancipation Proclamation in 1863. The plantation home was demolished in 1960, and its bell stands outside the public library. The town is now largely a federal military establishment.[39]

What happened to the personnel who settled outstanding claims between the two nations? American representative Nathaniel Upham continued his railroad activities, arbitrated a boundary dispute between the United States and the Republic of New Granada (now Columbia, Panama, Ecuador, and Venezuela), and served one year in the New Hampshire House of Representatives. He died on December 11, 1869, at sixty-eight.[40] After judicial postings to Constantinople and Shanghai, British representative Edmund Hornby retired to Devon in southwest England. He continued his interests in international law. He died in his sleep at age seventy-one in 1896 after a long mountain climb in northern Italy.[41]

After successful completion of his balancing act as umpire at the Anglo-American Commission during the mid-1850s, Joshua Bates continued his lucrative financial career with the Barings firm. He donated around $100,000 to the Boston Public Library. During the Civil War, he supported the Union through various fiscal policies and by blocking loans to the Confederacy. He bought residencies in the exclusive London neighborhood of Portland Place and in leafy suburban Sheen in Surrey, England. He claimed that he started life with $5 and ended worth $4 million. He died on September 24, 1864. His daughter Elizabeth married the Belgian ambassador to Great Britain. "Legacies of British Slave Ownership," the pioneering research project on West Indian slaveholders and compensation claims at University College London, has recently revealed that Bates was an unsuccessful co-claimant for financial compensation for the emancipation of slaves on the Spring Garden estate in British Guiana after British colonial abolition.[42]

---

[39] Frederick Bancroft, *Slave-Trading in the Old South* (Baltimore: J. H. Furst, 1931), 325–326, 341; "Belle Chasse, Louisiana," Wikipedia, https://en.wikipedia.org/wiki/Bell e_Chasse,_Louisiana

[40] "Nathaniel Gookin Upham," Wikipedia, http://en.wikipedia.org/wiki/Nathaniel_Gooki n_Upham

[41] "Edmund Grimani Hornby," Wikipedia, http://en.wikipedia.org/wiki/Edmund_Griman i_Hornby

[42] Ralph W. Hidy, *The House of Baring in American Trade and Finance: English Merchant Bankers at Work, 1763–1861* (New York, Russell & Russell, 1970), 84; "Joshua Bates (1788– 1864) *Encyclopedia Britannica* 1911, www.theodora.com/encyclopedia/b/josh

In contrast to these details about the great personas involved in the saga of the *Creole* revolt, we know less about what happened to some of the ordinary male and female participants. The 1850 federal census does not list Captain Robert Ensor. It does list thirty-year-old Eliza Ensor and three children ranging from eleven months to twelve years living in Richmond. It is possible that Eliza and the twelve-year-old were the wife and daughter who were aboard the *Creole* nine years earlier. In 2001, a local researcher sent out a request for information on Captain Ensor of Richmond but elicited no response.[43] We can assume that the *Creole*'s officers and crew served out their days at sea. It is clearly difficult to track down what happened to individual local administrators in Nassau, members of the Second West India Regiment, and Bahaman boatmen and locals. One important task of *Rebellious Passage*, though, has been to rescue them *collectively* from the obscurity of the past.

We have some clues as to what happened to some of the captives on coastal slavers. On June 30, 1854 Richard Henry Dana recorded an afternoon visit from a certain Mr. Robinson. The visitor explained that he was formerly the foreman for Robert Lumpkin of Richmond who had overseen forty-eight slaves on a journey to New Orleans before the vessel [*Hermosa*] was driven into a British port and the slaves liberated. He went to Boston after which he went to New Orleans because he had given his word to his owner. After the owner's no-show, he returned to Boston. In 1842, Lumpkin visited Boston inquiring after him. Robinson was concerned that he might have been carried off. Dana explained that he was free, although this might be tested by a claim under the recently passed Fugitive Slave Act. Robinson's trail ends here.[44]

Mary Warfield was one of five children kidnapped from the Warfield plantation and put aboard the *Enterprise* in 1835. After the slaver was grounded in Bermuda, local authorities helped liberate Mary and her fellow captives. Her descendants included Esther DeShield Pitt, a retired Ohio schoolteacher, and Reverend Cyril Butterfield, head of the African Methodist Episcopal church in

ua_bates.html; "Joshua Bates," Legacies of British Slave Ownership, University College London, www.ucl.ac.uk/lbs/person/view/1326456588.

[43] Downey, *Creole Affair*, 208n14; Seagrave, Ronald R. "Captain Robert Ensor, 1840, Richmond, Virginia," Genealogy.com, www.genealogy.com/forum/surnames/topics/ensor/237/.

[44] Charles Francis Adams, *Richard Henry Dana: A Biography*, vol. 1 (Boston: Houghton, Mifflin, and Company, 1891), 287–288. My thanks to Richard Blackett for this reference.

Bermuda. Mahaley Warfield's granddaughter, Elizabeth Colyer "Bessie" McKenzie, was born in 1875 and married Albert C. Jackson, a grocer in Hamilton. They moved to New York City around 1914. Their only granddaughter Madeline Johnson migrated to Bermuda. Other Warfield descendants included American and Bermudian singers and musicians.[45]

The fate of twenty-four-year-old Rachel Glover, eighteen-year-old Mary Scroggins, the other two women and the child who opted to stay aboard the *Creole* remains undetermined. They were probably sold on the New Orleans slave market to join many thousands gone.

As we have seen, some of the *Creole*'s former captives spread across the Bahamas, while others ended up in Jamaica. They probably had families whose descendants may or may not know of their remarkable journey to freedom. Rebel leaders Benjamin Johnson and Dr. Ruffin probably shared similar personal stories. It is unclear what exactly happened to Madison Washington. He fades away after the revolt in most accounts with one exception. Self-emancipator Thomas Thomas worked as a porter in the Springfield, Massachusetts, warehouse of radical abolitionist John Brown. At one point, he was sent by his employer "to look up Madison Washington, the leader of the courageous slaves of the vessel 'Creole,' who was wanted as a leader among the colored recruits that were to join the band of liberators; but Washington, when found, proved to be an unfit person for such a task."[46] This intriguing reference begs several questions. Where was Washington living? When did he return to the United States, and why? And what was this forty-year-old former rebel doing that now rendered him unsuitable to join Brown's prospective rebellion? Or was this simply the construction of a fictive link among antislavery freedom fighters in a post-abolitionist publication?

Fellow rebel leader Elijah Morris and his family left more of a trace in the historical records. As noted in Chapter 7, Morris bought several plots of land in the village of Gambier outside Nassau. There is no record of his death in the local Bahamian newspapers. This is hardly surprising given his social obscurity. His son Alexander Morris inherited his father's real estate. The son also purchased land in the village

---

[45] Nellie Eileen Musson, *Mind the Onion Seed: Black "Roots" Bermuda* (Hamilton, Bermuda: Musson's, 1979), 66.

[46] Franklin Benjamin Sanborn, *The Life and Letters of John Brown* (1885; New York: Negro University Press, 1969), 133.

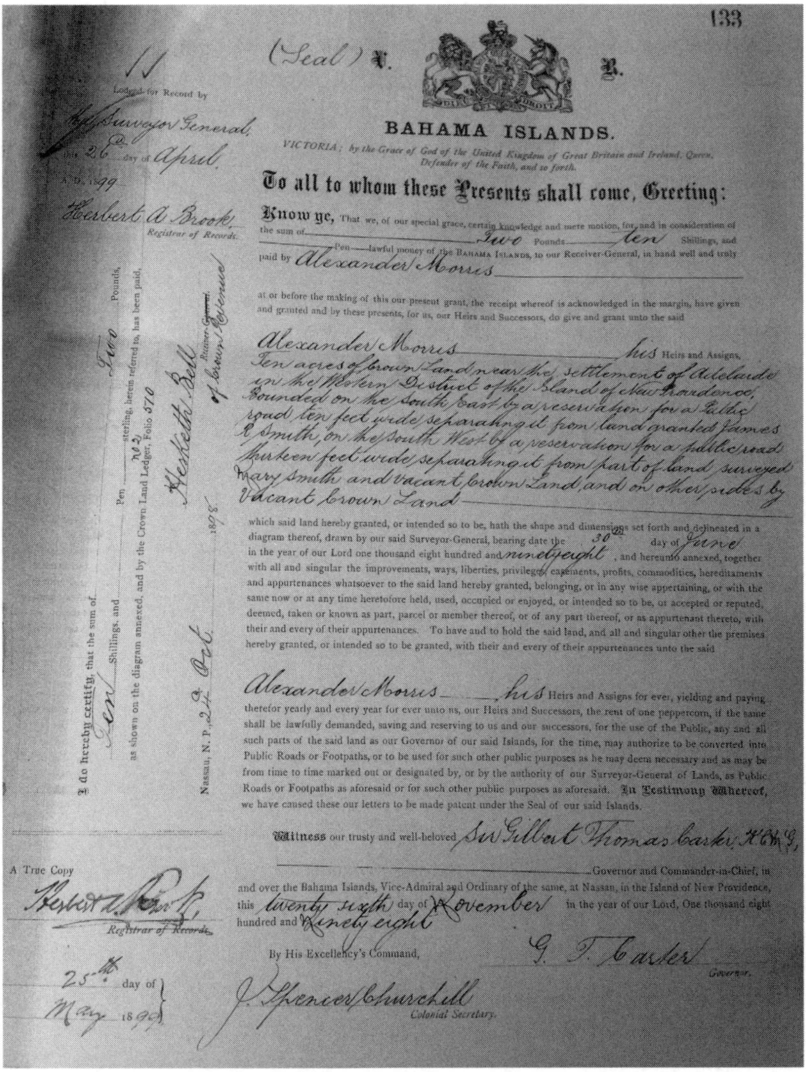
133

(Seal) V. R.

BAHAMA ISLANDS.

VICTORIA; by the Grace of God of the United Kingdom of Great Britain and Ireland, Queen, Defender of the Faith, and so forth.

To all to whom these Presents shall come, Greeting:

Know ye, That we, of our special grace, certain knowledge and mere motion, for, and in consideration of the sum of Two Pounds ten Shillings, and Pen lawful money of the Bahama Islands, to our Receiver-General, in hand well and truly paid by Alexander Morris

at or before the making of this our present grant, the receipt whereof is acknowledged in the margin, have given and granted and by these presents, for us, our Heirs and Successors, do give and grant unto the said

Alexander Morris his Heirs and Assigns, Ten acres of Crown Land near the settlement of Adelaide in the Western District of the Island of New Providence, Bounded on the South East by a reservation for a Public road ten feet wide separating it from land granted James R Smith, on the South West by a reservation for a public road thirteen feet wide separating it from part of land surveyed Mary Smith and Vacant Crown Land, and on other sides by Vacant Crown Land

which said land hereby granted, or intended so to be, hath the shape and dimensions set forth and delineated in a diagram thereof, drawn by our said Surveyor-General, bearing date the 30th day of June in the year of our Lord one thousand eight hundred and ninety eight, and hereunto annexed, together with all and singular the improvements, ways, liberties, privileges, easements, profits, commodities, hereditaments and appurtenances whatsoever to the said land hereby granted, belonging, or in any wise appertaining, or with the same now or at any time heretofore held, used, occupied or enjoyed, or intended so to be, or accepted or reputed, deemed, taken or known as part, parcel or member thereof, or of any part thereof, or as appurtenant thereto, with their and every of their appurtenances. To have and to hold the said land, and all and singular other the premises hereby granted, or intended so to be granted, with their and every of their appurtenances unto the said

Alexander Morris his Heirs and Assigns for ever, yielding and paying therefor yearly and every year for ever unto us, our Heirs and Successors, the rent of one peppercorn, if the same shall be lawfully demanded, saving and reserving to us and our successors, for the use of the Public, any and all such parts of the said land as our Governor of our said Islands, for the time, may authorize to be converted into Public Roads or Footpaths, or to be used for such other public purposes as he may deem necessary and as may be from time to time marked out or designated by, or by the authority of our Surveyor-General of Lands, as Public Roads or Footpaths as aforesaid or for such other public purposes as aforesaid. **In Testimony Whereof,** we have caused these our letters to be made patent under the Seal of our said Islands.

Witness our trusty and well-beloved Sir Gilbert Thomas Carter, K.C.M.G., Governor and Commander-in-Chief, in and over the Bahama Islands, Vice-Admiral and Ordinary of the same, at Nassau, in the Island of New Providence, this twenty sixth day of November in the year of our Lord, One thousand eight hundred and Ninety eight

By His Excellency's Command,

G. T. Carter
Governor.

J. Spencer Churchill
Colonial Secretary.

11
Lodged for Record by
Surveyor General,
this 26 day of April
A.D. 1899
Herbert A. Brook,
Registrar of Records.

I do hereby certify, that the sum of Two Pounds, Ten Shillings, and Pen sterling, herein referred to, has been paid, as shown on the diagram annexed, and by the Crown Land Ledger, Folio 370
Hesketh Bell
Receiver General
of Crown Revenue
Nassau, N. P., 24 Oct 1898

A True Copy
Herbert A. Brook,
Registrar of Records.
25th day of May 1899

FIGURE E.4 Alexander Morris's land grant, Adelaide Village, New Providence Island, Bahamas, November 26, 1898.
Source: Index to Crown Grants, 1862–1944, Registrar General's Department, Nassau, Bahamas.

of Adelaide in 1898. He sold his property in 1923 and died in 1928. Harold Morris, born May 16, 1925, was a carpenter who remembered dances such as the Ring Play, Jumping Dance and Quadrille, which were performed accompanied by the drum during nocturnal festivals at the village of Gambier. Members of the Morris family still reside in Gambier.[47] Some of the Morris family eventually relocated to the United States. Today, their descendants live somewhere in America, either aware or unaware of their connection to a remarkable slave ship revolt.

---

[47] Saunders with Fernandez, September 11, 1970, Oral History Transcripts Collection, BNA; Gail Saunders, *Gambier Village: A Brief History* (UNESCO, Nassau, Bahamas, 2007), 18–19. I could find no references to newspaper reports of the deaths of Elijah Morris and Alexander Morris in Thompson's *Marriage, Birth, and Death Notices*.

APPENDIX I
Captives aboard the *Enterprise*, March 1835

1	Anderson, Lloyd	12 years old
2	Brent, Sarah	14
3	Briscoe, George	13
4	Brooks, Louisa	8
5	Brown, Maria	10
6	Brown, Nancy	16
7	Buckingham, Dinah	25
8	Dinah's infant	?
9	Buckingham, Emiline	8
10	Buckingham, Jane	6
11	Burch, Sarah	12
12	Butler, Eliza	20
13	Butler, Harriet Ann (daughter)	2
14	Carter, Abram	14
15	Chase, William	16
16	Counter, Hamilton	14
17	Dent, Charlotte	20
18	Dobbins, Mary	10
19	Dorsey, Charles	19
20	Fendall, Ann Maria	18
21	Fisher, Harriet	9
22	Gray, Dafney	20
23	Gray, Grace (daughter)	6 months old
24	Groom, Easter	14
25	Groom, Louisa	2
26	Groom, Martha-Lean	4

(continued)

(continued)

27	Groom, Patsey	31
28	Groom, Thomas	9
29	Hale, Henry	18
30	Hammet, George	25
31	Holiday, Stephen	9
32	Jackson, Daniel	30
33	James, Samuel	12
34	Johnson, Henson	10
35	Johnson, Lucy	23
36	King, Calbert	9
37	Lancaster, Maria	19
38	Lyles, Easter	25
39	Lyles, Henrietta	3
40	Lyles, John	8
41	Mahoney, Charles	24
42	Mason	19
43	Parker	20
44	Pinney, Eliza	24
45	Pinney, John	7
46	Pinney, Mary	8
47	Pinney, Phil	4
48	Pinney, Rachael	2
49	Pinney, Richard	3 weeks old
50	Potson, Charles	7 years
51	Potson, Ned	6
52	Powell, Mahaley Ann	13
53	Reed, Shade	7
54	Reeder, Julia	24
55	Ridgley, Ann	5 months old
56	Ridgley, Betsy	3 years old
57	Ridgley, Helen	7
58	Ridgley, Mahaley	5
59	Ridgley, Matilda	25
60	Ridgley, Martha	10
61	Ridout, Phil	25
62	Ruffin, John	14
63	Sallsbury	6

(continued)

(continued)

64	Smith, Betty	15
65	Spencer	22
66	Stewart, Abram	21
67	Thrift, Peter	10
68	Thomas, Ben	12
69	Warfield, Charles R.	8
70	Warfield, Elizabeth	12
71	Warfield, Mahaley	12
72	Warfield, Mary	9
73	Warfield, Mary Ann	15
74	Washington, George	10
75	Wilson, Susan	5
76	Wood, Thomas	23
77	Woodley, John	7
78	Worthy, Oscar	12

Source: Nellie Eileen Musson, *Mind the Onion Seed: Black "Roots" Bermuda* (Hamilton, Bermuda: Musson's, 1979), 67.

Manifest of the *Hermosa*, October 10, 1840

Manifest of slaves intended to be transported on board the Schooner *Hermosa*, John L. Chattin, Master, of the burthern of one hundred and thirty-three 66/95 tons, and bound from the Port of Richmond, State of Virginia – for the Port of New Orleans, Louisiana, this 10th day of October 1840.

Names	Sex	Age	Shippers	Residence	Consignee
Sarah Willy	Female	16	Lancaster, Denby & Co.	Richmond	A. Ladeux
Lucy	Female	13			
Mariah	Female	13			
Eliza	Female	12			
Horace	Male	11			
John	Male	12			
Tazewell	Male	13			
Issac	Male	15			
David	Male	13			
Chip Smith	Male	19	H. N. Templeman	Richmond	
Fountain Alers?	Male	24			
James Douglas	Male	25			
Jason Morris	Male	26			
Dan Holmes	Male	26			
Madison Edwards	Male	22			
Sam Johnson	Male	19			
Ben Jackson	Male	23			
Epey? West	Male	21			

(continued)

Names	Sex	Age	Shippers	Residence	Consignee
Edmond Page	Male	25			
Frank Dickenson	Male	17			
Joshua Brown	Male	17			
Reuben Francis	Male	16			
William Lewis	Male	15			
Henry Lacy	Male	17			
Tom Jones	Male	30			
William Robertson	Male	23			
Tom Young	Male	25			
William Nelson	Male	25			
Betsy Green	Female	30			
Jane Williams	Female	22			
Ann Morris	Female	27			
Isabella Allen	Female	22			
Harriet Young	Female	16			
Lisa Goode	Female	15			
Mary Henderson	Female	17			
Rachel Bower	Female	16			
Lucy Rawlins	Female	27			
Priscilla Ellen?	Female	20			
Malinda Gibbs	Female	25			
Louisa Gibbs	Female	10			
Dicey Lumpkin	Female	10			
France Toublin	Female	10			
Edward Parker	Male	35			
Malinda ?	Female	22			
William Smith	Male	22			
? Smith	Female	27			
Lewis Johnson	Male	45	L. C. Read	Richmond	J. H. Daly

We do solemnly swear – to the best of our knowledge and belief – the above mentioned slaves were not imported or brought into the United States from and after the first day of January, one thousand eight hundred and eight, and that under the laws of the state are held to service or labour, so help us God.

Sworn to   H. N. Templeman
This 10th day of October   Laudon? L. Read
1840 – before me   T. Tenby
Geo. B. Read   J. L. Chattin
Dg. Coll.

John L. Chattin, Master of said Schooner *Hermosa,* having sworn to the above document [sic] manifest, consisting of forty-seven slaves and delivered a duplicate thereof according to law, and permission is hereby granted to the Schooner *Hermosa* to proceed with the above described slaves to the Port of New Orleans, as her aforesaid port of destination.

John L. Chattin.
Given under my hand at Richmond
this 10th day of October 1840.
George B. Read

Source: Manifest of the *Hermosa,* October 10, 1840, Bahamas 1840 vol. 1, January to December, Governor Sir Francis Cockburn, CO 23/107, TNA.

APPENDIX 3
Creole's Captives and Shippers, October 20 to 28, 1841

No.	Name	Sex	Age	Height	Color	Trade	Value	Shipper
1	Anderson, Caroline	F	16	5-4	Black			Thos. McCargo
2	Bankhead, Andrew	M	25	5-7	Black			Thos. McCargo
3	Beldin, Lucy	F	24	5-1	Black	Wash/iron	700	Geo. W. Apperson
4	Bell, Adelaide	F	8	3-9	Dark			Shields & Hall
5	Bell, Hester	F	25	5-3	Dark			Shields & Hall
6	Beverly, Horace*	M	19	5-9	Black		800	Rbt. Lumpkin
7	Bird, A.	M	35	5-8	Black		800	Rbt. Lumpkin
8	Blair, Ben	M	15	4-11	Brown			Thos. McCargo
9	Brown, Harry	M	21	5-7	Black			Thos. McCargo
10	Brown, Nelly	F	18	5-1	Black		666.33	Rbt. Lumpkin
11	Brown, Walter*	M						
12	Bruce, James	M	18	5-4	Black			Thos. McCargo
13	Bryant, William	M	23	5-4	Black			Thos. McCargo
14	Burton, George*	M	19	5-5	Brown		800	Geo. W. Apperson
15	Butler, Benjamin	M	16	5-2	Black		700	Geo. W. Apperson
16	Butler, Richard*	M	23	6-1	Brown			Thos. McCargo
17	Butt, George	M	19	5-4	Black	Blacksmith	900	Geo. W. Apperson
18	Callen, Elizabeth	F	14	5-1	Black			Thos. McCargo
19	Carling, Harriet	F	16	4-10	Brown	Domestic	700	Geo. W. Apperson
20	Carney, Adam*	M	25	5-7	Black		800	Geo. W. Apperson
21	Carp?, William	M	16	5-2	Black		700	Geo. W. Apperson

(continued)

No.	Name	Sex	Age	Height	Color		Value	Owner
22	Carter, C.	M	16	5–3	Black		800	Rbt. Lumpkin
23	Carter, Lewis	M	18	5–6	Yellow			Thos. McCargo
24	Carter, Lucy	F	17	5–4	Brown		666.33	Rbt. Lumpkin
25	Carter, R.	M	17	5–4	Brown		800	Rbt. Lumpkin
26	Carter, William	M	20	5–6	Black		800	John Hagan
27	Clarke, L.	F	10	4–6	Black		666.33	Rbt. Lumpkin
28	Clarke, William	M	17	5–4	Yellow		800	Rbt. Lumpkin
29	Collins, Mary	F	13	4–8	Yellow		700	Geo. W. Apperson
30	Corbin, M.	F	17	5–6	Black		666.33	Rbt. Lumpkin
31	Crew, Agnes	F	15	5–5	Black		666.33	Rbt. Lumpkin
32	Davis, Fanney	F	16	5–2	Black		700	Geo. W. Apperson
33	Dawley, Gilbert	M	18	5–5	Black		800	Geo. W. Apperson
34	Denby, William	M	18	5–5	Black			Thos. McCargo
35	Dorsey, P.	M	23	5–5	Brown		800	Rbt. Lumpkin
36	Ellis, L.	F	16	5–3	Black		666.33	Rbt. Lumpkin
37	Evan, Mary Ann	F	17	5–1	Black			Thos. McCargo
38	Evans, Rebecca	F	30	5–4	Black			Thos. McCargo
39	Ferguson, Frankey	F	40	5–1	Black			Thos. McCargo
40	Fields, Ann	F	17	5–2	Black			Thos. McCargo
41	Foster, Reuben	M	18	5–5	Black		800	John Hagan
42	Francis, Julia Ann	F	16	5–2	Brown		666.33	Rbt. Lumpkin
43	French, Lucy	F	21	5	Black	Wash/iron	700	Geo. W. Apperson

(continued)

No.	Name	Sex	Age	Height	Color	Trade	Value	Shipper
44	Gaines, H.	M	25	5–8	Brown		800	Rbt. Lumpkin
45	Gaines, Milla	F	15	4–10	Black			Thos. McCargo
46	Garret, H.	M	30	5–4	Black		800	Rbt. Lumpkin
47	Garrison, Pompey *	M	19	5–2	Black			Thos. McCargo
48	Glover, Isah	M	9	4–1	Black			Thos. McCargo
49	Glover, Rachel	F	24	5–1	Black			Thos. McCargo
50	Glover, Wiley	M	22	5–5	Black			Thos. McCargo
51	Gibson, B.	M	17	5–7	Black		800	Rbt. Lumpkin
52	Gordon, L.	F	17	5–5	Brown		666.33	Rbt. Lumpkin
53	Grandy, George *	M	26	5–8	Brown			Shields & Hall
54	Grigsby, C.	M					800	Rbt. Lumpkin
55	Grigsby, H.	F	8	4–6	Black		666.33	Rbt. Lumpkin
56	Grigsby, Lucy	F	26	5–2	Black		666.33	Rbt. Lumpkin
57	Hardister, E.	F	28	5–2	Black		666.33	Rbt. Lumpkin
58	Harrell, Cloe	F	18	5–2	Black			Shields & Hall
59	Haywood, Jacob	M	17	5–4	Black			Thos. McCargo
60	Hemming, Albert	M	9	4–4	Brown		500	John Hagan
61	Henley, Rachel	F	37	5	Dark			Shields & Hall
62	Hilliard, Mary	F	20	5	Yellow			Thos. McCargo
63	Jackson, Andrew	M	24	5–7	Brown			Thos. McCargo
64	Jenkins, Williams *	M	21	5–7	Black			Thos. McCargo

(continued)

No.	Name	Sex	Age	Height	Color	Value	Owner
65	Jewett, Milla	F	26	5-1	Black		Thos. McCargo
66	Johnson, Benjamin *	M	23	5-8	Black		Geo. W. Apperson
67	Joiner, Milinda	F	21	5-3	Brown		Shields & Hall
68	Jones, Charlotte	F	10	4-4	Yellow		Thos. McCargo
69	Jones, J.	M	22	5-6	Black	800	Rbt. Lumpkin
70	Jones, Philip *	M	17	5-6	Black	800	Rbt. Lumpkin
71	Jones, Rachel	F	17	5-4	Black	700	John Hagan
72	King, Dick	M	25	5-9	Black	800	Rbt. Lumpkin
73	King, Israel	M	18	5-6	Black	800	John Hagan
74	King, Roddy	F	18	5-3	Black	700	John Hagan
75	Larson, Mary Anne + child	F	18	5-1	Light Black	700	Geo. W. Apperson
76	Lattimore, Margaret + child	F	18	5	Yellow	700	Geo. W. Apperson
77	Leatherbury, Martha	F	13	4-10	Dark		Shields & Hall
78	Lester, A.	F	15	5-2	Brown	666.33	Rbt. Lumpkin
79	Lewis, Harriet	F	18			700	John Hagan
80	Liddy	F				700	John Hagan
81	Lindsay, John	M	21	5-8	Black		Thos. McCargo
82	Long, Myer	M	17	5-2	Black		Thos. McCargo
83	Lonry, Lewis	M	21	5-8	Black		Thos. McCargo
84	Loyde, Mary	F	10	4-7	Black	666.33	Rbt. Lumpkin
85	Lucy, Robert	M	19	5-8	Black	800	Rbt. Lumpkin
86	Lumpkins, Robert *	M				800	Rbt. Lumpkin

(continued)

No.	Name	Sex	Age	Height	Color	Trade	Value	Shipper
87	Moore, Bill	M	20	5-11	Black		800	Rbt. Lumpkin
88	Moore, C.	F	19	5-2	Black		666.33	Rbt. Lumpkin
89	Morris, Elijah *	M	23	5-5	Black			Thos. McCargo
90	Muerdaugh, Elizabeth	F	18	5-1	Yellow	Seamstress	900	Geo. W. Apperson
91	Oliver, Charles	M	18	5-6	Black			Thos. McCargo
92	Overton, H.	M	33	5-5	Black		800	Rbt. Lumpkin
93	Page, P.	F	17	5-4	Black		666.33	Rbt. Lumpkin
94	Palmer, Elisa	F	20	5-6	Black			Thos. McCargo
95	Parker, David	M	18	5-4	Black			Thos. McCargo
96	Pendleton, Marshall	M	22	5-6	Brown			Thos. McCargo
97	Phillips, Jourdan	M	21	5-6	Black		800	John Hagan
98	Portlock, George *	M	21	5-6	Black			Thos. McCargo
99	Pullen, Robert	M	22	5-5	Black		800	Rbt. Lumpkin
100	Ray, Julia	F	13	4-11	Dark			Shields & Hall
101	Reynard, Lewis	M	19	5-3	Brown			Shields & Hall
102	Right, Ruben	M	11	4-3	Black		500	Geo. W. Apperson
103	Robinson, G.	M	25	5-9	Black		800	Rbt. Lumpkin
104	Robinson, Monroe	M	24	5-7	Black			Thos. McCargo
105	Robinson, Pinky	F	16	5	Yellow			Thos. McCargo
106	Ross, B.	M	17	5-5	Black		800	Rbt. Lumpkin
107	Ruffin, D. *	M	25	5-6	Brown		800	Rbt. Lumpkin

(continued)

#	Name	Sex	Age	Height	Color	Value	Owner
108	Sallo, Argyle	M	16	5–2	Black	700	Geo. W. Apperson
109	Scott, Violet	F	26	5–3	Brown		Shields & Hall
110	Scott, William	M	10	4–7	Yellow		Thos. McCargo
111	Scroggins, Mary E.	F	18	5–6	Black		Thos. McCargo
112	Shields, Susan	F	28	5–1	Brown		Lancaster, Denby
113	Shields, Sylla	F	11	4–3	Dark		Shields & Hall
114	Smallwood, Peter*	M	23	5–10	Brown	800	Rbt. Lumpkin
115	Smith, Alley	F	13	4–10	Black		Thos. McCargo
116	Smith, Warner*	M	24	5–7	Black		Thos. McCargo
117	Sonry, Lemis	M	21	5–8	Black		Thos. McCargo
118	Tallafino, Edmond	M	21	5–6	Black		Thos. McCargo
119	Thompson, Martha	F	22	5–4	Black		Thos. McCargo
120	Twine, James	M	23	5–7	Brown	800	Rbt. Lumpkin
121	Tyler, Addison*	M	23	5–5	Black	800	Rbt. Lumpkin
122	Walker, Nelson	M	18	5–4	Black	800	Rbt. Lumpkin
123	Washington, Madison*	M	22	5–9	Black		Thos. McCargo
124	Washington, Sarah	F	15	5–1	Brown	666.33	Rbt. Lumpkin
125	White, Henry	M	23	5–11	Brown		Thos. McCargo
126	White, Monroe	M	10	4–8	Black		Thos. McCargo
127	White, P.	M	18	5–6	Black	800	Rbt. Lumpkin
128	Wiley, Winney	F	16	5–3	Black	700	Geo. W. Apperson
129	Wilks, William	M	26	5–8	Black		Thos. McCargo

(continued)

No.	Name	Sex	Age	Height	Color	Trade	Value	Shipper
130	Williams, Margaret	F	9	4–3	Yellow			Thos. McCargo
131	Wilson, Ann	F	15	5–3	Black			Thos. McCargo
132	Wilson, Hester	F	13	4–8	Black		500	Geo. W. Apperson
133	Wilson, Leonora	F	9	4–3	Black		400	Geo. W. Apperson
134	Wilson, Melvina	F	18	5–2	Yellow	Seamstress	900	Geo. W. Apperson
135	Wood, H.	M	22	5–7	Black		800	Rbt. Lumpkin
136	Woodis, America *	M	23	5–10	Black		800	Geo. W. Apperson
137	Yancy, Mahala	F	14	5	Brown			Thos. McCargo
138	Child							
139	Child							

* Rebels: Robert Lumpkins and Walter Brown, two of the rebels, are not listed in any of the documents.

Sources: *Creole* ship manifest, October 28, 1841, (Consolidated Cases, Docket Nos. 4413, 4414, 4419), NOPL.

Robert Ensor, Bill of Lading for forty-one Negroes shipped by Robert Lumpkin to Edward Lockett on the *Creole*, Richmond, October 20, 1841, ARC. Memorandum of valuation of forty-one slaves shipped on the *Creole*, claim of Edward Lockett, n. d., ARC. This memo also lists the captives by value and gender.

Robert Ensor, Bill of Lading for nine Negroes shipped by John Hagan on the *Creole*, Richmond, October 20, 1841, ARC. Memorandum of twenty-one Negroes shipped by G. W. Apperson on the *Creole*, Norfolk, October 28, 1841, ARC. This memo also lists the value of the captives.

Robert Ensor, Bill of Lading for eight Negroes shipped by C. H. Shields & W. W. Hall on the *Creole*, Norfolk, October 28, 1841 (ARC); October, 28, 1841, (Consolidated Cases, Docket Nos. 4413, 4414, 4419), NOPL.

Robert Ensor, bill of Lading for forty-nine slaves to be delivered to Thomas McCargo, September 5, 1842, ARC. This was a copy used in the CCNO trial because the original document could not be located.

Richmond Citizens' Ten Resolutions, January 27, 1842

Resolved, 1st, That the People of Virginia will never submit to any other people or nation the question of their right of property in their slaves, and that they hold as enemies to their peace all who meddle therewith.

Resolved, 2nd, That the Statute of New York, passed the 6th day of May, 1840, entitled an act, to extend the trial by jury, is a flagrant violation of the Constitution of the United States, and an act of hostility to the Slaveholding States – the practical effect of which is to form a bond of union, fellowship, and alliance, between the State of New York and Foreign Fanatics, tending to the subversion of Southern institutions.

Resolved, 3rd, That under whatever pretext, whether of securing trial by jury, or any other, we cannot but regard the legislation of some of the States of this Union as acts of hostility to our institutions; and as those States by their laws and practice justify and give protection and encouragement to those who feloniously abduct our slaves, we must look to ourselves for protection in the enactment, and prompt and vigilant execution of such laws as will secure the offender before he reaches his sanctuary – And believing that the present laws of this Commonwealth are in this respect insufficient,

Resolved, therefore, That we respectfully and earnestly recommend to the Legislature of Virginia, to revise all the existing laws in relation to slaves, free negroes, and mulattoes, and to remodel and amend the same, as more effectually to secure the slave property of Virginia, and protect the same from either domestic or foreign molestations; and we particularly request the General Assembly so provide such additional enactments as they may deem advisable, to prevent the escape of slaves by railroads and steamboats – at the same time exempting railroad companies from any damages to which they might be subjected, for refusing to transport in their care any persons of color, who may present themselves under suspicious circumstances.

Resolved, 5th, That we protest against any attempt on the part of Congress to interfere with the rights of property in slaves, either in the States, in the Territories of the United States, or in the District of Columbia; and that we deprecate, in the strongest terms, any action on the petitions of Abolitionists who are attempting to meddle with our own property and our own institutions.

Resolved, 6th, That the flag of the United States, in time of peace, and in pursuit of lawful commerce, wherever it waves, should be a protection and guarantee of safety of the property and persons under it.

Resolved, 7th, That the aggressive policy of the British Government, and their Colonial authorities upon the rights of property, especially in the recent case of the *Creole*, sailing from our own port, and thrown by the mutiny of the slaves on board thereof, and the murder of its passengers into the port of Nassau, calls loudly for remonstrance and redress.

Resolved, 8th, That our confidence in our Senators and Representatives in Congress forbids us to fear, that the rights of American citizens and the honor of the American flag will suffer at their hands.

Resolved, 9th, That we look to the firmness and discretion of the Government of the United States for a just vindication of our national honor. We look to the General Assembly of Virginia for the adoption of such resolutions, as may call for the legitimate action of the Federal Government in appealing to the justice of Great Britain; and we pledge ourselves for a hearty cooperation in such proper measures, as the constituted authorities may think it most advisable to adopt.

Resolved, 10th, That copies of the proceedings of this meeting be furnished to our Senators and Representatives in Congress, our State Senator, and Delegate from this City.

Source: *Richmond Enquirer,* January 29, 1842.

APPENDIX 5

Joshua Giddings's Nine Resolutions, March 21, 1842

[1] *Resolved*, That prior to the adoption of our Federal Constitution, each of the several States composing this Union exercised full and exclusive jurisdiction over the subject of slavery within its own Territory, and possessed full power to continue or abolish it at pleasure.

[2] *Resolved*, That by adopting the Constitution, no part of the aforesaid powers were delegated to the Federal Government, but were reserved by, and still pertain to each of the several States.

[3] *Resolved*, That by the 8th section of the 1st article of the Constitution, each of the several States, surrendered to the Federal Government all jurisdiction over the subjects of commerce and navigation upon the high seas.

[4] *Resolved*, That slavery being an abridgment of the natural rights of man, can exist only by force of positive municipal law, and is necessarily confined to the territorial jurisdiction of the power of creating it.

[5] *Resolved*, That when a ship belonging to the citizens of any State of this Union leaves the waters and territories of such State and enters upon the high seas, the persons on board cease to be subject to the slave laws of such State, and thenceforth are governed in their relations to each other by, and are amenable to, the laws of the U.S.

[6] *Resolved*, That when the brig *Creole*, on her late passage from New Orleans, left the territorial jurisdiction of Virginia, the slave laws of that State ceased to have jurisdiction over the persons on board of said brig, and such persons became amenable only to the laws of the U.S.

[7] *Resolved*, That the persons on board the said ship, in preserving their natural rights of personal liberty, violated no law of the U.S., incurred no legal penalty, and are justly liable to no punishment.

[8] *Resolved*, That all attempts to regain possession of, or to re-enslave, said persons, are unauthorized by the Constitution or the laws of the U.S., and incompatible with our national honor.

[9] *Resolved*, That all attempts to exert our national influence in favor of the coastwise slave trade, or to place this nation in the attitude of maintaining a "commerce in human beings," are subversive of the rights and injurious to the feelings and the interests of the free States; are unauthorized by the Constitution and prejudicial to our national character.

Source: *US Congressional Globe*, 27th Congress, 2nd Session, March 21, 1842, 342

Bibliography

I ARCHIVES

Amistad Research Center, Tulane University, New Orleans, LA (ARC)
Creole Affair Collection, 1854–1941, Box 106.
Dispatches from United States Consuls in Nassau, New Providence Island, 1821–1906, Microfilm Roll 5, vol. 5, January 9, 1840–December 28, 1841.
Bahamas National Archives, Nassau, Bahamas (BNA)
The Creole Case.
Department of Land & Surveys, Plans of Villages, Photographs.
Historical Notes on Fox Hill Community.
Index to Crown Land Grants Records, 1862–1944 (microfilm).
Oral History Transcripts Collection.
Bahamas Registrar General's Department, Nassau, Bahamas
Index to Crown Grants, 1862–1944.
British Library, London, England (BL)
Aberdeen Papers.
Library of Virginia, Richmond, VA (VL)
Personal Property Tax Records for City of Richmond, 1835–1850.
Louisiana State Museum, New Orleans, LA
Log Book of the Brig Creole.
National Archives and Records Administration, Washington, DC (NARA)
Bureau of Marine and Navigation, Record Group 41.
Dispatches from the US Consul in Nassau, British West Indies, Record Group 59.

Records of the US Customs Service, 1745–1997, Record Group 36.
The National Archives, London, England (TNA)
Colonial Office 23, Bahamas Original Correspondence, 1807–1900.
Colonial Office 27, Bahamas: Miscellanea, 1804–1900.
Colonial Office 137, Original Correspondence of Jamaican Governors.
Foreign Office 84, General Correspondence before 1906: Slave Trade, 1816–1892.
New Orleans Notarial Archives, New Orleans, LA (NONA)
Edward Barnet, Public Notary, 1840 Acts, 1841 Acts, 1842 Acts.
William Boswell, Public Notary, 1826 Acts, 1829 Acts, 1831 Acts, 1838 Acts.
William Christy, Public Notary, 1842 Acts.
Carlile Pollock, Public Notary, 1841 Acts, 1842 Acts.
New Orleans Public Library, City Archives, New Orleans, LA (NOPL)
Louisiana, Orleans Parish, Commercial Court of New Orleans (CCNO), Suits Relating to Slave Mutiny aboard the Brig Creole, 1841, Microfilm.
Registrar Generals Office, Nassau, Bahamas.
Crown Land Grants, Books 9, 11
University of New Orleans, Archives and Special Collections, New Orleans, LA
Louisiana State Supreme Court Dockets, Box 256.
Williams Center, New Orleans, LA
New Orleans Newspaper Collection, Microfilm.

II GOVERNMENT PUBLICATIONS

"Decree of Abolition of Slavery in Mexico," in Junius Rodriguez, ed., *Encyclopedia of Emancipation and Abolition in the Transatlantic World.* Armonk, NY: Sharpe, 2007.
Louisiana Supreme Court, "Louisiana Supreme Court History," http://www.lasc.org/about_the_court/history.asp
UK Government, Past Prime Ministers, George Hamilton Gordon Earl of Aberdeen. www.gov.uk/government/history/past-prime-ministers/george-hamilton-gordon-earl-of-aberdeen.
US Bureau of the Census, Population Returns, 1830, 1840, 1850.
US Congress, Biographical Directory, "Benjamin, Judah Philip." http://bioguide.congress.gov/scripts/biodisplay.pl?index=b000365
US Congress, Biographical Directory, "Bullard, Henry Adams." http://bioguide.congress.gov/scripts/biodisplay.pl?index=B001049

US Congress, Senate, Executive Document 51, 27th Congress, 2nd Session. *Message from the President of the United States, Communicating, in Compliance with a Resolution of the Senate Copies of Correspondence in Relation to the Mutiny on Board the Brig Creole, and the Liberation of the Slaves Who Were Passengers in the Said Vessel.* Washington, 1842.

Executive Document 103, 34th Congress, 1st Session. *Report of the Decisions of the Commissioner of Claims under the Convention of February 8, 1833, between the United States and Great Britain, Transmitted to the Senate by the President of the United States, August 11, 1856.* Washington: A. O. P. Nicholson, 1856.

US *Congressional Globe*, 27th Congress, 2nd Session, December 6, 1841 to August 31, 1842.

US Department of State, *Register of the Officers and Agents, Civil, Military, and Naval, in the Service of the United States.* Washington: J & G. S. Gideon, 1843.

Office of the Historian, "Biographies of the Secretaries of State: John Forsyth (1780-1841)," http://history.state.gov/departmenthistory/people/forsyth-john.

Office of the Historian, "Biographies of the Secretaries of State: Daniel Webster (1782–1852)," https://history.state.gov/departmenthistory/people/webster-daniel.

US House of Representatives, "Giddings, Joshua Reed," http://history.house.gov/People/Listing/G/GIDDINGS,-Joshua-Reed (G000167)/

History, Art & Archives, "Smalls, Robert," http://history.house.gov/People/Detail/21764

III NEWSPAPERS

American Beacon and Norfolk and Portsmouth Daily Advertiser (Norfolk)

Baltimore Afro-American (Baltimore)

Bee (New Orleans)

Belfast News-Letter (Belfast, Ireland)

Boston Courier (Boston)

Caledonian Mercury Edinburgh (Edinburgh, Scotland)

Charleston Mercury (Charleston)

Chatham Journal (Chatham, Canada)

Cleveland Daily Herald (Cleveland)

Commercial Bulletin (New Orleans)

Cork Examiner (Cork, Ireland)

Courrier de la Louisiane (New Orleans)

Daily Picayune (New Orleans)

Debow's Review (New Orleans)

Devizes and Wiltshire Gazette (Devizes, England)
Emancipator (New York City)
Freeman's Journal and Daily Commercial Advertiser (Dublin, Ireland)
Hampshire Advertiser (Southampton, England)
Liberator (Boston)
Mobile Register & Journal (Mobile)
Morning Post (London, England)
National Anti-Slavery Standard (New York City)
National Era (Washington, DC)
New Hampshire Patriot and State Gazette (Concord)
New York Evangelist (New York City)
New York Times (New York City)
Niles Register (Baltimore)
Norfolk and Portsmouth Phenix (Norfolk)
The North American and Daily Advertiser (Philadelphia)
North Devon Journal (Barnstaple, England)
North Star (Rochester)
Northern Star and Leeds General Advertiser (Leeds, England)
Richmond Enquirer (Richmond)
Richmond Whig (Richmond)
Standard (London, England)

IV PRIMARY PUBLISHED

"An Act to Prohibit the Importation of Slaves into Any Port or Place within the Jurisdiction of the United States," in The Avalon Project: Documents in Law, History and Diplomacy. New Haven: Yale Law School, http://avalon.law .yale.edu/19th_century/sl004.asp.

Andrews, Ethan. *Slavery and the Domestic Slave Trade in the United States.* Boston: Light & Stearns, 1836.

Arthur, Max and Imperial War Museum, eds., *Forgotten Voices of the Great War.* London: Ebury Press, 2014.

Berlin, Ira, Barbara Fields, Steven F. Miller, Joseph P. Reidy, Leslie S. Rowland, eds., *Free at Last: A Documentary History of Slavery, Freedom, and the Civil War.* New York: New Press, 1992.

Blassingame, John, ed., *The Frederick Douglass Papers, Series 1, Vol. 3, 1855–63.* New Haven: Yale University Press, 1985.

"Book of Negroes," in Black Loyalists: Our History, Our People, Canada's Digital Collections, http://blackloyalist.com/cdc/documents/official/book_of_ne groes.htm.

Brotten, Jerry. *The Renaissance: A Very Short Introduction*. New York: Oxford University Press, 2006.

Brown, William Wells. *A Description of William Wells Brown's Original Panoramic Views of the Scenes in the Life of an American Slave, from His Birth in Slavery to His Death or His Escape to His First Home of Freedom on British Soil*. London: Charles Gilpin, 1850.

The Negro in the American Rebellion: His Heroism and His Fidelity. 1880, rpr., New York: Krause Reprint Co., 1969.

Calhoun, John C. "John C. Calhoun Letter to Richard Pakenham, April 18, 1844," Econospeak, http://econospeak.blogspot.com/p/mr.html

Catterall, Helen Tunnicliffe, ed., *Judicial Cases Concerning American Slavery and the Negro*. Washington, DC: Carnegie, 1926–1936.

Channing, William E. *Dr. Channing's Last Address, Delivered at Lenox, on the First of August, 1842, The Anniversary of Emancipation in the British West Indies*. Boston: Oliver Johnson, 1842.

Conrad, Robert Edgar, ed. *Children of God's Fire: A Documentary History of Black Slavery in Brazil*. University Park, PA: Pennsylvania State University Press, 1994.

De Bow, James D. B. "Art. I.—Marine Insurance." *Debow's Review*, vol. 2, no. 1 (July 1846): 2–21.

"The Merchant Fleets and Navies of the World." *Debow's Review*, vol. 6, no. 4 (October-November 1848): 322–33.

Dickens, Charles. *American Notes*. 1842, rpt., London: Heron Books, n.d.

Dombey and Son. 1848, rpt., London: Penguin Classic, 2002.

Donnan, Elizabeth, ed. *Documents Illustrative of the History of the Slave Trade to America, Vol. 4, The Border Colonies and Southern Colonies*. Washington, DC: Carnegie Institution of Washington, 1935.

Douglass, Frederick. *The Heroic Slave*. 1853, rpt., in Ira Dworkin, ed. *Frederick Douglass: Narrative of the Life of Frederick Douglass, an American Slave*. London: Penguin, 2014.

Drew, Benjamin. *A North–Side View of Slavery. The Refugee or the Narratives of Fugitive Slaves in Canada. Related by Themselves, with an Account of the History and Condition of the Colored Population of Upper Canada*. Boston: J. P. Jewett, 1856.

Edwards, Bryan. *An Historical Survey of the French Colony in the Island of St. Domingo*. 1797, rpt., in Karina Williamson, ed. *Contrary Voices: Representations of West Indian Slavery, 1657–1834*. Mona, Jamaica: University of West Indies Press, 2008.

Ellyson's Business Directory and Almanac for the Year 1845. New Orleans: H. K. Ellyson, 1845.

Faust, Drew Gilpin, ed. *The Ideology of Slavery: Proslavery Thought in the Antebellum South, 1830–1860*. Baton Rouge: Louisiana State University Press, 1981.

Forbes, R. N. *Six Months' Service in the African Blockade, from April to October, 1848, in Command of H. M. S. Bonetta*. 1849, rpt., London: Dawsons, 1969.

"*Francois v. Jacinto Lobrano,*" in Merritt M. Robinson, ed. *Reports of Cases Argued and Determined in the Supreme Court of Louisiana, X, March 1–June 20, 1845.* New Orleans: Samuel M. Stewart, 1845.

Friends of the Cabildo. *New Orleans Architecture,* vol. 2,*The American Sector* (Faubourg St. Mary). Gretna, LA: Pelican Publishing Company, 1972.

"Ghent, Treaty of," 1814, in The Avalon Project: Documents in Law, History and Diplomacy. New Haven: Yale University, http://avalon.law.yale.edu/19th_c entury/ghent.asp.

Gibson's Guide and Directory of the State of Louisiana and the Cities of New Orleans and Lafayette. New Orleans: John Gibson, 1838.

Gienapp, William E. and Eruca L. Gienapp. eds. *The Civil War Diary of Gideon Welles, Lincoln's Secretary of the Navy.* Urbana: University of Illinois Press, 2014.

Greenberg, Kenneth S., ed. *The Confessions of Nat Turner and Related Documents.* New York: Bedford St. Martins, 1996.

Hicks, Granville. "Dr. Channing and the Creole Case," *American Historical Review,* vol. 37, no. 3 (April 1932): 516–525.

Higginson, Thomas Wentworth. *Army Life in a Black Regiment.* 1870, rpt., New York: Collier Books, 1972.

Hough, Franklin B. *The New York Civil List.* New York: Weed, Parsons, 1858.

J. C. "Art. IV – Case of the Creole." *American Jurist and Law Magazine,* 27 (April 1842): 79–110.

Jay, William. *The Creole Case, and Mr. Webster's Dispatch: With the Comments of the New York American.* New York: American, 1842.

   The Progress and Results of Emancipation in the English West Indies. London: Wiley and Putnam, 1842.

Jefferson, Paul, ed. *The Travels of William Wells Brown, a Fugitive Slave, and the American Fugitive in Europe, Sketches of Places and People Abroad.* New York: M. Wiener, 1991.

Knight, Frederick C. *Working the Diaspora: The Impact of African Labor on the Anglo-American World, 1650–1850.* New York: New York University Press, 2010.

"Legacies of British Slave-Ownership," University College London, www.ucl.ac .uk/lbs/.

"Lord Dunmore's Proclamation (1775)," Encyclopedia Virginia, www .encyclopediavirginia.org/Lord_Dunmore_s_Proclamation_1775.

Marx, Karl. *The Eighteenth Brumaire of Louis Bonaparte.* 1852, rpt., New York: International Publishers, 1984.

McNair, Baron and Arnold Duncan. "Slavery and the Slave Trade," in *International Law Opinions.* New York: Cambridge University Press, 1956.

Newman, Richard, Patrick Rael, Phillip Lapsansky, eds. *Pamphlets of Protest: An Anthology of Early African American Protest Literature, 1790–1860.* London: Routledge, 2001.

Northup, Solomon. *Twelve Years a Slave: Narrative of Solomon Northup, a Citizen of New York, Kidnapped in Washington City in 1841, and Rescued in 1853.* 1853, New York: W. W. Norton, 2017.

Pennington, James W. C. *An Address Delivered at Newark, N.J. at the First Anniversary of West India Emancipation, August 1, 1839.* Newark, NJ: Aaron Guest, 1839.

Phillips, Wendell. "Freedom's Jubilee." *Herald of Freedom*, August 5, 1842.

"Pitts & Clarke's Directory for 1842 New Orleans; and John Hagan, Bill of Lading, October 20, 1841," in *New Orleans Directory for 1842: Comprising the Names, Residences and Occupations of the Merchants, Business Men, Professional Gentlemen and Citizens of New Orleans, Lafayette, Algiers and Gretna.* New Orleans: Pitts & Clark, 1842.

Potter, Hon. B F. "Slavery, Ancient and Modern." *Debow's Review*, vol. 2, No. 5 (November 1846): 351–354.

Purdue, Charles L. Jr., Thomas E. Barden, Robert K. Phillips, eds. *Weevils in the Wheat: Interviews with Virginia Ex-Slaves.* Charlottesville, VA: University of Virginia Press, 1976.

Race and Slavery Petitions Project, Digital Library on American Slavery, University of North Carolina Greensboro, http://library.uncg.edu/slavery/petitions/details.aspx?pid=1573.

Ripley, Peter C., ed. *The Black Abolitionist Papers, Vol. 2 Canada, 1830–1865.* Chapel Hill, NC: University of North Carolina, 1985.

Rose, Willie Lee, ed. *A Documentary History of Slavery in North America.* 1976. Athens, GA: University of Georgia Press, 1999.

S. F. D. "Art. V – The Right of Visitation and Search in Time of Peace." *American Jurist and Law Magazine*, 27 (April 1842): 110–146.

Story, Joseph. *Commentaries on the Conflict of Laws, Foreign and Domestic, in Regard to Contracts, Rights, and Remedies, and Especially in Regard to Marriages, Divorces, Wills, Successions, and Judgments*, 2nd ed. London: A. Maxwell, 1841.

Thom, Adam Bissett. *The Upper Ten Thousand, An Alphabetical List.* London: Routledge, 1875.

"Thomas McCargo v. The New Orleans Insurance Company", in Merritt M. Robinson, *Reports of Cases Argued and Determined in the Supreme Court of Louisiana*, vol. 10, *(March 1 to June 20, 1845).* New Orleans, LA: Samuel M. Stewart, 1845.

"Treaty of Ghent, 1814," in The Avalon Project: Documents in Law, History and Diplomacy, New Haven: Yale University, http://avalon.law.yale.edu/19th_century/ghent.asp

"Treaty of Paris, 1783" The Avalon Project: Documents in Law, History and Diplomacy, New Haven: Yale University, http://avalon.law.yale.edu/subject_menus/parismen.asp.

Wadstrom, Carl Bernard. *An Essay on Colonization, Particularly Applied to the Western Coast of Africa with Some Free Thoughts on Cultivation and Commerce.* London: Darton and Harvey, 1794.

Walker, Jonathan. *Trial and Imprisonment of Jonathan Walker, at Pensacola, Florida, for Aiding Slaves to Escape from Bondage.* Boston: Anti-Slavery Office, 1845.

Ward, Samuel R. *Autobiography of a Fugitive Negro.* London: John Snow, 1855.

"Webster-Ashburton Treaty 1842 and Associated Documents" in The Avalon Project: Documents in Law, History and Diplomacy, New Haven: Yale Law School, http://avalon.law.yale.edu/subject_menus/br1842m.asp

Wylly, William. *A Short Account of the Bahama Islands, Their Climate, Productions,* etc. n.p. 1789.

V SECONDARY

"Aberdeen, George Hamilton Gordon, 4th Earl of," *Encyclopedia Britannica,* vol. 1, Wikisource, http://en.wikisource.org/wiki/1911_Encyclop%C3%A6 dia_Britannica/Aberdeen,_George_Hamilton_Gordon,_4th_Earl_of.

Ackroyd, Peter. *Dickens.* London: Sinclair-Stevenson, 1990.

Adams, Charles F. *Richard Henry Dana: A Biography.* vol. 1. Boston: Houghton, Mifflin, 1891.

Adams, E. D. "Lord Ashburton and the Treaty of Washington." *American Historical Review* 17, no. 4 (July 1912): 764–782.

Adderley, Rosanne Marion. *"New Negroes from Africa": Slave Trade Abolition and Free African Settlement in the Nineteenth-Century Caribbean.* Bloomington, IN: Indiana University Press, 2006.

Altoff, Gerald T. *Amongst My Best Men: African-Americans and the War of 1812.* Put-in-Bay, OH: Perry Group, 1996.

Aptheker, Herbert. *American Negro Slave Revolts.* 1943, rpt., New York: International Publishers, 1970.

"Ashburton, Baron (UK 1835)," Cracroft's Peerage, www.cracroftspeerage.co.uk /online/content/ashburton1835.htm;

Bailey, Thomas A. *A Diplomatic History of the American People.* New York: Appleton-Century-Crofts, Inc. 1955.

Bancroft, Frederic. *Slave-Trading in the Old South.* Baltimore, MD: J. H. Furst, 1931.

Baptist, Edward E. *The Half Has Never Been Told: Slavery and the Making of American Capitalism.* New York: Basic Books, 2014.

"Baring Family," *Encyclopedia Britannica,* www.britannica.com/EBchecked/top ic/53302/Baring-family#ref212753

Beckert, Sven. *Empire of Cotton: A Global History.* New York: Alfred A. Knopf, 2014.

Beckles, Hilary McD. "'An Unfeeling Traffick': The Intercolonial Movement of Slaves in the British Caribbean, 1807–1833," in Walter Johnson, ed. *The Chattel Principle: Internal Slave Trades in the Americas.* New Haven: Yale University Press, 2004.

Berlin, Ira. *Generations of Captivity: A History of African-American Slaves.* Cambridge MA: Harvard University Press, 2003.

Many Thousands Gone: The First Two Centuries of Slavery in North America. Cambridge, MA: Harvard University Press, 1998.

Berlin, Ira and Philip D. Morgan, eds. *Cultivation and Culture: Labor and the Shaping of Slave Life in the Americas*. Charlottesville, VA: University of Virginia Press, 1993.

Bemis, Samuel Flagg. *A Diplomatic History of the United States*. New York: Henry Holt, 1936.

Bergad, Laird W. *The Comparative Histories of Slavery in Brazil, Cuba, and the United States*. New York: Cambridge University Press, 2007.

Berquist, Harold E. "Henry Middleton and the Arbitrament of the Anglo-American Slave Controversy by Tsar Alexander I." *South Carolina Historical Magazine*, 82, no. 1 (January 1981): 20–31.

Bethell, Leslie. *The Abolition of the Brazilian Slave Trade: Britain, Brazil and the Slave Trade Question, 1807–1869*. New York: Cambridge University Press, 1970.

Black, Jeremy. *Slavery: A New Global History*. Philadelphia: Running Press, 2011.

Blackburn, Robin. *The American Crucible: Slavery, Emancipation and Human Rights*. London: Verso, 2011.

The Making of New World Slavery: From the Baroque to the Modern, 1492–1800. London: Verso, 1997.

The Overthrow of Colonial Slavery, 1776–1848. London: Verso, 1988.

Blackett, R. J. M. *Building an Antislavery Wall: Black Americans in the Atlantic Abolitionist Movement 1830–1860*. Baton Rouge: Louisiana State University Press, 1983.

Making Freedom: The Underground Railroad and the Politics of Slavery. Chapel Hill, NC: University of North Carolina Press, 2013.

Bolster, Jeffrey W. *Black Jacks: African American Seamen in the Age of Sail*. Cambridge, MA: Harvard University Press, 1997.

Brinkley, Alan. *The Unfinished Nation: A Concise History of the American People, Vol. 1 to 1877*. New York: McGraw Hill, 1993.

Brooks, Corey M. *Liberty Power: Antislavery Third Parties and the Transformation of American Politics*. Chicago: University of Chicago Press, 2016.

Brotton, Jerry. *The Renaissance: A Very Short Introduction*. New York: Oxford University Press, 2006.

Brown, Christopher Leslie. *Moral Capital: Foundations of British Abolitionism*. Chapel Hill, NC: University of North Carolina Press, 2006.

Brown, Christopher Leslie and Philip D. Morgan, eds. *Arming Slaves: From Classical Times to the Modern Age*. Yale University Press, 2006.

Buba, Tony, dir. *Ghosts of Amistad: In the Footsteps of the Rebels*. Pittsburgh, PA: University of Pittsburgh, 2014, DVD video.

Buckley, Roger N. *Slaves in Redcoats: The British West India Regiments, 1795–1815*. New Haven: Yale University Press, 1979.

Bullard, Mary R. *Black Emancipation at Cumberland Island in 1815*. Athens, GA: University of Georgia Press, 2008.

Butler, Pierce. *Judah P. Benjamin*. Philadelphia: G. W. Jacobs, 1907.

Calderhead, William. "The Role of the Professional Slave Trader in a Slave Economy: Austin Woolfolk, A Case Study." *Civil War History* 23, no. 3 (September 1977): 195-211.

Campbell, Randolph B. *An Empire for Slavery: The Peculiar Institution in Texas.* Baton Rouge: Louisiana State University Press, 1989.

Candido, Mariano P. *An African Slaving Port and the Atlantic World: Benguela and Its Hinterland.* New York: Cambridge University Press, 2013.

Canizares-Esguerra, Jorge, Matt Childs and James Sidbury, eds. *The Black Urban Atlantic in the Age of the Slave Trade.* Philadelphia: University of Pennsylvania Press, 2013.

Carroll, Joseph Cephas. *Slave Insurrections in the United* States *1800–1865.* 1938, rpt., Mineola, NY: Dover Publications, 2004.

Cassell, Frank A. "Slaves of the Chesapeake Bay Area and the War of 1812." *Journal of Negro History* 57, no. 2 (April 1972): 144-155.

Cecelski, David S. *The Waterman's Song: Slavery and Freedom in Maritime North Carolina.* Chapel Hill, NC: University of North Carolina Press, 2001.

Cesaire, Aime. *Discourse on Colonialism.* 1955, rpt., New York: Monthly Review Press, 2000.

Chakrabarty, Dipesh. *Rethinking Working-Class History: Bengal 1890 to 1940.* Princeton, NJ: Princeton University Press, 1990.

Chamberlain, Muriel E. *Lord Aberdeen: A Political Biography.* New York: Longman, 1983.

Chernow, Ron. *The House of Morgan: An American Banking Dynasty and the Rise of Modern Finance.* New York: Grove Press, 1990.

Childress, Boyd. "*Hermosa* Case (1840)" in Junius P. Rodriguez, ed., vol. 1, *Historical Encyclopedia of World Slavery.* Armonk, NY: M. E. Sharpe, 2007.

Christopher, Emma. *Slave Ship Sailors and Their Captive Cargoes, 1730–1807.* New York: Cambridge University Press, 2006.

Clavin, Matthew J. *Aiming for Pensacola: Fugitive Slaves on the Atlantic and Southern Frontiers.* Cambridge, MA: Harvard University Press, 2015.

Clayton, Ralph. *Cash for Blood: The Baltimore to New Orleans Domestic Slave Trade.* Bowie, MD: Heritage Books, 2002.

Colley, Linda. *Britons: Forging the Nation 1707–1837.* New Haven: Yale University Press, 1992.

Collins, Winfield H. *The Domestic Slave Trade of the Southern States.* New York: Broadway Publishing, 1904.

Conrad, Robert. *The Destruction of Slavery in Brazil, 1850–1888.* 1972, rpt., Malabar, FL: Krieger Publishing Company, 1993.

Crane, Elaine F. "'The First Wheel of Commerce': Newport, Rhode Island and the Slave Trade, 1760–1776." *Slavery and Abolition* 1 (1980): 178-198.

Crapol, Edward P. *John Tyler: The Accidental President.* Chapel Hill, NC: University of North Carolina Press, 2006.

Carney, Judith, *Black Rice: The African Origins of Rice Cultivation in the Americas.* Cambridge, MA: Harvard University Press, 2001.

Craton, Michael. "Caribbean Vice Admiralty Courts and British Imperialism," in *Empire, Enslavement, and Freedom in the Caribbean.* Kingston, Jamaica: Ian Randle, 1997.

A History of the Bahamas. New York: Collins Press, 1962.

"Hobbesian or Panglossian? The Two Extremes of Slave Conditions in the British West Indies, 1783–1834," in *Empire, Enslavement, and Freedom in the Caribbean.* Kingston, Jamaica: Ian Randle, 1997.

Testing the Chains: Resistance to Slavery in the British West Indies. Ithaca, NY: Cornell University Press, 1982.

Craton, Michael and Gail Saunders. *Islanders in the Stream: A History of the Bahamian People,* vol. 1. Athens, GA: University of Georgia Press, 1992.

Islanders in the Stream: A History of the Bahamian People from the Ending of Slavery to the Twenty-First Century, vol. 2 Athens, GA: University of Georgia Press, 1998.

Daunton, Martin and Rick Halpern, eds. *Empire and Others: British Encounters with Indigenous Peoples, 1600–1850.* Philadelphia: University of Pennsylvania Press, 1999.

Dawson, Kevin. "The Cultural Geography of Enslaved Ship Pilots," in Jorge Canizares-Esquerra, Matt D. Childs, James Sidbury, eds. *The Black Urban Atlantic in the Age of the Slave Trade.* Philadelphia: University of Pennsylvania Press, 2013.

Deconde, Alexander. *A History of American Foreign Policy.* New York : Charles Scribner, 1963.

Deyle, Steven. *Carry Me Back: The Domestic Slave Trade in American Life.* New York: Oxford University Press, 2005.

Diouf, Sylviana Anna. *Dreams of Africa in Alabama: The Slave Ship Clotilda and the Story of the Last Africans Brought to America.* New York: Oxford University Press, 2007.

Diouf, Sylviana Anna, ed. *Fighting the Slave Trade: West African Strategies.* Athens, OH: Ohio University Press, 2003.

Donald, David Herbert, Jean Harvey Baker, Michael F. Holt. *The Civil War and Reconstruction.* New York: W. W. Norton, 2001.

Douglass, Frederick. "The Heroic Slave," in *Autographs for Freedom.* Boston: John P. Jewett & Company, 1853.

Dow, George F. *Slave Ships and Sailing.* Salem: MA: Marine Research Society, 1927.

Downey, Arthur T. *The Creole Affair: The Slave Rebellion That Led the U.S. and Great Britain to the Brink of War.* London: Rowman and Littlefield, 2014.

Dubois, Laurent and John D. Garrigus. *Slave Revolution in the Caribbean, 1789–1804.* Boston: Bedford, 2006.

Dubois, W. E. B. *Black Reconstruction in America, 1860–1880.* 1935, rpt., New York: Atheneum, 1992.

The Suppression of the African Slave-Trade to the United States of America, 1638–1870. 1896, rpt., New York: Library of America, 1986.

Dunn, Richard S. *A Tale of Two Plantations: Slave Life and Labor in Jamaica and Virginia.* Cambridge, MA: Harvard University Press, 2014.

Dupuy, Alex. *Haiti in the World Economy: Class, Race, and Underdevelopment since 1700.* Boulder, CO: Westview Press, 1979.

"Edmund Grimani Hornby," Wikipedia, http://en.wikipedia.org/wiki/Edmund_Grimani_Hornby

"Edward Law, 1st Baron of Ellenborough," Wikipedia, https://en.wikipedia.org
   /wiki/Edward_Law,_1st_Baron_Ellenborough
Egerton, Douglas R. *Death or Liberty: African Americans and Revolutionary
   America*. New York: Oxford University Press, 2009.
   He Shall Go Out Free: The Lives of Denmark Vesey. 1999. rpt., London:
   Rowan & Littlefield, 2004.
   "Slave Resistance," in Robert L. Paquette and Mark M. Smith, eds. *The Oxford
   Handbook of Slavery in the Americas*. New York: Oxford University Press,
   2010.
Ellison, Rhoda Coleman. *History and Bibliography of Alabama Newspapers in
   the Nineteenth Century*. Tuscaloosa, AL: University of Alabama Press, 1954.
Eltis, David. *Economic Growth and the Ending of the Transatlantic Slave Trade*.
   New York: Oxford University Press, 1987.
Eltis, David and David Richardson. *Atlas of the Transatlantic Slave Trade*. New
   Haven: Yale University Press, 2010.
Engs, Robert F. *Freedom's First Generation: Black Hampton, Virginia,
   1861–1890*. 1979, rpt., New York: Fordham University Press, 2004.
Engs, Robert F. and Randall M. Miller, eds. *The Birth of the Grand Old Party:
   The Republicans' First Generation*. Philadelphia: University of Pennsylvania
   Press, 2002.
Evans, Eli N. *Judah P. Benjamin: The Jewish Confederate*. New York: Free Press,
   1988.
Faragher, John Mack, Mari Jo Buhle, Daniel Czitrom, and Susan H Armitage. *Out
   of Many: A History of the American People*, 4th ed., vol. 1. Upper Saddle
   River, NJ: Prentice Hall, 2005.
Farrison, William Edward. *William Wells Brown: Author and Reformer*. Chicago:
   University of Chicago Press, 1969.
Fehrenbacher, Don E. *The Slaveholding Republic: An Account of the United
   States Government's Relations to Slavery*. New York: Oxford University
   Press, 2005.
Fenton, Laurence. *Frederick Douglass in Ireland: The Black O'Connell*.
   New York: Collins Press, 2014.
Fields, Barbara Jeanne. *Slavery and Freedom on the Middle Ground: Maryland
   during the Nineteenth Century*. New Haven: Yale University Press, 1985.
Finkenbine, Roy. "The Symbolism of Black Mutiny: Black Abolitionist Reponses
   to the *Amistad* and *Creole* Incidents," in Jane Hathaway, ed. *Rebellion,
   Repressions, and Reinvention: Mutiny in Comparative Perspective*.
   Westport, CT: Praeger Publishers, 2001.
Fitz, Caitlin A. "The Hemispheric Dimensions of Early U.S. Nationalism: The War
   of 1812, Its Aftermath, and Spanish American Independence." *Journal of
   American History* 102, no. 2 (September 2015): 356–379.
Fogel, Robert W. and Stanley L. Engerman. *Time on the Cross: The Economics of
   American Negro Slavery*. 1974, rpt., London: Little, Brown, and Company,
   1984.
Foner, Eric. *Free Soil, Free Labor, Free Men: The Ideology of the Republican Party
   before the Civil War*. New York: Oxford University Press, 1970.

Freedom's Lawmakers: A Directory of Black Officeholders during Reconstruction. Baton Rouge: Louisiana State University Press, 1993.

Reconstruction: America's Unfinished Revolution. New York: Harper and Row, 1988.

Franklin, John Hope. *From Slavery to Freedom: A History of African Americans,* 7th ed. New York: McGraw Hill, 1994.

Franklin, John Hope and Evelyn Brooks Higginbotham. *From Slavery to Freedom: A History of African Americans,* 9th ed., New York: McGraw Hill, 2011.

Freedmen and Southern Society Project. College Park, MD: University of Maryland, www.history.umd.edu/Freedmen/

Freehling, William W. *The Road to Disunion: Secessionists at Bay, 1776–1854.* New York: Oxford University Press, 1990.

Frey, Sylvia R. *Water from the Rock: Black Resistance in a Revolutionary Age.* Princeton, NJ: Princeton University Press, 1991.

Friends of the Cabildo. *New Orleans Architecture, IV, The Creole Faubourgs.* Gretna, LA: Pelican Publishing Co., 2002.

Fryer, Peter. *Staying Power: The History of Black People in Britain.* London: Pluto, 1984.

Frykman, Niklas. "The Mutiny on the *Hermione*: Warfare, Revolution, and Treason in the Royal Navy." *Journal of Social History* 44, no. 1 (Fall 2010): 159–187.

Gaffield, Julia, ed. *The Haitian Declaration of Independence: Creation, Context, and Legacy.* Charlottesville, VA: University of Virginia Press, 2016.

Gaspar, David Barry and David P. Geggus, eds. *A Turbulent Time: The French Revolution and the Greater Caribbean.* Bloomington, IN: Indiana University Press, 1997.

Geiger, John O. "A Scholar Meets John Bull: Edward Everett as United States Minister to England, 1841–1845." *New England Quarterly,* 49, no. 4 (December 1976): 577–595.

Genovese, Eugene D. *From Rebellion to Revolution: Afro-American Slave Revolts in the Making of the Modern World.* Baton Rouge: Louisiana State University Press, 1979.

The Political Economy of Slavery: Studies in the Economy and Society of the Slave South. New York: Vintage Press, 1967.

Roll, Jordan, Roll: The World the Slaves Made. New York: Vintage Press, 1972.

The Slaveholders' Dilemma: Freedom and Progress in Southern Conservative Thought, 1820–1860. Columbia, SC: University of South Carolina Press, 1992.

The Southern Front: History and Politics in the Cultural War. Columbia, MO: University of Missouri Press, 1995.

Gilje, Paul A. *Free Trade and Sailors' Rights in the War of 1812.* New York: Cambridge University Press, 2013.

Goodman, Jordan. *Tobacco in History: The Cultures of Dependence.* London: Routledge, 1993.

Gould, Eliga H. *Among the Powers of the Earth: The American Revolution and the Making of a New World Empire.* Cambridge, MA: Harvard University Press, 2012.

Grant, Douglas. *The Fortunate Slave: An Illustration of African Slavery in the Early Nineteenth Century.* New York: Oxford University Press, 1968.

Greene, Lorenzo J. "Mutiny on the Slave Ships." *Phylon,* 5, no. 4 (1944): 346–354.

Greenspan, Ezra. *William Wells Brown: An African American Life.* New York: W. W. Norton, 2014.

Gudmestad, Robert H. *A Troublesome Commerce: The Transformation of the Interstate Slave Trade.* Baton Rouge: Louisiana State University Press, 2003.

Guterl, Mathew Pratt. *American Mediterranean: Southern Slaveholders in the Age of Emancipation.* Cambridge, MA: Harvard University Press, 2008.

Hahn, Steven. "Did We Miss the Greatest Slave Rebellion in Modern History?" in *The Political Worlds of Slavery and Freedom.* Cambridge, MA: Harvard University Press, 2009.

A Nation under Our Feet: Black Political Struggles in the Rural South from Slavery to the Great Migration. Cambridge, MA: Harvard University Press, 2003.

Hall, Gwendolyn Midlo. *Africans in Colonial Louisiana: The Development of Afro-Creole Culture in the Eighteenth Century.* Baton Rouge: Louisiana State University Press, 1992.

Hall, Neville A. T. *Slave Society in the Danish West Indies: St. Thomas, St. John and St. Croix.* Barry W. Higman, ed. Mona, Jamaica: University of West Indies Press, 1992.

Hall, Stephen G. *A Faithful Account of the Race.* Chapel Hill, NC: University of North Carolina Press, 2009.

Hamer, Philip M. "British Consuls and the Negro Seamen Acts, 1850 to 1860." *Journal of Southern History* 1, no. 2 (May 1935): 138–168.

"Great Britain, the United States, and the Negro Seamen Acts, 1822 to 1848." *Journal of Southern History* 1, no. 1 (February 1935): 3–28.

Hamilton, Keith and Patrick Salmon, eds. *Slavery, Diplomacy and Empire: Britain and the Suppression of the Slave Trade, 1807–1975.* Brighton, England: Sussex Academic Press, 2009.

Harding, Vincent. *There Is a River: The Black Struggle for Freedom in America.* New York: Vintage Books, 1983.

Harris, Charles Alexander. "Pakenham, Richard" in *Dictionary of National Biography, 1885–1900,* vol. 43, https://en.wikisource.org/wiki/Pakenham,_Richard_(DNB00)

Harrold, Stanley. *The Abolitionists and the South, 1831–1861.* Lexington, KY: University Press of Kentucky, 1995.

"Romanticizing Slave Revolt: Madison Washington, the *Creole* Mutiny, and Abolitionist Celebration of Violent Means," in John R. McKivigan and Stanley Harrold, eds. *Antislavery Violence: Sectional, Racial, and Cultural Conflict in Antebellum America.* Knoxville, TN: University of Tennessee Press, 1999.

Hay, Douglas. "Poaching and the Game Laws on Cannock Chase," in Douglas Hay, Peter Linebaugh, John G. Rule, E. P. Thompson, Cal Winslow, eds., *Albion's Fatal Tree: Crime and Society in Eighteenth-Century England*. New York: Pantheon Books, 1975.

Hendrick, George and Willene Hendrick. *The Creole Mutiny: A Tale of Revolt aboard a Slave Ship*. Chicago: Ivan R. Dee, 2003.

Hidy, Ralph W. *The House of Baring in American Trade and Finance: English Merchant Bankers at Work, 1763–1861*. 1949, rpt., New York: Russell & Russell, 1970.

Hill, Christopher. *The Collected Essays of Christopher Hill*, vol. 1, *Writing and Revolution in Seventeenth Century England*. Amherst, MA: University of Massachusetts Press, 1985.

Hobsbawn, Eric. *The Age of Empire, 1875–1914*. New York: Vintage Books, 1987.

On Empire: America, War, and Global Supremacy. Pantheon, 2008.

Hochschild, Adam. *Bury the Chains: Prophets and Rebels in the Fight to Free an Empire's Slaves*. New York: Mariner, 2005.

Holt, Michael F. *The Fate of Their Country: Politicians, Slavery Extension, and the Coming of the Civil War*. New York: Hill & Wang, 2004.

The Rise and Fall of the American Whig Party: Jacksonian Politics and the Onset of the Civil War. New York: Oxford University Press, 1999.

Holt, Thomas. *Black over White: Negro Political Leadership in South Carolina during Reconstruction*. Urbana, IL: University of Illinois Press, 1979.

The Problem of Freedom: Race, Labor, and Politics in Jamaica and Britain, 1832–1938. Baltimore, MD: John Hopkins University Press, 1992.

Horne, Gerald. *Confronting Black Jacobins: The United States, the Haitian Revolution and the Origins of the Dominican Republic*. New York: Monthly Review Press, 2015.

Fighting in Paradise: Labor Unions, Racism, and Communists in the Making of Modern Hawai'i. Honolulu: University of Hawai'i Press, 2011.

Negro Comrades of the Crown: African Americans and the British Empire Fight the U.S. before Emancipation. New York: New York University Press, 2012.

Race to Revolution: The United States and Cuba during Slavery and Jim Crow. New York: Monthly Review Press, 2014.

Horton, James O. and Lois E. Horton. *In Hope of Liberty: Culture, Community and Protest among Northern Free Blacks, 1700–1860*. New York: Oxford University Press, 1997.

Howard, Warren S. *American Slavers and the Federal Law, 1837–1862*. Berkeley, CA: University of California Press, 1963.

Hughes, Jonathan and Louis P. Cain. *American Economic History*, 5th ed. New York: Addison Wesley, 1998.

Hunt, Tristram. *The Frock-Coated Communist: The Revolutionary Life of Friedrich Engels*. London: Allen Lane, 2009.

Huzzey, Richard. *Freedom Burning: Anti-Slavery and Empire in Victorian Britain*. Ithaca, NY: Cornell University Press, 2012.

Jackson, Maurice and Jacqueline Bacon, eds. *African Americans and the Haitian Revolution: Selected Essays and Historical Documents.* London: Routledge, 2010.

James, C. L. R. *The Black Jacobins: Toussaint L'Ouverture and the San Domingo Revolution.* 1938, rpt., New York: Vintage Book, 1963.

Jervey, Edward D. and C. Harold Huber. "The Creole Affair." *Journal of Negro History* 65, no. 3 (Summer 1980): 196–211.

Johnson, Clifton H. "The Creole Affair," *Crisis* 78, no. 8 (October 1971): 248–251.

Johnson, Howard. *The Bahamas in Slavery and Freedom.* Princeton, NJ: Ian Randle, 1991.

Johnson, Walter. *Soul By Soul: Life inside the Antebellum Slave Market.* Cambridge, MA: Harvard University Press, 1999.

Jones, Gareth Steadman. *Karl Marx: Greatness and Illusion.* Cambridge, MA: Harvard University Press, 2016.

Jones, Howard. "The Creole Mutiny: A Tale of Revolt aboard a Slave Ship by George Hendrick; Willene Hendrick, (Review of)," *Journal of Southern History* 70, no. 2 (May 2004): 427–428.

Mutiny on the Amistad: The Saga of a Slave Revolt and Its Impact on American Abolition, Law, and Diplomacy. New York: Oxford University Press, 1987.

"The Peculiar Institution and National Honor: The Case of the *Creole* Slave Revolt." *Civil War History* 21, no. 1 (March 1975): 28–50.

To the Webster-Ashburton Treaty: A Study in Anglo-American Relations, 1783–1843. Chapel Hill: University of North Carolina Press, 1977.

Jones, Wilbur D. "The Influence of Slavery on the Webster-Ashburton Negotiations." *Journal of Southern History* 22, no. 1 (February 1956): 48–58.

Jonsson, Patrik. "In Wake of Eric Garner Case, Should Grand Jury System Be Reformed?" *Christian Science Monitor*, December 6, 2014. http://snews i.com/id/1449060385/In-wake-of-Eric-Garner-case-should-grand-jury-sys tem-be-reformed.

"Joshua Bates, Financier," Wikipedia, http://en.wikipedia.org/wiki/Joshua_Bate s_%28financier%29

Joshua, R. *Giddings and the Tactics of Radical Politics.* Cleveland, OH: Case-Western Reserve University Press, 1970.

Judd, Denis. *Empire: The British Imperial Experience, from 1865 to the Present.* London: Fontana, 1996.

Kale, Madhavi. *Fragments of Empire: Capital, Slavery, and Indian Indentured Labor in the British Caribbean.* Philadelphia: University of Pennsylvania Press, 1998.

Kambourian, Elizabeth. "Slave Traders in Richmond." *Richmond Times-Dispatch* (February 24, 2014), www.richmond.com/slave-traders-in rich mond/table_52a32a98-9d56-11e3-806a-0017a43b2370.html.

Karp, Matthew. "Arsenal of Empire: Southern Slaveholders and the U.S. Military in the 1850s." *Common-Place*, 12, no. 4 (July 2012): 1–15, www.common-place.org/vol-12/no-04/karp/.

Kars, Marjoleine. "Dodging Rebellion: Politics and Gender in the Berbice Slave Uprising of 1763." *American Historical Review*, 121, no. 9 (February 2016): 39–69.

Kaye, Anthony. "The Second Slavery: Modernity in the Nineteenth-Century South and the Atlantic World." *Journal of Southern History* 75, no. 3 (August 2000): 627–650.

Keegan, John. *The Face of Battle*. London: Penguin, 1978.

Kelly, Robin D. G. *Race Rebels: Culture, Politics, and the Black Working Class*. New York: Free Press, 1994.

"Kenyon, Lloyd Kenyon, 1st Baron," *Encyclopedia Britannica*, 11th ed., 15: 748–749, https://archive.org/stream/encyclopaediabri15chisrich#page/748/mode/2up

Kerr-Ritchie, Jeffrey R. "Black Abolitionists, Irish Supporters, and the Brotherhood of Man." *Slavery and Abolition*, 37: 3 (September 2016): 599–621.

Freedom's Seekers: Essays on Comparative Emancipation. Baton Rouge: Louisiana State University Press, 2014.

Freedpeople in the Tobacco South, Virginia, 1860–1900. Chapel Hill: University of North Carolina Press, 1999.

"Reflections on the Bicentennial of the Abolition of the British Slave Trade." *Journal of African American History*, 93, no. 4 (Fall 2008): 532–542.

Rites of August First: Emancipation in the Black Atlantic World. Baton Rouge: Louisiana State University Press, 2007.

"Slaves Supplicant and Slaves Triumphant: The Middle Passage of an Abolitionist Icon," in Ana Lucia Araujo, ed. *Paths of the Atlantic Slave Trade: Interactions, Identities, and Images*. Amherst, NY: Cambria Press, 2011

King, Dean. *A Sea of Words. A Lexicon and Companion for Patrick O'Brien's Seafaring Tales*. New York: Henry Holt, 1997.

Kolchin, Peter. *American Slavery, 1619–1877*. New York: Hill and Wang, 1993.

Laird, Matthew R. "Lumpkin's Jail," *Encyclopedia Virginia*, https://www.encyclopediavirginia.org/Lumpkin_s_Jail#).

Landry, Harral E. "Slavery and the Slave Trade in Atlantic Diplomacy, 1850–1861." *Journal of Southern History* 27, no. 2 (May 1961): 184–207.

Law, Robin. *Ouidah: The Social History of a West African Slaving "Port" 1792–1892*. Athens, OH: Ohio University Press, 2004.

Levy, Jonathan. *Freaks of Fortune: The Emerging World of Capitalism and Risk in America*. Cambridge, MA: Harvard University Press, 2012.

Lewis-Jones, Huw. "The Royal Navy and the Battle to End Slavery," British Broadcasting Corporation, www.bbc.co.uk/history/british/abolition/royal_navy_article_01.shtml

Lightner, David L. *Slavery and the Commerce Power: How the Struggle against the Interstate Slave Trade Led to the Civil War*. New Haven: Yale University Press, 2006.

Lindsay, Arnett G. "Diplomatic Relations between the United States and Great Britain on the Return of Negro Slaves, 1783-1828." *Journal of Negro History*, 5, no. 4 (October 1920): 391–419.

Lofton, John. *Denmark Vesey's Revolt: The Slave Plot That Lit a Fuse to Fort Sumter*. Kent, OH: Kent State University Press, 1964.

Logan, Rayford W. *The Diplomatic Relations of the United States with Haiti, 1776–1891*. Chapel Hill: University of North Carolina Press, 1941.

Lovejoy, Paul E. *Transformations in Slavery: A History of Slavery in Africa*. 1983, rpt., New York: Cambridge University Press, 2012.

"Lumpkin's Jail," Wikipedia, https://en.wikipedia.org/wiki/Lumpkin%27s_jail;

Lynch, John. *The Spanish American Revolutions, 1808–1826*. New York: W. W. Norton, 1973.

"Madison Washington," *Liberator*, June 10, 1842

"Madison Washington," Wikipedia, https://en.wikipedia.org/wiki/Madison_Washington#cite_note-williams-2

Mack Smith, Denis. *Mazzini*. New Haven: Yale University Press, 1994.

Manuel, Gladys. *Historical Notes on the Fox Hill Community*. n.p., 1988.

Mannix, Daniel P. and Malcolm Cowley. *Black Cargoes: A History of the Atlantic Slave Trade*. 1962, rpt., London: Penguin, 1976.

Martin, Thomas P. "Cotton and Wheat in Anglo-American Trade and Politics, 1846-1852." *Journal of Southern History*, 1, no. 3 (August 1935): 293–319.

Martínez-Fernández, Luis. "The Rise of the American Mediterranean, 1846–1905," in Stephan Palmié and Francisco A Scarano, eds. *The Caribbean: A History of the Region and its Peoples*. Chicago: University of Chicago Press, 2011

Mason, Mathew. "Keeping Up Appearances: The International Politics of Slave Trade Abolition in the Nineteenth Century Atlantic World." *William and Mary Quarterly*, 66, no. 4 (October 2009): 809–832.

Slavery and Politics in the Early American Republic. Chapel Hill, NC: University of North Carolina Press, 2006.

Matthews, Gelien. *Caribbean Slave Revolts and the British Abolitionist Movement*. Baton Rouge: Louisiana State University Press, 2006.

Mattoso, Katia M., de Queiros. *To Be a Slave in Brazil, 1550–1888*. New Brunswick, NJ: Rutgers University Press, 1986.

May, Gary. *John Tyler*. New York: Henry Holt, 2008.

McDowall, Angus. "Saudi Arabia Steps Up Beheadings; Some See Political Message," October 2014, www.reuters.com/article/2014/10/20/us-saudi-execution-idUSKCN0I91G220141020.

McFeely, William S. *Frederick Douglass*. New York: Touchstone, 1991.

McKenna, ed., "Cockburn, Sir Francis," *Dictionary of Canadian Biography*, v.9, www.biographi.ca/en/bio.php?id_nbr=4357.

McMillan, Richard. "Savannah's Coastal Slave Trade: A Quantitative Analysis of Ship Manifests, 1840–1850." *Georgia Historical Review* 78, no. 2 (Summer 1994): 339–359.

McNair, Arnold Duncan. "Slavery and the Slave Trade," in *International Law Opinions*. New York: Cambridge University Press, 1956.

McPherson, James M. *The Negro's Civil War: How American Negroes Felt and Acted during the War for the Union*. New York: Vintage Book, 1965.

Miller, Hubert W. "The Colonization of the Bahamas, 1647–1670." *William and Mary Quarterly* 3rd Ser., II (1945): 33–46.

Mintz, Sidney. *Caribbean Transformations*, 1974. Baltimore, MD: John Hopkins University Press, 1984.

Mixon, Gregory. *Show Thyself a Man: Georgia State Troops, Colored, 1865–1905*. Gainesville, FL: University Press of Florida, 2016.

Mohr, Clarence. *On the Threshold of Freedom: Masters and Slaves in Civil War Georgia*. Athens, GA: University of Georgia Press, 1986.

Moniz, Amanda Bowie. "A Radical Shrew in America: Mary Wilkes Haley and Celebrity in Early America." *Common Place* 8, no. 3 (April 2008), www .common-place.org/vol-08/no-03/moniz/.

Morgan, Edmund S. *American Slavery, American Freedom: The Ordeal of Colonial Virginia*. New York: W. W. Norton, 1975.

Morgan, Lynda J. *Emancipation in Virginia's Tobacco Belt, 1850–1870*. Athens, GA: University of Georgia Press, 1992.

Morgan, Philip D. and Andrew Jackson O'Shaughnessy. "Arming Slaves in the American Revolution," in Christopher Leslie Brown and Philip D. Morgan, eds. *Arming Slaves: From Classical Times to the Modern Age*. New Haven: Yale University Press, 2006.

Musson, Nellie Eileen. *Mind the Onion Seed: Black "Roots" Bermuda*. Hamilton, Bermuda: Musson's, 1979.

Mustakeem, Sowande' M. *Slavery at Sea: Terror, Sex, and Sickness in the Middle Passage*. Urbana, IL: University of Illinois Press, 2016

"Nathaniel Gookin Upham," Wikipedia, http://en.wikipedia.org/wiki/Nathaniel_ Gookin_Upham

Nicholls, David. *From Dessalines to Duvalier: Race, Color and National Independence in Haiti*. New Brunswick, NJ: Rutgers University Press, 1979.

Northrup, David. "Identity among Liberated Africans in Sierra Leone," in Jorge Canizares-Esguerra, Matt D. Childs, James Sidbury, eds. *The Black Urban Atlantic in the Age of the Slave Trade*. Philadelphia: University of Pennsylvania Press, 2013.

Oakes, James. *Freedom National: The Destruction of Slavery in the United States, 1861-1865*. New York: W. W. Norton, 2013.

O'Malley, Gregory E. *Final Passages: The Intercolonial Slave Trade of British America, 1619–1807*. Chapel Hill, NC: University of North Carolina Press, 2014.

Owsley Jr., Frank L. *Struggle for the Gulf Borderlands: The Creek War and the Battle of New Orleans, 1812–1815*. Tuscaloosa, AL: University of Alabama Press, 2000.

Palmer, Colin A. *Freedom's Children: The 1938 Labor Rebellion and the Birth of Modern Jamaica*. Chapel Hill, NC: University of North Carolina Press, 2014.

Slaves of the White God: Blacks in Mexico, 1570–1650. New York: Cambridge University Press, 1976.

Pargas, Damian Alan. *Slavery and Forced Migration in the Antebellum South*. New York: Cambridge University Press, 2015.

Parsons, Timothy H. *The Rule of Empires: Those Who Built Them, Those Who Endured Them, and Why They Always Fall*. New York: Oxford University Press, 2010.

Penningroth, Dylan C. *The Claims of Kinfolk: African American Property and Community in the Nineteenth-Century South*. Chapel Hill: University of North Carolina Press, 2003.

Peerthum, S. "Resistance against Slavery," in U. Bissondoyal and S. B. C. Servansing, eds., *Slavery in the South-West Indian Ocean*. Moka, Mauritius: Mahatma Ghandi Institute, 1989.

Phillips, Ulrich B. *American Negro Slavery: A Survey of the Supply, Employment and Control of Negro Labor as Determined by the Plantation Regime*. 1918, rpt., Baton Rouge: Louisiana State University Press, 1966.

Life and Labor in the Old South. 1929, rpt., Boston: Little and Brown, 1963.

Picketty, Thomas. *Capital in the Twenty-First Century*. Cambridge, MA: Harvard University Press, 2014.

Pons, Frank Moya. *History of the Caribbean: Plantations, Trade, and War in the Atlantic World*. Princeton, NJ: Markus Wiener, 2007.

Popkin, Jeremy D. *You Are All Free: The Haitian Revolution and the Abolition of Slavery*. New York: Cambridge University Press, 2010.

Postma, Johannes. *Slave Revolts*. Westport, CT: Greenwood Press, 2008.

"Preliminary History of the Lumpkin's Jail Property," www.richmondgov.com/CommissionSlaveTrail/documents/historyLumpkinJail.pdf.

Pryor, Elizabeth Stordeur. *Colored Travelers: Mobility and the Fight for Citizenship before the Civil War*. Chapel Hill: University of North Carolina Press, 2016.

Quarles, Benjamin. *Black Abolitionists*. New York: Oxford University Press, 1969.

The Negro in the Making of America. 1964, rpt., New York: Collier, 1987.

Rasmussen, Daniel. *American Uprising: The Untold Story of America's Largest Slave Revolt*. New York: Harper, 2011.

Rediker, Marcus. *The Amistad Rebellion: An Atlantic Odyssey of Slavery and Freedom*. New York: Viking, 2012.

The Slave Ship: A Human History. New York: Viking, 2007.

Reidy, Joseph P. The Business of Slavery and the Rise of American Capitalism, 1815–1860 by Calvin Shermerhorn (Review of), *Journal of American History*, 103, no. 2 (September 2016).

Reis, Joao Jose. *Slave Rebellion in Brazil: The Muslim Uprising of 1835 in Bahia*. Baltimore, MD: John Hopkins University Press, 1993.

Richards, Leonard L. *The Slave Power: The Free North and Southern Domination, 1780–1860*. Baton Rouge: Louisiana State University Press, 2000.

Who Freed the Slaves? The Fight over the Thirteenth Amendment. Chicago: University of Chicago Press, 2015.

Richardson, David. "Shipboard Revolts, African Authority, and the Transatlantic Slave Trade," in Sylviane A. Diouf, ed. *Fighting the Slave Trade: West African Strategies*. Athens, OH: Ohio University Press, 2003.

Richardson, David, Anthony Tibbles, Suzanne Schwartz, eds., *Liverpool and Transatlantic Slavery*. Liverpool: University of Liverpool Press, 2007.

Roberts, J. M. *Europe 1880–1945*. London: Longman, 1967.

Robinson, Armstead L. *Bitter Fruits of Bondage: The Demise of Slavery and the Collapse of the Confederacy, 1861–1865*. Charlottesville, VA: University of Virginia Press, 2005.

Rodney, Walter. *How Europe Undeveloped Africa*. 1972, rpt., Washington DC: Howard University Press, 1982.

Rood, Daniel B. *The Reinvention of Atlantic Slavery: Technology Labor, Race, and Capitalism in the Greater Caribbean*. New York, NY: Oxford University Press, 2017.

Rose, Willie Lee. *Rehearsal for Reconstruction: The Port Royal Experiment*. New York: Oxford University Press, 1964.

Rouleau, Brian. *With Sails Whitening Every Sea: Mariners and the Making of an American Maritime Empire*. Ithaca, NY: Cornell University Press, 2014.

Rupprecht, Anita. "'All We Have Done, We Have Done for Freedom': The *Creole* Slave-Ship Revolt (1841) and the Revolutionary Atlantic." *Internationaal Instituut voor Sociale Geschiedenis*, 58 (2013): 253–277.

Sale, Maggie Montesinos. *The Slumbering Volcano: American Slave Ship Revolts and the Production of Rebellious Masculinity*. Durham, NC: Duke University Press, 1997.

Sanborn, Franklin Benjamin, ed. *The Life and Letters of John Brown*. 1885, rpt., New York: Negro University Press, 1969.

Saunders, Gail. *Gambier Village: A Brief History*. n.p., 2007.

Schama, Simon. *Rough Crossings: The Slaves, the British, and the American Revolution*. New York: Harper Collins, 2006.

Schermerhorn, Calvin. *The Business of Slavery and the Rise of American Capitalism, 1815–1860*. New Haven: Yale University Press, 2015.

Schlesinger, Jr., Arthur M., ed. *The Almanac of American History*. New York: Barnes & Noble Books, 2004.

Schweninger, Loren. "Property Owning Free African-American Women in the South, 1800 to 1870," in Darlene Clark Hine, Wilma King, Linda Reed, eds. *"We Specialize in the Wholly Impossible,": A Reader in Black Women's History*. Brooklyn, NY: Carlson, 1995.

Scott, James C. *Domination and the Arts of Resistance: Hidden Transcripts*. New Haven: Yale University Press, 1990.

Sellers, Charles. *The Market Revolution: Jacksonian America, 1815–1846*. New York: Oxford University Press, 1991.

Shepherd, Verene A. *Maharani's Misery: Narratives of a Passage from India to the Caribbean*. Mona, Jamaica: University of West Indies Press, 2002.

Sinha, Manisha. *The Counter-Revolution of Slavery: Politics and Ideology in Antebellum South Carolina*. Chapel Hill: University of North Carolina Press, 2000.

Smallwood, Stephanie E. *Saltwater Slavery: A Middle Passage from Africa to American Diaspora*. Cambridge, MA: Harvard University Press, 2007.

Smith, Gene Allen. *The Slaves' Gamble: Choosing Sides in the War of 1812*. New York: Palgrave Macmillan, 2013.

Smith, Mark M. "Time, Slavery and Plantation Capitalism in the Ante-Bellum American South." *Past and Present* 150 (February 1996): 142–168.

Snyder, Jennifer K. "Revolutionary Refugees: Black Flight in the Age of Revolution," in Brian Ward, Martyn Bone, William A. Link, eds. *The American South and the Atlantic World*. Gainesville, FL: University Press of Florida, 2013.

"Somerset House," Wikipedia, https://en.wikipedia.org/wiki/Somerset_House.

Soulsby, H. G. *The Right of Search and the Slave Trade in Anglo-American Relations, 1814–1862*. Baltimore. MD: John Hopkins University Press, 1933.

Spears, John R. *The American Slave Trade: An Account of Its Origin, Growth, and Suppression*. New York: Charles Scribner, 1900.

Stampp, Kenneth. *The Peculiar Institution: Slavery in the Ante-Bellum South*. New York: Vintage, 1956.

Stark, James H. *Stark's History of and Guide to the Bahama Islands*. Boston: Photo-Electrolyte Company, 1891.

Steckel, Richard H. "Demography and Slavery," in Robert L. Paquette and Mark M. Smith, eds. *The Oxford Handbook of Slavery in the Americas*. New York: Oxford University Press, 2010.

Stein, Robert Louis. *The French Slave Trade in the Eighteenth Century: An Old Regime Business*. Madison, WI: University of Wisconsin, 1979.

Stephenson, Wendell H. *Isaac Franklin: Slave Trader and Planter from the Old South*. Baton Rouge: Louisiana State University Press, 1938.

Stewart, James B. *Holy Warriors: The Abolitionists and American Slavery*. New York: Hill and Wang, 1976.

Joshua R. Giddings and the Tactics of Radical Politics. Cleveland, OH: Case-Western Reserve University Press, 1970.

Sweig, Donald. "Alexandria to New Orleans: The Human Tragedy of the Interstate Slave Trade," *Alexandria Gazette Packet*, 4 Parts, (October 2014).

Tadman, Michael. "Internal Slave Trades," in Robert L. Paquette and Mark M. Smith, eds. *The Oxford Handbook of Slavery in the Americas*. New York: Oxford University Press, 2010.

Speculators and Slaves: Masters, Traders, and Slaves in the Old South. Madison, WI: University of Wisconsin Press, 1996.

Taylor, Alan. *The Internal Enemy: Slavery and War in Virginia, 1772–1832*. New York: W. W. Norton, 2013.

Taylor, Eric Robert. *If We Must Die: Shipboard Insurrections in the Era of the Atlantic Slave Trade*. Baton Rouge: Louisiana State University Press, 2006.

Taylor, Nikki M. *Driven Toward Madness: The Fugitive Slave Margaret Garner and Tragedy on the Ohio*. Athens, OH: Ohio University Press, 2016.

Thomas, Hugh. *The Slave Trade: The Story of the Atlantic Slave Trade*. New York: Simon & Schuster, 1997.

Thomas, Keith. *Religion and the Decline of Magic: Studies in Popular Beliefs in Sixteenth and Seventeenth Century England*. New York: Oxford University Press, 1971.

Thompson, Edward P. *Customs in Common: Studies in Traditional Popular Culture*. New York: New Press, 1993.

Thompson, Sharyn. *Marriage, Birth and Death Notices from Newspapers of the Bahamas*. Nassau, Bahamas: Off Island Press, 2002.

Tomich, Dale W. "The 'Second Slavery': Bonded Labor and the Transformation of the Nineteenth-Century World Economy," in Francisco O. Ramirez, ed. *Rethinking the Nineteenth Century: Contradictions and Movements*. New York: Praeger, 1988.

Tomich, Dale W. ed. *The Politics of the Second Slavery*. Binghamton, NY: State University Press of New York, 2016.

Towers, Frank. "Job Busting at Baltimore Shipyards: Racial Violence in the Civil War- Era South." *Journal of Southern History*, 66, no. 2 (May 2000): 221–256.

Trent, Hank. *The Secret Life of Bacon Tait, a White Slave Trader Married to a Free Woman of Color*. Baton Rouge: Louisiana State University Press, 2017.

Trevelyan, G. M. *British History in the Nineteenth Century and after, 1782–1919*. 1937. London: Longmans, 1956.

Troutman, Philip. "Grapevine in the Slave Market: African American Geopolitical Literacy and the 1841 *Creole* Revolt," in Walter Johnson, ed. *The Chattel Principle: Internal Slave Trades in the Americas*. New Haven: Yale University Press, 2004.

Tucker, Spencer. Review of William E. Gienapp and Erica L. Gienapp, eds. *The Civil War Diary of Gideon Welles, Lincoln's Secretary of the Navy*, ed., *Journal of American History* 102, no. 2 (September 2015): 566.

Turley, David M. "'Free Air' and Fugitive Slaves: British Abolitionists versus Government Over American Fugitives, 1834–61," in Christine Bolt and Seymour Drescher, eds. *Anti-Slavery, Religion, and Reform: Essays in Memory of Roger Anstey*. Folkestone, Kent, England: Dawson, 1980.

Underdown, David. *Revel, Riot, and Rebellion: Popular Politics and Culture in England 1603–1660*. New York: Oxford University Press, 1985.

Unsworth, Barry. *Sacred Hunger*. New York: W. W. Norton, 1993.

Vega, Philine Georgette. "Creole Case (1841)," in Junius P. Rodriguez, ed. *Encyclopedia of Emancipation and Abolition in the Transatlantic World*, 1. Armonk, NY: M. E. Sharpe, 2007.

Voyages Database, Emory University, www.slavevoyages.org/voyage/.

Walvin, James. *Fruits of Empire: Exotic Produce and British Taste, 1660–1800*. Basingstoke, Hampshire, England: MacMillan, 1997.

The Zong. New Haven: Yale University Press, 2011.

Ward, Brian, Martyn Bone, William A. Link, eds. *The American South and the Atlantic World*. Gainesville, FL: University Press of Florida, 2013.

"Waterloo Bridge," Wikipedia, https://en.wikipedia.org/wiki/Waterloo_Bridge.

Wax, Darold D. "Negro Resistance to the Early American Slave Trade." *Journal of Negro History*, 51, no. 1 (January 1966): 1–15.

Wesley, Charles H. "Manifests of Slave Shipments along the Waterways, 1808–1864." *Journal of Negro History*, 27, no. 2 (April 1942): 155–174.

Wharton, Vernon Lane. *The Negro in Mississippi, 1865–1890*. 1947, rpt., New York: Harper and Row, 1965.

White, Ashli. *Encountering Revolution: Haiti and the Making of the Early Republic*. Baltimore, MD: John Hopkins University Press, 2010.

White, Richard. *"It's Your Misfortune and None of My Own": A New History of the American West*. Norman, OK: University of Oklahoma Press, 1991.

Whitfield, Harvey Amani. *Blacks on the Border: The Black Refugees in British North America, 1815–1860*. Burlington, VT: University of Vermont Press, 2006.

Wiencek, Henry. *An Imperfect God: George Washington, His Slaves, and the Creation of America*. New York: Farrar, Strauss, and Giroux, 2003.

Wilentz, Sean. *The Rise of American Democracy: Jefferson to Lincoln*. New York: W. W. Norton, 2005.

Williams, Eric. "The British West Indian Slave Trade after Its Abolition in 1807." *Journal of Negro History*, 27 (1942): 175–191.

Capitalism and Slavery. 1944, rpt., London: Andre Deutsch, 1964.

Williams, Gomer. *History of the Liverpool Privateers and Letters of Marque, with an Account of the Liverpool Slave Trade*. London: William Heinemann, 1897.

Williams, Patrice. *A Guide to African Villages in New Providence*. Nassau, Bahamas: Bahamas Department of Archives, 1979.

Williams, William Appleman. "Empire as a Way of Life." *Radical History Review*, 50 (1991): 71–102.

The Tragedy of American Diplomacy. New York: Dell, 1962.

Wish, Harvey. "American Slave Insurrections before 1861." *Journal of Negro History* 22, no. 3 (July 1937): 300–306.

Woodman, Harold D. *King Cotton and His Retainers: Financing and Marketing the Cotton Crop of the South, 1800–1925*. 1968, rpt., Columbia, SC: University of South Carolina Press, 1990.

Woodward, C. Vann. *Origins of the New South, 1877–1913*. Baton Rouge: Louisiana State University Press, 1951.

Worsley, Frank and Glyn Griffith. *The Romance of Lloyds: From Coffee House to Palace*. London: Hillman-Curl, 1937.

Wright, Gavin. *Slavery and American Economic Development*. Baton Rouge: Louisiana State University Press, 2006.

Ziegler, Philip. *The Sixth Great Power: A History of One of the Greatest of All Banking Families, The House of Barings, 1762–1929*. New York: Alfred Knopf, 1988.

Zimmerman, James Fulton. *Impressment of American Seamen*. Port Washington, NY: Kennikat Press, 1925.

Zinn, Howard. *A People's History of the United States, 1492 – Present*. 1980. New York: Harper Collins, 2001.

VI. UNPUBLISHED

Adderley, Rosanne Marion. Presentation at the American Historical Association, Atlanta, Georgia, January 2015.

Baxter, Jane Eva. "Negotiations for Compensations: Bahamian Slaveholders in 1834." Talk, 47th Annual Conference, Association of Caribbean Historians, Nassau, Bahamas, May 17, 2015.

Engs, Robert F. "The Great American Slave Rebellion." Lecture, University of Georgia, February 13, 1987.

"Who Freed the Slaves and Does It Matter: An Adventure in the Politics of Race and History," Talk, Association for the Study of African American Life and History, Charlotte, NC, October 6, 2007.

Headley, Marcia. "Imaging Haiti: Perceptions of Haiti in the Atlantic World, 1791–1875." PhD dissertation, Howard University, Washington DC, 2012.

Hooper, Jane. "American Yankees and Abolitionism in East Africa, 1840–1860." Paper Presentation, African Diaspora Seminar, Howard University, Fall 2017.

Levy, Jonathan Ira. "The Ways of Providence: Capitalism, Risk, and Freedom in America, 1841–1935." Vol. 1, PhD dissertation, University of Chicago, Chicago, Ill., 2008.

McMahon, Kate. "The Transnational Dimensions of Africans and African Americans in Northern New England, 1776–1865," PhD dissertation, Howard University, Washington DC, 2017.

Poole, William Joseph, Jr. "The Creole Case." MA thesis, Louisiana State University, Baton Rouge, 1970.

Stewart, Byron James. "Freedom's Orphans: A Discourse on the Fates of Black Loyalists from the Revolutionary Generation 1776–1836." PhD dissertation, Howard University, Washington DC, 2016.

Weise, Marcus S. "A Social History of the West India Regiments, 1795–1838." PhD dissertation, Howard University, Washington DC, 2017.

Index